The Pacific's New Navies

The initial creation of the United States' ocean-going battlefleet – otherwise known as the "New Navy" – was a result of naval wars and arms races around the Pacific during the late nineteenth century. Using a transnational methodology, Thomas M. Jamison spotlights how US Civil War-era innovations catalyzed naval development in the Pacific World, creating a sense that the US Navy was falling behind regional competitors. As the industrializing "newly made navies" of Chile, Peru, Japan, and China raced against each other, Pacific dynamism motivated investments in the US "New Navy" as a matter of security and civilizational prestige. In this provocative exploration into the making of modern US navalism, Jamison provides an analysis of competitive naval build-ups in the Pacific, of the interactions between peoples, ideas, and practices, and ultimately the emergence of the US as a major power.

Thomas M. Jamison is Assistant Professor of Strategic Studies at the Naval Postgraduate School. His work has been published by the *Journal of Military History* and *Technology and Culture*.

MILITARY, WAR, AND SOCIETY IN MODERN
AMERICAN HISTORY

Series Editors
Beth Bailey, University of Kansas
Andrew Preston, University of Cambridge
Kara Dixon Vuic, Texas Christian University

Military, War, and Society in Modern American History is a new series that showcases original scholarship on the military, war, and society in modern U.S. history. The series builds on recent innovations in the fields of military and diplomatic history and includes historical works on a broad range of topics, including civil-military relations and the militarization of culture and society; the military's influence on policy, power, politics, and political economy; the military as a key institution in managing and shaping social change, both within the military and in broader American society; the effect the military has had on American political and economic development, whether in wartime or peacetime; and the military as a leading edge of American engagement with the wider world, including forms of soft power as well as the use of force.

The Pacific's New Navies
An Ocean, its Wars, and the Making of US Sea Power

Thomas M. Jamison
Naval Postgraduate School

Shaftesbury Road, Cambridge CB2 8EA, United Kingdom

One Liberty Plaza, 20th Floor, New York, NY 10006, USA

477 Williamstown Road, Port Melbourne, VIC 3207, Australia

314–321, 3rd Floor, Plot 3, Splendor Forum, Jasola District Centre, New Delhi – 110025, India

103 Penang Road, #05–06/07, Visioncrest Commercial, Singapore 238467

Cambridge University Press is part of Cambridge University Press & Assessment, a department of the University of Cambridge.

We share the University's mission to contribute to society through the pursuit of education, learning and research at the highest international levels of excellence.

www.cambridge.org
Information on this title: www.cambridge.org/9781009559737

DOI: 10.1017/9781009559706

© Thomas M. Jamison 2025

This publication is in copyright. Subject to statutory exception and to the provisions of relevant collective licensing agreements, no reproduction of any part may take place without the written permission of Cambridge University Press & Assessment.

When citing this work, please include a reference to the DOI 10.1017/9781009559706

First published 2025

A catalogue record for this publication is available from the British Library

Library of Congress Cataloging-in-Publication Data
Names: Jamison, Thomas M., author.
Title: The Pacific's new navies : an ocean, its wars, and the making of US sea power / Thomas M. Jamison, Naval Postgraduate School.
Description: Cambridge, United Kingdom ; New York, NY : Cambridge University Press, 2025. | Series: Military, war, and society in modern American History | Includes bibliographical references and index.
Identifiers: LCCN 2024023226 | ISBN 9781009559737 (hardback) | ISBN 9781009559706 (ebook)
Subjects: LCSH: United States. Navy – History – 19th century. | Sea-power – United States – History – 19th century. | Navies – Pacific Area – History – 19th century. | United States – History, Naval. | War of the Pacific, 1879–1884 – Influence. | Sino-Japanese War, 1894–1895 – Influence. | United States – Military relations – Pacific Area. | Pacific Area – Military relations – United States.
Classification: LCC E182 .J36 2025 | DDC 359.00973–dc23/eng/20240711
LC record available at https://lccn.loc.gov/2024023226

ISBN 978-1-009-55973-7 Hardback
ISBN 978-1-009-55974-4 Paperback

Cambridge University Press & Assessment has no responsibility for the persistence or accuracy of URLs for external or third-party internet websites referred to in this publication and does not guarantee that any content on such websites is, or will remain, accurate or appropriate.

For Sarah and Matty

Contents

List of Figures and Table	*page* viii
Acknowledgments	ix
Introduction	1
1 The Confederate "Navy to Construct"	16
2 The Pacific's Civil War Inheritance	35
3 Pacific Naval Races and the Old Steam Navy	59
4 Pacific Wars and Their Lessons	85
5 The Californian Case for a New Navy	104
6 The US New Navy Wins a Race – Finally	127
7 The Sino-Japanese War and New "Yankees" in the Pacific	152
Conclusion	175
Notes	185
Bibliography	261
Index	286

Figures and Table

Figures

I.1	Pacific wars and naval races (1864–1895)	page 3
I.2	US naval expenditures (1855–1900)	4
1.1	Confederate rams	23
1.2	"Naval Architecture Sketch of the Peruvian Ironclad Monitor *Huáscar*"	26
2.1	*Stonewall*	50
3.1	*Cochrane*	64
3.2	Thomas Somerscales, *La Escuadra Chilena en 1879*	67
4.1	"Our Navy," *Harper's* (1881)	93
4.2	"Plans of the *Huáscar*"	101
5.1	US vs Chilean steel and armored warships	113
6.1	The Union Iron Works	131
6.2	"A Warning," *Puck* (1892)	141
6.3	Fred Cozzens, *New York Naval Parade*	146
7.1	ONI data comparing Qing and Japanese naval power (1895)	156
7.2	*Esmeralda*, *Diario de la Unión* (1894)	163

Table

C.1	Pacific naval battles and precedents set (1877–1895)	177

Acknowledgments

Many people supported this book – too many to mention, but here goes. Erez Manela was a conscientious and thorough dissertation adviser. He set standards as a scholar and teacher I strive to meet. Fredrik Logevall, Odd Arne Westad, and Dirk Bonker provided valuable and critical feedback as committee members. Thanks to the editor and staff at Cambridge University Press, Cecelia Cancellaro and Victoria Phillips. And to the series editors of Military, War, and Society in Modern American History, Beth Bailey and (especially) Andrew Preston, who coached me along. I am grateful to the press' anonymous reviewers, who presented fresh challenges to my thinking. Will Inboden was an essential mentor. Katherine Epstein, Jason Smith, and B. J. Armstrong gave course corrections along the way.

I began researching this project as a graduate student at Harvard, wrote most of it as a dissertation while on a fellowship at the University of Texas at Austin (UT Austin), and revised the final manuscript at the Naval Postgraduate School in Monterey, CA. At Harvard, David Armitage sparked my interest in the international history of the Pacific. Arunabh Ghosh and Andrew Gordon offered specific training in Chinese and Japanese history, respectively. Charles Maier and Sven Beckert first encouraged my work in the Harvard Weatherhead Initiative on Global History Seminar in 2014–2015. As importantly, thanks are due to my graduate cohort. I got good advice from Andrew Bellisari, Ian Kumekawa, Georgia Whitaker, Sally Hayes, Kai Thaler, Kimberly Wortmann, Mateo Jarquin, Pete Pellizzari, Jonathon Booth, Matthew Sohm, Maddie Williams, Aaron Bekemeyer, Ella Antell, Ben Goossen, and above all Lydia Walker. Thanks to Jorge Ortiz-Sotelo for his help with archives in Peru and Chile. My colleagues at Clements Center for National Security at the University of Texas at Ausin – Mary Elizabeth Walters, Alexandra Evans, Theo Milonopoulos, Jaehan Park, Silke Zoller, M. L. deRaismes Combes, and Alex Foggett – notched achievements at a furious pace, providing ample motivation. Texas also offered excellent mentors in Jeremi Suri, Aaron O'Connell, Mark Atwood Lawrence, Celeste Ward

Geventer, and Paul Edgar. At the Naval Postgraduate School, I appreciate Kalev Sepp, John Arquilla, Doug Borer, and Carter Malkasian for finding time and space for my research. I am equally grateful to my students in Monterey, who tolerate my digressions and remind me that war is a wretched thing done by (very often) deeply humane people. They ground my conviction that we should study war like a Marxist studies capitalism: with an eye toward eliminating it. I also received feedback from many colleagues at the Society for Military History, Society for the History of American Foreign Relations, and North American Society for Oceanic History, such as: Paul Fontenoy, Ryan Wadle, David Ulbrich, Heather Haley, Mark Folse, Aimée Fox, and Timothy Wolters.

My work was well funded throughout. Major grants included the Naval History and Heritage Command Hayes Predoctoral Fellowship, a Harvard Warren Center Term-Time Grant, the H. F. Guggenheim Dissertation Fellowship, the Weatherhead Center for International Affairs Dissertation Completion Fellowship, the Society for the History of American Foreign Relations Gelfand-Rappaport-LaFeber Fellowship, the Clements Center for National Security (UT Austin) Predoctoral Fellowship, and the Smith-Richardson World Statecraft and Politics Fellowship. I revised this work for publication using Research Initiation Program funds from the Naval Postgraduate School in 2021–2022. I completed final edits in Tokyo on a Council on Foreign Relations International Affairs Fellowship in 2024.

None of this would have been possible without my family. Thanks to my wife, Sarah, who saw this book from its first day in a graduate school seminar to the end. I would have abandoned the project (and maybe even a career as a historian) without her. It is fitting that as I am completing this story about trans-Pacific crossings and new beginnings, Sarah and I are making our own journey across the ocean (from California to Tokyo) with a new son in tow. Our dog Charlie was no help at all. My mother-in-law Margaret Townsley proofread many documents. My mom and dad – Liana and John – raised me in a house filled with books and taught me to be curious about the world. That gift shapes everything in my life, this book included.

Introduction

Union Square, San Francisco, 1903. Theodore Roosevelt had the place packed. Thousands had come to witness his dedication of the new "Dewey Monument": a column celebrating the titular George Dewey's victory over the Spanish at Manila Bay (1898). Beyond its military result (a lopsided affair in which the US squadron suffered only one fatality), the battle, Roosevelt noted, "showed once and for all that America had taken our position on the Pacific." Atop the column, Nike, goddess of victory, carried both a wreath and a trident – the latter apparently on loan from Poseidon. For anyone missing the symbolism, Roosevelt made the connection between naval power and victory explicit. Dewey's success at Manila was possible because "those who went before us had the wisdom to make ready for the victory" by investing in the peacetime construction of a modern, industrial fleet: the aptly named United States "New Navy." "In 1882," Roosevelt continued, "our navy was a shame and disgrace to the country … the ships and guns were as antiquated as if they had been the galleys of Alcibiades."[1] That changed – dramatically – in the intervening decades. The Old Navy's wooden hulls were broken up and steel New Navy ships built from scratch. Armed with vessels such as USS *Olympia*, Dewey had the hardware to make real all that *fin-de-siècle* puffery about destinies, doors, and doctrines. More naval building was necessary and logical; just look at what the United States Navy (USN) had already achieved in the War of 1898! In this respect, Roosevelt's 1903 commemoration was a prolog to the Great White Fleet's world cruise (1907), the battleships at Tokyo Bay (1945), and the enduring US dominance over the global commons of the sea, air, space, and cyberspace – for now.

This book explores the origins of the steel, steam-powered "New Navy" Dewey took to Manila. Unlike existing accounts, it does so by stressing the interactive relationships between the US, its post-Civil War navy (indeed navies "Old" and "New"), and several industrial naval wars and races around the Pacific in the last decades of the nineteenth century. Generally, shifting our perspective to the Pacific World allows for a better understanding of how relatively weak militaries outside of the North Atlantic influenced maritime development during a period of technological flux and accelerating globalization. More particularly, "looking outward" from the edges of the US Empire in California suggests a new argument for a long-standing question.[2] In the absence of overt hostilities or new "great power" rivals, what sparked the transformation of the US "Old Navy" from an assortment of wooden ships so archaic they inspired ridicule (notably from Roosevelt) into the cruisers, torpedo boats, and battleships that defeated Spain in 1898?

Historians who study the New Navy have offered a diverse set of explanations about its origins – discussed in greater detail in Section I.4. Those who focus on the international environment have long cohered into two broad camps. Some, such as Roosevelt, portray the building of the New Navy as farsighted preparation for transoceanic war and empire c. 1898 (the "wisdom to make ready for the victory").[3] More recent scholars have framed US naval modernization as a defensive and competitive reorientation against European threats to the Atlantic Coast and Caribbean.[4] These are compelling but incomplete arguments.

By shifting regional perspective, this book presents the early years (c. 1882–1897) of the US New Navy as neither imperial *preparation*, nor a *defense* against "great power" fleets, but rather as a *reaction* to the Pacific and its "newly made navies": a general type of small, industrial fleet built from little or no existing inventory and leveraging technological innovations. The narrative charts a wave of technology and knowledge flowing out from the US after the Civil War (1861–1865), catalyzing naval development in Chile, Japan, Peru, and China, and then flowing back by the 1880s as something dangerously destabilizing: an anxious sense that the US "Old Navy" was falling behind industrial newly made navies in the Pacific. Observations of Pacific wars created a widespread sense of physical and cultural insecurity (above all in California) that US navalists – advocates of peacetime naval expansion – seized on as their first, best argument for funding; an insecurity that by the 1890s also motivated naval deployments against regional competitors like Chile and Japan. Before it was a battleship-dominated "great power" force, the US New Navy was a race with Pacific rivals – newly made navies in their own right – with nothing less than physical security and civilizational superiority on the line.

I.1 A New Navy, among the Pacific's Newly Made Navies

During what was supposedly a "century of peace," there are a surprising number of wars to investigate across an ocean that was anything but Pacific.[5] While in the Atlantic naval battles were "few and far between,"

I.1 A New Navy, among the Pacific's Newly Made Navies 3

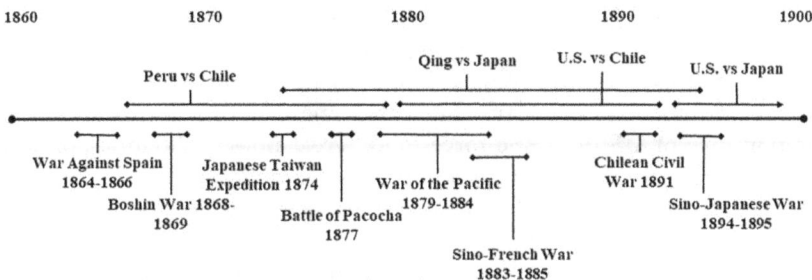

Figure I.1 Pacific wars and naval races (1864–1895)

in the latter half of the nineteenth century, a nearly continuous series of industrial naval races and conflicts played out in waters from Patagonia to Guangdong (Figure I.1).[6]

Even before the conclusion of the US Civil War (1861–1865), there was conflict on the Pacific slope between Chile, Peru, and Spain (1864–1866). Two years later, in Japan, Meiji revolutionaries consolidated national authority through the Boshin War and a naval expedition to Hokkaido (1868–1869). In 1874, Japanese leaders ordered a punitive expedition against Taiwan, catalyzing a naval race with the Qing Empire. In 1877, a rebellion in Peru led to a clash with the Royal Navy at the Battle of Pacocha. Shortly thereafter, Peru, Bolivia, and Chile fought the War of the Pacific (1879–1884) over their mutual frontier. Contemporaneously, across the Pacific, China and France clashed in the Sino-French War (1883–1885). In 1891, Chile fought a civil war. Three years later, the Sino-Japanese War established a new regional order in Northeast Asia (1894–1895). Hot war fought with industrial naval weapons was a more or less constant feature of the late nineteenth century not-so Pacific World.

To date, the Pacific's wars and the small but sophisticated navies that waged them are usually seen as peripheral to US (and global) naval development.[7] The *real* engine(s) of the "American Naval Revolution" in the 1880s and 1890s, the consensus holds, were trends in the industrial North Atlantic: the unification of Germany, British threats to the Caribbean Basin, US congressional politics, increased domestic steel production, the pursuit of overseas markets, and so on. Far removed from the centers of economic productivity, it seemed unlikely that conflicts once dismissed as the "Pigtail War" (Sino-Japanese War, 1894–1895) or "Guano War" (War of the Pacific, 1879–1884) could explain something as fundamental as the US New Navy or the force of "navalism" – the belief in the necessity of a large, peacetime battlefleet – that underwrote it.[8] That said, as scholars and policymakers increasingly (re)emphasize the United States as no "mere Atlantic nation," events in the Pacific seem ripe for reassessment.[9] Stipulating the overall importance of US domestic forces and "great power" Atlantic politics, this book argues that wars across an ocean Herman Melville called the "tide-beating heart of earth" affected the case for US naval expansion in underappreciated but critical ways.[10]

In the case of the US "New Navy" there are at least three reasons to marginalize Europe and stress coincident developments in Asia and the Americas. For a start, in the 1870s and 1880s it did not take a "great power" to challenge the almost astonishingly weak USN; regional, newly made navies in the Pacific were more than enough. Today, most Americans have grown so accustomed to maintaining "a navy second to none" that it takes some effort to imagine the "Old Navy" and its post-Civil War "demobilization and decrepitude."[11] After 1865, USN ships literally rusted or rotted away as Congress slashed budgets and a sclerotic bureaucracy ate up resources (Figure I.2). As often as not, international rankings of "great power" navies simply omitted the United States.[12] In 1887, as US New Navy reforms got underway in earnest, writers at the Chilean *Revista de Marina* could still dismiss the

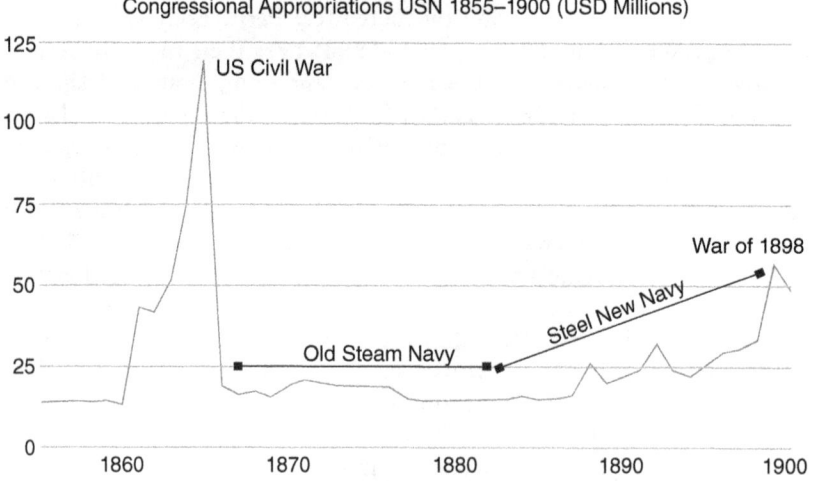

Figure I.2 US naval expenditures (1855–1900)
Source: "Naval Appropriation Laws," *Navy Yearbook* (Washington: Government Printing Office, 1904), 547. Also: *Annual Reports of the Secretary of the Navy* (Washington, DC: Government Printing Office).

I.1 A New Navy, among the Pacific's Newly Made Navies

"offensive and defensive power" of the USN as inferior to the fleets of Japan, Chile, China, and Argentina.[13] That weakness meant that small wars waged by Pacific navies could (and did) have big consequences for the United States as it transitioned from a wooden "Old Navy" to a steel "New" one. Indeed, when seen regionally, the US New Navy becomes one variant competing for influence and security among several, newly made navies building industrial naval power on the fly. Comparisons and intersections between the particular (proper noun US New Navy) and this general type (newly made navies in Peru, China, Chile, and Japan) run throughout the book.

As importantly, the Pacific's wars occurred in and around the chief target of US expansion in the late nineteenth century – the leading edge of "Manifest Destiny" or the "New Empire" of Latin America and the western Pacific.[14] After incorporating the Oregon Territory and California, US commercial interests, military planners, and politicians increasingly saw the Pacific not as an annex to Atlantic developments but rather, in William H. Seward's words, "the chief theater of events in the world's great hereafter."[15] In much the same way the historian Matthew Karp detected a Southern variant of navalism in the antebellum United States – one designed to promote and protect slavery – concerns on the Pacific coast shaped a regionally specific case for US naval building in 1880s: An argument focused not on preparing for a "great power" conflict with Germany or Great Britain but rather soothing anxiety about the proliferation of industrial power across small, newly made navies in the Pacific.[16]

Finally, the comparative peripherality of the Pacific is incongruous with the experiences of many of the New Navy's intellectual leaders. After the US Civil War, a glut of ex-officers, inventors, and advisers traveled out into the Pacific World, bringing with them new technologies and tactics. Alfred Thayer Mahan – the lead protagonist of the global turn toward navalism – was actually in theater for portions of the Boshin War (1868–1869) and the War of the Pacific (1879–1884).[17] He hatched the idea for *The Influence of Sea Power upon History* in Lima while war still smoldered in the Andes.[18] Theodorus B. Mason, the future head of US naval intelligence, and William S. Sims, Mahan's chief rival among USN intellectuals, documented battle damage to Peruvian and Chinese warships, respectively. These men, and many like them, manifest on a personal level some of the entanglements between the Pacific's wars and US naval development. What follows is an argument about those entanglements: about how the diffusion and adaptation of naval technologies in the Pacific shaped the first years of the New Navy and with it the emergence of the United States as a world power.

I.2 Major Themes

Four consistent themes emerge: demand, testing, threat, and opportunism. First, in the absence of major European wars, Pacific naval programs created demand for surplus and experimental weapons. As leaders from Peru to China attempted to build their own newly made navies, they drove production and innovation in the North Atlantic – above all the United States. The first impetus came immediately after the US Civil War as Confederate *materiel* and expertise spread across the Pacific. The torpedo boat commander Charles Read worked as an adviser in Chile; Japanese agents purchased the Confederate ironclad CSS *Stonewall*; the Chinese emissary Zhi Gang (志剛) studied US warships in Boston Harbor as a lesson for Qing naval reform.[19] These lessons and tools were employed in what Qing reformers called "self-strengthening" (自强) – building military and economic capacity to resist North Atlantic imperialism – in two overlapping patterns. Either a *symmetrical* acquisition of ships and artillery designed to compete ship-for-ship with the dominant state in the regional or international system (e.g., the Qing efforts to acquire or build "strong ships and powerful cannon" [船坚炮利]).[20] Or else *asymmetrically* by disrupting legacy platforms through the adoption or adaptation of new technologies (i.e., the torpedo as a means to sink armored warships). As one result of the latter pattern, many prototypical advances such as the torpedo boat and the protected cruiser were spearheaded by Pacific newly made navies hoping to capitalize on "disruptive" innovations during an era of "transcendental" and "unceasing" (日新月异) technological change.[21]

Second, war in the Pacific served as an operational laboratory for naval weapons such as ironclads, torpedoes, electrical apparatuses, and even submarines. Toward such empirical ends, the North Atlantic remained unhelpfully irenic.[22] Fortunately, if only for the navalist set, examples of "actual warfare" abounded across what the British historian (and United States Naval Institute honoree) William Laird Clowes called "hot and well-fought naval wars" from Callao (1866) to Weihaiwei (1895).[23] Even "scanty indications" from such engagements, Mahan contended, were "worth much more than the most carefully arranged programme" of study or war-gaming.[24] In 1879, no less than the first chief of the US Office of Naval Intelligence, Theodorus Mason, recorded a "careful and technical description" of battle damage to a Peruvian ironclad.[25] Fifteen years later, William Sims, one of the New Navy's key innovators, made similar observations of Chinese and Japanese vessels after the battle of Weihaiwei.[26] Like their counterparts in other federal departments, the "Progressives in Navy Blue" needed data with which to make policy and

I.2 Major Themes

found a ready supply of natural experiments in the Pacific.[27] The results were often contradictory, or bent through existing biases, but the Pacific disproportionately provided the raw evidence for navalist debate in the United States.

Third, the news these observers brought back created a great deal of anxiety, nowhere more so than on the comparatively isolated coast of California. Technological proliferation enabled Pacific newly made navies to threaten US territory and ambition; what the Chilean diplomat Benjamín Vicuña Mackenna called "the continual and little equitable division of the Pacific."[28] That sounds as incredible today as it was obvious to contemporaries. The onetime Secretary of the Navy John Long went so far as to rue that in 1882, the warships of "Little Chile" could have attacked San Francisco "and the United States would have been unable to repel them."[29] A decade later, warnings about Japan's threat to Hawaii echoed Long's concerns about Chile nearly word for word.

Material threats, while real enough, were probably most dangerous to assumptions about "Anglo-Saxonism" or what Mahan approvingly referred to as "race patriotism": the belief in the innate superiority of white, Anglophone peoples.[30] Most historians have dismissed all this as cynical threat exaggeration by naval officers, but in a period that reified power into "civilizational" standing, unfavorable comparisons between the Old Navy and Pacific newly made navies stung keenly and sincerely.[31] After all, as the founder of the US Naval War College Stephen Luce argued in 1883, "war led the way to civilization."[32] In his foundational study of arms racing, Samuel Huntington argued that the US "New Navy" was "apparently unrelated to the actions of any other power."[33] In fact, the first phase of expansion – building a handful of small, steel warships – was an explicit race to match power and prestige in the Pacific.

Lastly, these challenges were a crisis *and* opportunity for US navalists – especially on the West Coast. Real threats were sensationalized by men such as Mahan, Henry Cabot Lodge, and Theodore Roosevelt into a cultural force that in the 1880s first shook loose the inertia of Old Navy demobilization. Long before twentieth-century municipalities recruited military bases to spur economic development in "Fortress California," Pacific politicians and newspapers saw regional threats as a rationale for federally financed defenses.[34] The "Yankees" of South America (Chile) and Asia (Japan) may never have been existential dangers to the United States, but the relative standing of the Chilean and Japanese (and to a lesser extent Peruvian and Chinese) newly made navies vis-à-vis the US Old Navy provided an argument for peacetime military investment.[35] Novels forecasted the invasion of the United States by Chinese,

Japanese, and Chilean warships.[36] Congressmen browbeat their opponents with examples of US inferiority. Californian journalists savaged San Francisco's vulnerability to "little" Chile and Japan. In this sense, Pacific wars had an unusual influence: the ability to shame US institutions and politicians into action. Violence in the Pacific would, as Mahan wrote, "tickle the national vanity" of a nation in which "army and navy affairs are little regarded."[37] Ironically, then, the public campaign to sell the peacetime US New Navy hinged on the creative mobilization of actual war in the Pacific.

I.3 Sources and Methods: A *Transwar* History of the Pacific

The Pacific's wars were far-flung; so too are the sources. National archives in the US, UK, Chile, and Peru figure prominently, as documents from military institutions such as the US Naval War College and the Chilean Museo Marítimo Nacional. Corporate records and personal papers offer insights as well. For the Qing Empire, I have relied on published multivolume compilations of government documents as well as digital reproductions of vernacular newspapers, most notably *Shenbao* (申报): a periodical owned by British residents in Shanghai but nonetheless a useful window onto late Qing China.[38] Official records are supplemented by novels, memoirs, and pieces of visual culture.

It is a diverse collection. To make sense of it, I have applied the tools of international and new military history. Adjacent to "transimperial" history, these methods make for what might be called a *transwar* approach: an analysis linking together discrete conflicts, spilling past the conventional thematic, spatial, and temporal framings of war.[39] The term transwar is usually applied to Japan (or more recently Asia) to look for trends across the dividing line of 1945, but its potential ranges further afield.[40] For example, the US Civil War, in traditional accounts, was fought primarily within the continental United States between 1861 and 1865. A transwar perspective would (for a start) follow that conflict's transnational articulations with European shipyards and foreign cotton markets, as well as its postwar (or trans-temporal) connections with South American plantation economies, militaries, and eventually wars. For their part, Californians tended to lump the Pacific's wars together into a generation-long transwar experience, tracing developments from one conflict to another.

This project is "international" in that, like all studies of interstate conflict or oceans, it requires the researcher to transcend national boundaries and with them the blinders of the "logo-map."[41] Describing a war

I.3 Sources and Methods: A *Transwar* History of the Pacific

involving a border (and most do) as "transnational" is redundant, hence my preference for the term transwar. By viewing the Pacific as a coherent unit of analysis, I have also emphasized the erasure of geographic containers erected by area studies programs and military bureaucracies which divide the Pacific into Latin America, East Asia, North America, etc. In the same way Fernand Braudel saw the Mediterranean as an integral whole, the nineteenth-century Pacific was less a barrier between continents than a "freeway" connecting them.[42] That said, having opened the lens of analysis onto the Pacific one is left with the largest geographic feature on earth. To manage it, I have elected to focus on regional states and (mostly) exclude European warships or the growing colonial empires they supported. Stories of "great power" navies, the carving up of China, and the scramble for the Pacific are available elsewhere. The protagonists here are small or medium-sized states – what Immanuel Wallerstein described as "semi-peripheral" – that are too often obscured by interest in big powers and the big navies they wielded.[43] In the 1880s and 1890s these were the relevant peers against which the US New Navy had to measure up.

For an analysis of nineteenth-century naval war this level of oceanic and intermediate analysis has two clear advantages. First, it encourages engagement with a set of middle powers which are poorly captured by the dominant "Age of Empire" narratives.[44] Historians of the period typically describe a "great divergence" of industrial and military power in the late nineteenth century between a set of colonizing "haves" and colonized "have-nots."[45] "The West and the Rest," as Niall Ferguson put it.[46] The Japanese Empire has always been an anomaly because of how uneasily it fits into this division, but it was hardly unique.[47] At different points, Chile, the Qing Empire, Peru, and even the Confederacy occupied similar positions as "semi-peripheral" states and empires outside of the North Atlantic with considerable administrative and naval forces but without robust industrial economies.[48] Falling outside the clean bifurcation of "weak" or "strong" this sort of intermediate power – what US officials sometimes labeled as "semi-barbarian," "half-civilized," or "semi-civilized" – was the norm among newly made navies in the Pacific.[49] Second, and by close association, economic and geographic similarities between these states shaped their ability to organize naval forces, making them a compelling subject for comparative and transnational study. In much the same way the "imperial turn" has shed light on the United States as an empire "among empires" so too does a transwar history of the Pacific suggest that the US New Navy was one among several (inter)related examples of newly made navies.[50]

Most often, the actors who engaged with these developments were government officials from the US and Pacific states. It is a familiar set of diplomats and bureaucrats, but when staged in transwar context surprises abound. Among many intrigues, one finds the USN officer Robert Shufeldt loaning out his advice to the Chinese reformer Li Hongzhang and the Peruvian naval diplomat Aurelio Garcia y Garcia saber-rattling in Liverpool and Tokyo.[51] Arms-makers and innovators are common figures as well, be they corporations such as Armstrong or individual engineers, for example John Lay, peddling torpedoes from Lima to Tianjin. US domestic views are accessed primarily through congressional records and press reports, alongside the artists and propagandists who worked to market the New Navy to the public.

I.4 Implications

Most directly, this project engages the history of the US New Navy and its origins. The past hundred years have generated a small library of causal interpretations for nineteenth-century US naval expansion. There have been realists (emphasizing German unification and/or the British threat to a future Panama Canal) and economic historians (interested in the navy as a tool to absorb surplus domestic steel and secure markets overseas) as well as scholars of domestic (Congress) and institutional politics (most pointing to the advocacy of the US Naval Institute and Naval War College).[52] Accounts of specific individuals, squadrons, or weapons are common as well.[53] In the wake of the cultural turn, historians have favored ideological (navalism and progressivism) and social (sentiments about technologies and gendered anxieties, among others) forces.[54] In the aggregate, it makes for a convincing set of explanations, albeit one that lists toward the North Atlantic.

This project rejects none of these approaches and instead hopes to expand on them by more fully considering the Pacific. It is less "revision" than a geographic and temporal "reframing" of the New Navy. For instance, the defense of Panama against European competitors clearly mattered a great deal to US navalists, but the canal was valuable to the United States only inasmuch as it linked the Mississippi to the Pacific.[55] For another example, Dirk Bonker's *Militarism in a Global Age* ably traced strands of navalist ideology in the United States, Britain, and Germany.[56] A global perspective on this globalizing age, however, would have to account for the theorists in Chile, China, Peru, Japan, and beyond who produced their own ideas about naval war. Five years before Mahan published *The Influence of Sea Power upon History*, the inaugural issue of the Chilean *Revista de Marina* proclaimed, "*He who controls the*

I.4 Implications

sea, dominates the land" and that the "Peoples who have taken hold of the empire of the sea surpass all the others in their riches, power and civilization."[57] In 2012, one historian in China even contended that the Opium War-era (1839–1842) reformer Wei Yuan (魏源) anticipated Mahan's concept of sea power (海权) by half a century.[58]

An additional product of pivoting to the Pacific is relevance to the growing field of oceanic history, which to date has shown limited interest in military subjects.[59] Oceanic scholars have made clear that when seen as a regional unit (including the Americas), the nineteenth-century Pacific teems with circulating peoples, goods, and ideas. Naval developments mirrored that dynamism – a fact the maritime historian W. E. B. DuBois long ago recognized about the Atlantic.[60] In 1866, the ex-Confederate naval commander John Tucker was hired by Peruvian leaders to organize an attack on Spanish Manila.[61] During the Sino-Japanese War, the Chinese minister Li Hongzhang advocated buying a small fleet of warships from Chile wholesale.[62] While stationed in Japan in 1868, a young Mahan investigated "the most terrible and wonderful thing that has ever come within my experience": a group of half-starved Chinese laborers who had mutinied against their overseers and wended back from the coast of Peru to Hokkaido, Japan.[63] War fostered odd connections across the Pacific World.

Finally, a more thorough appreciation of the Pacific's wars challenges existing histories of technology and modern conflict. Historians and theorists have typically defined "modern warfare" by three criteria: (1) mass armies (usually national) using (2) industrial weapons in (3) a three-dimensional environment (in the air or under the sea).[64] To this particular "grammar of modernity" should be added the nocturnal or twenty-four-hour environment, as submarine war and illumination (searchlights and later radar) expanded the possibilities for violence after dark.[65] World War I offers a clear example of "modern warfare," but it is hardly a paradigmatic break.[66] If this four-part definition is applied to the hot wars of the nineteenth century, then the contours of "naval modernity" appear to take shape incrementally in the Pacific. Conflict in the region provided the first opportunities to push industrial naval *war* (not merely testing) into the undersea and nocturnal environment. Consider the precedents set: the first launch of a mobile torpedo (Pacocha, 1877), the first engagement between seagoing ironclads (Angamos, 1879), the first armored warship sunk by a torpedo (Caldera, 1891), the first battle between armored fleets (Yalu, 1894), and the first systematic use of automobile torpedoes as an offensive weapon (Weihaiwei, 1895).

More than semantics, interrogating the origins of "naval modernity" doubles as a provocation about power in the industrial age.

Conventionally, histories of the late nineteenth century explain the rise of North Atlantic imperialism by linking industrial productivity to military effectiveness.[67] As Jürgen Osterhammel has argued, in the nineteenth century, "instruments of power were directly related to industrial capacity. The widening economic disparity between countries went hand in hand with the gap in military technology."[68] Late nineteenth-century imperialists summed up the industrial/nonindustrial divide more succinctly: "Whatever happens we have got / the maxim gun and they have not."[69]

A history of naval war written from the Pacific muddies these Manichean depictions. Through the adoption of technologies, Pacific newly made navies could (and on occasion did) upset the "global dominance of the West" with the very products that built empires in the first place.[70] Note that the same Liverpool firm responsible for the steamship *Nemesis* in the First Opium War (1839–1842) also built CSS *Alabama* (1862) and the Peruvian *Huáscar* (1866) – themselves nemeses of North Atlantic navies.[71] This was not a simple case of passively receiving advanced weapons and doctrines from centers of North Atlantic industrial power but one of syncretism and adaptation.[72] Since the 1990s, historians of North America's borderlands have excavated the agency of indigenous peoples who mixed geographic advantages with Euro-US technologies to blunt continental imperialism.[73] Out on the watery frontier of the US "New Empire," newly made Pacific navies likewise adapted the tools of industrial militaries to underwrite programs of resistance and even territorial expansion. In doing so they also participated in the messy, global making of modern naval warfare. For politicians and naval officers in cities such as Tacoma and San Francisco, such developments were as stunning as the need to play catch-up was imperative.

I.5   Chapter Outline

In the 1860s and 1870s, US Civil War-era tactics and technologies proliferated out into the Pacific World where they enabled naval building and conflict. By the 1880s, those regional conflicts and the newly made navies that fought them generated an anxiety about the physical security and civilizational superiority of the United States. Angst about the Pacific, in turn, encouraged the first investments in and deployments of the US New Navy. The chapters here follow that basic process chronologically.

Chapter 1 frames Confederate naval strategy during the US Civil War as a form of "self-strengthening" that had much in common with efforts throughout the Pacific World in the 1860s and 1870s. Like the Confederacy, Pacific states faced the task of creating navies on weak

I.5 Chapter Outline

industrial foundations. To overcome their limitations, Confederate navy builders relied on radical innovations and foreign acquisitions to compete with the materially superior United States. The US Civil War was, in this sense, a vast practical experiment for small or industrially weak states confronting North Atlantic power. Beginning in the 1860s, the "template" set by the Confederacy – local adaptation with cheap asymmetric weapons and the overseas acquisition of qualitatively advanced systems – reached numerous newly made navies in the Pacific.

Chapter 2 follows veterans and surplus *materiel* after the US Civil War as both found employment in the Pacific: critically during the War against Spain (1864–1865), the Boshin War (1868–1869), and an early phase of Qing self-strengthening. New technologies and tactics deployed by the Confederate States Navy (CSN) – such as the torpedo and ironclad – were especially attractive to small navies facing materially superior adversaries. That was true for structural reasons but also because of transnational connections between firms and Civil War veterans. When viewed through a transwar lens, the 1860s and 1870s were less a "Dark Age" of USN stagnation and more a fit of US-inspired innovation in the Pacific World.

Chapter 3 investigates how the proliferation of advanced weapons catalyzed intra-regional naval races on both sides of the Pacific. One state's efforts to acquire naval power in response to European imperialists – self-strengthening – created classic security dilemmas for its neighbors. What began as efforts to accrue defensive capabilities in China and Peru soon morphed into spiraling naval races with Japan and Chile, respectively. Leveraging new technologies and international networks, these races were every bit as dynamic as their better-studied analogs in the North Atlantic. Both also led to war within a generation. For those looking out from San Francisco, the Pacific's naval races were further significant because they offered a contrast with the deterioration of the "Old Steam Navy." Even as it continued to perform useful missions as a constabulary force, the Old Navy was made up of ships built in the 1850s. By maintaining its status quo, the Old Navy was, in practice, falling behind newly made Pacific navies. Early instigators of naval reform in the United States took notice.

Chapter 4 puts the Pacific's naval races to the test by analyzing the War of the Pacific (1879–1884) and the Sino-French War (1883–1885). These two wars are rarely compared, despite occurring more or less contemporaneously and employing many of the same technologies. In the War of the Pacific, Chilean forces achieved a decisive victory at sea, securing lines of communication for an amphibious invasion of Peru and transforming the Chilean Navy into the "preponderant force in South

America."[74] In doing so, the Chilean newly made navy became a credible danger to the "Old Steam Navy" and the "New Navy's" future pacing threat. Across the Pacific, strategic defeat in the Sino-French War masked Chinese tactical successes that would guide the Qing Empire's self-strengthening efforts in the coming decades. Defeat was not a refutation but rather confirmation of the need to cultivate effective naval power. Modern naval warfare began to take shape, realigning the Pacific's geopolitics along the way.

Chapter 5 tracks the US reaction to these wars, with a focus on perspectives from the Pacific slope. When refracted through San Francisco, the story of naval expansion in the 1880s – the creation of a small but respectable force of steel cruisers and gunboats – becomes a form of racing against Pacific newly made navies and the crises they engendered. Californians howled for a New Navy, citing fears of Chile, China, and eventually Japan. Without Peru to balance against it, the Chilean Navy became at once a substantive threat to the USN and a challenge to the self-image of the United States as the dominant "civilization" in the Americas. Conversely, Qing defeat in the Sino-French War confirmed perceptions of Chinese "backwardness," reinforcing objections to Chinese immigration in the 1880s. Paradoxically, the latent potential of the Chinese Empire and its rapid acquisition of warships after 1885 also offered rationales for defending against Chinese military power. The "Yellow Peril" was a threat in more than one sense. Not coincidentally, the first appropriations for the New Navy *and* the Chinese Exclusion Act were both passed in 1882–1883.

Chapter 6 shows how naval leaders tested this first phase of US naval expansion against Pacific antagonists. Having raced with the Chilean newly made navy for a decade, US naval leaders were eager for a demonstration at the expense of "little Chili." As of 1891, the New Navy mattered little to North Atlantic powers but was sufficiently powerful to force Chile into diplomatic settlements during the Chase of the *Itata* (1891) and the *Baltimore* Incident (1891–1892) – the New Navy's first successful acts of "cruiser diplomacy." By 1893, as its sailors and marines intervened once more in Hawaii, the New Navy had a record of achievement in the Pacific to celebrate. Naval exhibitions from Astoria, OR to New York did just that, citing success in the Pacific as proof of the New Navy's value.

Chapter 7 tracks similar themes into the 1890s, as Japan replaced Chile in the role of Pacific bête noire – almost as if by necessity. As the relative power of the Chilean Navy faded after 1892, Japanese victory in the Sino-Japanese War (1895) created a new, still more racially salient threat. In the same way that California's security was a source of anxiety during the US–Chilean naval race in the 1880s, Hawaii served as a site of contestation between US and Japanese imperialisms, acutely in 1893 and 1897. US policymakers and naval officers were quick to notice the similarities and used recent experiences with Chile as a lens through which to understand Japan. The upshot was that the origins of the US–Japanese "Pacific Estrangement" were intimately tied to navalist politics and US–Chilean tensions in the 1880s.[75]

All this to say that events in the Pacific mattered disproportionately to the early origins of the New Navy and its employment. In the much the way that big-ship navalism was a transnational craze in late nineteenth-century Atlantic, so too does an emphasis on the Pacific World reveal multiple newly made navies driven by the intersecting imperatives of self-strengthening and intra-regional naval racing. As Pacific states raced against each other in the 1870s and 1880s, the growing delta between the post-Civil War Old Navy's stagnation and Pacific dynamism helped advocates justify naval investment as a matter of security and prestige. Only after this shift – modest in scope and reactive to the Pacific World – were conditions set for what the New Navy would eventually become and what historians most commonly recognize it as: a battlefleet for hemispheric defense and transoceanic offensive war.

1 The Confederate "Navy to Construct"

This is a story about the Pacific, and yet – in the first of many ironies – it begins not in Valparaiso, San Francisco, or Yokohama but on the river Mersey in the first year of the US Civil War. There, shuttling between Liverpool's banks and dockyards, the Confederate "secret agent" James Bulloch enjoyed a sense of well-earned satisfaction about his efforts to acquire a radical sort of newly made navy all his own. Dispatched to Britain in 1861, he had already overseen the conversion and construction of the Confederate cruisers *Florida* and *Alabama* – fast, lightly armed ships built to raid the US merchant marine. Returning to Liverpool in March 1862, he brought with him a wider mandate: to ink contracts for oceangoing armored warships that (he and his superiors hoped) would break the Union blockade. In the summer of 1863, Bulloch celebrated progress on the two 3,000 ton "rams" taking shape at the Laird Brothers Shipyard, fantasizing that after sweeping past the USN's wooden ships they could shell New York or Boston with impunity.[1] Here – in the metropolitan heart of the "Empire of Cotton" – was the nucleus of a newly made Confederate navy: a force built on little or no existing inventory and leveraging technological innovation to upset a numerically superior fleet.[2]

Unluckily (for him), by September 1863 Bulloch's agenda foundered on the question of British neutrality and the Foreign Enlistment Act.[3] The Laird-built cruiser *Alabama* escaped embargo under a fig-leaf cover story about its civilian utility. But unlike the Confederacy's cruisers, the armored warships being fitted out by Bulloch in Liverpool, or the "Scottish Sea Monster" in Glasgow, were unmistakably made for war.[4] Fearing the British government might seize the ships as contraband, Bulloch cut bait and abandoned the projects.

The experience left Bulloch embittered, but his frustrations worked to the advantage of many navy builders. In 1869, an eleven-year-old Theodore Roosevelt visited Liverpool – where Bulloch still lived in exile – taking in the "could-have-been" possibility of the CSN and with it the importance of naval power.[5] It was a lesson he never forgot. Even earlier, Bulloch's strategy found purchase among other navy builders – especially those in the Pacific World facing similar structural disadvantages. By 1863, agents from Pacific states arrived in Liverpool, working like Bulloch to conjure up newly made navies for defense against North Atlantic pressure. Even in failure, Bulloch and other Confederate leaders had articulated a vision of what a small, relatively unindustrialized state could accomplish through foreign acquisitions and radically innovative technologies. In the coming decades, that same sense of possibility – the chance to compete – spread across the Pacific World's self-strengthening movements as a template for naval power on the cheap. Similarities stemmed from common structural constraints, but as often as not the proliferation of the CSN model was also the result of explicit imitation or the transnational circulation of veterans and/or tactical manuals after 1865. Unlike Bulloch and the CSN, Pacific self-strengtheners achieved lasting results, building small but technically advanced newly made navies – some of which later challenged the USN.

This chapter makes little attempt to break new archival ground on the CSN per se but rather considers the Civil War's relevance to the Pacific by resituating the CSN in an international and comparative (i.e., transwar) context. Intersections with the Pacific World have been underestimated to date by the tendency to see the CSN as a (sub)national question of the US Civil War.[6] A transwar reframing brings into focus the CSN's position as one of many export-dependent economies building navies in the 1860s as a response to the shock of North Atlantic naval power. In this respect, the CSN offered a technical-strategic template – and indeed a practical experiment under the conditions of real war – for maritime self-strengthening against major industrial powers. Geographical and economic factors forced the Confederacy – as much as China or Peru – to turn to experimental technologies. As the technical and tactical legacies of the Civil War proliferated in the Pacific during the 1860s and 1870s, they inspired newly made navies, arms races, wars, and credible threats to the North Atlantic's monopoly on industrial naval violence. A case for the making of *the* US New Navy in response to all this activity was not far behind.

1.1 The Confederate Variant of Self-strengthening

Appreciating the extent to which Confederate tactics, *materiel*, and personnel mattered to the Pacific World requires a shift to a more capacious understanding of the CSN. Most obviously situating the CSN in an international context – much in the way transnational and comparative historians have reframed slavery and the Civil War in general – reveals parallels to what nineteenth-century Chinese reformers called "self-strengthening": a drive to acquire, build, or adapt industrial technologies to resist North Atlantic imperialism.[7] Because of its geographic and economic position, the Confederacy shared a great deal with other weak, coastal states – most often in the Pacific – pursuing new capabilities. While usually applied to the Qing, the impulse to self-strengthen was widespread. Though it varied according to specific cases, in a general sense self-strengthening appears as a global reaction to industrially backed imperialism.[8] Historians have used self-strengthening as an analytical category for late nineteenth-century China, Japan, Turkey, Egypt, and Ethiopia – but curiously not the Confederacy.[9]

The comparability of the CSN to contemporaneous self-strengthening movements (or newly made navies) has largely been obscured by methodological nationalism and a bias toward the continental history of the Civil War.[10] Owing to the raw scale of the violence on land, military historians usually portray the CSN as a subset of a subnational conflict.[11] Embedding the CSN in a transwar context forces a reexamination of its significance. Far from exceptional, the CSN experimented with a common model of self-strengthening. Because of its ambition and record of tactical (if not strategic) success against the USN, the CSN was not only representative of wider trends but prototypical of later movements that leveraged technological change and recent experience to "catch up." That fact becomes even clearer when CSN operations are contrasted against the Pacific wars and naval races of the 1860s and 1870s.

Two (primary) structural factors encouraged common strategies among Confederate leaders and other self-strengtheners: economic dependency and geographic vulnerability to the sea. Economically, the Confederacy's cotton crop made it similar to other "peripheral" and "semi-peripheral" states organized to extract – most often through coercive labor regimes – commodities such as sugar, guano, copper, cotton, tea, and silk in exchange for manufactured goods from the industrial "core" in the North Atlantic.[12] One result was to limit domestic industrial capacity and create dependency on European factories and yards.[13] As warships became more technically sophisticated, industrial dependency had obvious implications for newly made navy builders in the Confederacy and Pacific world alike. In a telling example of the Confederacy's comparative similarities to other self-strengthening states, Laird Brothers built warships in the 1860s for the CSN, China, Brazil, and Peru – more or less simultaneously.[14]

In the case of the US Civil War, the industrial asymmetry was striking. Even as Southern slaveholders pioneered cutting-edge techniques of capitalist exploitation, the Confederacy's export-driven economy

1.1 The Confederate Variant of Self-strengthening

lacked significant shipbuilding capacity.[15] During the antebellum period, "Southern Navalists" cultivated the federal USN as a force for the protection and expansion of slavery into and across the Americas.[16] But once stripped of this national protection, Confederate leaders faced the prospect of building a navy with little or no existing inventory or infrastructure.[17] Surveying the industrial potential of the Confederacy in 1862, Stephen Mallory, the Secretary of the CSN, enumerated the many ways in which material inferiority impeded the "speedy construction of a navy": The South had few mills, few yards, and fewer still engine-making facilities.[18] Bulloch lamented the challenge of building a navy when "the means for constructing and equipping a naval force for offensive warfare, or even for a vigorous resistance, were practically nil."[19] The Confederate Naval Academy – such that it was – had no campus and made do holding classes onboard the aging CSS *Patrick Henry*, anchored in the James River.[20] In 1862, Mallory summed up the issue by reporting to his superiors, "the United States have a constructed Navy; we have a Navy to construct."[21]

In this respect, the Confederacy resembled a number of states facing the threat of North Atlantic gunboats. Confronting a Spanish squadron in 1865, Chilean Foreign Minister Alvaro Covarrubias noted that Chile would have to "extemporize armies" after being caught unprepared and consequently "almost disarmed and without elements for a naval war."[22] That same year, Jose Manuel Pinto, the Minister of the Chilean Navy, complained that whatever ships Chile had "at present, or which we hope to have, they demand arsenals" without which "there is no service possible."[23] Even states with modern shipyards, such as those established by the Qing reformers Li Hongzhang and Zuo Zongtang in the 1860s, needed time to actually build warships and develop technical proficiency (人才).[24] As ironclad steamships improved in the 1860s, it was relatively easy to recognize naval power, Mallory wrote to the Confederate Committee on Naval Affairs, as "a matter of the first necessity."[25] "Strong ships and power cannons" (船坚炮利), agreed Li Hongzhang in 1867, were clearly an "existential matter."[26] Achieving that end was another story, impeded by material limitations. As the pace of North Atlantic industrialization accelerated, competitors faced a daunting task.

Geographic liabilities were as important as economic constraints. The Confederacy's port cities and coastal communities had to be defended from amphibious pressure. More dangerous still, in the same way that US river networks allowed for slavery's south–north expansion from the Caribbean ("our steamboat imperialism" in the words of the historian Maya Jasanoff), so too did the Confederacy's rivers and ports offer avenues of attack for Union gunboats.[27] USN ships steaming "up the

Yazoo" and other rivers threatened to carve up the Confederacy like a melon – indeed they eventually did.[28] Defending against that vulnerability was a persistent challenge and one the CSN never adequately solved.

Naval strategists in Chile, China, and Japan could (and sometimes did) empathize. In 1866, José Manuel Pinto, wrote that Chile was bound by the Andes to the east and the Atacama to the north, leaving its coast the "only flank to guard" and nowhere to retreat.[29] Li Hongzhang stressed similar vulnerabilities along China's "vast coastline" and river networks.[30] Well into the 1880s, Li could observe to the US naval diplomat Robert Shufeldt that "the geographical positions of the United States and China are fairly similar," owing to their coastlines and river networks, complicating defensive measures.[31] And of course, after the arrival of Perry's Black Ships in 1853, the "extreme vulnerability of Japan to maritime aggression" was self-evident to Tokugawa and Meiji officials.[32] With the benefit of historical perspective, Alfred Thayer Mahan theorized that an extensive coastline and deepwater ports were a useful element of "sea power" but only if defended by appropriate investments.[33] Nineteenth-century self-strengtheners in both the Pacific and the Confederacy had the coastline but scrambled to create newly made navies to match it.

For the CSN (and later imitators), material inferiority and geographical vulnerability were not, though, without their advantages. Given its structural constraints, CSN officers set about seizing the advantages at hand; first and foremost a willingness to innovate with new industrial technologies free of the institutional fetters and path dependencies of the USN.[34] Alongside desperation, that sense of liberation from convention produced a staggering degree of innovation. Mallory argued to Jefferson Davis that because of the Confederacy's inability to compete symmetrically with the Union, its newly made navy should instead focus on acquiring modern (if experimental) industrial weapons, "compensating by their offensive and defensive power for the inequality of numbers."[35] Against the power of Union industrial productivity and numerical advantage, Mallory proposed an asymmetric strategy relying on new and prototypical naval technologies; above all ironclad warships that would render wooden-hulled USN ships obsolete.[36]

Historians have called this a "technology strategy," or strategy of "technical surprise," but it might better be understood in a transwar context as the Confederate variant of self-strengthening: an attempt to seize on paradigmatically innovative technologies – namely ironclads (which could defeat wooden ships) and the torpedo (which could defeat ironclads) – to upset the inherited advantages of a North Atlantic power.[37] It was a form of technical-strategic synthesis, borne of material inferiority, institutional creativity, and geographic vulnerabilities. Here industrial technology would not just improve the military performance of warships; it was a revolutionary set of wonder weapons that could reshape the course of the war in a strategic sense. Just as the challenges to CSN self-strengtheners were common across Pacific states in the nineteenth century, so too (with variations) did this technical-strategic gamble travel widely. Structural challenges encouraged officials in Charleston, Callao, Valparaiso, and Fuzhou to rely on mirrored naval strategies: namely the foreign acquisition of armored warships and/or the local adaptation of new, asymmetric technologies such as the torpedo. This chapter's following sections explore how this all worked in practice.

1.2 Peru, the Confederacy, and the Liverpool Connection

In 1861, the CSN faced two existential and unenviable tasks. First, given the Confederate States of America's (CSA) export/import-dependent economy, the maintenance of sea lines of communication to Europe was critical.[38] The best means to run, or ideally break, the Union blockade was a constant source of debate and intrigue among Confederate leaders. The second challenge was to defend the Confederacy's coastline and river networks against Union amphibious attacks and penetration. Without a "constructed navy," Confederate naval strategy hinged on three technologies: (1) steam-powered commerce-harassing cruisers such as the *Alabama*; (2) ironclad warships to challenge USN sea control; and finally (3) torpedo-mines and shore batteries to resist Union amphibious attacks.

Locally produced warships such as CSS *Virginia* were the most obvious (and after the fact famous) manifestation of self-strengthening through novel technologies. As navies transitioned from wooden-hulled to armored warships, late adopters had major advantages. In 1862, at Hampton Roads, the CSN seized on exactly this ephemeral advantage, devastating wooden USN ships. But while CSS *Virginia* and its eventual fight with the USN ironclad *Monitor* inspired a great deal of excitement – poems, memorabilia, even *Monitor*-themed cheese boxes – the Confederacy's domestic production of ironclads was never a sustainable strategy for resistance.[39] Without shipyards and foundries, the Confederacy was unable to symmetrically compete with Union shipbuilding on a ton-for-ton basis. The Union had the shipyards to turn out monitors by the dozen; the Confederacy did not. Throughout the course of the war, the CSN managed to bolt together twenty ironclads of various shapes and sizes. The Union, by contrast, purpose built seventy-one ironclads.⁴⁰ In a revealing detail, a squadron of Confederate river defense "Cottonclads" resorted to using compressed bales of cotton for protection in lieu of metal armor.⁴¹ The export-dependent South had lots of cotton; ironworks were another matter.

This limitation encouraged a turn to asymmetric warfare and commerce raiding, enabled by European firms. Leveraging European industrial productivity and political sympathies, CSN agents fanned out across France and Britain to buy the ironclads, cruisers, and gunboats they were unable to build at home. Unsurprisingly, in Liverpool – likely the most pro-Confederate city in Europe – they found shipbuilders and bankers happy to oblige Confederate aims.⁴² Just over the river Mersey, the shipyard Laird Brothers first became involved in the US Civil War when it contracted with Bulloch to build the "rebel pirate" *Alabama*: a Confederate commerce-raider that captured or sank sixty-four US merchant ships and provoked a storm of diplomatic correspondence between Washington, London, and Richmond.⁴³ This program of cruiser warfare had some prospect of strategic success and was long seen as the "most effective" Confederate naval effort.⁴⁴ Economic hardship brought about by commerce raiding, the theory went, might force a northern political collapse. At the very least, the USN would have to divert warships to convoy merchant shipping, thereby lessening the effectiveness of the blockade of the Confederate coast.⁴⁵

Like CSS *Virginia*, such dreams amounted to little strategic consequence. While Confederate raiders destroyed large quantities of Union shipping, they never seriously eroded USN sea control or the blockade. As Mahan (who took part in the Union blockade) noted after the war, campaigns of commerce destruction tend to be only marginally effective next to fleet actions. His experience in the Civil War offered a near textbook example. Red tape mattered as well. US diplomats scrutinized foreign shipbuilding in an effort to snuff out would-be *Alabamas* before they could launch. A paperwork war over CSS *Alabama*'s record of destruction endured well after the conclusion of the Civil War, souring Anglo–US relations into the 1870s.⁴⁶

Domestically produced warships (*Virginia*) and maritime raiding (*Alabama*), then, had lackluster effects for the CSN; that left the promise of technological gambles. Laird was again a central player in the Confederacy's most technologically ambitious efforts. Undeterred by *Alabama*'s (Laird vessel No. 290) notoriety, Bulloch returned to Liverpool in 1862 to doubled down on the Confederate technology strategy, ordering Laird vessels No. 294 and No. 295: a pair of ironclad, seagoing "rams," with "shield and patent apparatuses" designed by the British naval architect Cowper Coles (Figure 1.1).⁴⁷

1.2 Peru, the Confederacy, and the Liverpool Connection

Figure 1.1 Confederate rams
Source: "HMS *Scorpion*," S27/002, WA/UK.[48]

Contracted in July 1862, only months after the Battle of Hampton Roads, these "Laird Rams" were an experiment in naval architecture building on recent technical lessons and the strategic imperatives of the US Civil War.[49] Designated as the "North Carolina" class, the ships were designed to engage directly with the USN, hoping that, as Mallory had advocated, "inequality of numbers may be compensated by invulnerability."[50] Unlike the largely improvisational (if locally effective) CSS *Virginia*, these ships were cutting edge and purpose built to upset USN numerical preponderance. Their blueprints were so novel (and the pressures to obscure their military utility from US officials so intense) that the contracts Laird provided to Bulloch warned they could only "show *generally* the class of vessel and machinery."[51] That same technological ingenuity produced rampant optimism about the rams' potential.[52] Bulloch claimed that in contrast to the *Virginia* – limited by range, endurance, and firepower – the Laird Rams promised "something more than harbor or even coast defense ... they could sweep away the entire blockading fleet of the enemy."[53] Raids by Confederates such as Charles Read – a future mercenary in South America's newly made navies – against Portland Maine (1863) highlighting the Union seaboard's vulnerability.[54] Perhaps, as the Confederate historian Thomas

Scharf argued, the rams could even "break the blockade of the Southern ports, and lay some of the Northern cities under ransom."[55] The assistant Secretary of the USN, Gustavus Fox, took the threat seriously and ordered every diplomatic effort be made to prevent their release to the Confederacy.[56]

Unhappily for the CSN, the stipulations of the Foreign Enlistment Act eventually frustrated Bulloch's ambitions.[57] British law prohibited the building and arming of naval vessels for a belligerent state. Bulloch might have skirted the letter of the law with *Alabama*, but the armored Laird Rams were weapons in and of themselves. What civilian purpose could there be for the vessels' titular rams – designed to rip into the hulls of opposing ships – or proprietary gun turrets? After Whitehall prohibited their sale to the Confederacy in 1863, the Royal Navy purchased the rams, recommissioning them as HMS *Scorpion* and HMS *Wivern* in October 1865.[58] For Bulloch and his backers, it was a heavy blow given the financial and emotional investment. Many at the time believed, as the historian Frank Merli later noted, that "September [1863] at Birkenhead no less than July at Gettysburg, doomed the Confederacy."[59] In what should be an inspiration to every staff officer, good paperwork won the USN perhaps its most important victory in the Civil War.

It was not, however, all gloom in Liverpool for would-be navy builders. The Confederate foray into ironclad shipbuilding was a prolog to a steady stream of self-strengtheners looking to acquire modern forms of naval power. In 1863, Laird launched the screw-steamer *Tien Tsin* and the armed paddle steamer *Kwang Tung* for Qing China; part of an ill-fated attempt to buy the ready-made, foreign-built Lay-Osborne Flotilla.[60] In 1865 Laird contracted the *Bahia* and *Lima Baros* for Brazil.[61] And in 1866 Laird delivered the *Huáscar* to Peru: an ironclad monitor for use in the then ongoing conflict between Peru, Chile, and Spain.[62] The Confederate Laird Rams were exceptional because of the diplomatic fury that attended them, but as artifacts of naval power through the applications of new technologies they were representative of a trend on which Laird happily capitalized. In what became a theme in the coming decade, Confederate distress was to the advantage of the Pacific's newly made navies.

Consider the Peruvian ironclad *Huáscar*. Laird completed the vessel in 1866, but its origins belong to the comparative world of the Civil War and the Confederate strategy of self-strengthening through novel technologies: of "fighting with iron against wood."[63] As early as May 1862, Peruvian representatives in the United States had entertained offers from the shipbuilder John Ericsson for "a vessel of war with

1.2 Peru, the Confederacy, and the Liverpool Connection

revolving turrets on the 'Monitor' system," then used by the USN.[64] The Peruvian agent in New York assumed that this was the "best system yet invented" and had exposed the "comparative inferiority" of CSS *Virginia*.[65] That sale was blocked by questions of neutrality and resource availability but nonetheless reflected an attempt by Peruvian agents to seize on advances from the US Civil War mere weeks after the Battle of Hampton Roads.

The Peruvian drive to acquire an armored warship turned more urgent in 1864, when a Spanish fleet sailed into the Pacific with ominous demands for its former colonies (see Chapter 2). Having been turned away by the United States, Peruvian agents traveled to Liverpool, following the same logic and incentives that motivated Bulloch. Jose Maria Salcedo arrived at Laird's doorstep fast on the heels of his Confederate counterpart.[66] Like Bulloch, he came with an order for small cruising ships but quickly expanded his objectives. What Peru really needed, Salcedo concluded, was an oceangoing armored ram – something state of the art – that would allow Peru to meet the Spanish threat. In an effort to do just that, Salcedo contracted the *Huáscar* in the summer of 1864.[67] Just one year after the launch of the Confederate rams, "vessel No. 321" was built with the benefit of experience gained at the Confederacy's expense (Figure 1.2).[68] Key, iterative improvements included a centrally located, rotating armored turret. Coles, the ship's architect, considered it one of his finest inventions.[69] Cheerleading for its local industrialists, the *Portsmouth Times and Naval Gazette* as well as *Liverpool Albion* approved of *Huáscar* as the world's first proof that an "armour-clad ship ... can be built of Captain Cowper Coles' turret principle to combine speed and sea-going qualities of the first order."[70]

During the same period, the British firm Samuda Brothers built the 3,000 ton armored frigate *Independencia* under the supervision of the Peruvian officer Aurelio Garcia y Garcia. This ship, too, benefited from Confederate self-strengthening effort – in its own way. Early in the war, Samuda built a turreted ironclad warship with Coles' technology in a speculative endeavor to attract Confederate buyers.[71] Snarled in red tape, that ship eventually became the Prussian *Arminius*, but it prepared Samuda for similar contracts. For Garcia y Garcia, Samuda's practice appeared to have paid off in the making of *Independencia*. Ordered in 1864, *Independencia*, he contended, represented the apogee of naval construction, featuring innovations such as "a magnificent propeller steam engine" and a "water distillation apparatus that could keep the ship at sea for fifty days at a time." The British engineer Edward J. Reed (a chief rival and critic of Cowper Coles' turreted concept, featured on the *Huáscar*) celebrated *Independencia* as "one of the best ships of its class

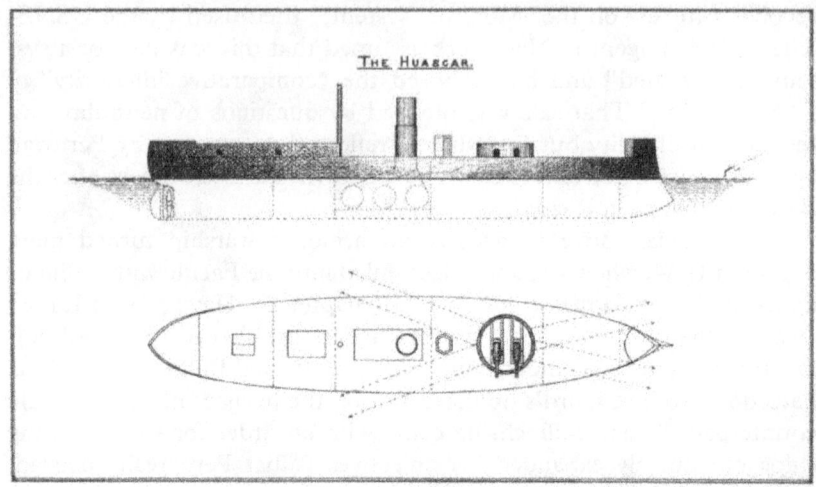

Figure 1.2 "Naval Architecture Sketch of the Peruvian Ironclad Monitor *Huáscar*"
Source: "Peruvian Ironclad Monitor *Huáscar*," James Wilson King, *The War-Ships and Navies of the World* (Boston: A. Williams, 1880).

to leave an English shipyard." Most importantly, Garcia y Garcia wrote in an echo of Mallory and Bulloch that by concentrating "the most offensive and defensive power in one ship," *Independencia* could overcome North Atlantic advantages.[72]

Forecasting the impact of the ironclads on the War against Spain from his hotel in Great Britain, Garcia y Garcia had high hopes. Mirroring Bulloch's aspiration to "sweep away" the Union blockade, Garcia y Garcia reported that the *Huáscar* and *Independencia* were exactly what Peru needed to rid the Pacific of the "declared enemies of America and highwaymen." He argued, furthermore, that if *Huáscar* and *Independencia* were to attack Spanish possessions in the West Indies, Peru would "conquer much glory to our flag."[73] That was less a boast than an ambition to exploit the paradigmatic significance of the moment. It was no more grandiose than Confederate dreams of raiding New York and Boston.

Of course, for Coles and Laird Brothers, both Salcedo and Bulloch's efforts to acquire an ironclad fleet were reciprocally advantageous. For a start, there was money to be made. The *Huáscar*'s turret alone (the most distinctive feature of Coles' design) cost £5,700.[74] More notably, Peruvian (and CSN) demand supplemented lukewarm British interest, offering a practical test of his designs.[75] Coles complained that while the Admiralty had hesitated, "foreign governments ... besides private firms have proved the principle by building new and seaworthy turret vessels" such as the *Huáscar*.[76] Captain Sherard Osborn, RN likewise accused Admiralty officials, in contrast to foreign ones, of providing Coles with nothing but "ignorance and red tape."[77] The Peruvian "navy to construct," like the CSN, could afford no such reticence about innovation.[78] In practice, the experimental *Huáscar*'s "most satisfactory" performance en route to Peru was valuable proof (it seemed) of the design's seaworthiness, then under (rightful) skepticism in Britain.[79] Laird Brothers wrote to the *Times* that it had already built ironclad monitors for Peru and Brazil, so there was nothing holding up the private sector from producing said weapons for the Royal Navy. As it was, the only turreted warships in British hands were the Laird Rams, originally built for the CSN.[80] Foreign experience, from the Confederacy to Peru, had validated the concept; perhaps the Royal Navy would finally take note.

In all, Bulloch's and Mallory's attempts to attain naval power in Liverpool set precedents for a number of self-strengthening states in the Pacific confronting similar economic limitations and geographical vulnerabilities. Even before the conclusion of the Civil War, Confederate machinations mirrored Peruvian ones. By seizing on paradigmatically new technologies, new navy builders hoped to use the rate of naval development to catch up and even surpass established North Atlantic powers. Reciprocally, Confederate demand stimulated experimental technology in Britain and created surplus weapons and capacity for the Pacific World as early as 1864. The implications echoed throughout the 1860s and 1870s.

1.3 The Torpedo as a Campaign of Technological Asymmetry

Sensibly, naval historians like to study ships. As a result, seagoing combatants such as *Alabama* have captured headlines and historiographical attention about Civil War navies to the detriment of other technologies.[81] At the same time as Bulloch fantasized about the strategic implications of his rams in Liverpool, a campaign of comparable innovation bubbled up from the swampy ground along the Confederate coast: torpedo warfare. Cheap, novel, and often crude, the CSN's turn to (semi-)submersible weapons was ultimately a more effective and enduring technical response to USN material superiority than foreign-built ironclads. Reflecting its prototypical nature, the term torpedo covered a confusingly wide range of innovations. Primarily, the weapons came in the form of floating torpedo-mines or spar torpedo boats: small ships with an explosive device attached to their bows via a pole or spar.[82] What the CSN historian Thomas Scarf called "subaqueous and subterranean infernal machines" promised to level Union naval power by cheaply distributing lethality into new dimensions.[83] Hence the danger that made Farragut's command, "damn the torpedoes, full speed ahead" so remarkable.[84] As the CSA General Matthew Butler noted, "[under] the pressure of dire distress and great necessity, the Rebels turned their attention to torpedoes as a means of defense against such terrible odds."[85] It was a paradigmatic departure in the history of naval war, motivated by desperation and enabled by freedom from legacy investments.

The record of the CSA/N's crash innovation program in undersea warfare was dramatic. Confederate torpedoes first sunk USS *Cairo* on the Yazoo in December 1862 and grew steadily in importance to coastal and river defense.[86] Consider the precedents set during the defense of Charleston, SC (1861–1865) alone. It was there that William T. Glassell and James. H. Tomb built the semi-submersible craft CSS *David* and used its spar torpedo to attack an enemy combatant (the "much dreaded naval Goliath" USS *New Ironsides*).[87] Ordered out by John R. Tucker "with a view of destroying as many of the enemy's vessels as possible," Glassell and Tomb managed to detonate a torpedo against USS *New Ironsides*' hull.[88] It was hailed as a success, no matter that in doing so the Confederates capsized their boat leaving Glassell in enemy hands – hoisted, rather literally, by his own petard. Charleston also saw the first modification of ironclads with spar torpedoes for offensive war – an attempt to amalgamate two paradigmatic technologies in one.[89] Incredibly, the CSN even deployed the world's first metal-hull submarines. These had a distressing habit of sinking.[90] The most famous of the bunch, CSS *Hunley*, struck and sunk USS *Housatonic* with a spar torpedo but foundered before its return to port – a pathetic but predictable result after a dismal run of tests.[91] Inspired by Charleston's example, the Confederate innovator Hunter Davidson built a network of electrically fired submarine mines to defend the James River, still another precedent in the history of warfare.[92]

Adaptations such as these were not merely the product of pluck or quixotic optimism. Rather, the CSN's use of submersible mines and spar torpedoes to deny the Union access to ports and river networks represented the world's first campaign of industrial, asymmetric naval warfare in three-dimensional and nocturnal space. CSN officers and engineers sought to apply advances in industrial technology to upset the Union's investment in conventional platforms – and did so with some success.[93] During the war, torpedoes sank or disabled more Union ships than any other weapon.[94] Were it not for Sherman's overland army, Charleston's coastal defenses may have resisted indefinitely.[95] The point was one of

1.3 The Torpedo as a Campaign of Technological Asymmetry 29

great pride to the Confederate self-strengtheners – and a proportionate embarrassment for the USN. Mallory believed that "nothing in the history of naval warfare so humiliating to a proud people" as the Union's inability to take Charleston by sea.[96] It was a remarkable step driven not by generous research budgets or careful staff planning but the articulations of "great necessity" with the opportunities created by paradigmatic shifts in industrial technology.[97]

From Washington to Beijing, many took note. The Union commander at Charleston, John A. Dahlgren – a critical figure himself in the history of USN development, known as the "founding father of naval ordnance" – was so impressed by the CSN's torpedo program that he proposed imitating it.[98] After blockade ships captured the crew of the foundering *David*, he forwarded a sketch to the Navy Department outlining the CSS *David* as a model for the United States. "The torpedo element as a means of certain warfare," Dahlgren admitted, "can be ignored no longer." The torpedo boat was a weapon of the weak but one the United States should mass-produce with its industrial establishment. "By all means," Dahlgren urged, "let us have a quantity of these torpedoes, and thus turn them against the enemy. We can make them faster than they can."[99] Not long after, an intrepid group of USN officers and engineers did exactly that, using a spar torpedo boat to destroy an upriver Confederate ironclad.[100]

Whatever its operational and tactical import, the torpedo could only do so much to affect the war's outcome. But thinking beyond the conventional boundaries of the war suggests a global significance. The CSN/A failed in its bid for independence, but its effort at asymmetric self-strengthening produced the crude outlines of modern, three-dimensional naval war which would feature prominently in nineteenth-century naval races and beyond.[101] James Hamilton Tomb – the CSN torpedo engineer onboard the *David* – recognized as much. In 1916, as World War I's U-boat campaign reached its nadir, he and a colleague marveled that their primitive experiments at Charleston were "the real start in the present development" of submarine war.[102]

More immediately, Pacific states in comparable economic and geographic predicaments took note of the Confederate experience and its possibilities. Foreign acquisitions of experimental *materiel* and local adaptation of asymmetric technologies made for a potent combination – one with the potential to upend the dynamic of North Atlantic gunboat imperialism. With the torpedo's potential in mind, Vicuña Mackenna offered command of the allied Peruvian–Chilean squadron to a very junior W. T. Glassell, stressing his "heroic action" piloting a torpedo boat against USS *New Ironsides*; proof positive of the torpedo's "extraordinary results" in the minds of one Pacific self-strengthener.[103] Likewise, Chinese officials touring Boston in 1868 could look out over a fleet of decommissioned USN monitors and take away the need to invest in torpedoes as a means of stopping up rivers against foreign warships.[104] The Confederate "navy to construct" responded to the particular exigencies of the Civil War (a blockade and the threat of riverine penetration), but the threat of North Atlantic naval power as well as economic and geographic vulnerability were common in the Pacific. As it turned out, the solution – self-strengthening through the acquisition of advanced hardware and adaptation of local technologies for coastal defense – was common as well.

1.4 The Civil War on the Edge of the US Empire

Beyond revealing a suite of technological options, the Civil War demonstrated something else about the Pacific to regional self-strengtheners: the strategic opportunities and vulnerabilities of its raw separation from the North Atlantic.[105] That was true, in particular, for the US citizens huddled along the Pacific slope and largely denuded of USN presence by the existential struggle in the Atlantic. From the Mexican American War to the opening of the Panama Canal, US residents on the California coast expressed a chronic sense of separation; a sentiment that spiked acutely during the Civil War. In 1847, Kit Carson attempted a speed record when he crossed overland from California to Washington, DC in sixty days by mule – the most convenient means available, unless you asked the mules.[106] A decade later, passengers had to brave a bone-rattling trip by stagecoach across West Texas, New Mexico, and Arizona. During the Civil War, Confederate raids severed what rudimentary roadways connected California to Texas.[107] French intervention in Mexico further attenuated matters.[108] By sea, the route of many gold-seeking "49ers" through "the dread malaria of the tropics" remained time-consuming and expensive – though not so much as the weeks-long journey around the horn of South America.[109] It was a long, hard way, but at least San Francisco's preferred whiskey, Cyrus Noble, benefited from almost a year of barrel aging en route by ship from its distillery in Ohio.[110] Attempts to knit together, or "territorialize," the United States with railroads and telegraphy in the 1850s and 1860s did little to alleviate the immediate sense of alienation. While funded during the Civil War, the transcontinental railroad was not completed until after Appomattox – and even then it was more a technical achievement than means of transportation.[111] Jules Verne's

1872 *Around the World in Eighty Days* still imagined the transcontinental train journey interrupted by failing bridges and raids by plains Indians.[112] As a result of distance and violence, Civil War-era Anglo-Californians felt more divided than connected by the American continent, making California an overseas colony in all but name.

For these "overseas" Californians, it was distressingly unclear if the United States had the ability to protect its maritime appendage in the Pacific World. The US Navy Yard at Mare Island was never well supplied in the best of times. Demand for resources by the war in the Atlantic made things worse. In 1863, Rear Admiral Bell, commanding the Pacific Squadron, expressed ambivalence about his capacity to defend sea routes to Panama from Confederate privateers leaking out from South or Central America.[113] A year later, stretching to protect US citizens and interests from Mexico to Peru, Bell pleaded with the Navy Department to station *one* cruiser in San Francisco to pursue suspicious vessels.[114]

The Confederate cruiser CSS *Shenandoah* realized Bell's fears in the last year of the war when it began a months-long attack on US commercial interests in the northern Pacific. Its commander, James Waddell, ran the Union blockade to Britain in August 1863, placing himself at Bulloch's disposal just as the Laird Rams came to grief.[115] Taking command of the *Shenandoah* in October 1864, he accepted orders for "the far-distant Pacific" to raid the US whaling fleet.[116] When CSS *Shenandoah* reached the Pacific in 1865, Waddell found no serious opposition and began his depredations. A "cowardly, mercenary and utterly perfidious system of warfare," CSS *Shenandoah* was, the *Sacramento Daily Union* stewed, of "of special interest to California."[117] Frustrated news reports swirled that *Shenandoah* was on the prowl, threatening "terrible havoc" among US ships from the Arctic Circle to New Zealand.[118] Waddell's ambitions were more modest, but he did his worst burning ships and whale oil. Beyond this, Californian newspapers worried he would fit out captured vessels as privateers and "sail for the American coast" in an effort to strike at Californian shipping.[119] As a maritime satellite of the continental United States, Californians were keenly alive to such threats. Out of contact with his superiors, Waddell's war in the Pacific actually continued for months after the official conclusion of hostilities. Distrusting news of Lee's surrender at Appomattox from Yankee whalers, he continued apace until August, 1865.[120] New Bedford ship-owners and San Francisco wharf masters predicted the unaccountable Waddell would "soon destroy the whole Arctic fleet."[121] USN officials noted "great apprehensions felt by the mercantile community of San Francisco" – but who could blame them?[122]

As for the USN, whatever its success in the Atlantic, it was ill-prepared for the Pacific and its demands. CSS *Shenandoah* was only lightly armed, certainly relative to the entire Pacific Squadron, but it was fast and would demand resources to catch. Everyone could remember how, the *Sacramento Daily Union* noted, "quite a formidable squadron of our gunboats vainly ... pursued the *Alabama*."[123] No such force was available in the Pacific. As of May 1865, the commander of the Pacific Squadron would lamely report that his flagship, USS *Lancaster*, had nonfunctioning boilers and had been reduced to sail power.[124] So much for industrialization. Secretary of the Navy Gideon Welles fumed, threatening to charter a civilian vessel and arm it in order to pursue the last Confederate warship afloat.[125] "Whereabouts of Uncle Sam's Navy – What is to be Done!" read headlines from San Francisco to Honolulu.[126] Others papers transmitted taunts from Waddell – "give the [US] naval officers my compliments" – which must have stung.[127] The handful of USN vessels that eventually did sortie after *Shenandoah* failed to locate it. Fortunately for all involved, on August 2, 1865, a British ship captain crossed paths with Waddell and managed to convince him that the war was *really* over.[128] Waddell turned – naturally – for pro-Confederate Liverpool, where he expected a hero's reception.

It was a ragged end to the Civil War on the far and isolated edge of the US Empire. Waddell had confined himself to raiding at sea, but left unchecked he also threatened to attack Pacific ports. California had its own (recent) tradition of maritime vulnerability. In the 1840s, the USN Pacific Squadron seized then Mexican Monterey in Alta California – *twice*: once by mistake in 1842, when Commodore Catesby Jones dashed up from Lima under the false impression that British forces might occupy California,[129] and again in 1846, this time in deadly earnest, as part of the wider Mexican American War.[130] As Waddell cruised the North Pacific, older residents of Monterey could recall the raid of Hippolyte Bouchard – an French-born, Argentine captain – whose forces occupied the city in 1818 for the better part of a week.[131] In one generation the capital of California had been attacked from the sea three times. What guarantee did the people of San Francisco have that something similar would not befall the California coast in the 1860s? Technological change coupled with geographic distance made the Pacific alive with ephemeral asymmetries of power.

Such worries, fortunately, remained unrealized. Waddell surrendered it to British authorities on the river Mersey six months after Appomattox.[132] As CSS *Shenandoah* crept up the river excited crowds peered through fog to catch a glimpse of the "last of the Anglo-rebel pirates."[133] Waddell hauled down the flag not so far from where *Alabama* and the Laird Rams had put to sea earlier in the war. Liverpool was an origin point of the Confederate naval self-strengthening effort and the site of its last stand. Waddell understood the moment. Among his achievements he counted the fact that the "last gun in defense of the South was fired from her deck" in June 1865.[134] The Civil War at sea – while fought primarily in the Atlantic and on the rivers of North America – ended in the Pacific.

The war's many afterlives began there as well. A month before Waddell surrendered, the Laird-built *Huáscar* launched into the Mersey. The Peruvian agent overseeing construction could admire the last of Confederate raiders, even as he followed the Confederate self-strengthening template, building ironclads and impatiently making preparation for a looming war with Spain. The CSN had mostly remained a "navy to construct," but other self-strengtheners managed to build their own newly made navies on the foundation of similar technical-strategic foundations. The Pacific's wars and newly made navies would provide ample tests of the Confederate Navy's dreams. Indeed, as CSS *Shenandoah* surrendered, new competitions were already underway across the Pacific World that would soon be accelerated by a wave of Civil War *materiel* and knowledge flowing out to the region.

1.5 Conclusion

Confederate self-strengtheners started the Civil War with a basic challenge: How to mobilize a plantation society and economy to build an industrial navy? They shared this problem with a number of agricultural and pre-industrial economies contemporaneously facing the threat of North Atlantic gunboats. The CSN's solution was to extemporize a form of newly made navy that relied on prototypical innovations and local adaptation, thereby compensating for numerical inferiority with technological sophistication (or at least ingenuity). Bulloch came to Liverpool to contract cruisers but soon moved on to ironclad rams that might sweep the USN from the sea and shell the East Coast into surrender. Bulloch's optimism seems incredible in hindsight, but new technologies have a way of encouraging vaulting ambitions; witness twentieth-century airpower theorists who believed strategic bombing could independently win wars. Locally, innovators such as William Glassell built torpedo weapons in the harbors of the Confederacy – using an asymmetric technology to disrupt the USN.

Self-strengtheners from Chile to China noticed all this progress. Because their own "navies to construct" shared so many foundational similarities with the Confederacy's predicament, the CSN's tactics and strategies offered a possible model as well. After 1865, CSN personnel, their expertise, and even equipment were in high demand as Pacific self-strengthening movements seized on innovations from the Civil War. One result, the US Civil War's losers nevertheless gained a valuable prize in the form of demand for services that would endure into the 1880s. Reciprocally, the transnational circulation of Civil War expertise and material in the Pacific accelerated self-strengthening programs from Peru to China in the 1860s and 1870s, shaping the newly made navies and the origins of regional wars. For veterans, shipyards, and inventors, the Pacific's newly made navies provided a second and often more ambitious act for the Confederate strategy of naval resistance. Those afterlives are the subject of Chapter 2, and they may well have greater significance for the history of the USN than the Civil War at sea between 1861 and 1865.

2 The Pacific's Civil War Inheritance

The conclusion of the US Civil War left many loose ends. For a start, it put the CSN out of work. Consider John Randolph Tucker, the erstwhile commander of the CSN at Charleston, SC. He had spent years deterring the Union's amphibious assaults, only to be outflanked by William T. Sherman's overland army. Understandably, he and his colleagues found a chilly reception in the re-United States.[1] Likewise, a rapidly demobilizing USN imperiled the careers of Union officers, particularly those with skill sets at odds with the demands of the professional, bluewater force. John Lay, for example – the Union's most successful torpedo engineer – faced limited career opportunities as the USN returned to its prewar cruising stations or else drifted into a more general "naval slumber."[2] A small flotilla of ships, too, entered limbo. Union steam-powered monitors built to penetrate the riverine interior of North America rusted at their berths. Confederacy-bound cruisers and ironclads waited, unclaimed, in European shipyards and sundry ports around the world.

Luckily for Tucker et al. (if no one else), just as the US Civil War concluded, a rash of wars broke out in the Pacific creating demand for weapons and personnel. The template of Confederate self-strengthening looked useful to other "navies to construct" – especially if that technical template came supported by hard-won practical experience. Tucker took a position as a flag officer in the Peruvian Navy. Hunter Davidson outfitted a torpedo ship for Chile. The would-be Confederate ironclad CSS *Stonewall* wended its way from Bordeaux to Yokohama. These were not isolated cases. Indeed, after 1865 officers, *materiel*, and tactics from the US Civil War proliferated widely around the Pacific World as self-strengtheners confronted wars of national consolidation and the predations of North Atlantic imperialists.

This chapter traces the transnationally entangled afterlives of Civil War veterans, tactics, and equipment in the Pacific. Exploring Confederate naval innovations in transwar context – a comparative perspective that escapes the conventional temporal (1861–1865) and geographic (continental US) boundaries of the Civil War – it links the CSN to three conflicts: (1) the Peru/Chile-led War against Spain (1864–1866) and the latter's imperial designs on the Pacific slope; (2) the Boshin War (1868–1869), fought between political factions in Japan during the Meiji Restoration; and finally (3) an early phase of Qing industrial military development, stimulated by the Japanese invasion of Taiwan (1874). As the Confederate war effort collapsed and the USN demobilized, the Pacific's "navies to construct" picked up (often literally) where the CSN had left off.

Like the concept of Confederate "self-strengthening," the proliferation of ex-Civil War expertise and *materiel* to the Pacific has attracted mostly parenthetical attention. The raw trauma of the US Civil War tends to focus historians on events inside the US logomap.[3] What interest in the postwar CSN that does exist is generally directed at its "European inheritance."[4] The *Times* of London had a sense of this as early as 1865 when it reassured readers, "we have lost our cotton, but we are getting wise in military science."[5] What a consolation prize!

European militaries did, of course, refine doctrine and tactics using lessons from the US Civil War, but foreign interest was hardly limited to the industrializing North Atlantic. The historian David Werlich demonstrated as much by chronicling the postwar service of the CSN officer John Tucker as a naval officer and hydrographer in Peru.[6] Tucker, in fact, was representative of a wider phenomenon: the spread of ex-Civil War expertise and equipment as a catalyst for regional naval development.[7] A transwar perspective suggests that the CSN's template for self-strengthening and the Union's response to it were not merely subplots in an internal rebellion but rather strategic and tactical experiments with international resonance. After 1865, comparative similarities between Confederate and Pacific self-strengthening programs became an increasingly thick web of transnational connections. The CSN offered a model (technical surprise via asymmetric advantages) for Pacific navy builders while Confederate defeat provided *materiel* and expertise to accelerate self-strengthening. Many seized that opportunity, finding in Confederate defeat a chance to build newly made navies and defend against North Atlantic power.

2.1 Peru and Chile Profit from Confederate Failure (1862–1866)

Nowhere was the effect of Civil War technology and expertise more apparent (or urgently sought) than along the Pacific slope of South America. In 1863, Spain dispatched a naval squadron to South America under orders to enforce long-standing territorial and financial claims against Peru and Chile.[8] With the US Civil War in the balance and

French forces entrenched in Mexico, the United States seemed unlikely (or unable) to enforce the Monroe Doctrine against European gunboats. In April the following year, Spanish forces occupied the guano-rich Chincha Islands (Peru) as collateral, precipitating a crisis and eventually an allied "War against Spain" or *Guerra Hispano-Sudamericana*.[9]

As relations between Peru, Chile, and these "Last Conquistadores" deteriorated in 1864, leaders in Lima and Santiago looked abroad for munitions and experienced personnel.[10] Animated by the same logic that motivated Mallory in 1861 – namely using weapons which compensated "by their offensive and defensive power for the inequality of numbers" – Chile and Peru dispatched agents to Great Britain, France, and the United States with instructions to purchase or commission modern naval weapons capable of upsetting the numerical advantages of the Spanish fleet.[11] The ironclad warships *Huáscar* and *Independencia* contracted in 1864 (detailed in Chapter 1) were the clearest examples: attempts to buy advanced technologies which could overmatch legacy Spanish investments. The end of the US Civil War supercharged the process. In 1866, the allies' "Confidential Agent" in New York, Benjamin Vicuña Mackenna, reported optimistically that the US Civil War had "introduced considerable alterations in the military arts, principally by the invention of armored ships, torpedoes, heavy cannons and sea-rams," which could be appropriated by the allied Chilean-Peruvian fleet.[12] Aurelio Garcia y Garcia, while contracting for the ironclad *Independencia* in Britain, agreed, stressing the "necessity of equipping our nascent navy only with ships at the height of the most recent innovations."[13] At the outset of their respective conflicts, the maritime forces of Chile, Peru, and the CSA were all "navies to construct" facing a "constructed navy."[14] As a result, a strategy of self-strengthening through novel technologies appealed to all three.

For these Pacific navy builders, the CSA's frustrations in Europe's shipyards came at an opportune moment. The Peruvian wooden corvettes *Unión* and *America*, for example, were originally commissioned by the CSA in France, but, in 1864, Peru purchased both after pressure from the US interrupted sale to the Confederacy.[15] The Peruvian Navy also took advantage of US Civil War's conclusion to buy the ironclad river monitors *Oneota* and *Catawba* (renamed *Manco Capac* and *Atahualpa*) surplus from the United States, skirting neutrality concerns via the aid of a private US firm.[16] Delivered to the USN in June 1865, too late for the Civil War, the ironclads were sold on the cheap. Chilean agents, too, worked with less spectacular success to acquire ex-Confederate blockade runners, recommissioning them as armed transports and cruisers.[17] In the wake of the Civil War, it was a buyers' market.

All told, the material composition of the Peruvian Navy in the late 1860s was largely a transwar by-product of the US Civil War. Just count the hulls. By 1867, Peru had managed to acquire a small armada of six warships. Four – the *Unión*, *America*, *Manco Capac*, and *Atahualpa* – were commissioned by either the Union or the CSA. One – the *Huáscar* – was built by a firm which had profited through CSA contracts and which employed a turreted design featured on a pair of CSN-commissioned ironclad rams. Another, *Independencia*, followed on speculative experiments for the Confederate agents. Given these connections, one could forgive the USN officer who in 1866 sighted *Huáscar* and *Independencia* and erroneously assumed they were, in fact, the very same rams "built by Messrs. Laird of Liverpool for the Confederate Navy."[18] By leveraging insights from the CSN and availability of surplus weapons, the Peruvian "navy to construct" became a fully realized newly made navy in a matter of months. Connections between the allied Republics and the US Civil War veterans ran deeper still as the War against Spain entered a more violent phase. In terms of personnel as well as warships, the CSN's loss was Lima's gain.

2.2 The Bombardment of Valparaiso and the Limits of International Law

While Peruvian and Chilean agents worked to acquire naval arms, Spanish frustrations with their Pacific campaign stoked new bellicosity.[19] On November 26, 1865, Chilean forces captured the Spanish schooner *Covadonga*; a small tactical reversal with deep psychological and political ramifications. Humiliated by the loss – and the halting pace of the war more broadly – the commander of the Spanish fleet, Vice Admiral José Manuel Pareja, committed suicide.[20] His death opened the way for a change in strategy. Pareja's successor, Casto Méndez-Núñez wasted little time in demanding concessions from the Chilean government and threatening to bombard Valparaiso in retaliation for the *Covadonga*. He had the spirit of the moment. In Madrid, even the "most moderate of journals" advocated for reducing Valparaiso and Callao "into a heap of ashes."[21]

Facing Méndez-Núñez's threats – and as agents abroad still scrambled to find naval weapons – Chile's diplomatic representatives appealed to the nascent structure of international law for protection. Legal historians have detected a growing (if limited) ability in the nineteenth century of "semi-peripheral" diplomats to resist industrial violence through the appropriation of European legal customs and ideals.[22] Valparaiso in 1866 offers a test case of that proposition, as well as a sharp contrast to the decidedly "hard-power" self-strengthening at port cities such as

2.2 Bombardment of Valparaiso and International Law 39

Charleston (1862–1865) and later (as will soon be seen) Callao (1866). Where Chilean diplomats turned to the law, soldiers in Carolina and Peru preferred guns and torpedoes.

What, then, was Chile's theory of the case? According to the consensus at the time, an unfortified port was legally immune to bombardment because it offered no military utility. Citing Andres Bello's *Principles of International Law* (1832), the Chilean Foreign Minister Alvaro Covarrubias contended that shelling an unfortified city such as Valparaiso "constitutes a recourse to hostilities contrary to civilization, to human rights and to the most weighty duties of humanity."[23] It was an appeal befitting Chile's self-image as a satellite of the European community *and* (more tangibly) its military inferiority to Spain. Without a symmetrical answer to the Spanish squadron, options were limited. If Chile could not beat Spain with weapons, perhaps it could stave off an attack with words? As the Chilean Legation in Paris noted, Chile was the world's only state without a navy and yet possessing "all the signs of those countries ranked as civilized and advanced."[24] Covarrubias' argument gained considerable sympathy, not least from the British commander on scene who "threatened to blow every Spanish vessel out of the water if [Méndez-Núñez] fired one shot on the city."[25]

Chile's legal position, however, was eroded almost immediately by (false) rumors that its military had mined Valparaiso with torpedoes and other "insidious engines of this nature."[26] In essence, Spanish officers accused the Chileans of having it both ways: Diplomats claimed Valparaiso was unfortified while the Chilean military hedged its bets with hidden weapons. Fears that US-made torpedoes and other arms had been shipped to Valparaiso exacerbated matters, particularly after the Chilean President José Joaquín Pérez studiously refused to deny their existence.[27] Amid the confusion, in February 1866 a concerned British representative in Santiago took pains to "impress upon [President Pérez] the evils to which the fortified towns on the coast of Chile ... would be subjected" if the Chilean military deployed torpedoes against the Spanish fleet.[28] For his part, Méndez-Núñez threatened to fire on the city without notice if his forces were attacked by torpedo-mines.[29] Less than a year after the Confederate defeat, Civil War tactics were a potent menace – if only in the minds of Spanish commanders.

But unlike at Charleston, the threat of new naval technologies at Valparaiso amounted to a self-defeating bluff. Valparaiso's harbor had not been mined but failure to clarify that fact allowed Spanish commanders to claim the city had military defenses and was therefore a legitimate target. On March 31, after a series of ultimatums, the Spanish fleet opened fire on Valparaiso. Casualties were light, owing to the city's partial evacuation, but damage to property was reckoned in the millions of dollars.[30]

Confronted in London, the Spanish minister in Britain "declined all moral responsibility" and defended the legality of the squadron's actions as a proportional response to "reprobate means of warfare," that is, torpedoes and privateering.[31] The Confederate defenders of port cities such as Charleston had put those means to good effect. The Chileans had not, and the results told the tale.

If the limits of the "Law of Nations" were apparent in the embers of Valparaiso, so too were the empty pretensions of the Monroe Doctrine.[32] In a circular, the Chilean Foreign Ministry attacked the passivity of the United States and Britain in the face of this "unprecedented international crime."[33] "The protection of the United States," the Chilean *Mercurio del Vapor* observed acerbically, "is nowhere to be seen."[34] Subsequent offers by the United States to mediate the dispute, the Peruvian Foreign Ministry concluded, "cannot truly be taken seriously."[35] Royal Navy ships, too, had watched idly as Spain shelled "the opulent and elegant emporium of the commerce and navigation of the Pacific."[36] Public outrage in Britain to the thought of its ships cowering before a Spanish ironclad became a powerful argument for British naval construction.[37] After the attack, Covarrubias excoriated the British ambassador in Santiago for depriving Chile of a means of defense by making the "unequivocal insinuation" that if Chile did not mine the port, the foreign powers would defend its neutrality.[38] Even as British agents held up Chilean arms purchasing in Europe, no help came from the British fleet in the Pacific.

The lessons of Valparaiso were manifest: International law was an insufficient check to North Atlantic gunboats and a more concrete means of resistance was necessary. Chile's Foreign Ministry declared, "if this cowardly abuse of force" was tolerated by "the great powers of Europe and America, the weaker states will have to completely change their attitude and views in their international relations."[39] Chile did just that. Shortly after the Spanish attack, engineers began installing fortifications along the Chilean coast, replacing the supposed power of European legalism with that of North Atlantic armaments.[40] Peru's military took the same lesson years earlier, leveraging CSN innovations and hard-won expertise as a means of defense.

2.3 The Charleston Template in Callao (1866)

As the Spanish fleet menaced Valparaiso, military preparations in Lima's seaport Callao assumed a fevered pitch. On land, the hills above the port sprouted an assortment of artillery, including Armstrong and Blakely cannon capable of hurling artillery shells nine miles.[41] At sea, naval technologies and expertise deployed in the US Civil War found immediate application. As agents such as Salcedo and Garcia y Garcia hurried along their warships to completion in Britain, the local acquisition of ironclads, torpedoes, and even the ex-commander of the CSN forces at Charleston transplanted a form of the CSN's technical-strategic template to the Pacific slope.

Ironically enough, the first steps in this effort were taken not by CSN personnel but by the ex-USN engineer and torpedo expert John Lay – one of the earliest converts to the CSN's strategy of industrial, asymmetric war.[42] At Valparaiso, the Spanish fleet faced mere rumors of torpedo-mines, but John Lay brought real expertise to Callao. This, too, was largely a product of Confederate innovation. Lay gained that experience through observation of Confederate advances in the Civil War and some aggressive self-promotion to his USN superiors. In 1863, responding to Confederate torpedo boat attacks against Union blockade ships, Lay was singled out by Union officers to present his "plan of a torpedo" as a means of defending against a Confederate ironclad on the Roanoke River.[43] A year later, he helped convert discarded boiler tubes into a spar torpedo used to sink one of the few seaworthy CSN armored warships – CSS *Albemarle*. It was a feat that earned Lay's partner in the scheme (William Cushing) a global reputation, he claimed, as a "new Nelson" and Lay a lifetime of work as a torpedo engineer.[44]

Despite these precocious steps, in the summer of 1865, Lay found himself in a similar predicament to his adversaries in the CSN: underemployed and attractive to foreign militaries. Demand for asymmetric weapons dried up as the USN demobilized.[45] Lay resigned in May 1865. Months later, while traveling in Peru in search of work, he came to the attention of the Chilean Consul in Paita who offered him an "advantageous position in Chile" as a torpedo expert.[46] As was obvious to one British official, Lay's reputation as the inventor of an "efficient class of torpedo" carried considerable weight with the allied Republics.[47] Lay jumped at the chance. In 1866, he traveled to Callao where the Peruvian government contracted him to defend that port with torpedo-mines.[48] Lay's experience, as Chile's agent in the United States put it, as a "truly intelligent engineer in the construction of this article of war" made him immediately valuable to an alliance facing a materially superior Spain.[49]

In Callao, as he had during the US Civil War, Lay set about modifying metal tubes from steamship engines for use as naval mines. The need for this fundamental but scarce material brought him into almost immediate conflict with the Peruvian staff. On February 27, 1866 (a month before the Spanish attack on Valparaiso) Lay wrote the Peruvian Naval

Command that he had discovered 325 boiler tubes in storage and hoped to convert them into torpedo-mines.[50] It was an expensive proposition. While the Peruvian construction commissions in Britain worked to acquire steamship engines, Lay proposed to cannibalize the literal engine of nineteenth-century industrial power in order to build asymmetric weapons.[51] The arsenal in Callao rejected the notion as an affront, insisting that the tubes were "of great necessity for the ships of our squadron."[52] Lay, the arsenal, and the Peruvian staff traded notes for several days, before reaching an agreement to provide "the inventor Juan Lay" with the necessary materials for his efforts.[53] Having made his mark transforming boilers into torpedoes for the USN, John Lay picked up in Callao where he left off, ruffling feathers.

Along with torpedoes, Peruvian authorities hastily attempted to produce what the CSN's Bulloch would have called "improvised armored vessels" modeled on those tested during the US Civil War.[54] While the *Huáscar* and *Independencia* received their finishing touches in Britain, Peruvian military officials in Callao turned to organic improvisation. In 1864, engineers worked to modify two hulls, the *Loa* and *Victoria*: an ironclad monitor and ram suitable for coastal defense.[55] Foreign military officials in the region instantly recognized the "Peruvian Iron-Clad" as derivative of Civil War technology.[56] They were, the British naval historian Herbert Wilson wrote in 1896, using the names for the warships at Hampton Roads, "a small monitor," and a "diminutive Merrimac."[57] Also using the vocabulary of the Civil War, Commodore John Rodgers, of USS *Vanderbilt*, reported that "the Peruvians have two armored ships": one, the *Loa*, was a monitor "and the other, the *Victoria*, [was] constructed in the style of the Confederate monitors, covered with rails from the railway."[58] In the same way Lay had repurposed the steamship engines to build torpedoes, so too did constructors in both Peru and the Confederacy use railroad tracks and steam engines to build crude ironclads.[59] Together, these torpedoes and locally produced ironclads meant that Peru's naval defenses at Callao were much closer in inspiration and appearance to the CSN's strategy at Charleston than the legalistic defense at Valparaiso.

When put to the test, Callao's defenses – like those at Charleston before it – proved remarkably effective. On May 2, 1866, the Spanish squadron attacked Callao where, in contrast to Valparaiso, it met stiff Peruvian resistance. Under fire from coastal defense batteries, Méndez-Núñez's forces were repulsed with heavy casualties.[60] No ships were sunk, but Peruvian shellfire did considerable damage. For several days thereafter, timbers shot away from Spanish warships washed ashore in Callao.[61] Méndez-Núñez attempted to save face, claiming to have "chastised Peru," but his argument evoked mostly "pity" from foreign observers.[62] The Spanish fleet had been beaten back. Méndez-Núñez died not long after in 1869, at least in part as a result of wounds he received in the battle.[63]

The political implications were substantial. May 2 (*El Dos de Mayo*) remains the namesake of Peruvian plazas and provinces – with good reason. Not only did the battle check Spanish war aims, it also upset the conventional wisdom about power in the Pacific. Armed resistance to European maritime imperialism through the local adaptation of industrial technologies was suddenly possible. The US South Pacific Squadron commander George Pearson assessed that "the Peruvians in this conflict have proved to the South American Republics that with energy and bravery and heavy guns they can not only protect themselves, but the foreign residents who conduce so much to their welfare, against wooden ships at least."[64] Ecuadorian officials were so impressed that they proposed a "confederation of the Southern American Republics on the Pacific" or "Confederation of the Andes" as a long-term security pact.[65] The Chilean *Mercurio del Vapor* reported that Callao proved the republics of South America were not dependent on Britain or the Monroe Doctrine for protection: "Spain has been humbled without such aid."[66] At Valparaiso, diplomats and politicians had appealed to international law, without result. At Callao, Peru demonstrated the possibility of mobilizing the Confederate template against North Atlantic militaries for local defense.

All that said, the value of the naval technology at Callao was likely less important than land-based coastal defense batteries. Spanish and Peruvian accounts stressed as much.[67] "The feats of the [ironclad *Loa*] and its first test of arms" were remembered mostly by vendors, inflating the ship's importance while soliciting remuneration from the Peruvian government.[68] John Lay's most significant contribution to the defense of Peru was his reputation for "villainous torpedoes."[69] Though it was true, as Vicuña Mackenna noted in his memoir, "none of [Lay's torpedoes] managed to bring to the bottom any of the Spanish ships on the 2nd of May, it is no less evident that the idea of their danger did much to impede" the Spanish fleet.[70] Lay's 1899 obituary counted his "distinguished" service in Callao among his chief achievements.[71] His example at Callao certainly strengthened Peruvian aims to acquire and deploy modern, submersible weapons. On May 5, 1866, the Spanish flagship *Numancia* captured a Peruvian spar torpedo launch outside of Callao; a near mirror image of the tactics and technology used by Lay and his Confederate colleagues (and similarity acknowledged by Spanish officials).[72] In the following months, Lima's naval commission in the United States attempted to purchase not only "floating batteries" (armored warships) but also asymmetric weapons such as the "torpedo" and a "submarine boat."[73] A decade later, Lay would win repeat business from Peruvian leaders for his torpedoes, this time for use in the War of the Pacific (1879–1884).

That, though, is a later story. In May 1866, officials in Santiago and Lima had more pressing concerns: namely what to do with success? After Callao, military officers pondered their next steps amid uncertainty about Spanish intentions. Contradictory reports swirled: Méndez-Núñez would retire from the Pacific; he would regroup in Manila; or perhaps reinforcements would arrive from the Atlantic.[74] Not content to wait, the Peruvian leader Mariano Ignacio Prado nurtured an ambition to seize the initiative after Callao and launch an offensive war against Spain. As the ironclads *Huáscar* and *Independencia* arrived in the Pacific, this looked like a real possibility. Right on time, a small cohort of ex-CSN advisers reached in Callao ready to counterattack the Spanish Empire in the Pacific, armed now with a Peruvian newly made navy that to them looked eerily familiar.

2.4 Tucker and Peru on the Offensive against Spain (1866)

As with other self-strengthening movements, Peru's demand for European-built armored warships was matched by a drive to acquire the technical expertise needed to employ them. For obvious reasons, the United States looked like a promising place to start. CSN officers there had, after all, just spent four years resisting a materially superior USN and laying out a basic template for resistance. That, moreover, as the diplomat Benjamín Vicuña Mackenna reported, Confederate defeat had left "some of the most notable leaders" of the CSN without prospects was an opportunity too good to pass up. In January 1866, Vicuña Mackenna notified his superiors that "some of the most eminent officials of the Confederate Navy" had offered services to Chile, including Glassell, "who was the first to use torpedoes," and "Commodore Tucker, who commanded the Southern squadron."[75] Though Glassell eventually demurred, he vouched for Tucker as a man who "would take advantage with *gusto* the opportunity … to abandon forever this country and look for his fortune in Chile."[76] The USN certainly wasn't hiring.

Given the conditions on the Pacific slope, Tucker's credentials were almost certain to attract attention. During the Civil War he achieved familiarity with the full suite of CSN innovations: ironclads, torpedoes, and semi-submersible boats.[77] After Appomattox, Tucker spent several months in a fruitless search for employment in the United States and the merchant marine.[78] Unsatisfied with civilian life, he eagerly accepted a Peruvian offer of a military command. Hired by Peru, Tucker set about recruiting other CSN officers with experience employing modern industrial weapons.[79] David Porter McCorkel – who served with Tucker on CSS *Patrick Henry* – took a position as "captain of the fleet," while Walter Raleigh Butts – an officer from CSS *Virginia* – proffered his services as a "commander and aide."[80] They brought with them their expertise from the CSN and even key doctrinal publications from the conflict, such as Foxhall Parker's *Squadron Tactics under Steam*, which would live on in Chile and Peru long after the ex-Confederates had left.[81]

Once in South America, Tucker's ambitions were proportionate to the extraordinary concentration of naval power entrusted to him.[82] He arrived on the Pacific slope to find the *Huáscar* and *Independencia* along with several ships originally built for the Confederacy or the Union. For him, the possibilities seemed almost incredible, since as early as 1864, Tucker had conserved newspaper articles about British-built ironclad warships, fantasizing about the power they would afford him.[83] The Peruvian fleet – most of it a holdover from or derivative of the Civil War – offered a chance to translate CSN rhetoric into reality. Reaching Peru shortly after the Battle of Callao, he installed his command aboard *Independencia* and began preparing, the Peruvian government hurriedly cabled its consulates, "for offensive war."[84] By 1866, a curious derivation of the Confederate "navy to construct" appeared – through transnational exchange and coincidence – in Peru as a newly made navy. Tucker was ready to use this small industrial force, not merely for defense against North Atlantic imperialists but to strike back at the empire.

As a holdover from the Civil War, Tucker's plans continued to emphasize the use of novel weapons to upset North Atlantic power. Adding another layer to the Civil War's afterlife in Peru, Tucker planned to augment this fleet with offensive torpedo weapons – a logical outgrowth of the technologies he had overseen at Charleston.[85] Details are sketchy, but the ex-CSN officers fitted some combatants with torpedo launches that could be deployed at sea. Other warships had torpedo spars attached directly to their hulls.[86] The senior British official in the South American Pacific reported that Tucker and the Peruvians placed "considerable reliance on their torpedoes and have three steam launches fitted for them in *Independencia*."[87] Requisitions for the ironclad *Independencia* in 1866 suggested exactly these sorts of modifications.[88] The adaptation of Peruvian warships was a testament to the lasting influence of the CSN's asymmetric war against the Union transplanted (on a larger scale) to the Pacific.

How Tucker would use this ironclad and torpedo-armed newly made navy was hotly debated. Nervous reports about his intentions passed between consulates. One suggested an expedition against Cuba.[89] Another warned of an attack against unspecified "Spanish Colonies."[90] Still another predicted the *Huáscar* and *Independencia* would be employed in the Atlantic as "corsairs, in order that [Peru and Chile] may reap some of the pecuniary advantages."[91] In fact, Tucker and his Peruvian employers hatched something altogether more extraordinary: a plan to destroy Spanish morale by steaming the allied armored force across the Pacific and attacking (like a proto-Dewey) Spanish Manila.[92] There was a logic to it, noted Powell, "the Philippine islands being farthest from Spain and most convenient for [Tucker]."[93] The very same Lima–Manila connections which had long made the Pacific a "Spanish Lake" now rendered it vulnerable to industrial weapons proliferating in the region.[94] With any luck, the allied fleet would then deploy additional vessels to attack Spanish colonies in the Caribbean and, perhaps, even bombard the Iberian Peninsula.[95]

It was a moment of possibility – one envisioned by men such as Mallory and Bulloch but fully realized only after the war in Peru. With the CSN template in hand and enabled by Civil War-era expertise, Tucker seized on an ephemeral inversion of conventional power relations between the Pacific and industrial North Atlantic. The British representative in Rio de Janeiro believed that "there is not one of the Spanish vessels of war in the Pacific, not even the ironclad *Numancia*, which is a match individually either in offensive or defensive armament or in speed for either of the above mentioned Peruvian ironclads."[96] The senior US officer on the Brazilian Station was more equivocal but admitted that "by appearance [the Peruvian ships] are very formidable."[97] One US officer wondered how "Peru and Chili would crow if they should happen to get the second great Spanish Armada under."[98] Confederate dreams of bombarding New York with the Laird Rams looked tame by comparison but they followed the same logic.

Tucker's plans, as his biographer and colleague recorded, were "favorably considered by the Governments of the allied Republics," but ultimately abandoned.[99] Internal political disagreements between Chile, Peru, and Tucker's "*Yanquis del Sur*" (as they were incongruously known) played a role.[100] Staffing disagreements had bedeviled discipline for months. Tucker and his colleagues had offered their letters of resignation three times before they were finally – and according to President Prado "painfully" – accepted.[101] *El Comercio* (Lima) concluded that it was simply "incompatible with the decorum of Peru ... that the naval operations of the republic, in the moment of a foreign war, were entrusted to a foreign chief."[102] Nationalism cut the transwar ties which had been forged by military exigency between the Allied Republics and the CSN. In any case, military operations were soon overcome by diplomacy. Shocked by the growing expense of its expedition and bloodied by Peruvian coastal defenses, Madrid began to extricate itself from the conflict, just as Tucker's preparations got underway.[103]

Regardless of its (in)feasibility, Tucker's audacity makes for a curious and underdocumented subcurrent against the tide of nineteenth-century European maritime hegemony. While imperial powers relied on industrial naval weapons to subdue colonial dependencies, Tucker and his transnational forces plotted to counterattack the Spanish Empire with a modern, ironclad, and torpedo-armed fleet. Uncertainty created by technological change and the international circulation of industrial weapons made competition between a postcolonial state and a European power a realistic possibility. As with the Confederate "navy to construct," technical advances stoked strategic aims. By appropriating CSN technology, tactics, and even personnel, Pacific self-strengtheners believed they could strike back. That belief was not an unreasonable one. In November 1866, the senior British naval commander in South America reported that, whatever its aim, this CSN-led Peruvian squadron was capable of doing "considerable mischief to the enemy."[104] It was a prescient assessment. A decade later, the *Huáscar* would, in fact, do mischief to none other than the Royal Navy at the Battle of Pacocha (1877) discussed in Chapter 3.

Little of this was lost on Rear Admiral John Dahlgren, the USN commander who had witnessed the CSN strategy firsthand during the blockade of Charleston.[105] While passing through the Pacific in 1866, he smarted at the idea of extending to his ex-enemy Tucker "customary courtesies" and worried (erroneously) that Tucker held "the rank of Vice Admiral, a good deal superior to my own."[106] His bitterness was understandable: a product of frustrations about his failure at Charleston and an incredulous sense of USN inferiority to Peruvian forces in the region. Sensing a gap, Dahlgren requested additional US warships for Pacific, noting that "the Peruvians have two, *Independencia* and the *Huáscar*, so that our flag alone will be without an ironclad."[107] Secretary of the Navy Gideon Welles denied his request, but Dahlgren's complaint and the sentiments behind it would echo in the coming decades as the demobilizing USN reckoned with the proliferation of newly made navies.[108] Having defeated the CSN in the Atlantic, the CSN's template caused fresh headaches for the USN in the Pacific.

2.5 Hunter Davidson's Torpedoes Arrive Too Late

Chilean officials made their own efforts to appropriate lessons and tactics from the US Civil War. Initially, strategists proposed a *guerre de course* to interrupt Spanish commercial and military lines of communication. For the Chileans and Spanish alike, the potential of cruiser warfare had been vividly illustrated by the Confederate commerce raiders – CSS *Alabama* in particular. In 1865–1866, the parallels stalked the imagination of the Spanish diplomatic corps. Spain's legation in London reported that Captain Raphael Semmes, *Alabama*'s ex-commander, had outfitted a ship on behalf of Peru and Chile "for the purpose of going to the Spanish West India Islands."[109] In New York, diplomatic representatives protested that Chilean agents had been "sent to the United States for the purpose of organizing vessels of *marque* to act against the Spanish Commerce of Cuba and West Indian Islands."[110] There were even rumors that a joint-stock company had been formed in the Pacific with "the object of commissioning privateers from California to act against the Spanish commerce in the Philippine Islands."[111] For the *New York Herald*, the situation was uncannily familiar: "It appears that England, actuated by a love of Chilean copper and guano, as she was formerly by a love of Southern cotton, has consented to furnish Chile with vessels of war, as she formerly served the rebel Confederacy."[112]

Spanish protests had their desired effect. Attempts to outfit privateers and commerce raiders exposed Chilean agents to the same neutrality concerns and sanctions which had curtailed CSN shipbuilding in Europe. With Anglo–US litigation regarding *Alabama* still pending, the British government proclaimed "a strict and impartial neutrality in the contest between" Spain, Peru, and Chile.[113] Thereafter, British municipal police officers surveilled the construction of potential Chilean combatants at Victoria Docks, lest they be shipped out to a belligerent party.[114] CSN agents in Liverpool would, no doubt, have empathized with the challenges faced by the Chileans. Contemporaneously, in New York, the outfitting of the Chilean privateer *Meteor* provoked a related transatlantic legal debate that scuttled its departure.[115] The frustrated Vicuña Mackenna (with some justification) decried the "famous *neutrality* of Mr. Seward," while facing criminal indictment in the United States for illegally organizing arms shipments to Chile and Peru.[116]

After failing to arm privateers and cruisers, Chilean agents overseas turned next (like the CSN and Peru) to the torpedo. The weapon's potential in mind, Vicuña Mackenna worked unsuccessfully to organize an abortive "expedition of four Confederate officials, expert in the use of torpedoes" to South America.[117] Chilean agents in Europe made a more productive contract with Hunter Davidson, the ex-commander of the electric torpedo-mine network on the James River. As tensions with Spain festered, the Chilean representative in London, Ambrosio Rodriguez, commissioned Davidson and an associate named H. H. Dotty

2.5 Hunter Davidson's Torpedoes Arrive Too Late

to man and equip the commercial steamer *Henrietta* for torpedo warfare.[118] Davidson, like other CSA/N officers, was attractive because of his firsthand experience with the modern, asymmetric weapons "born in the South."[119] His most prominent achievement during the Civil War was his responsibility (he tirelessly pointed out) for "the *first* vessels ever *injured or destroyed in war* by electrical torpedoes."[120] Perhaps more notable to Chilean arms-buyers, Davidson's spar torpedo attack against USS *Minnesota* was, by his reckoning, the first time a torpedo boat had attacked another combatant without destroying itself.[121]

Davidson and Dotty's basic concept was to modify the *Henrietta* to carry smaller steam launches equipped with torpedoes, and then to deploy them as flotilla once at sea; a mirror of the modifications proposed by Tucker to *Independencia* in Peru.[122] In the winter of 1865–1866, Dotty and Davidson set to work, sailing from London in February 1866, under Davidson's command but with a "British certificate of captaincy" in order to evade neutrality laws.[123] The unhappy transit took four months, impeded by secrecy, weather, and several inauspicious mechanical failures (at one point Dotty was forced to work the pumps to avoid foundering). Still, on arrival in Valparaiso, Dotty, ever the salesman, hoped to satisfy the "high expectations of the government with respect to the future utility of this ship."[124]

As it happened, Dotty and Davidson's plans – like Tucker's – were overcome by events. Spanish forces retreated from the region just as *Henrietta* arrived. Without a materially superior enemy to confront, asymmetric naval war was a dubious investment for the Chileans. John Lay separated from the USN in 1865 for much the same reason. In July 1866, the Ministry of the Navy terminated the contract, informing Dotty and Davidson that their "services here were already unnecessary."[125] Davidson spent a month in Valparaiso (at $3 *per diem*) turning over the ship in order "to enable the Chilean government to prepare her for service," ideally along the lines he and Dotty had intended.[126] He was disappointed. Chilean officials converted the *Henrietta* into a dispatch ship and distributed its complement of torpedo boats across the fleet for miscellaneous tasks.[127] Davidson, whatever the promise of his inventions, found himself without a navy to serve for the second time in as many years.

Failure aside, Davidson's value as a naval adviser endured for some time in South America. That was true at least in part because he never missed an opportunity to defend his place in the historical record as one of the torpedo's first and most successful adopters. As late as 1906, he would write to the magazine *Confederate Veteran* vaingloriously highlighting his contributions to the making of modern war.[128] That self-promotion paid off. A decade after the Chilean disappointment, the Argentine government hired Davidson to organize a system of torpedo defenses. In 1875, retracing his steps to Britain, Davidson placed orders for steam launches suited to torpedo warfare from the shipbuilder Yarrow and Hedley.[129] The launches in question were, as Alfred Yarrow's biographer noted, the first time "we find the torpedo and the torpedo-boat united in an indissoluble bond."[130] Having flowed out to the Pacific, technological innovations and practical experience flowed back. It would become a familiar pattern in the Pacific's wars during the following decades.

2.6   A Confederate Ironclad in Hokkaido

Beyond the Americas, the Confederate ironclad CSS *Stonewall* was likely the most notable piece of military hardware left stranded by the conclusion of the Civil War (Figure 2.1). Notable for its design, surely, but more so for its deeply ironic origin and ends. The armored ram *Stonewall*

Figure 2.1 *Stonewall*
Source: "The Dano-Rebel Ram Sphynx," *New York Herald*, February 15, 1865.

2.6 A Confederate Ironclad in Hokkaido

was a French-built weapon, intended to undermine the United States, but which ultimately became one of the primary instruments of national consolidation during Japan's Boshin War (1868–1869): the final act of the Meiji Restoration, fought between the imperial government and the remnants of the Tokugawa on the island of Hokkaido.[131]

Built in France by the "eminent constructor" L'Arman in Bordeaux, CSS *Stonewall* was a small ship, which compensated for its lack of size and "disposition to act the part of the leviathan" with heavy armor.[132] Originally ordered by the CSA, the vessel (due to neutrality complications) was briefly purchased by Denmark (1864) before coming under Confederate control in January 1865.[133] That spring, CSA propagandists celebrated the ship as a miracle weapon; a sort of *deus ex machina* of the flagging Confederate war effort. In March 1865, as Confederate armies retreated, the *Dallas Herald* comforted readers with slim hopes, writing: "What is to prevent the Confederate iron-clads from entering the harbor of New York?"[134]

Timing, as it turned out. After crossing the Atlantic, the ram arrived in Havana in May 1865, just as the Confederacy collapsed. The cruise of CSS *Shenandoah* went on in the Pacific, but the war was over in the Atlantic. In an instant CSS *Stonewall*, as its commander Thomas J. Page recalled, "found herself a useless hulk."[135] Cuban authorities seized the vessel and later surrendered it to the United States.[136] After a period of refurbishment, the Department of the Navy concluded that because it was "liable to rapid deterioration," retaining the ship was inadvisable.[137] The USN had too many ironclad monitors as it was, selling some for scrap and others – as detailed earlier – to Peru.

Saddled with the ship, another Pacific state came to USN officials' rescue: Japan. In 1866, the Japanese Shogunate was yet another of the world's navies to construct in the market for advanced warships.[138] Just as Peruvian and Chilean agents snapped up ships left undelivered to the Confederacy, Japan's representatives in the United States saw an opportunity to capitalize on innovation and surplus capacity.[139] Japanese leaders had installed hundreds of coastal defense fortifications in the wake of Commodore Perry's visits (1853, 1854) but, as the historians David Evans and Mark Peattie noted, saw their greatest opportunity in "the rapid and revolutionary changes in naval technology" – a chance made all the more attractive by the fact that the Japanese "navy to construct" was unburdened by obsolete equipment and costs.[140] It was an opportunity for US officials as well, eager to discard surplus material after the war.[141] In that spirit, in the summer of 1867, Tokugawa agents purchased *Stonewall* for $400,000 and arranged for George Brown, a USN officer, to sail it to Japan.[142] The CSN had contracted the vessel in an attempt to use technological novelty to compensate for its numerical inferiority. That logic appealed to the Japanese as well, and for similar structural reasons. US reports were incredulous that a weapon built "to destroy the American Navy" was now in the hands of "our Celestial friends."[143] In addition to conflating China with Japan, such coverage demonstrated a lack of imagination given the number of ex-Union and Confederate warships already in the Pacific. Indeed, Japanese interest in *Stonewall* seemed entirely reasonable to at least one other Pacific navy. US sailors nursing *Stonewall* around Cape Horn reported that Chilean authorities in Valparaiso (already coveting Peru's ironclads) "would like to have purchased the vessel, and would have given for her twice what she cost."[144]

After a mammoth transpacific crossing, *Stonewall* reached Japan in April 1868, only to again enter a state of legal limbo on account of an ongoing civil war.[145] Defeated in the Meiji Restoration (or more rightly Revolution), the residual forces of the Tokugawa Shogunate (*Stonewall*'s titular owners) retreated to the northern island of Hokkaido. There, in January 1869, Admiral Enomoto Takeaki established the Republic of Ezo as, the commander of the US Asiatic Squadron noted, "an asylum for those who had forfeited their heads in the rebellion."[146] Arriving in the main island of Honshu, it was not immediately clear to Brown whether this rump government to the north or the Meiji had a rightful claim to ex-Confederate vessel. Most of the Shogunal Navy followed Enomoto north, increasing Meiji officials' desperation to acquire ironclad warships capable of overcoming their adversary's numerical superiority at sea.[147] Unluckily for this new regime in Tokyo, the US Minister in Japan Robert Van Valkenburgh cited US neutrality (and was perhaps concerned about "the Japanese in their present irritable frame of mind against foreigners") and refused to surrender *Stonewall* to the Meiji government while it was still at war with the Shogunate.[148] The same problems that had so frustrated Confederate rebels in Liverpool had come to Tokyo.

The *Stonewall* was thus left ownerless and manned by a caretaker US crew in Yokohama Bay.[149] A then very junior Alfred Thayer Mahan (no less) complained about diverting crew members to the ex-CSN vessel, "fearing that it would interfere with my exercising."[150] The comparably decrepit state of the US forces in the western Pacific deepened his aggravation. While USN engineers and firemen kept *Stonewall* in working order, the wooden ships of the US Asiatic Squadron rotted away. William Cushing, the USN hero behind a successful torpedo attack in the Civil War, worried that USS *Maumee* "might soon be too rotten to sell."[151] Mahan faced similar problems onboard USS *Aroostook*, a gunboat condemned and auctioned off in July 1869.[152]

2.6 A Confederate Ironclad in Hokkaido

The mutually dissatisfying situation was resolved in March 1869, when an ephemeral peace broke out between the Meiji and Tokugawa forces. With a tentative truce in hand, US authorities released *Stonewall* to the Imperial government, where it was renamed *Kōtetsu* ("ironclad"); the first of its kind in the Japanese Navy. Foreign observers were skeptical about its capabilities, noting that it was "manned and officered by Japanese exclusively."[153] One *New York Herald* correspondent assessed that "the Japs have got a sort of wild elephant in the shape of the *Stonewall*" – powerful, but unlikely to be managed toward productive ends.[154]

Contrary to such racist expectations, the Meiji government would soon put the *Kōtetsu* to decisive use in its campaign to retake Hokkaido. As intended, when engaged with enemy forces, the *Kōtetsu* proved impervious to shot and "more than a match for a score" of Enomoto's wooden ships.[155] A raid by Shogunate forces to capture the ironclad by boarding party ended in fiasco.[156] After Meiji victory at the Battle of Miyako Bay (1869), the Shogunate's surviving ships took refuge beneath the city fort.[157] As the commander of the US Asiatic Squadron, Rear Admiral (RADM) Stephen Rowan, reported, "having lost his navy and had his fort knocked down by the fire of the *Stonewall*, [Enomoto] surrendered to save useless loss of life."[158] In 1865, the *Dallas Herald* had dreamed of *Stonewall* shelling New York and Boston with "impunity."[159] It was at once incredible and yet wholly consistent with the moment that in 1869 the Meiji's newly made navy would reap the benefit of the CSN's optimism. Self-strengtheners in Peru and Chile had already led the way. *Stonewall* was built to win a war through technological novelty and – US commanders thought at least – so it had in Japan.

Like Peruvian victory at Callao in 1866, imperial success at Hokkaido demonstrated a shift in regional hierarchies. As power proliferated, perceptions changed. A generation before the Sino-Japanese War, Rowan predicted the rise of a new regional order, heralded by Meiji naval capabilities. He wrote: "Already have the Japanese outstripped the Chinese in progress towards Western Civilization ... The naval ships are well armed ... The coal mines are successfully worked and supply our squadron with coal."[160] By taking advantage of a variant of the CSN self-strengthening strategy to leapfrog stages of naval development, Japan began to take shape as an industrial newly made navy in its own right.[161] Just as Tucker brought Foxhall Parker's texts to the Pacific slope, by 1870, less than a year after Meiji officials assumed control of *Stonewall*, *Squadron Tactics under Steam* went into print in Japan.[162] *Kōtetsu*, which in 1874 the *North China Herald* continued to assess as "the most formidable vessel of the Japanese navy," played a critical role in that process.[163] As late as 1897, US industrialists would still claim *Stonewall* (most often using its original Civil War-era name) as the "foundation of the Japanese Navy."[164] Thinking more symbolically in 1907, A. T. Mahan argued that what forty years later he *still* called *Stonewall* was "the beginning of [Japan's] armored navy," earning the ship "a place in history."[165] Retrospectives aside, though, the more immediate consequence of Japanese naval ascendancy would be to goad the Qing Empire into naval reforms which mirrored the CSN technical-strategic template or were themselves based on CSN innovations.

2.7 The Japanese Invasion of Taiwan (1874) and the Confederate Influence on the Qing

Qing interest in industrial maritime defense antedated the US Civil War by many years, at least to the threat of European gunboats in the Opium War.[166] Various schools of thought contended, proposing self-strengthening as the means by which to make a "prosperous and strong" (富强) country – watchwords of "the Chinese Dream" still in use today.[167] Naval power, or at least a meaningful coastal defense, was a key component of that vision. During the First Opium War, Lin Zexu (林则徐), the Qing commissioner in Guangdong, advocated for a coastal defense navy capable of resisting British steamships after his appeals to morality and an incipient international law fell on indifferent ears (officials in Valparaiso c. 1866 would have done well to study his example).[168] Beginning in the 1860s, Li Hongzhang – soon to become China's most significant reformer – agreed, proposing a network of fortifications in concert with shallow-draft coastal defense ships and torpedoes.[169] Others, such as Wei Yuan, were more ambitious, arguing for the expansion of Chinese maritime and industrial power as a means to "control the barbarians" at sea.[170] Toward that end, following the Taiping Civil War (1850–1864) and the Second Opium War (1856–1860), military officials such as Zuo Zongtang (左宗棠) founded a series of naval arsenals and academies launching the Qing "Self-Strengthening" movement in earnest.[171] Looking out into the Pacific, the Qing's officials had another "navy to construct" and ambitions to do so with the benefit of new technologies.

Halting progress in China took on a new urgency in 1874, after Japanese forces invaded the Ryukyus and Taiwan, shocking the consciousness of the Qing.[172] Launched ostensibly in retaliation for the murder of shipwrecked sailors, the Japanese invasion of Taiwan precipitated a military and political crisis in China unlike that caused by earlier (and more famous) incursions from the sea.[173] In 1867, for example, US sailors and marines from the Asiatic Squadron landed in Taiwan, investigating the murder of the crew of the US ship *Rover*. Once ashore,

2.7 Japanese Invasion and Influence on the Qing

the US force was harried by indigenous Taiwanese who, the officer commanding noted, "displayed a strategy and courage equal to North American Indians."[174] Taking fire and subject to heat exhaustion, the Americans withdrew, citing "the inutility of such an expedition against a savage enemy in a wild country."[175] From a US perspective, the 1867 action warranted prominent inclusion and appendices in the Secretary of the Navy's Annual Report, alongside coverage in leading journals and newspapers. But in China, Qing officialdom mostly shrugged off the US landings as just another among many such insults. This apathetic reaction stands in sharp contrast to Qing debates prompted by the Japanese 1874 expedition. European and US gunboats were one matter, but an attack by the Japanese "dwarfs" [倭奴] on Chinese territory signaled something else about the broader hierarchy of power in East Asia.[176] A livid Li Hongzhang wrote that if Taiwan had been properly fortified, "the Japanese would not have dared to have come." Looking forward, he asked: "Can the acquisition of defensive equipment be delayed for even one day!?"[177] Competing with the Europeans could wait, but the exigencies of competition with Japan demanded an immediate response.

Li's frustration spoke to a disorienting asymmetry of power vis-à-vis Japan which would have been familiar to men such as Dahlgren and others who confronted newly made navies in South America. How could it be that little Japan – beset by reactionary rebellions until 1877 – had forms of naval power that the vast Qing Empire did not? As Li Hennian (李鹤年) – an official sent to review defenses on Taiwan – noted laconically, Japan had ironclad warships "and we have none."[178] Despite the expansion of naval arsenals in the late 1860s, officials at the Zongli Yamen – the body responsible for foreign affairs – agreed that Chinese forces were unable to defend Taiwan because as of 1874 they still lacked armored warships.[179] Put another way, even with its head start, China was a "navy to construct" facing an (albeit recently) constructed Japanese newly made navy. In a fitting coincidence of global proportions, the *Kōtetsu* (ex-CSS *Stonewall*) was among the Japanese assets dedicated to the Taiwan Expedition.[180]

As it had for Peru and Chile, vulnerability to foreign ironclad warships encouraged Qing interest in the CSN's campaign of naval resistance. Chinese knowledge of the Confederate torpedo service dated at least to 1868, when the Qing delegate traveling with the Burlingame Mission to the United States, Zhi Gang noted how Confederate coastal artillery had been unable to impede the movement of ironclad warships during the US Civil War. An effective defense, he recorded, was achieved "only through the concealed emplacement of torpedoes."[181]

Still more significant was the 1874 publication of the Chinese-language version of the Prussian engineer Viktor von Scheliha's (希理哈) text *A Treatise on Coast Defense* (防海新论) – coincident with the Japanese Expedition to Taiwan.[182] Though often described as a "Prussian" manual, Scheliha's analysis derived its authority from his personal experience in the US Civil War.[183] Scheliha served with the Confederacy, helping to construct maritime defenses at Mobile, AL (the very torpedoes David Farragut supposedly damned).[184] In the process, he became one of the world's leading advocates for torpedo defenses against numerically or technically superior forces. Li Hongzhang read the Chinese version of *Coast Defense* in 1874, no doubt sympathizing with the experience of another industrially weak military striving for defensive power against steamships.[185] Thus mediated by Scheliha, the CSN technology strategy found a Chinese audience in high places. That same year, front-page articles in the vernacular Qing newspaper *Shenbao* began attributing a host of naval inventions to the US Civil War, including the ironclad warship and the torpedo-mine.[186] Both would be central to Qing self-strengthening in the next decades.

Scheliha's chief tactical insight (as interpreted by Qing reformers) was that fortifications alone were no defense against ironclad warships. After the fiascos at the Dagu Forts (1860) and Taiwan (1874), that conclusion made good sense. In 1874, Li Zongxi (李宗羲) argued that during the US Civil War, "[a]lthough [the Confederacy] had extremely good fortifications ... they could only destroy one or two enemy ships, and could not prevent the easy comings and goings of the [Union] fleet. This is clear proof that cannons alone are insufficient to be too deeply relied upon."[187] Li Hongzhang agreed, writing, "when *Coast Defense* discusses the era of the US Civil War ... although the forts were hardened and equipped with numerous guns, they still offered no means of resisting the great enemy."[188] Citing Scheliha, he contended that without asymmetric defenses located at key strategic points enemy ironclads would always get through coastal batteries. The solution, Li Hongzhang argued (reflecting Zhi Gan's observations in 1868), was to supplement port defenses with torpedo-mines and ironclad ships.[189] On the ground in Taiwan, Li Henian recommended that "in terms of weapons for the defense of Taiwan's ports, nothing is as good as the torpedo-mine."[190]

Of course, in 1874 such plans were mostly aspirational. They certainly came too late to be of use against the Japanese expedition. In November, Meiji forces withdrew from Taiwan having extracted minor concessions and an indemnity. Japan would later annex the Ryukyus (1879) en route to its emergence as a regional rival to the Sinocentric order in the western Pacific.[191] For Li Hongzhang and others, the crisis began a lifelong fascination with Japan as a "hypothetical enemy" and the torpedo as a means of resistance.[192] The race was on, and technologies and knowledge from the US Civil War were relevant from start to finish. Three years after he read Scheliha, another Civil War (and Callao) veteran, John Lay, arrived in Tianjin with a proposal to sell Li Lay torpedoes.[193] He was the first of many. Naval technologies, developed through transwar connections from Mobile to Callao to Tianjin, took root in the Qing Empire.

2.8 Civil War Afterlives in the Pacific

After 1865, naval technology and expertise flowed out of the North Atlantic in response to demand from the not-so-Pacific World. Confederate defeat and USN demobilization created a surplus of *materiel* and expertise. Both were in hot demand in the Pacific by various navies to construct, providing opportunities for CSN veterans, shipyards, and even a generation of USN officers caught in a period of demobilization. Ex-US and CSN ships were foundational to the industrialization of the Peruvian and Japanese navies in the 1860s. CSN and Union personnel sold advice about engineering, strategy, and tactics in Callao, Valparaiso, and beyond. Still more enduring, doctrinal texts developed during the Civil War, such as *Coast Defense* and *Squadron Tactics Under Steam*, shaped thinking about modern naval war across the region. While nationally bound histories of the USN portray the decade after Appomattox as a "naval slumber," a transwar perspective reveals that the afterlife of the Confederacy in the Pacific's newly made navies was, in many respects, more interesting than the Civil War itself.[194]

This same proliferation of technology and expertise made for a set of developments that are at odds with most depictions of power and its distribution in the industrial era. This chapter has attempted to texture the long-standing (if deterministic) conventional wisdom by recovering the transwar history of the Civil War in the Pacific. At Charleston, the CSN leveraged paradigmatic departures in naval technology – the ironclad, torpedo, and submersible warship – to resist the asymmetries of US industrial power. When exported to the Pacific, ex-CSN expertise and *materiel* provided Peru with the means to compete against Spanish gunboats at Callao. Tellingly, the CSN commander at Charleston Harbor, John Tucker, *and* his Union antagonist, John A. Dahlgren, were physically present at both Charleston and Callao. The inversion of traditional assumptions about power was all the more glaring as Tucker and his South American colleagues planned a transoceanic assault on the Spanish Empire in 1866. Across the Pacific, in Japan, the ex-CSS *Stonewall* became a key tool of national consolidation and a symbol of Japanese power (1868–1869). For Qing reformers confronting that power in Taiwan (1874), the Confederate experience offered – quite literally – a manual for naval resistance.

The conclusion of the US Civil War had unpredictable effects on Pacific newly made navies, but in general it accelerated investments and experiments in modern military technology and force structure. US demobilization created surpluses of expertise and weapons that then catalyzed naval development – the building of newly made navies – in Peru, Chile, Japan, and China. As Chapters 3 and 4 argue, demobilization also made the USN so weak that this same military activity could (and soon did) weigh disproportionately on the minds of US navalists. As the USN retrogressed in the late 1860s to its prewar missions in defense of commerce and expatriates, its ability to protect national "prestige" began to atrophy.[195] John Dahlgren's 1866–1867 complaints about the relative superiority of Tucker and his Peruvian ironclads are a fine example; Alfred Thayer Mahan gazing out on ex-*Stonewall* in Japan another. At least they were not alone in the coming years, being joined by dozens of US officials who were surprised, insulted, and eventually inspired by the power of Pacific states and the relative deterioration of the USN after the Civil War.[196] More proximately, in the 1870s Japanese and Peruvian military progress sparked intra-regional naval races and conflicts as officials and Chile and China did what their counterparts in the United States would not for at least a decade: catch up by building newly made navies of their own.

3 Pacific Naval Races and the Old Steam Navy

The spread of ex-US Civil War technology and personnel during the 1860s catalyzed naval development around the Pacific. This chapter documents how, in the following decade, Pacific navy building and experimentation accelerated as China, Japan, Peru, and Chile engaged in intra-regional arms races. For a sense of the moment and its possibilities, consider the 1873 notes of Aurelio Garcia y Garcia – the Peruvian officer who had overseen *Independencia*'s construction in Britain (1864–1866). In 1872, Lima appointed Garcia y Garcia as Peru's diplomatic representative in East Asia. On arriving in Tokyo, his immediate concern was a question of Peru-bound Chinese laborers in Japanese ports.[1] When Japanese officials considered intervening against Peruvian traffickers, Garcia y Garcia raised the possibility of a port call to Yokohama by *Independencia* and *Unión* – a Peruvian example of gunboat diplomacy by two of its "best warships."[2] Assessing the situation ahead of a possible conflict, Garcia y Garcia also produced intelligence on the Japanese Navy, noting the ironclad *Azuma* (ex-*Stonewall*) first and foremost.[3] The crisis eventually found a diplomatic resolution. As it turned out, the only arms exchanged were a "collection of antique Japanese arms" destined for a Lima museum.[4] Nonetheless, Garcia y Garcia's threat illustrates the diffusion of industrial power in the Pacific (including two ships initially slated for the CSN) and its instrumentalization as a tool outside of the usual club of North Atlantic imperialists. The self-strengtheners had started with navies to construct and could now boast newly made navies.

Unluckily, in a recurring tragedy of international relations, successful examples of defensive self-strengthening against North Atlantic power combusted into bilateral naval races on both sides of the Pacific. Officials in Chile and China could not help but look to the newly made navies of Peru and Japan (respectively) and aspire to similar capabilities. And just as the CSN and Peru were able to leverage technological shifts (the ironclad and the torpedo) to compete with materially superior forces in the 1860s, so too did the pace of technical change create chances for local rivals to "catch up." What Peruvian and Qing officials, respectively, called "improvements of transcendental importance" and the "ceaseless change" (日新月异) of naval technology were real opportunities.[5] While understudied, (notably when compared to the Anglo-French and Anglo-German races), the competitions between the newly made navies of Chile/Peru and China/Japan were key causal variables for coming wars of regional ordering (the War of the Pacific [1879–1884] and the Sino-Japanese War [1894–1895]).

Against Pacific naval racing, the USN slid into what one textbook called "a stage of decline and senescence." The force demobilized from 700 ships in 1865 to 200 in 1870 – of which only fifty-two were in commission. Most of these were "obsolete" and antedated the Civil War – befitting the sobriquet "Old Steam Navy."[6] True, this "Old Navy" or "Smooth Water Navy" continued to show the flag with reasonable competence: patrolling foreign ports, safeguarding missionaries and merchants, protecting commerce, and so forth.[7] But by treading water during a moment of fecund technological invention, the USN began to fall behind even as smaller Pacific states – and some budding empires – were racing ahead. US officers had noted curious manifestations of Pacific naval power at Callao (1866) and Hakodate (1869).[8] Examples multiplied as Pacific arms races deepened, carving out a sort of "little divergence": an ephemeral gap in military capability between the fading US Old Steam Navy and four newly made navies in the Pacific.[9] The relative decline was particularly jarring next to growing US commercial and territorial ambitions in the region; what the USN officer and diplomat Robert W. Shufeldt in 1868 called "the ocean bride of America."[10]

Taken together, the story of the Pacific in the 1870s was one of acceleration and deceleration – of races and stagnation – encouraged by the conclusion of the US Civil War. USN/CSN demobilization accelerated arms races in East Asia and Latin America by freeing up expertise and *materiel*. Postwar US demobilization, conversely, meant stagnation for the US Old Steam Navy: a force so weakened by neglect that qualitative advances in small state newly made navies could matter a great deal. By the 1870s, Pacific self-strengthening movements had flattened the imbalance of power with the North Atlantic world, a fact made vivid by the Battle of Pacocha (1877) between Peru and Great Britain. Even as "New Empire" builders remade the Pacific into a frontier of US expansion, the "Old Navy" sagged into a position of comic inferiority (literally, jokesters found in the Old Navy a frequent point of inspiration). These ironic gaps, between new imperial aspirations and old military capabilities, between newly made Pacific navies and the US Old Navy, became the best fodder for navalist arguments in the 1880s and 1890s.

3.1 Technology, Geography, and the Pacific's Age of Empire

This chapter continues a comparative story of self-strengthening from the 1860s and follows its transition into intra-regional arms races between Chile/Peru and China/Japan – preludes to the War of the Pacific (1879–1884) and the Sino-Japanese War (1894–1895) respectively. For the Pacific World it was a period of possibilities, and one more unpredictable than accounts of the "Age of Empire" usually suggest. In a general sense it is of course true that beginning in the 1840s, European military innovations and industrial productivity underwrote the partition of the globe into (semi-)colonial dependencies.[11] But the Pacific fits awkwardly into simple narratives about the "West and the Rest."[12] For Pacific navy builders in Callao, Fuzhou, Valparaiso, and Yokohama, power was not clearly bifurcated between what Eric Hobsbawm called the "strong and the weak, the 'advanced' and the 'backward.'"[13] Rather, by acquiring and adapting the core technologies of North Atlantic expansion, Peru, Chile, Japan, and China obtained real military capabilities, in some cases transforming into regional empires in and of themselves. Few, Japan aside, managed to catch up – compete as peers – with the North Atlantic's great powers, but the relative growth of Pacific newly made navies startled North Atlantic observers who confronted them; especially those Americans on the decks of the Old Navy's ships or the quays of San Francisco.

Textbook security dilemmas and escalation spirals followed self-strengthening as a matter of course. Processes that began as self-strengthening efforts against North Atlantic gunboats – or perhaps "arms chasing" – morphed into regional "arms races" within a decade.[14] For example, in 1866 Garcia y Garcia celebrated the Peruvian ironclad *Independencia*'s value against Spain, but that ship's arrival on the Pacific slope created a new set of asymmetric vulnerabilities for Chilean leaders. Just as Japanese ironclads inspired the Qing to accelerate naval acquisitions in 1874, Peru's new warships provided a rationale for Chilean naval expansion. Pacific states fought to catch up with North Atlantic industrial power – and in relative terms they did – even at the cost of local suspicion and competition. Matters spiraled from there leading (eventually) to war.[15]

Against a paucity of comparative work on self-strengthening movements, arms races are a better-studied subject – not least because they are so central to the origins of both World Wars.[16] Samuel Huntington's definition of an arms race still serves: "[A] progressive, competitive peacetime increase in armaments by two states or coalition of states resulting from conflicting purposes or mutual fears."[17] Within the category, Huntington delineated two modes of arms racing: quantitative (more stuff) and qualitative (better stuff). The latter mode dominated naval arms races in the nineteenth century because of the rate of "technological breakthrough" and confusion attendant to naval industrialization.[18] There was always something better or that seemed better to obtain. Measuring balances of power – always an inexact business – was deeply complicated by what A. T. Mahan in 1875 called the "unsettled, transition state" of naval technology.[19] That uncertainty bred races to acquire the latest and greatest thing, or else fall behind.

Despite its many examples, Pacific arms races remain on the periphery of historiographical attention relative to intra-European competitions before World War I and World War II.[20] The historian Johnathan Grant's *Rulers, Guns and Money* is an exception in a field that generally addresses extra-European arms races (sometimes literally) parenthetically.[21] Perhaps the lack of attention owes to the fact that in the Pacific self-strengthening crossed with arms races creating category errors. Should we count the Qing's warships as self-strengthening against Europe or arms racing against Japan? More likely, it reflects the interests of military historians in "big things": be they warships or the great powers that tended to build them. Failure, too, creates its own teleology, obscuring genuine achievements. The Qing defeat in 1894–1895 is the best example, but it is mirrored by experiences in Peru and Chile given the relative decline of Latin American sea power in the western hemisphere in the twentieth century.[22] All these trends conspire to muddy the achievements of Pacific arms chasers and racers. But whatever the condescension of later generations, the relevance of the Pacific's newly made navies was obvious to contemporary observers – indeed they were topics of global speculation and debate.

For US policymakers, geography and ambition made the Pacific's arms races all the more relevant. The most basic question was how to balance investments in the Atlantic and Pacific, given the continent dividing them. Oceanic vastness, interruptible sea lanes through the Straits of Magellan, and the limits of coal-fuel impeded power projection from the North Atlantic to the Pacific, even after the opening of the Suez Canal and the completion of North American transcontinental railways.[23] Looking out from the California coast, insecurities stoked by isolation – recall the depredations of CSS *Shenandoah* – remained unaddressed in the 1870s. There was profit to be made, but who could be sure the federal government could protect or support commercial and civic interests in the Pacific? After the Civil War, the USN had managed to coax an ironclad warship around Cape Horn (with liberal grog rations to reward workers in the overheated engine spaces), but the result proved more "remarkable" than replicable.[24] Moving warships from Atlantic to the Pacific would be time-consuming and expensive, if not impossible. The festooned notoriety surrounding the battleship USS *Oregon*'s dash from California to Key West around Cape Horn proved as much in the run-up to the War of 1898.[25] Her run was exciting because no one was sure if she could make it in time to be useful. That contingency was fun for casual newspaper readers but imagine the anxiety of naval officers as they tracked USS *Oregon*'s odyssey around South America. Matters were much more challenging in 1869, when Secretary of the Navy George Robeson wrote: "The Pacific Station is one of great extent and importance ... It still is evident that our force in the Pacific is inadequate for the duties required of it. Our trade on that ocean is constantly and rapidly increasing, and our citizens are found located everywhere on its shores and among its islands."[26] Not so the newly made navies of the Pacific that had acquired hardware at a blistering clip, increasing the gap between USN stagnation and Pacific acceleration.

3.2   The Andean Security Dilemma (1867–1879)

Peruvian self-strengthening in the wake of the US Civil War netted it the region's most capable naval force: two armored warships, cruisers, auxiliaries, and technical experts for support. It was enough power to plot a transpacific counterattack against the Spanish Empire in 1866. That status was short-lived. The same warships that encouraged Garcia y Garcia's irascible bellicosity against Spain (1866) and Japan (1872–1873) created a dilemma for Peru's onetime ally Chile. Lacking a common Spanish antagonist after 1866, political fissures soon split Peru and Bolivia from their erstwhile partner. The commercial development of nitrate deposits in the Atacama Desert on the three nations' mutual frontier exacerbated diplomatic strains.[27] Frictions worsened over the rights to exploit and tax the Atacama's resources.[28] For the global nitrate market the stakes of this debate were significant; for Peru, Chile, and Bolivia the matter was existential.[29]

Facing an increasingly confrontational and better-armed rival, the Chilean government under President Federico Errázuriz Zañartu sought to improve its security situation.[30] The Pacific slope's geography and recent history encouraged leaders in Santiago and Valparaiso to capitalize on experimental foreign naval developments and leapfrog years of trial and error; it had, after all, worked for Peru.[31] The failure of the United States and Great Britain to defend Valparaiso from Spanish bombardment in 1866, as one historian notes, likely played a role as well by demonstrating "the danger of expecting more from the Monroe Doctrine than it actually promised."[32] Flanked by the Andes to the east and protected by a nearly trackless desert in the Atacama to the north, naval weapons were the key measure of power between Peru and Chile. The US Office of Naval Intelligence (ONI) analyst Theodorus Mason summed up the situation, noting how the Chilean government:

> was fully alive to the vital importance of this branch of the national defense, surrounded as Chile was by nations more or less hostile, but who ... would be forced to attack her by sea. Willing to profit by the costly experience carried on in other countries ... she sent her officers abroad—the older ones to examine the latest ships and guns, the younger ones to enter the foreign services and gain experience in their duties.[33]

The chief lesson of all this, the Ministry of the Marine noted in 1871, was that the Chilean Navy was "still little prepared to make a defense of our coast in case of war with a maritime nation" and that at least two armored ships "of the first class" were immediately necessary;[34] two armored ships, perhaps, to match the Peruvian *Huáscar* and *Independencia*.

Responsively enough, the following year the Chilean agents in Europe contracted with Earle's Shipbuilding in Hull, UK for twin armored frigates: *Cochrane* and *Blanco Encalada/Valparaiso* (Figure 3.1).[35] Though a mere decade younger than *Huáscar* and *Independencia*, these vessels were a marked improvement over their Peruvian counterparts, fitted

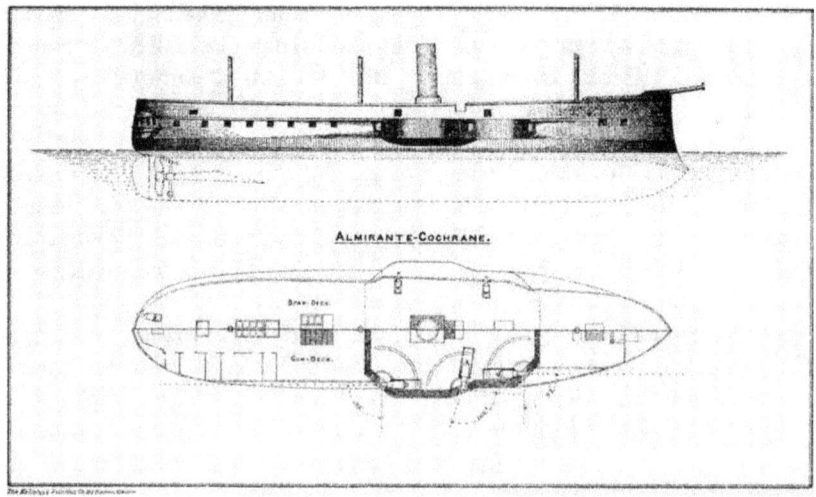

Figure 3.1 *Cochrane*
Source: *The War-Ships and Navies of the World*, 1880.

out with what the *Hull Times* admired as "the most modern appliances of war."[36] Designed by Edward Reed (a rival to Cowper Coles – the *Huáscar's* architect) and "considered by him among his best conceptions," the ships featured Armstrong guns, nine inches of armor and – in a revealing detail of their sophistication – electrical control systems which would be updated throughout the decade.[37] The commander of the US South Pacific Squadron, George Preble, observed *Blanco Encalada* lying at Mejillones, Bolivia in 1877, reporting enviously that though "somewhat peculiar" it was "a fine casemented ship with all the modern improvements": electrically fired guns, rifled artillery, and a hull covered with wood and zinc to resist fouling in the South Pacific.[38] For perspective, not until 1883 did the USN retrofit its first ship – USS *Trenton* – with electric lighting.[39] In 1879, Mason concluded that *Cochrane* and *Blanco* were experiments "of the very best sea-going type," representing a qualitative improvement over *Huáscar* and *Independencia*.[40] They were a concrete example, as the Peruvian Ministry of the Marine sullenly admitted in 1878, of the "improvements of transcendental importance" in naval architecture which had been achieved between the 1860s and 1870s.[41] In other words, the same rate of technological change which allowed Peru to compete with Spanish gunboats in the 1860s made it vulnerable to Chile's strategy of catching up through qualitative arms racing.

As in Peru during the 1860s, a number of foreign-built auxiliary ships and coastal defenses supported the fleet "nucleus" of *Cochrane* and *Blanco Encalada*.[42] Most were holdovers from the 1866 coalition war against Spain, but Chile also made additional purchases from Europe between 1872 and 1881, to include a squadron of torpedo boats built by Yarrow in London.[43] Augmenting its combatant ships was a merchant marine which nearly doubled in size during the 1870s and served as a contingent reserve for the Chilean Navy.[44] Heavy-gun emplacements went in ashore. By the early 1870s, Valparaiso looked nothing like the undefended port of 1866.[45] Even the Chilean Naval Academy's library went on a European spending spree.[46] Having absorbed the bombardment of Valparaiso and the lessons of Callao in 1866, Chilean Navy builders spared little expense.

Foreign observers followed the Chile–Peru rivalry closely, not least because it increased transnational interdependence on technical expertise and strategic raw materials. The same need for technical expertise that brought Tucker to the Pacific slope in 1866 endured, creating a race for human talent nested within the larger arms race. Ships such as the Peruvian *Unión* were commanded by local officers but relied "almost exclusively" on foreigners to fill its engineering and technical billets: John

Mackinley, chief fireman, Harry Withfield, stoker, James Clark, *artillero*, etc.[47] A number of Chilean officers trained – US officials were surprised to learn – in the Royal Navy, but they were an elite minority.[48] One newspaper covering *Cochrane*'s launch sniffed that it was still necessary to deliver the vessel with the aid of British technicians because Santiago needed time to "accustom such seamen as the Chilean government possess to the duties required of them in so massive a vessel."[49] A mountain of labor contracts were necessary just to transport *Cochrane* and *Blanco Encalada* to Chile in 1874.[50] On board *Huáscar*, the Irish émigré "Don Carlos M'Arti" served as a gunner for thirteen years, becoming something of an institution.[51] Ships bearing the names of Inca emperors or nineteenth-century revolutionaries were at once monuments to South American independence from Spain and testament to the interdependence of the Pacific and the industrial North Atlantic.[52]

Access to naval-grade coal was another entanglement – the literal fuel – of this naval race. At the time, South American coal was generally considered inferior to that mined in the North Atlantic. It tended to burn coolly and produce more smoke. Both the Chilean and Peruvian navies imported large quantities of coal from Britain, the United States, and Australia.[53] In 1877, one US commander sent back a specimen of coal mined from Chimbote to the United States for chemical evaluation, with lackluster results.[54] Efforts to develop mines in South America did little to dampen military demand for what the *Union*'s commander in 1879 called "indispensable" Welsh coal.[55] As late as 1894, speakers at the US Naval War College could observe that coal remained "the *only article of raw material* going in bulk to the Pacific."[56] In a wrinkle to Wallerstein's model of global economic integration, here the operation of industrial naval weapons by resource-exporting states such as Chile and Peru were linked not only to imported finished goods but also to strategic raw materials from the US and Europe. Technological changes meant dependency on European shipyards for vessels *and* coal mines for fuel.

Dependency should not, though, distract from the remarkable expansion of Chilean naval capabilities by the late 1870s, befitting its position as what one historian labeled an "Indigenous Latin American Sea Power."[57] Supported by a network of connections to Europe and North America, the Chilean newly made navy had reshuffled regional (and even global) calculations of power. As the historian Carlos López noted, Santiago's investments in its race with Peru converted the Chilean fleet into the best in South America "and one of the ten premier fleets in the world."[58]

The scope and significance of that expansion was not lost on maritime artists (Figure 3.2) nor international military observers. In 1877, the commander of the US South Pacific Station called special attention

3.3 *Shah*, *Huáscar*, and the Pacific's Hampton Roads

Figure 3.2 Thomas Somerscales, *La Escuadra Chilena en 1879*
Source: Museo Histórico Nacional, Santiago, Chile.

to the fact that "the naval force of Chili is larger ... in proportion to the commerce it protects than that of the United States."[59] A contemporary French military analyst stressed in a letter to the *Revue Maritime* that the Chilean Navy must "enter into the calculations of any nation intending to undertake a war by sea."[60] It was a stunning transformation, anticipating that achieved by Japan in the 1890s: from navy to construct to newly made navy in a generation. The impending War of the Pacific (1879–1884) would put that nominal strength to the test. But before it did, the Royal Navy had a chance preview the military effectiveness of the Peruvian ship *Huáscar* – the ironclad that had started all this racing – with results indicative of a flattening of naval power between the North Atlantic and Pacific World.

3.3   *Shah*, *Huáscar*, and the Pacific's Hampton Roads (1877)

By the late 1870s, it seemed on paper that Chile's newly made in place of built navy surpassed Peru's in both tonnage and sophistication. This relative decline did not mean, however, that Peruvian self-strengthening efforts "failed" in absolute terms. Weapons acquired to upset Spanish material advantages in the 1860s remained relevant against North Atlantic warships into the 1870s and 1880s. The naval force that had inspired bellicosity in Tucker's war plans against Spain or Garcia y Garcia's diplomatic bluff in Japan gave confidence for sound reason.

As if to prove the point, in 1877 a clique of Peruvian officials put the promise of their newly made navy into practice against the world's pre-eminent sea power: Great Britain. That May, a Peruvian political faction supporting Nicolas de Piérola commandeered *Huáscar*, mutinied against the central government, and took the ship to sea.[61] Unmoved by the harangues of the Peruvian President M. J. Prado, loyal naval officers seemed unwilling or unable to recapture the ironclad.[62] Frederick Bedford, commander of HMS *Shah* (the most advanced British ship in South American waters), guessed that they probably preferred keeping "a whole skin" to a forlorn hope.[63] After *Huáscar* interrupted British shipping, the Royal Navy admiral on station, A. F. R. de Horsey, had no such reservations and quickly declared his intention "to put a stop to [*Huáscar's*] depredations."[64] British spirits were high, edging on over-confidence. Bedford confided in his diary, "this is the day we have all been looking forward to."[65] Ultimately, like the Spanish before him, he would be frustrated by the unexpected material sophistication of a Pacific navy.

On May 29, 1877, HMS *Shah* and HMS *Amethyst* engaged *Huáscar* near Ilo, Peru. During the inconclusive battle which followed the "beautifully handled" *Huáscar* was struck multiple times but escaped serious harm.[66] Reciprocally, the inexperienced Peruvian gunners, despite "valor and energy," failed to damage either of the British ships.[67] Frustrated by the fecklessness of naval artillery against *Huáscar*'s armor, *Shah* fired a Whitehead torpedo at the Peruvian ship – a first in history.[68] The attempt fizzled out, allowing *Huáscar* to escape into shallow water at dusk. Unwilling to risk *Shah* in unfamiliar shoals, the British force organized a torpedo flotilla to search for and sink *Huáscar*.[69] Two small boats sortied from *Shah* but neither managed to locate *Huáscar* before it surrendered to Peruvian authorities.[70] It was an inconclusive but incredible outcome: the crew of the Peruvian *Huáscar* had fought two British warships, kitted out with state-of-the-art technologies, and lived to tell about it.

Overnight, Piérola and his men became national heroes set against British imperial arrogance. By competing successfully with the dominant maritime state in the international system, Piérola appeared to snatch victory from the jaws of indecision. Newspapers printed reams of diplomatic correspondence about the event; protests arrived at the Peruvian legation in London; chants of "death to the English" were reported in

3.3 *Shah*, *Huáscar*, and the Pacific's Hampton Roads

Lima's streets.[71] In July – their transgressions against the state transmuted by the alchemy of nationalism – ex-rebels from *Huáscar* marched through Lima under a shower of bouquets tossed from roadside balconies.[72] *Huáscar* was proof, one placard in Lima read, that "the force of patriotism has conquered English Haughtiness."[73] Bedford rued that the rebel Piérola had somehow been "elevated into a hero and kind of martyr."[74] One (predictable) side effect of anti-British sentiment was to exaggerate the purported significance of the "victory of the *Huáscar* over the combined forces of Her Majesty's steam-ships."[75] Here, the *South Pacific Times* argued, were the real defenders of the *Doctrina Monroe*: the policy of "'America for the Americans.'"[76] It was an encore, in this sense, to the Spanish defeat at Callao in 1866 and a measure of the success of Peru's self-strengthening program.

True to the moment, a memorial commissioned from the French artist Luis Boudat Du Collier depicted the battle as an almost religious experience. Held today in the collection of the Peruvian Foreign Ministry, *Alegoría del Combate de Pacocha* depicts winged Nike – goddess of victory – delivering laurels to Peru while Britannia looks on. Clio – the muse of history – takes note beside Peru; the "victor" dictating history and the muse transcribing it. *Alegoría del Combate de Pacocha* was a melodramatic reading of the event but it was grounded in a real upending of assumptions about naval power. By seizing qualitative technological advances, Peru competed above its weight. If the Civil War had Hampton Roads, the Pacific had Pacocha: a localized, precedent-setting battle in which a self-strengthening power fought a North Atlantic adversary to a stalemate.

None of this was lost on foreign observers. The *New York Herald*'s account described Pacocha as "one of the most glorious phases in Peruvian history" and a "heroic defense of the national honor against a powerful and disciplined enemy."[77] The Chilean *Mercurio de Valparaíso* agreed, writing, "the British ships were powerless" against *Huáscar*.[78] In London, the *Times* warned the battle demonstrated that wooden corvettes were "utterly useless" against Latin American ironclads.[79] Bedford betrayed similar sentiments, confessing to his mother (of all people), "I am secretly glad it is all over … if [*Huáscar*'s] gunnery had been as good as the way she was handled, she would have knocked the *Shah* in pieces."[80] "What a position," he still stewed weeks later, "in which to place the name and prestige of a nation like ours!"[81] Dahlgren voiced to a similar incredulity as he confronted Tucker (another rebel) in command of *Huáscar* in 1867.[82] Like Confederate navy builders, Peruvian leaders in the 1860s had sought to use technological shifts and geographic distance to compete with European (Spanish) warships.

Pacocha demonstrated the fruits of those endeavors. For those in command of the US Old Navy's wooden ships, the failure of the Royal Navy was a warning of things to come.

3.4 Qing "Strong Ships and Powerful Cannon" (1874–1884)

Contemporaneously, across the Pacific, the Qing Empire engaged in a mirrored and occasionally intersecting project. Just as the acquisition of the Peruvian ships *Huáscar* and *Independencia* touched off an intraregional naval race with Chile, the 1874 Japanese Expedition to Taiwan highlighted maritime defense as the Qing Empire's "most urgent matter."[83] Reformers such as Li Hongzhang, Zuo Zongtang, and others debated points of emphasis but were united in their concern about Japan "swallowing up the Ryukyus" and "drooling" (垂涎) over Taiwan.[84] The Qing encounter with North Atlantic naval power in the Opium Wars created interest in self-strengthening but the regional arms race with Japan dramatically accelerated it. Arsenals (established at Nanjing [1865], Jiangnan [1865], Fuzhou [1866], and Tianjin [1867]) and foreign missions abroad sought to build and/or obtain armaments "for a long term victory" against Japan and other maritime threats.[85] In naval circles, the watchwords of this race were "strong ships with powerful cannon" (船坚炮利), supplemented almost always by torpedoes and technical proficiency.[86] Toward that end, the "ceaseless change" of technological development was – as on the Pacific slope – both a challenge and an opportunity.[87] It produced heated debate about the dangers of "mistakenly purchasing obsolete warships" but also – like other naval programs from Charleston to Callao – a chance for navies to construct to leverage new weapons against constructed navies.[88]

Historians have, until recently, taken a dim view of the late Qing's "Tongzhi Restoration" (同治中兴) and associated self-strengthening efforts.[89] Mao-era depictions in the People's Republic of China were almost uniformly damning, portraying the "Foreign Affairs Movement" (洋务运动) as a conspiracy by corrupt Qing bureaucrats to use foreign technologies in order to suppress the Chinese people.[90] Skepticism about Qing self-strengthening is particularly evident relative to the apparent "success" of Japanese naval modernization.[91] The general tendency, as Benjamin Elman and Meng Yue argued, has been to read defeat in Sino-French and Sino-Japanese Wars backward, obscuring a more nuanced set of Qing achievements.[92] The result has been less an analysis of the Foreign Affairs Movement than, as the historian Allen Fung complained, a "witch hunt for the inadequacies of the Chinese

3.4 Qing "Strong Ships and Powerful Cannon"

army and navy," with Li Hongzhang serving as a much maligned scapegoat. Put bluntly, Japan appeared to succeed at building a newly made navy, while China failed.[93]

A more useful perspective, as the historian David Pong wrote, is to explore "the degree of the failure" in the Qing attempt to build a newly made navy of its own.[94] Success in self-strengthening should not be seen as a high-jump bar – cleared successfully or not – but as a hurdle race in which competitors could complete the race at different speeds. The Qing cleared many barriers cleanly, building reasonably impressive armies, and all the while maintaining frontier security through vicious continental campaigns into central Asia.[95] As for its maritime defenses, with transwar context in mind, the Qing Navy was one of several Pacific newly made navies engaged in the halting and experimental development of industrial naval war. Some failure should be expected, surely.

In this respect, contemporaneous reports from US naval observers in the 1870s require little revision; the Qing Navy's record of measured achievement and innovation is clear throughout. Perhaps from a position of relative stagnation, US observers were more sensitive to the incremental improvements in China's navy to construct. As early as 1871, the USN officer L. A. Kimberly surveyed the "Chinese arsenal at Nakin [sic]" commenting favorably on its achievements, albeit with reservations. Already machinery existed there for the production of industrial weapons, including torpedoes and rifled artillery pieces.[96] What subsequent officers called "very certain progress" followed.[97] By 1877, a USN officer observing the Fuzhou arsenal found five steamships "well armed" and "of superior build" with "one [the *Yangwu*] being larger and the remainder a trifle smaller than the *Kearsarge*" (one of the primary US warships in the western Pacific).[98] News made its way across the Pacific. China, *The Daily Alta California* argued in 1881, "may yet become a formidable naval power" and "no longer depends upon and puts her trust in old wooden junks as formerly" – that last observation a not-so-veiled swipe at the wooden hulls of the US Old Steam Navy.[99] Just a few years after the Japanese Expedition to Taiwan, "strong ships and powerful cannon" were on display in China, keeping pace with the intra-regional naval race. All things were possible, the US official H. E. Mullan noted in 1882, since the threat of lagging behind Japan had "spurred China on in the field of competitions."[100]

Self-strengthening within China's ports was matched by efforts overseas to acquire armored and steel warships. Qing agents purchased the light cruisers *Chaoyong* and *Yangwei* in 1881 from British builders; "the first to bear the Dragon Flag from those shores to the Far East," as one Edinburgh paper romanticized it.[101] These comparably small and lightweight ships were unlikely to threaten British naval power – the Chinese official accepting them assured an audience in northern England that they were tokens "of peace" – but were clearly relevant in the intra-regional arms race with Japan.[102] Reciprocally, Armstrong and his designers held up *Yangwei* and *Chaoyong* as "the pioneers of a certain class of vessels combining great power with great speed."[103] Once again, demand from the Pacific World provided industrial manufacturers with an opportunity to experiment with new technologies and profit by their testing in foreign navies. Naturally, these "pioneers" were also a technical advance on the antiquated gunboats of the US Asiatic and Pacific squadrons.

Cruisers were one thing, but by the late 1870s reformers such as Li Hongzhang and Xue Fucheng still saw armored battleships as their outstanding priority.[104] As early as 1874, Japanese naval actions inspired the goal of acquiring ironclads.[105] The 1877 launch of the Japanese ironclad *Fuso* under the supervision of Tōgō Heihachirō at Samuda Brothers in London – the same firm which had built the Peruvian *Independencia* – was a further "stimulus" for the intra-regional arms race.[106] Mirroring the motivations that prompted Chile to order its two "*buques blindados*," Li Fengbao inked contracts in 1881 with Vulcan for *Dingyuan* (定远) and *Zhenyuan* (镇远): armored warships "among the newest styles of all the nations."[107] Li Hongzhang had nurtured the dream of acquiring ironclads for a frustrating seven years and here at last was real progress.[108] Readers in *Shenbao* could follow the details of their construction and testing; one article happily concluded that they compared favorably to *Huáscar*, which had just recently proved its mettle against the British.[109] In fact, the vessels were larger and (on paper) more powerful than the first US battleships (USS *Maine* and USS *Texas*) built a decade later in the 1890s.[110]

Beyond ships, the Chinese search for human talent – what Li Hongzhang called the "fundamental root of China's navy" (人材为水师根本) – began to show returns on years of investment.[111] Foreign advisers remained vital to the Chinese military well into the twentieth century, but the Qing placed a heavy emphasis on developing indigenous expertise as well.[112] In 1875, USN Captain John Reynolds called attention to a Chinese steam frigate he encountered, "manned and officered exclusively by Chinese."[113] While others were skeptical, Reynolds assessed that China's cadre of naval officers was a "great advance on their part in the very few years which have elapsed since they took the first step beyond their banks."[114] That same year, a Shanghai newspaper, which was forwarded to the US Secretary of the Navy, worried that if trends continued, "the Celestial would be the man of the future" erecting a new

3.4 Qing "Strong Ships and Powerful Cannon"

order on the ruins of London.[115] Two years later, Reynolds reported on a Chinese-built corvette (likely *Yangwu*) "of almost 2000 tons, armed with twenty guns, all rifled breech loaders of Krupp's latest model ... and her entire *personnel* is made up of Chinese."[116] True, the Beiyang (North Sea) Fleet's eventual commander, Ding Ruchang, had little or no experience with ships, but he was a tested veteran of the Taiping Civil War.[117] Benjamin Franklin Tracy, the US Secretary of the Navy (1889–1893) who did more than any other to encourage US navalism, was likewise a Civil War general, but service affiliation did little to impede his cheerleading for naval investment. Continental powers found talent where they could. By 1879, as war broke out on the Pacific slope and Japan annexed the Ryukyus, Li Hongzhang felt confident that China's "human talent will be more flourishing by the day" (人才日盛).[118]

The early life of Yan Fu (严复) – a translator and national hero – encapsulates the Qing search for talent, its promise, and its results. Yan Fu is usually remembered as a leader of Chinese "ideological development," but he began his professional life as a naval officer caught up in the currents of self-strengthening and regional arms racing. As a boy, he studied at the Fuzhou Naval College, graduating to a position onboard the domestically constructed *Yangwu* – then under the command of an English captain.[119] Patrolling the Sea of Japan in 1872, Yan noted crowds of thousands who gathered to see the ship in Nagasaki and Yokohama; an early twist of a competitive spiral. When Japanese forces invaded Taiwan in 1874, Yan deployed to the island to review the military situation there, concluding that whatever its efforts, the Qing self-strengthening movement was clearly insufficient to meet the Japanese challenge. Three years later, Yan was among a cadre of Fuzhou Naval College graduates sent to France and Britain to study shipbuilding and naval tactics. Along with some of the leading characters of the Sino-Japanese War – such as Deng Shichang and Lin Taizeng – Yan took courses at Portsmouth and later Greenwich. Japanese students were there as well as the race for talent accelerated.[120] Always a good student, Yan and his Chinese compatriots proved "generally 'clever fellows' and good seamen."[121] He graduated in 1879 and returned to China to a teaching position, "developing talent" in Fuzhou and later the Beiyang Naval College outside of Tianjin. Though he eventually grew disillusioned with the material emphasis of Qing self-strengthening – advocating instead for deeper, almost spiritual reforms – his professional success was a by-product of arms racing with Japan. Had he learned French instead of English as a boy in Fuzhou (Zuo Zongtang believed the French were best at shipbuilding and the British best at seamanship, splitting students on two tracks), the intellectual world of late Qing China might have looked very different.[122]

Between the arsenals, ships, and experts it was a moment of tremendous, if protean, potential; one clear enough to the leading US naval diplomat of his era, Commodore Robert W. Shufeldt. When Shufeldt arrived in China in 1880 on a diplomatic mission to the region, he was immediately impressed with the possibilities of the Qing newly made navy.[123] If managed properly, Shufeldt argued to Li Hongzhang, China "should dominate the waters which wash its shores and exercise a commercial influence upon the Pacific Rim ... It may be taken for granted that with a proper system of coast defense – both naval and military – no western power could attack China from the sea with any prospect of permanent success."[124] Shufeldt's 1881 analysis of construction at the Fuzhou arsenal reflected the sincerity of that sentiment.[125] He even briefly considered taking a position as the commander of the Beiyang Navy – China's most sophisticated regional fleet.[126] From his perch on the aging USS *Ticonderoga* – an unarmored steam sloop – China's newly made navy left an impression. Surely a position in command of the Beiyang's steel warships would be more enticing, the *Daily Alta California* rationalized in 1881, than a career mired in the stagnation of "our poor apology for a navy."[127]

In parallel with efforts to acquire ships, guns, and human talent – the usual expression of navalism – Qing reformers stood out for their embrace of three-dimensional, asymmetric technologies to resist armored ships – most notably the torpedo-mine and the automobile or "fish torpedo."[128] This weapon used a new dimension (the undersea environment) to upset conventional assessments of power, encouraging torpedo races within navies the world over. Qing reformers were a touch literal in their translation: In 1882, the official uniform insignia for an "assistant torpedo workman" was an arm patch displaying the image of a carp.[129] "Fish" torpedo, indeed. Balancing finite resources, asymmetric weapons such as the torpedo provided a means of maritime defense on the cheap – a strategy first articulated by CSN/A self-strengtheners during the US Civil War. In 1875, one official argued that as long as China remained an unconstructed navy (ironclads were too "expensive" and port defense "mosquito-boats" too weak) it should "attack ironclad warships with automobile torpedoes."[130] That same year, a USN engineer in China took time to note the capabilities of Chinese-built torpedo-mines.[131] Two short years later, Tianjin already boasted a small arsenal of experimental "fish torpedoes."[132] By 1881, Chinese agents had purchased more effective variants in Berlin, while also building static torpedoes in "native arsenals" – so many, in fact, that in 1884 the large "quantity of torpedo stores" in Chinese arsenals moved one British officer to envy.[133] As the Sino-French War approached, the Qing historian and official Qin

3.4 Qing "Strong Ships and Powerful Cannon"

Xiangye (秦缃业) identified the torpedo's fundamental appeal in an era of growing naval expenditures. He argued: "The weapons of yesterday are not as good as today's, and the weapons of the future will surpass the advantages of those of today ... For this reason if the foreigners are inclined to ironclad ships, we must consider new methods for destroying armored vessels."[134] As it had been for the CSN, Peru, and other self-strengtheners, the torpedo was a fundamental component of that effort.

In addition to structural factors, Qing interest in the torpedo was encouraged by the transnational circulation of asymmetric warfare experts. Two Americans stood out, blending state and commercial motivations: John Lay (the Civil War veteran) and Daniel Mannix. In 1877, Lay brought an example of his newly designed locomotive torpedo to China, attracting the attention of Li Hongzhang and many others. The vernacular newspaper *Shenbao* treated readers to Civil War-era stories about Lay and his use of a "spar torpedo to attack an armored warship."[135] On the basis of that experience, Chinese officials in Tianjin contracted Lay and a small cadre of engineers "at great expense" to prepare for a series of "spectacular trials of the automobile torpedo."[136] The results failed to meet expectations. Apparently Chinese agents were "quite unsatisfied" and sought to recover their deposit on the weapons.[137] Nonetheless, Li Hongzhang's interest endured. A world-touring Ulysses S. Grant recorded in 1879 that Li asked specifically about the Lay and "stated 'that he had given much attention to torpedo defenses and watched with interest all the developments of the science in other nations.'"[138] The Lay torpedo – an almost preposterous mass of gears and over two miles of wires and cables – was a key vector of that knowledge and a stepping stone toward China's acquisition of more effective automobile torpedo weapons.[139] For Lay, Qing interest was, like Peruvian contracts in the 1860s, a means of funding his livelihood.

Li Hongzhang was apparently undeterred by the Lay torpedo's underwhelming performance. There were other models to choose from, and the weapon's promise was too great to ignore. In 1881, he hired another North American torpedo expert, Lieutenant Daniel P. Mannix, United States Marine Corps – an officer who had served under Commodore R. W. Shufeldt on the first US steam vessel to circumnavigate the world – to act as an instructor at the Tianjin torpedo corps.[140] A US perspective on the matter was welcome, Li stressed, because unlike European nations, the "geographical position of the United States nations and China are fairly similar" – both possessed long coastlines and far-reaching riverine networks – making the torpedo relevant.[141] *Shenbao* was optimistic about the "great fortune" the American adviser portended.[142] Caught in the Old Navy's doldrums, for Mannix it was a plush assignment.

He brought his family and an ex-slave to serve as a housekeeper in a walled estate ("for fear of dogs and the Chinese," his son later remembered).[143] Credit where it was due, Mannix earned a "Double Dragon" award from Li Hongzhang for his efforts (though Congress refused to let a commissioned US officer accept the "emolument").[144]

Subsequent attempts by US firms to use Shufeldt's relationship with Li Hongzhang as a conduit for more experimental torpedo technologies were less successful. After John Ericsson's torpedo boat *Destroyer* (or "*Sea Devil*") received mixed reviews from the USN, one entrepreneur hoped that Shufeldt might help "in inducing our Chinese friends to buy [it]."[145] Nothing came of the effort, but the hope was understandable. Surplus and experimental arms built by Ericsson (who had attempted to sell monitors and torpedoes to Peru in the 1860s and 1870s) often found a home among Pacific self-strengtheners.[146]

Of course, as in Chile and Peru, the autonomy gained through self-strengthening went hand in hand with new entanglements. Ever more capable weapons brought increased dependency on technical advice and strategic materials. Despite encouraging trends, in 1881 Li Hongzhang could still review the North Sea Fleet and conclude, "in all matters there is a need for talent" (事事需才).[147] What the American L. C. Arlington called a "weird set" of European advisers trickled in to address that need, with limited success.[148] When the Qing newly made navy went to sea and even to war it did so with North Atlantic experts onboard. Coal, again as in South America, was another liability.[149] In 1879, Wang Xianqian observed that for naval purposes, "China's coal production is scarce, and thus that used by its steamers must be obtained from overseas."[150] That dependency created a far-reaching drain on Chinese resources (漏卮); one with which naval leaders in Lima and Santiago could sympathize.

What then did all this amount to in terms of Qing naval power after a decade of racing and on the eve of the Sino-French War (1883–1885)? In the spring of 1882, the USN produced its most extensive survey of "Chinese Naval and military establishments," attempting to answer exactly that question.[151] It highlighted the tensions between domestic production of warships and ongoing technical dependency. US observers argued that Fuzhou possessed a credible naval force but, as a result of staffing limitations, the fleets at Shanghai and Canton were "useless for any kind of work which a man-of-war would be called upon to perform."[152] Asymmetric defenses in the North Sea looked more promising. The deployment of torpedoes at Tianjin and Port Arthur, one US report noted, made it "evident they don't intend that an enemy shall have such an easy walk over as did the English and French in 1858."[153]

In 1883, British intelligence officials agreed, reporting that whatever the Qing's limits, France's navy in East Asia stood "face-to-face with a formidable foe."[154]

Contrary, then, to retrospective analyses that search for the origins of failure, contemporaneous perceptions of Qing capabilities were mixed. Foreign observers eagerly awaited to see how Qing submarine defenses would be "practically tested by the French," precisely because the outcome of a future war was an uncertain one.[155] Perhaps another Callao or Pacocha was in the offing. Narratives of "failure" not only strip this moment of its contingency but underestimate China's role (alongside other Pacific newly made navies) as an early investor in prototypical naval technologies. How those weapons would fare in practice was an open question. The Sino-French War soon provided answers.

3.5 The Mismatch of New Empire and Old Navy

Against the trend lines of intensifying naval races in the Pacific, the USN entered a period of comparative deterioration. Budgets tightened amid the demobilization of what, in 1865, had likely been the second most powerful navy in the world. What Civil War-vintage ships and cruisers survived cutbacks remained the mainstay of the USN order of battle for a generation – at least those hulls that did not rot away. The naval historian Robert Albion summed up the historiographical tone when he described the post-Civil War era as the USN's "dark ages."[156] Promotion opportunities vanished as older officers cluttered up the ranks. USN hardware was an object of nostalgia to French admirals ("ah, the old cannons!").[157] In an often-cited example, USN ships even served as the butt of an Oscar Wilde joke. To paraphrase the exchange in an 1887 Wilde short story, an American visitor to Britain notes that, unlike in Europe, the United States had no "ruins or curiosities." Another character replies that, to the contrary, there was the United States Navy (a ruin) and American etiquette (a curiosity).[158] That Wilde's audience "got" the joke speaks to how obvious US naval decline was in the late nineteenth century. By contrast, we savvy moderns struggle to find the humor after nearly a century of global naval preponderance.[159] No comment on whether or not American manners remain a curiosity.

The contrast between the Old Navy's general stagnation and the achievements of small, Pacific newly made navies was especially jarring to USN officials and their boosters. By as early as 1871, the Admiral of the Navy David D. Porter lamented, "nearly every nation of consequence is outstripping us in the race for naval supremacy." He brooded that in the American Pacific, "Chili and Peru have quite a large force of ironclads, more than the combined forces of all foreign nations on their coasts."[160] By 1882, the naval diplomat and future president of the US Naval Advisory Board Robert W. Shufeldt reported (a la Wei Yuan) that China "is slowly learning the Western arts in order that by means of them she may sometime not only exclude foreign goods, but the foreigner himself from the country."[161] In Japan, the Meiji reformers' ambitious industrial program gathered steam – literally.[162] The effect of the end of the US Civil War was thus twofold: USN and CSN demobilization spread technology in the region, catalyzing arms races while also making the USN weak enough for the Pacific's newly made navies to matter a great deal.

In most historical surveys of the period, the Old Steam Navy's stagnation was crystallized in the public mind by the 1873 *Virginius* affair with Spain. *Virginius* was a Civil War-era blockade runner hired by insurgents to land munitions in Spanish Cuba. Captured by the Spanish corvette *Tornado*, authorities in Cuba tried the predominantly American crew as pirates. British diplomatic intervention averted war, as did the fact that the USN inspired very little in the way of a credible threat. Why would Spain get defensive if there was nothing to fear? Domestically, the crisis served as a shock to popular US opinion – though naval officers were already well aware of the Old Navy's relative decline.[163] In this sense, the *Virginius* affair (1873) appears more or less analogous to the Japanese punitive expedition to Taiwan a year later (1874): In both cases a maritime threat forced a major continental power into action. Less well known, this crisis was also a legacy of the US Civil War and its connections to the Pacific. The Spanish ship *Tornado* was originally built as the *Texas* for the CSN in 1863. It was purchased by Chilean agents in 1866 and captured by Spanish forces during the War against Spain.[164] Testament to a transwar web of entanglements, a Confederate vessel, purchased by Chile and captured by Spain, caused a stir in the United States about the extent of the Old Navy's decay.

The *Virginius* was a good story, and clearly mattered to US public awareness, but examples of USN decline were still more emotive in the Pacific. Falling behind Europe was one thing, but lagging regional powers in the Pacific was an indignity few USN officers could accept. Again, the comparison to the Japanese invasion of Taiwan in 1874 seems appropriate: losing the Opium War to Britain was a shock that could be rationalized by Qing officials, but an attack by little Japan required a response. Likewise, for USN commanders, inferiority to war-mongering European empires could be excused by the particularity of American geography and identity. Failure to measure up to "insignificant" states such as Chile and Japan, however, cut deep.[165]

3.5 The Mismatch of New Empire and Old Navy

A young Alfred Thayer Mahan experienced this rather personally while deployed to the Pacific. Demoralized, wrestling with what he assumed was a drinking problem, and forced to conduct upkeep on ex-*Stonewall*, he was an intimate witness to the "little divergence" in naval power beginning in the late 1860s between the US Old Steam Navy and the Pacific's newly made navies. Mahan served on the soon-to-be-condemned USS *Aroostook*: a gunboat built hastily during the Civil War that had nearly rotted away within a single deployment.[166] Mahan's billiards partner in Nagasaki, William Cushing, the first USN officer to use a torpedo boat in the Civil War, formally objected to taking out his gunboat USS *Maumee* because it was in worse shape yet: "I do not think it is the intention of our government to send its men and officers to sea in rotten ships," he complained.[167] Perhaps not, but it was an increasingly routine practice as demobilization shrank the Old Steam Navy to a position of insignificance.

Human resourcing posed equally consequential challenges. Promotion opportunities became dubious as positions onboard ships declined. Mahan seethed to his friend Samuel Ashe about the "deplorable condition" of the USN, so often officered by men of "grossly disreputable character." Not least his predecessor on USS *Wasp* – an "incompetent blackguard."[168] For the meritocratic or ambitious, as the historian Donald Chisholm noted, advancing was a matter of "Waiting for Dead Men's Shoes."[169] Competition for engineers and technical experts was another challenge as the Old Navy struggled to keep its boilers working. Mahan, once again for example, worried about "serious embarrassment" if he was unable to replace engineers onboard USS *Wasp* once their contacts expired – so hot was the competition for experience with industrial technology in the South American cone.[170] It may have been a "golden age" for the "Naval Aristocracy" at Annapolis, but the intellectual ferment and advocacy of Mahan and his messmates would take a decade or more to show results.[171]

Still, these manifest deficiencies should be kept in perspective. The Old Steam Navy was weak but it was also reasonably well suited to the task of continental consolidation and commercial expansion. As the historian Kenneth Hagan's classic work on "gunboat" imperialism notes, the Old Navy was in many respects the right tool for the job. Here was a small adjunct or constabulary force for an imperial project that was predominantly continental.[172] Congress alleviated some of the material stress by making minor investments in the 1870s, refurbishing pre-Civil War wooden steamships. It also authorized seven small gunboats and the "screw corvette" USS *Trenton* in 1873.[173] More revealing still, whatever its weakness in absolute terms, between 1866 and 1879 the United

States intervened militarily on thirty occasions in Latin America and the Pacific basin with relative impunity.[174] Mahan is, again, a representative example. In 1872, he assumed command of USS *Wasp*, patrolling indifferently off the South American cone, protecting "American interests" without much trouble.[175] Merchants and missionaries the world over appealed for protection; the cruisers of the Old Navy as what historians have called an "imperial constabulary" or "police of the world" offered it.[176]

Stipulating success at "policing," though, misses the sense of relative inferiority that laid the groundwork for USN naval transformation in the 1880s. In a nutshell, being good at policing was a poor standard for a navy interested in deterring or fighting wars. Against these goals, the Old Steam Navy lagged the capabilities of Pacific newly made navies. Policing was still worse as a bar for any navy with aspirations to represent a nation's civilizational standing or technological prowess (as they so often did). Even the most sophisticated USN vessels built in the 1870s soon fell behind international standards. In 1889, USS *Trenton* foundered in Apia Harbor, Samoa in a storm, its crew watching enviously as the British HMS *Calliope* managed to steam ahead of the weather while they could not.[177] For US naval officers and their backers, anxiety, humiliation, and even a legitimate sense of vulnerability followed material deterioration. These sentiments, as much as the hardware in question, were key explanatory factors in arms races around the world during the industrial era.[178]

Moreover, Hagan's standard account of the Old Navy's achievements is too categorical when arguing that during 1860s and 1870s, "local peoples – Africans, Chinese or Latin Americans – simply could not challenge wooden American warships, let alone the well-armed cruisers of Europe."[179] When read from a Pacific perspective, challenges were, in fact, common. *Huáscar*'s record at Pacocha represented a "challenge" to the Royal Navy during the apogee of "British Naval Mastery."[180] Dahlgren's feelings of inadequacy after confronting Tucker in Peru were born of personal frictions but also a real sense that the USN had been outclassed by Peru. And of course, the guns, ironclads, and torpedoes at Callao turned back the Spanish Navy in 1866, while the USN did little or nothing to enforce the Monroe Doctrine and its promises. Combining this record with the basic contingency of battle and Pacific threats appeared real enough to the officers of the Old Steam Navy.

The challenge of Pacific acceleration and USN stagnation was more worrying because of growing US territorial and strategic commitments to the region. The post-Civil War era saw an almost ideological commitment to the Pacific World as an arena for commercial interests and

3.5 The Mismatch of New Empire and Old Navy

empire builders. Much of this preceded the US Civil War, notably the pursuit of furs, whale oil, and guano.[181] The Gold Rush reinforced the Pacific in the American imagination. So too the transcontinental railroads: What was the transcontinental – built from San Francisco on the backs and bones of Chinese workers – other than a link to the Pacific? In 1868, the Burlingame Mission from China to the United States hoped to build a mutually "harmonious" relationship between the "land of Washington" and the "land of Confucius."[182] Shufeldt had similar dreams about Californian "vigor and industry infusing new life" in China.[183] Seward spoke in Hong Kong in 1871 of the vital "absolute necessity [of] the regeneration of the Pacific coast" and the possibilities of commerce and emigration from China.[184] He would know having also acquired Midway and Alaska as a bridge to Asia: what he called the "chief theater of events in the world's great hereafter."[185]

The "Old Navy" was a poor match for the grand intentions and ideological underpinnings this "New Empire," even if it was a reasonably good police force. Sending pre-Civil War gunboats and steamships to represent the prestige or enforce the hegemony of the United States was, on its face, a contradiction in terms. The Old Navy's ships, the US Secretary of the Navy warned in 1871, "our cruising navy, now by no means powerful, indeed scarcely respectable for a nation of our rank and responsibilities, will soon almost wholly pass out of existence as an arm of our national power."[186] How could Old Navy ships represent the US Empire and its civilization if its ships ranked behind the newly made navies of the Pacific?

Debates (contemporary and historiographical) about the significance of the Old Navy's "victory" in the first US–Korean War (1871) speak to the limits of policing as a marker of naval or civilizational standing. On the one hand, even as US naval officers began to find an audience for their complaints about decline, the Asiatic Squadron was still able to project force ashore in Korea, participating in the sort of violent punitive expeditions typical of "gunboat diplomacy." In 1871, responding to the wreck and disappearance of the merchant ship *General Sherman*, US sailors attacked and destroyed the Korean fortifications at Ganghwa Island. This event, as the historians Gordon Chang and Christoph Nitschke have argued, was as much about preforming the rites of "civilized" powers at the expense of the "barbarous" Koreans as it was opening markets or protecting US sailors.[187] "Barbarism," concluded the Secretary of the Navy after reviewing reports from the expedition, "will still respect nothing but power."[188] Inspired by a sense of mission over the Pacific peoples, RADM John Rodgers was willing and even eager to bombard the Korean peninsula and land troops against woefully overmatched defenders. The British did as much in China, and surely the US Old Navy should try to keep up. Leveraging their advantages, US sailors and marines assaulted the beach and killed hundreds of Korean soldiers (picking up a handful of cheaply won Medals of Honor along the way). Befitting the wider mission as a performance of civilization, Secretary of the Navy Robeson was proud to stress how the "punishment" inflicted "has not failed to make an impression upon the people of the Chinese coast, and to contribute materially in its effects to the consideration and comfort and perhaps to the safety of our citizens located there."[189]

On the other hand, in drawing attention to its ships, the Old Navy showed its vintage character. If this was how civilized powers behaved, what could one make of the atrophying and creaking technology underwriting it? The Old Navy could perform civilizational standing by inflicting violence on the Koreans. But just by showing up, it revealed technological retrogression next to British, French and increasingly to Qing and Japanese newly made navies as well. The US "victory" in Korea may have highlighted the Old Navy's success as a police force but it also showcased its limitations as a navy, let alone a marker of American "progressive civilization."[190]

The experience of William P. McCann in California a decade later captures this incongruous period of growing imperial ambition and declining naval power. A Civil War veteran, McCann was assigned to the Pacific Squadron as it reached a low point in the early 1880s. He was enchanted by California – the first duty station where he could afford to live on his pay (how times have changed).[191] He took sightseeing trips to Napa, marveling at the fecundity of the landscape.[192] California was a wonderland, but the naval forces he found guarding this western edge of empire left him seething into his journal. In February 1880, he was disgusted by the sight of USS *Ranger*: "another worthless vessel for our navy" that was not so much a warship as a "helpless craft" that had barely escaped foundering in a gale off Japan.[193] In port, he negotiated the crowding of officers and men onboard USS *Independence* to accommodate long-overdue maintenance. Jamming together, he groused, "the navy is at a very low condition as to discipline and efficiency especially."[194] Even genuine achievements, such as Commodore Shufeldt's around-the-world journey on USS *Ticonderoga*, were, McCann sulked, "supposed to be in the interest of trade and commerce" but in reality served "the interest of no one but Shufeldt."[195] As the forces of demobilization, territorial expansion, and the proliferation of qualitatively advanced armaments to Pacific states collided, they created an untenable position and with it an acute crisis of confidence. The answer to all this – to technical stagnation, the erosion of prestige, and the proliferation of threats – was for the United States to match the Pacific's newly made navies with a New Navy of its own.

3.6 Newly Made Navies in the Pacific and an Old One

Throughout the 1870s, two parallel naval races set off on both sides of the Pacific Rim: between Chile and Peru and Japan and China. Weak, relatively unindustrialized states found in the Confederate model (via direct experience or imitation) a means accelerating expansion and modernization. Radical changes in technology also created uncertainty. Peruvian reformers noted changes of "transcendental importance."[196] Qing self-strengtheners saw "unceasing change."[197] So too Mahan, who described "unresting progress" – even as the USN opted out of the race.[198] This rate of change and obsolescence made newly made navies in the Pacific disproportionately powerful. They also stoked fears in neighboring states about falling behind qualitatively; including a growing group of observers in the United States. As they did in the North Atlantic, arms races flowed from this sense of technological uncertainty and fear.

By the late 1870s, Pacific self-strengthening and arms racing had netted Peru, Chile, China, and Japan credible forms of naval power, somewhere in between the "west and the rest." The frustrating inability of the Royal Navy to capture or sink *Huáscar* in 1877 illustrated the matter dramatically – echoing the frustrations voiced by USN officers outside of Charleston, SC and the Spanish off Callao, Peru. The Pacific World could strike back owing to new technologies and geographic separation. As the "great divergence" swept over the world, the Pacific newly made navies offered small eddies in the tide: ephemeral pockets of parity achieved by the international proliferation of advanced technologies and the diffusion of power over space.

The contrast with the United States Old Navy was telling. As political and commercial voices in the newly consolidated and industrializing United States emphasized the markets of the Asia-Pacific, the relative weakness of USN forces emerged as a persistent source of irritation for the USN bureaucracy and the denizens of the Pacific slope. The Old Steam Navy was, in organization and function, an "imperial constabulary" performing some missions well. But its deterioration was an existential threat to the image of US primacy and progress. By the 1870s, US ambitions made it not strong but vulnerable in the ocean, competing for influence with both European and Pacific warships. There was a sense of anxiety among US naval officers and their backers who saw in the Pacific's newly made navies an erosion of US prestige and influence; to say nothing of an increasingly relevant marker of just how far the USN had declined relative to global competitors. Just as the Qing reacted more energetically to "little Japan" than Great Britain, civilizational condescension about Latin America and Asia fueled the most potent navalist rhetoric in the United States.[199] If *even* a Peruvian warship could hold its own against the most powerful navy in the world, what could it do against the United States? What did it mean for popular assumptions about US hemispheric leadership? As a decade of intra-regional security competition boiled over into war, the world was about to find out.

4 Pacific Wars and Their Lessons

In the 1880s, two conflicts put the Pacific's newly made navies to the test: the War of the Pacific (1879–1884, Chile/Peru and Bolivia) and the Sino-French War (中法战争) (1883–1885). Though more or less contemporaneous, these wars are usually siloed into discrete regional containers, obscuring their transwar comparability and occasional intersections. Having previously traced the efforts of self-strengtheners to build small but capable newly made navies in the 1860s and 1870s, this chapter (re)evaluates the War of the Pacific and Sino-French War as parallel "tests" of both the military effectiveness of Pacific fleets and the state of global maritime development more broadly. From Washington to San Francisco, officers of the "Old Steam Navy" and their political backers waited anxiously for the results of what Alfred Thayer Mahan would later call the "test of war": hard data to cut through decades of speculation about the effects of naval industrialization on tactics, strategy, and the balance of international power.[1]

Two trends stand out. First, wars in the Pacific during the opening years of "High Imperialism" demonstrate the contested nature of Europe's monopoly on industrial naval technology. Much as the CSN and Peru were able to use technological shifts to compete with industrializing empires in the 1860s, so too did the rapid pace of technical change destabilize local as well as global power balances in the 1870s and 1880s. Practically speaking, Peruvian victories at Callao against Spain (1866) and Pacocha against the Royal Navy (1877) had echoes in the Qing successes at Tamsui (1884) and Zhenhai (1885) during the Sino-French War. Far from checking Chinese naval growth, strategic defeat to the French in 1884–1885 stimulated further Qing naval expansion. More consequently still, the Chilean Navy capitalized on novel technologies to become a regional empire in its own right – foreshadowing a similar transformation by Japan after victory in 1895. Competition and friction with the United States followed in the wake of these transformations, especially off the Pacific slope as the Old Navy suffered the indignity of unflattering comparisons to the Chinese and Chilean newly made navies.

Second, the proliferation of advanced technologies in the Pacific produced an ever clearer outline of modern naval war: the use of industrial weapons in the three-dimensional and nocturnal environment. Narrowly, both wars tested the merits of self-strengthening movements in Chile, Peru, and China, but the conflicts were also experiments in naval warfare writ large. In much the same way that conflict in the Pacific during the 1860s generated demand for US Civil War innovations, regional violence in the late 1870s and early 1880s gave fresh impetus to radical technologies (often developed locally) which pushed the temporal and spatial boundaries of warfare. Incredibly, some of the same actors spanned both periods, stitching together transwar connections across the decades. Assumptions about marginal or "failed" modernizations in Asia and Latin America underestimate or misread those contributions to the internationally entangled production of modern war at sea well before World War I. True, the vast majority of naval investment and construction took place in the North Atlantic in the late nineteenth and early twentieth centuries, but the action – actual naval combat – was in the Pacific.

The import of such developments was worryingly obvious to incipient US navalists, who rightly recognized their own Old Navy as "a subject of ridicule at home and abroad."[2] The proliferation of modern weapons and their effective use by newly made Pacific navies created new rationales for USN transformation. The ONI was founded in 1882 in order to metabolize insights from European shipyards but made its best arguments for naval expansion out of conflicts in the Pacific. Naval officers patrolling the Pacific slope confronted Chilean naval power first hand, at once anxious and incredulous about how the USN had come to lag behind another naval power in the Americas. Other naval officers and marines considered positions as advisers in China – an empire building and buying warships while the US Old Navy idled. Together, wars in the Pacific made for a jolt, crystallizing the stagnation of the Old Steam Navy and the need for a new, steel fleet that could not only police a maritime space but compete for power and prestige with the Pacific's newly made navies.

4.1   The War of the Pacific (1879–1884)

The decade-long naval race on the Pacific slope culminated in the War of the Pacific (1879–1884): a protracted but often acutely violent conflict between Chile, Peru, and Bolivia over their mutual frontier in the Atacama Desert.[3] Chilean victory at sea in the opening months of the war proved a decisive first step. In 1881, after occupying Lima, Santiago

4.1 The War of the Pacific (1879–1884)

seized control of a band of Peruvian and Bolivian coastal territory, redrawing the political geography of South America in the process.[4] It was a pivotal event, not only for its territorial upshots but also because of the precedents it set in recognizably modern naval warfare. For USN observers these were all anxiety-inducing results and fodder for arguments in favor of naval modernization.

The naval phase of the war opened with a series of amphibious operations and dueling engagements between individual warships. Almost immediately, Peru suffered a major setback when one of its ironclads, *Independencia*, ran aground at Punta Gruesa in May 1879. It was an anticlimactic end for the ship at least one Peruvian officer – Garcia y Garcia – had hoped could strike out at the Spanish Empire from the Caribbean to Manila in the 1860s. For several months, Peruvian warships, led by Miguel Grau and *Huáscar*, kept up harassing operations, but eventually Chilean advances netted results. Matters turned decisively in October 1879 when the Chilean Navy's ironclads captured *Huáscar* at the Battle of Angamos. In doing so the Chileans achieved, as the French minister in Santiago cabled his government, "a success which assures them preponderance in the southern waters of the Pacific Ocean."[5]

Engagements involving armored warships – what the *New York Times* called the "most dramatic of modern contests on the sea" – have been well documented, not least by maritime artists and memorialists in Lima and Valparaiso.[6] Less well traversed are the conflict's messy and unpredictable steps toward modern naval violence, in which Peru was as much a co-participant as a defeated enemy. Just as many of the most forward-looking technologies of the US Civil War originated in the Confederacy, so too did Peruvian desperation translate into innovation. After Chile established naval supremacy along the Pacific slope in 1879–1880, the war entered a new phase which pushed the dimensional and temporal boundaries of naval violence. An asymmetry of power forced Peruvian officials to rely on local experimentation and the acquisition of prototypical armaments overseas; almost as if the CSN's strategy mutated once again the Pacific slope. Fittingly, a handful of US Civil War veterans found yet another opportunity to deploy their skills in South America, fifteen years after Appomattox.

Unable to compete symmetrically with the Chilean ironclads *Cochrane* and *Blanco Encalada*, in 1879 Peruvian naval leaders turned first to automobile torpedoes as a means of resistance. Almost perversely, the same class of weapon which in 1877 had been used for the first time in the history of war by the Royal Navy to attack *Huáscar* became the core of the Peruvian war effort after 1879. In the 1860s, static or floating torpedo-mines were key to the CSN defense against Union gunboats and armored warships – a strategy adopted by military leaders from Peru to China. By the late 1870s, inventors such as John Lay and Robert Whitehead had improved upon the concept, creating self-propelled or "automobile" torpedoes that could be aimed and launched at other ships. It was a weapon of immense potential, and one that would shape global debates about naval strategy and force structure for several generations.

Absent the ability to buy armored ships, acquiring competing versions of this new weapon became a top priority for Peruvian naval defense. Subterfuges flourished as smugglers shipped the weapons overland across the Panamanian Isthmus. At least one torpedo boat sailed from Panama under the Hawaiian Flag bound for Callao.[7] In turn, policing the isthmus became an unceasing concern for Chilean diplomats (like US ones in Liverpool during the Civil War) hoping to preserve their country's supremacy at sea.[8] Slipping past this "constant vigilance," a number of "formidable torpedoes" made their way over the isthmus, most often in the care of "American engineers."[9] Among these shipments came a stock of Lay torpedoes. For Lay, as it had in the 1860s, the outbreak of hostilities in South America came as a potential windfall. He and his associates aggressively marketed their locomotive torpedoes and expertise to Peru as a solution to Chilean preponderance at sea.[10] Lima took the bait. By August 1879, Manuel Palacio reported that there were eight Lay torpedoes in Peru and another two en route, cared for by three US experts.[11] Palacio stressed the Lay torpedo's "great utility" and advocated taking full advantage of "the services of the experts that are so costly."[12] Wasting no time, *Huáscar*'s commander, Miguel Grau, actually used a Lay torpedo to attack the Chilean ships *Magallanes* and *Abtao*, but the weapon fouled; "we launched one of them," Grau reported phlegmatically, "but with bad result."[13] After collecting the machine, Grau recorded that he "had occasion to note the necessity of repeated exercises and study in order to manage these apparatuses with skill and overcome those obstacles which occur frequently in its machinery."[14] Li Hongzhang had witnessed similar setbacks two years earlier in Tianjin.[15]

These underwhelming beginnings did little to dampen official interest. With *Huáscar*'s loss in October 1879, the Peruvian Navy requested additional torpedoes from multiple firms in an increasingly desperate and internationalized effort.[16] As was obvious to the *New York Times*, after Angamos, "the hope of the Peruvians is now in their torpedo service."[17] Peru's last remaining oceangoing warship, *Unión*, was fitted out with such a variety of torpedoes that the Ministry of the Navy apparently lost track.[18] Responding to the demand, private entities (and several charlatans) in Great Britain and the United States rushed to cash in on Peruvian desperation.[19] Weapons from the "US Torpedo Company" competed with the Lay for Peruvian interest.[20] The former CSA torpedo expert Charles Read traveled to Peru as an adviser in an unsuccessful effort to organize the torpedo service.[21] As the war dragged on, sales pitches arrived in Lima promising ever more impressive weapons. In January 1881, Peru's onetime representative in Britain, John H. Evans, forwarded an incredible proposal for a fully operational "*Submarine* torpedo boat," capable of "ten to twenty knots per hour whilst underwater."[22] Reports even suggested that John Ericsson had developed a new generation of gunpowder-propelled torpedo explicitly for Peru.[23]

At sea, the Peruvian *Unión*'s commanding officer was more skeptical about the possibilities of the automobile torpedo, given its complexity and the friction of war. After receiving a Lay torpedo in November 1879, Captain Nicolás Portal complained "that the good application of those artifacts of war [torpedoes] require perfect knowledge of their machinery and practice in their application, and that the crew members of this ship are completely unfamiliar with these circumstances."[24] British observers concluded from the Peruvian experience that "expensive and complicated torpedoes" such as the Lay were useless without specialized personnel.[25] One US expert who had helped ship Lay torpedoes to Peru claimed that if Grau had had the "improved" version "he could have cleaned out the whole Chilian fleet." Unfortunately for him, the iteration available was too large, too heavy, and too "complicated" for the "inexperienced" crew.[26] The "great destruction which the invention promises" – namely the chance to apply paradigmatic advances in naval technology to overcome material inferiority – was as of yet highly exaggerated.[27] Deficiencies in human talent, as Li Hongzhang might have put it, stymied the Peruvian war effort and the technical possibilities of the weapon.

Various forms of torpedo sparked Chilean interest as well. Not unlike the Union's imitation of the CSN torpedo program, Peruvian experiments encouraged Chilean military leaders to consider similar tactics. As early as 1879, Chilean agents solicited design specifications from Yarrow (the firm which had benefited from the ex-CSN officer Hunter Davidson's interest on behalf of the Argentinian military in 1875).[28] In quick succession, shipping agents in Hamburg and San Francisco offered sea-mines and torpedo boats to Chilean diplomats.[29] Hoping (as always) to profit, John Lay shamelessly proffered something better than the torpedoes which had so recently failed the Peruvians: the Lay Marine Projectile, what he called "the most reliable and predictable naval weapon of modern times either for the purposes of offense or defense or for coast service."[30] In Santiago and Valparaiso, officials demurred, citing the locomotive torpedo's complexity and (one suspects) recent evidence from Peru's war effort.[31] By comparison, spar torpedo boats, like those used by the CSN at Charleston a generation earlier, soon found a niche. As the Chilean Navy enforced a blockade of Callao Harbor, spar torpedo boats served as "the eyes of the blockading squadron during the dark hours."[32] Night raids took on a heroic cast in the press, catching international attention and reprints in naval intelligence publications.[33] Six years later, officers at the newly founded US Naval War College found the Peruvian and Chilean torpedo boat operations at Callao an example "particularly worthy of notice."[34] Qing reformers and British technicians also took note of this practical experiment in the Pacific.[35]

Defeat in conventional naval battles and the teething problems of the torpedo meant Chilean sea control was essentially secure by 1880 – with an important coda. Peru's inability to contest Chile's position symmetrically led it to organically pursue measures decades ahead of their time. Peruvian weakness (much as it had for the Confederacy) provided an incentive for paradigmatic innovation. Against the asymmetries of Chilean military and economic power, Peruvians locally adapted industrial technologies into creative and often prescient forms of resistance: the submarine, the airship, and the improvised explosive device. The results held great but ultimately specious promise. As in Qing China, "failure" was ironically compatible with forward-thinking about modern war.

In 1879, while proposals and weapons arrived from abroad, the Peruvian resident Federico Blume launched something altogether more ambitious: the submersible ship *Toro Submarino* or "Underwater Bull."[36] The vessel, while basic, was an unmistakable forerunner of future submarines and an asymmetric response to Chilean conventional naval power.[37] As *Huáscar* was to the Laird Rams, *Toro Submarino* constituted a considerably more sophisticated iteration of industrial naval technology originally tested during the US Civil War: the primitive submarine CSS *Hunley*. Due to the ship's unseaworthiness – an understandable limitation given its precocity – *Toro Submarino* never managed to target a Chilean vessel and was eventually scuttled to prevent capture.[38] Still, *Toro Submarino* marked a conceptual step in submarine development; an innovation made not in Europe or the United States but Peru.

Unshaken by failure, the Peruvian national leader Nicolas de Piérola (who had inspired the revolt of *Huáscar* in 1877) explored still more fantastic means to challenge Chilean superiority at sea. He reportedly turned next to a charlatan Tennessean who spent months and an unknown sum investigating designs for an airship capable of attacking the Chilean fleet.[39] The story could well be apocryphal but it built on the basic experience and aspirations of the Union and Confederate armies using "aeronautics" during the US Civil War.[40] In 1881, after frustratingly little progress, the plan was quietly dropped. Its technical feasibility aside, the concept, like Blume's submarine, was a precocious one hinting at the coming three-dimensionality of aerial violence. The airship and the submarine were akin in this effort to erode Chilean sea power by paradigmatically shifting the spatial bounds of modern naval war.

Peru's greatest success, though, came with a more basic adaptation of industrial products. The limitations of the propelled torpedo and the failure of novel weapons programs forced the Peruvians to investigate a yet more asymmetric form of violence – what can best be described as waterborne improvised explosive devices. In July 1880, the Chilean transport *Loa* was sunk by an abandoned launch carrying fresh fruit, vegetables, and a tremendous quantity of gunpowder. Two months later, a similar subterfuge destroyed the warship *Covadonga*.[41] The Chilean press was rabid: "VENGEANCE! VENGEANCE!" read one headline.[42] Another brooded that while in battle the "Peruvians were impotent ... now they sink the *Covadonga* with treachery."[43] Like the submarine and naval aviation, this tactic would also play a role in future campaigns of asymmetric resistance; it was difficult to argue with results.

Unluckily for Lima, none of these programs, however inventive, could upset Chilean maritime primacy. Guerrilla resistance in the Andes held up for months, but for Peru defeat followed defeat after the naval campaign of 1879–1880: a months-long "test" of naval technologies and strategies acquired in the course of a decade-long naval race. Chilean officers and *materiel* (most notably the ironclads *Cochrane* and *Blanco Encalada*) excelled in the moment. Peru failed, as had the CSN/A before it, despite innovations in modern naval violence. The template had its limits, even if it did provide insights into the future of naval war for anyone who cared to look.

The more obvious upshot of the war was Chile's break out as a sea power dominating the South American Pacific slope. The Peruvian Navy, as US naval intelligence concluded, "practically ceased to exist since the termination of the disastrous war with Chili."[44] At the same time, ONI reports continued, Chile emerged as "the preponderating Naval Force on the west coast of South America."[45] In Valparaiso, military leaders in Chile reflected confidently on their newfound power in South America. Five years before A. T. Mahan published *The Influence of Sea Power upon History* (and while Mahan himself patrolled sullenly off the Peruvian coast), the inaugural issue of Chile's *Revista de Marina* crowed: "The trident of Neptune is the scepter of the world ... *he who controls the sea, dominates the land.*"[46] That same brimming confidence would have substantial implications for US policy during the 1880s, as the USN reacted to a new rival in the Pacific.

4.2 The Old Navy Confronts Chilean Sea Power

On scene in the South American Pacific, the chief task for the USN during all this was twofold: protect US interests and encourage a war settlement between the belligerents. For the officers of the Old Steam Navy, accomplishing that mission proved a difficult and often humiliating challenge. The self-image of the United States as a hemispheric leader (or hegemon) was ill-matched by the Old Navy's obvious deficiencies next to Chile's newly made navy. US attempts to mediate on behalf of Peru fell flat, largely as a result of naval inferiority. In 1880, as Peru's army collapsed, Chilean diplomats rebuffed US attempts to mediate a peace settlement and prevent the dismemberment of Peru and Bolivia.[47] Gunboat diplomacy failed without real gunboats. The commander of USS *Pensacola* worried that US Secretary of State James Blaine had "disgraced and belittled us abroad by his 'vigorous' foreign policy" that promised more than the Navy could deliver.[48] The *Los Angeles Herald* feared that Blaine's "dictatorial tone" would "embroil" the United States in an unnecessary war – in the meantime "Chili, almost at any moment, might turn around and tell the United States to go to Hades."[49] James Blaine may have aspired to a "peace congress" to "remove all possibility of war on the Western Hemisphere," but without credible force, *Yanqui* leadership rang hollow.[50]

Judging by popular media, the US public as much as its naval officers saw the Chilean Navy as a marker of US naval impotence. Sundry insults flew – often exaggerated in the retelling of events. *Harper's* caught the spirit in an 1881 cartoon (Figure 4.1). In it, a Chilean ironclad warship sinks a wooden USN tub – making metaphors about the unseaworthy nature of the Old Steam Navy rather literal. President Arthur might have claimed that same year in an address to Congress that the United States would be the world's "chief Pacific power," but its navy made a literal mockery of that rhetoric.[51] The *New York Times* pondered the Jesuitical riddle of the USN as "a navy without ships."[52] Even anti-military publications such as *The Nation* got in on the act, mocking the Old Navy while advocating for reform as a matter of national prestige.[53] If "*Even* Chili" was superior to the USN, what did it mean for US identity and ambition in the hemisphere?[54]

Beyond damaging egos, Chilean naval power also allowed for more direct resistance on the Pacific slope. Most significantly, in 1881 Chilean forces claimed to have frustrated the US acquisition of a coaling depot at Chimbote, Peru: a port considered since the 1870s as a possible supply base for the USN.[55] Responding to rumors that the United States would move on the harbor in 1881, Chilean military leaders preemptively

Figure 4.1 "Our Navy," *Harper's* (1881)

dispatched troops and the armored warship *Blanco Encalada*.[56] To his evident surprise, George Balch – the commander of the US Pacific Squadron – arrived in Chimbote to find *Blanco* and Chilean forces occupying the port with instructions to prevent the United States from establishing a naval station there.[57] McCann, onboard USS *Pensacola*, recorded in his journal that "the Chilians have information that we were to seize this harbor and hoist the US flag over Chimbote" and had deployed *Blanco* "to prevent our doing so."[58] McCann found a popular consensus on shore that "the *Pensacola* was about to land a force and occupy Chimbote, but that the timely arrival of the *Blanco* with a Chilian force prevented this."⁵⁹ In his first contribution to *Revista de Marina*, the diplomat and onetime gunrunner Vicuña Mackenna remembered how the "magnificent bay of Chimbote" was saved from US predation by the "alive and happy vigilance" of the Chilean Navy, which arrived just minutes before Balch's forces.⁶⁰ Here (and certainly in the retelling of it) was a successful example of resistance to US hemispheric aspirations.

As Chilean officers hosted their USN counterparts, the latter got a closer look at the gap between a victorious newly made navy in the Pacific and the state of USN atrophy. Touring HMS *Triumph* four days later, McCann noted advanced firing mechanisms and torpedoes. By comparison, he was still obligated to send twenty-five men on deck "dragging about by *brute force* the 8 inch muzzle loading rifle – quite disheartening to us to say the least!"⁶¹ He felt the same onboard Chilean warships in April that year, visiting *Huáscar* and *Cochrane* armed with Elswick-made rifles, "probably the best guns now afloat."⁶² Drilling Chilean torpedo boats and launches raised apprehensions of about an inadvertent attack on USS *Pensacola* given that, unlike the Chilean, British, and German ships in the harbor, its commander vented, "the *Pensacola* is unprepared with either torpedoes or electric lights … of any kind against torpedoes!"⁶³ Mahan, too, privately ruminated about the situation, writing that, in 1882, the USN was so weak it "could not have controlled Chili's men of war."⁶⁴ While some – including a number of historians with the benefit of hindsight – could dismiss the War of the Pacific as a minor affair or "guano war," for USN officers on scene the conflict showcased an obvious qualitative contrast between a Chilean newly made navy with the state of the US "Old" one. A case for naval expansion (not so far removed from the self-strengthening plans of other Pacific states) came fast on the heels of that realization.

4.3 Reassessing Defeat in Asia's First Modern Naval War (1883–1885)

Across the Pacific, the Qing followed the "Chili-Peru War" with some interest.⁶⁵ Most reports documented the shameful treatment of Chinese laborers by the belligerent armies, but news about the performance of novel weapons filtered through as well.⁶⁶ It was suitable advanced reading. Between 1883 and 1885, while the War of the Pacific still ground on in the Andes, France and China fought a sprawling conflict in Southeast Asia, mainland China, and Taiwan featuring many of the same technologies deployed by Peru and Chile.⁶⁷ In this sense, the war was a mirrored "test" of a Pacific naval program after an intra-regional arms race (versus Japan).

4.3 Reassessing Defeat in Asia's First Modern Naval War

Qing officials had long predicted French aggression. As early as 1881, Li Hongzhang, Zhang Zhidong, and others worried that French forces would spread beyond Southeast Asia, cross "the sea and the rivers and penetrate Yunnan (China)."[68] Those fears proved prescient. In 1883, French military expansion collided with "Black Flag" and regular Chinese soldiers in Tonkin, precipitating a confused, often undeclared war between the French and Qing Empires.[69] In the end, decisive – though hardly inevitable – French victories ushered in a new era of formal imperialism and a fresh round of soul-searching among Qing reformers.

In the conventional telling, Qing defeat in the Sino-French War represented the failure of the self-strengthening movement and even a "secret betrayal" (私订卖国) by Qing officials who sold out to the French.[70] The People's Republic of China (PRC) anthology of diplomatic records from the war argued those forces "that were defeated in battle were precisely the ones extensively trained in new methods and armed with modern weapons." Limited success, it continued, could be found only in examples of popular or "people's war" against the French; a lesson for anticolonial movements in the twentieth century.[71] More dispassionately, Bruce Elleman (in one of the few English-language accounts of the conflict) concluded that "the Sino-French War of 1884–1885 was China's first test of its newly modernized army and navy .... Clearly China failed this test."[72] Chinese arsenals and fleets collapsed like vast Potemkin villages against the hard power of the industrial North Atlantic.

The empirical record bears much of this out. In August 1884, French warships under the command of Admiral Amédée Courbet ascended above the Min River's defenses and destroyed the South Sea Fleet at Fuzhou (马江之役). Courbet reported triumphantly, but with little exaggeration, that "nothing but wreckage is left of the Chinese flotilla," – what had theretofore been the chief material achievement of self-strengthening.[73] French torpedo boat attacks in February 1885 against the Chinese fleet outside of Shipu (石浦) were likewise effective, sinking two of the Qing Navy's most capable ships.[74] These defeats were nearly unmitigated fiascos.[75] "Little more than slaughter," wrote one nineteenth-century historian.[76]

Headlines about Qing naval defeat, though, obscure moments of contingency and in the wider war. The Battle of Fuzhou was a disaster, but Qing coastal defense operations were far more successful. With the examples of Charleston (1862–1865) and Callao (1866) in mind, Chinese port defense at Tamsui (1884), Keelung (1884), and Zhenhai (1885) take on new meaning as further instances of naval resistance and of the possibilities three-dimensional weapons used in concert with shore-based defenses.[77] Often, as with the Peruvians at Callao (1866) or

Pacocha (1877), inconclusive results were transformed by nationalistic retellings into dramatic victories against foreign powers. That such developments were illegible to most North Atlantic observers – and therefore downplayed in French or British sources – made them no less real. More significantly, given the extent to which China's so-called problem of modernization is bound up in its failure to "create an adequate modern naval defense," a rethinking of the Sino-French War encourages fresh perspectives on Qing history more broadly.[78]

Consider, for a start, the uneven record of the French amphibious assaults on Taiwan; Courbet's prime objective after destroying the Chinese Southern Fleet at Fuzhou. In August 1884, French forces attempted to capture the port of Keelung (基隆) and its adjacent coal deposits.[79] Writers at *Shenbao* reckoned that "France's cunning plan" was to occupy the mines and ransom them for financial concessions.[80] In August 1884, French forces managed an amphibious landing but failed to occupy the adjacent heights or coal fields, leaving the shore parties little option but withdrawal.[81] Chinese sources, searching for encouraging news, argued that it was "virtually a defeat inasmuch as [the French] were driven back to their ships with considerable loss."[82] A subsequent and better-prepared attack in October was more successful, at least superficially. Telegraphic reports lamented, "the Keelung batteries have been destroyed by French bombardment, without the French ships even suffering any injury. Events have come to this, what is to be done!"[83] *Shenbao* spared no feelings, ascribing the "instant flight" of Chinese forces to the failings of a local commander – a convenient scapegoat.[84]

That criticism was overblown and certainly premature. The withdrawal from Keelung was, in fact, a tactical retreat, effectively containing French forces to the port and maintaining (for a time) Chinese control of the inland coal mines – the only meaningful French objective.[85] US military officers noted "heavy" French losses in Taiwan to little end; "with the failure to get possession of the coal mines. Kelung [sic] lost all of its strategic value."[86] For Qing officials, the symbolic value of denying coal to the French was yet more important than its concrete effect on operations.[87] So much so that in August 1884, the Chinese commander had ordered the mines destroyed lest they be captured.[88] The French eventually took the port but to little concrete benefit.

The French fared even worse at Tamsui (淡水) in October 1884, where an amphibious force was stymied by waterborne obstacles and stiff resistance ashore. This defeat at (like Callao for Spain and Pacocha for Great Britain) was objectively a minor setback but was interpreted as an ill omen for French regional influence. British War Office intelligence observed, "there can be no question that [the French] have received a

4.3 Reassessing Defeat in Asia's First Modern Naval War

severe check."[89] It was, the report predicted, "a turn in the tide" of the war.[90] *Shenbao*'s coverage of "The Glorious Victory" was nigh ecstatic.[91] Similar reports in the *North China Herald* and *New York Times* about "The French Repulse at Tamsui," struck a discordant note with the pretensions of European industrial power.[92] In France, by contrast, the "decided failure of Tamsui" was deemed too sensitive for public release.[93] Spanish officials censored coverage about the defeat at Callao, Peru (1866) for similar reasons. The Union failure to take the port of Charleston in 1863 had equally profound psychological import.[94] North Atlantic gunboats were powerful – but not omnipotent.

Qing resistance at Zhenhai (the grandiosely styled "Zhenhai Campaign" [镇海之役]) offered another example of successful competition, using a mix of naval weapons. The Qing leader Xue Fucheng (薛福成) commanded the campaign: a pillar of the self-strengthening movement, skilled, as a propaganda movie from 2013 stresses, at "using foreign means to control the foreigners."[95] Xue's deployment of submerged defenses and torpedoes at this "gateway to Ningbo" were routine news in both the Chinese- and English-language press in the summer of 1884.[96] As at Tamsui, or Charleston and Callao for that matter, Chinese officials hoped underwater obstacles would impede French movement, providing opportunities for Chinese shore batteries. "Although the French flaunt their superiority (逞强) how will they deal with this!" *Shenbao* asked overconfidently in August 1884.[97]

Those defenses came to the test in March 1885 after Chinese warships retreated beneath Zhenhai's coastal fortifications. Throughout the "campaign" that followed, Chinese preparations held against probing attacks by French ships hoping to finish the job and sink the Chinese fleet. As *Shenbao* framed it, "the French warships lie in wait after the battle at Ningbo, not brave enough to approach the batteries" and did so chiefly because "they were very concerned about our secret emplacement of torpedoes."[98] The stalemate's significance was apparent in Chinese (if not Anglophone) historical accounts which transformed the standoff into a dramatic anti-imperial victory. Zhenhai was even appropriated by a 2013 film celebrating the "Zhenhai Defensive Battle" (镇海保卫战) as a victory for the Chinese military against European imperialism; an "Alegoría del Combate de Pacocha" for the western Pacific.[99] Today, a memorial on site reads "Monument to the Victory (胜利) in the Zhenhai Battle in the Sino-French War."[100] Far from a defeat of self-strengthening, the Sino-French War was evidence of the diffusion of industrial military power outside of the North Atlantic. To one American adviser, en route to fight for the Qing, the French war effort had "certainly done little towards the demonstration of the superiority of the systems and materials of European warfare over the Asiatic. After treacherously bombarding [Fuzhou] ... keeping up an insufficient and mismanaged blockade of the north coast of Formosa and ... being defeated in battle after battle."[101]

Moreover, contrary to most assessments of Chinese naval development, French victory at Fuzhou did little to shake Qing faith in the possibilities of modern naval war as a means to resist North Atlantic industrial power. Defeat was not synonymous with a repudiation of naval modernization but rather a stimulant.[102] Most immediately, Qing reformers absorbed hard lessons about tactics, technology, and the utility of torpedoes in naval war; "the more the better!" ("多多益善哉!") one official emphatically declared.[103] Days after news of French frustration at Tamsui broke in the mainland, one writer in *Shenbao* argued that defensive preparation there should be adopted as a model: With torpedoes in place, French forces "would be cautious and not dare" drive into Chinese ports.[104] Li Hongzhang agreed, citing the US Civil War and recent experience against France as evidence that "torpedo-mines" were the "most effective means" to restrict foreign penetration of Chinese rivers and ports.[105] Given the success of Chinese asymmetric weapons at Zhenhai and Tamsui, he advocated for the distribution of Tianjin-built torpedo-mines across the empire.[106] Liu Mingyu's (刘名誉) account of the war likewise noted that if China "could defend itself with torpedo-boats, what need is there to be in awe of the French ironclads!"[107]

Liu and Li soon got their wish. After 1884, asymmetric weapons proliferated along the Chinese coast while overseas commissions in Europe redoubled efforts to acquire advanced weapons. At Guangzhou, an ex-USN official was reportedly employed by the Chinese government to emplace torpedoes.[108] *Shenbao* expressed optimism about the possibilities of defending Tianjin through "densely placed static and automobile torpedoes."[109] British intelligence assessed that "Port Arthur has been made almost impregnable" (an opinion shared by the *North China Herald*) and that torpedo defenses laid at Fuzhou and the Min River rendered those positions "stronger and better organized than before the French bombardment."[110] Overseas, Chinese emissaries purchased Yarrow torpedo boats, along with "electrical torpedo apparatuses ... torpedoes and every other mechanism."[111] British naval intelligence surveyed Chinese activities in European shipyards, concluding that the Qing reformers "evidently do not intend to stand still."[112] An American adviser predicted, "if the present viceroy remains in power, a marked change in China's military and naval administration will be observable. Four hundred millions of souls ... are not to be ignored when, as one nation, trained to the use of modern arms."[113]

For the Qing, the Sino-French War was not a repudiation of self-strengthening but an early test with mixed results. In 1874, Civil War-era doctrinal texts reprinted in China predicted the utility of submarine defenses; a decade later the Sino-French War provided firsthand evidence, guiding Qing efforts and investments. That same year, Japanese warships impressed upon Qing reformers the need to acquire new weapons. Defeat in 1885 made naval expansion appear all the more imperative – a trend with implications for both the United States and Japan in the coming years as the intra-regional naval race picked up again.

4.4 Seeing Like a Modern Navy

All this activity in the Pacific mattered in the United States, in large part, because of new institutions built to understand innovation and obsolescence in naval technology. Information flowed back from the Pacific in the form of official dispatches and newspaper correspondence at an accelerating rate. Transforming all that information into technical or strategic knowledge called for new bureaucracies: namely, intelligence services. In 1882, the USN carved out funding for the ONI – the first US national intelligence agency – to do exactly that. Ahead of the Naval War College (1884), or the publication of *Influence of Sea Power upon History* (1890), information about war in the Pacific became intelligence, pointing to the necessity of US naval reform and expansion. In the following years, US naval attachés and "intelligence officers" (itself a neologism) fanned out across the world armed with a new set of formalized requirements and institutional support.[114] Their target was less specific capabilities or intentions of potential adversaries (the textbook definition of military intelligence) than the state of global naval technology, ideally validated by observed performance under combat conditions.[115] In this sense, they were as much "technologists" or propagandists as "spies."[116] In other words, violence in the Pacific helped build the infrastructure necessary to track global naval developments and "see" like a modern navy.[117] The news these officials brought back provided insight into the future of technology and also evidence in the tendentious case for US naval expansion.

In this sense, the 1880s marked the professionalization of the ad hoc and often perfunctory intelligence reporting produced by US officials in the 1860s and 1870s. It was, like the creation of the US New Navy itself, a halting process. Indeed, not until 1883 did members of the United States Naval Institute (USNI) define "intelligence" as a discrete priority for USN officers.[118] Small wonder that a year later, while on patrol in the South American Pacific, A. T. Mahan still seemed blasé about his mandate to collect information. Responding to memos from Washington, he feebly apologized for having "neglected to obtain the necessary data, mainly through forgetting to do so."[119] Attitudes about intelligence changed quickly, keeping pace with the need to understand the naval races from which the USN had abstained in the 1870s. By March 1895, many speculated that the now famous navalist Mahan (so indifferent to intelligence collection a decade earlier) would find his "intellectual and literary tastes" fulfilled by an assignment as ONI's chief intelligence officer.[120] The billet had a fresh sheen to it, reflecting its relevance to the New Navy.

Intelligence reporting on the War of the Pacific was fundamental to this transformation and the coming naval expansion it supported. The US Naval Attaché service made its initial forays to European capitals and shipyards in the 1880s, but ONI's exposure to what Mahan valued as "the experience of actual warfare" hinged on the Pacific's wars.[121] Tellingly, the foundation of ONI (1882) coincided with the War of the Pacific (1870–1884) and the creation of a global US Naval Attaché system came as a direct response to the Sino-Japanese War a decade later (1894–1895).[122] As significantly, the Pacific's wars shaped the nature of intelligence requirements and standards, in the process making the careers of key officers such as Theodorus B. Mason and later William S. Sims – Alfred Thayer Mahan's chief rival for intellectual influence in the New Navy.

Consider the career trajectory of Mason – a meteoric rise in contrast to the slow and frustrated progress experienced by most of his peers. On assuming command of the US Pacific Squadron in 1878, RADM Christopher R. P. Rodgers recruited Mason as one of a coterie of young officers interested in foreign military developments; many hand-selected from his tenure as the superintendent of the US Naval Academy.[123] It was a sensible priority given the amount of naval dynamism in the region. Rodgers seized on naval encounters at Iquique and Angamos (1879) as natural experiments in modern warfare. Just days after Angamos, he ordered a team of junior officers to visit the captured *Huáscar* – Mason among them – in order to "make a careful examination of the injuries she has sustained and the effect produced upon her armor and hull by the Chilian projectiles."[124] He then forwarded technical descriptions of the ship's battle damage to the Secretary of the Navy, both as a specific example of "actual war" and a general missive on the possibilities of foreign intelligence collection (Figure 4.2).[125]

It was a formative moment, both for US naval intelligence and Mason's career.[126] During the late 1870s, Mason had explored

4.4 Seeing Like a Modern Navy

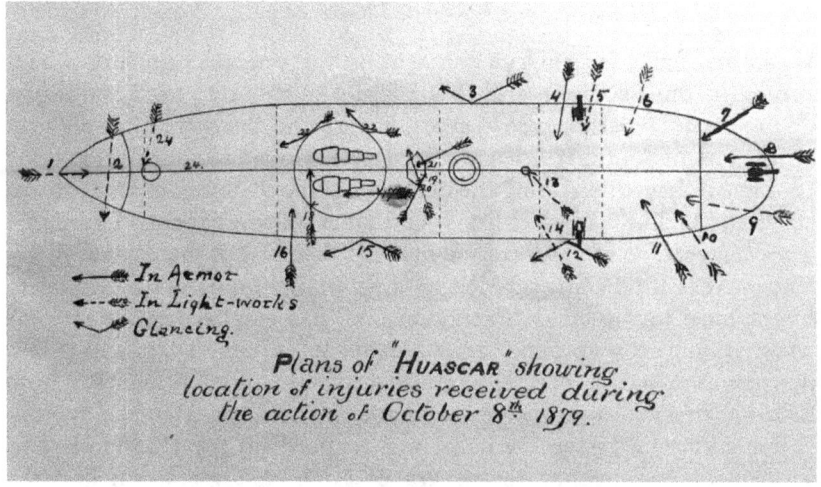

Figure 4.2 "Plans of the *Huáscar*"
Source: R. R. Ingersoll, "Plans of the *Huáscar*" (1879), NARA.

European shipyards on his own initiative, but his analysis of the War of the Pacific represented a departure: a new experience documenting actual violence.[127] He was quick to appreciate the difference. Mason saw Angamos as "one of the most important in modern naval warfare," precisely because it put novel technologies to a concrete test.[128] His work documenting that engagement – alongside a "board of very competent officers" – filtered back to the United States where it was repurposed and published not only for senior leaders in the USN but the wider reading public.[129] In 1881, James Wilson King, the USN's ranking engineering officer, cited Mason's "succinct account" of Angamos as the basis of his assessment that it was "the only engagement fought at sea ... between armor-clads, since their first introduction from which students of maritime warfare and naval architects can draw any lessons of value."[130] Mason's firsthand experience also formed the core of his 1883 account of "The War on the Pacific Coast of South America," one of the earliest Anglophone histories of the conflict with wide-ranging citations.[131] The New Navy's leadership was apparently satisfied. In recognition of his work in the Pacific, Secretary of the Navy William Hunt named Mason the inaugural chief intelligence officer of ONI in 1882.[132] What ONI "saw" in the Pacific – dynamism in contrast to Old Navy stagnation – had disproportionate consequences that were soon instrumentalized by advocates for US naval expansion.

4.5 Conclusion

When the region is seen as a coherent unit, there was a great deal happening in the Pacific in the 1870s and 1880s. After 1865, industrial weapons and expertise spread across the Pacific, sparking intra-regional naval races in South America and East Asia. Hot and sophisticated naval conflicts followed, featuring the defining weapons of modern war at sea: armored warships, steel cruisers, and submarine weapons. Through a transwar perspective, it was a moment of limited but intense naval violence across the Pacific, hidden by area studies containers. The historiographical turn toward "Pacific history" has emphasized the region's transnational economic and social dynamism.[133] In the 1870s and 1880s, that complexity was matched by naval experimentation and war from Santiago to Tianjin with wide-ranging if underdocumented effects.

For a start, a history of naval war focused on the Pacific restores a sense of contingency to the era of gunboat imperialism and the attendant "eclipse of the Non-European world."[134] Like the post-Appomattox period, the 1870s and 1880s represented another moment of shifting possibilities created by both the diffusion of industrial technology and the raw geographic distance between the Pacific and the North Atlantic. Unpredictability followed as a result. The War of the Pacific and Sino-French War were both hard tests of naval programs in the Pacific. The record was far from uniform – that is rather the point about contingency. Complicating deterministic accounts of the industrial revolution's tidal effect on naval war were eddies of localized resistance at battles such as Pacocha and Zhenhai. The proliferation of industrial weapons even underwrote the emergence of new, extra-European empires in their own right, such as Chile after 1880 and (as will be seen by the 1890s) Japan. The Qing's self-strengtheners actually used naval defeat in the Sino-French War to justify a more ambitious program of maritime expansion.

Win or lose, a constant throughout was that war in the Pacific produced an ever clearer outline of modern naval warfare. Facing asymmetries of power, Peruvian and Qing military officials experimented with novel forms of three-dimensional, industrial violence. Reciprocally, war in the region offered testing opportunities for North Atlantic navies during a period of technological uncertainty: The former used spar torpedo boats to surprise and overcome the Qing Navy and the latter launched an automobile torpedo against a Peruvian ironclad – a first in the history of war and one soon imitated by the Peruvian Navy. Naval building in the 1870s and 1880s may have been, as one historian argued, "fad-oriented, unplanned, intermittent and a waste of resources," but if so, the Pacific's

4.5 Conclusion

wars provided valuable tests for developmental technologies – much as the US Civil War had before them.[135] Far from the proving grounds and laboratories of the North Atlantic, the Pacific became the primary *locus in quo* of modern naval warfare in practice during the 1870s and 1880s. The US ONI understood as much, dispatching agents to document "intelligence" from these prototypically modern engagements. How to respond to the ocean's naval activity would soon drive discussions about the US New Navy.

5   The Californian Case for a New Navy

Wars and naval races across the Pacific made for remarkable strategic and technical dynamism in the decades following the US Civil War. Contemporaneously (and by obvious contrast), the deteriorating "Old Navy" sagged to a nadir. By the late 1880s, US post-Civil War demobilization had not only stimulated maritime development in the Pacific but it also made the USN weak enough for those developments to matter back home. National ambition in the Pacific made matters worse. A growing chorus complained about the weakness of what the *United Service* called "Our Little Navy" next to all "powers claiming to be maritime," including (in key respects) the newly made navies of "insignificant" and "inferior nations" such as Chile, China, and Japan.[1] Looking out from an "isolated and helpless" San Francisco – the western edge of US territorial expansion – it all made for an ominous set of trends.[2]

The threats that US observers found in the Pacific during the 1880s are typically rationalized by historians as a form of hype; a rhetorical means adopted by naval officers or Californian boosters to attract federal investment.[3] Advances in "little Chili" or big China were, indeed, sensationalized by naval advocates for political effect, but the rhetoric only worked because it tapped into something sincere. The reaction to the Pacific's wars by politicians, editors, and officers was no case of nineteenth-century "missile-gap hysteria": of fears cynically manipulated to secure larger budgets. Real anxieties were at play about physical security, prestige, and racial superiority – especially out on the far reaches of US Empire in California.

Viewing the Pacific through a transwar lens brings these anxieties into focus while also revealing a regionally specific, West Coast case for naval expansion. In much the same way that antebellum "southern navalists" saw "sea power" as a means to expand and protect slavery, so too did the settler colonists on the Pacific coast argue for a small but efficient navy in the 1880s as a response to regional threats and opportunities.[4] As early as 1881, the San Francisco Chamber of Commerce warned, "the idea of a great American city being at the mercy of China or Japan is not pleasing, but it is a sober truth, and it must be faced. Even little Chile could hold San Francisco to ransom tomorrow, and in case of war would no doubt do it."[5] West Coast politicians never gained the prominence or sway over the federal bureaucracy that Southern slaveholders did (just count the eligible senators), but their advocacy was ceaseless and their assumptions often adopted by national leaders.[6]

This chapter explores how US and, in particular, West Coast anxiety about Pacific newly made navies – punctuated by the War of the Pacific (1879–1884), the Sino-French War (1883–1885), and the Chilean Civil War (1891) – shaped the case for investing in the US "New Navy" as a reactive measure to defend territory and national prestige. It identifies three impetuses to US naval expansion: (1) threat assessments (often exaggerated) of Pacific newly made navies; (2) friction between the *Raza Chilena* ("Chilean race"), Chinese diaspora, and Anglo-Saxonism; and finally (3) the political opportunism of local and national officials searching for enemies against which to posture. After the War of the Pacific, Chile broke out as what ONI called, the "preponderating Naval Force on the west coast of South America."[7] In highlighting Chilean naval power, advocates found a convenient rhetorical argument, but rhetoric was only effective because it reflected real anxieties about the safety of Pacific cities and (most importantly) the US self-image as the hemisphere's most "advanced" civilization.[8] Across the Pacific, Qing defeat in the Sino-French War had a more nebulous meaning. In one sense, it reinforced prejudices about Chinese "backwardness" and the undesirability of Chinese migration to the United States. Often in the same breath, however, USN officials and their supporters worried what China's immense human resources might accomplish if properly armed and directed. As the Qing reformers continued to build and acquire advanced technologies in the late 1880s, the "Yellow Peril" took on a double meaning: a potential wave of nonwhite migration *and* a military threat to the Pacific. It was no coincidence that the New Navy's first appropriations and the Chinese Exclusion Act were passed in 1882–1883; both responded to perceived dangers on the maritime frontier in the Pacific. By the 1890s, navalists such as Roosevelt and Mahan would articulate a vision for a great power battlefleet, but the initial investments in the US New Navy were up to something at once more humble and yet essential: reactively safeguarding a sense of physical and civilizational superiority over the Pacific World and its newly made navies.

5.1 Sea Power from San Francisco, not New York

In the late nineteenth century, an ideology of "navalism" swept across the North Atlantic: a loose (originally pejorative) shorthand for the belief in the "national necessity" of a steel, battleship-heavy navy.[9] The US was no exception – at least eventually. In 1882, Congress passed appropriations bills for the first steel vessels in the USN; what the historian Charles Oscar Paullin called the "dividing-line between the old-steam navy and the New Navy."[10] Despite technical difficulties and infighting, US naval funding grew during Democratic and Republican administrations throughout the 1880s and 1890s, fueling what Walter Herrick described as "The American Naval Revolution."[11] That "revolution" was less quantitative expansion than qualitative transformation. Obsolete wooden frigates and Civil War-era monitors were decommissioned. New steel cruisers and battleships replaced them, leapfrogging a generation of half-baked innovations in Europe. US policy, observed Royal Navy intelligence in 1889, was "not so much to increase, as to re-create the Navy."[12] In 1883, one Massachusetts Republican surveyed the US fleet, concluding that, in effect, "we have no navy" and "should vote the appropriations necessary to build one."[13] In this, it was very much like the naval transformation of the Confederate and Pacific self-strengthening movements: from navy to construct, to newly constructed navy, starting from scratch.

By the close of the decade, results were promising. Capitalizing on decades of trial and error in Europe, the US New Navy "caught up" just as fast as the Pacific newly made navies had in the 1870s. By 1890 – the same year Alfred Thayer Mahan published *The Influence of Sea Power upon History* – the *New York Herald* reckoned the USN as the sixth most powerful fleet in the world and climbing.[14] A year later, the then Secretary of the Navy Benjamin Tracy felt sure enough to crow, "the sea will be the future seat of empire. And we shall rule it as certainly as the sun doth rise."[15]

The question of *why* the United States began this campaign in the 1880s has long been a playground for competing theories of state behavior. Scholars have identified material, political, and cultural explanations for the "navalist turn" in the United States.[16] This project rejects none of those arguments but rather subordinates domestic and intra-Atlantic factors to forces in the Pacific World.

The Pacific's influence on US navalism has some – albeit skeptical – acknowledgment in the historiography.[17] Histories of the transformation "from the Old Navy to New" commonly include parenthetical references about the rhetorical function of Chilean naval power in US national debates.[18] How could one miss it? A much quoted line from the historian George Davis (c. 1940) reads: "There was not a single day of the debate on navy bills in the decade of the eighties in which the Chilean affair was not summoned to support the case for naval expansion."[19] That said, for Davis and subsequent historians, the "Chilean affair" was less of a

5.1 Sea Power from San Francisco, not New York

threat than a cynical foil.[20] Bilaterally focused histories of US–Chilean relations give more credit to the role of serious inter-American competition on US navalist politics.[21] But while such texts acknowledge Chilean (if not Peruvian) agency in shaping US attitudes about sea power, they leave considerable room for explorations of cultural and material factors in the transwar Pacific – including Asia. Chile was only one example of a broader reaction to the Pacific World.

What influence coincident naval developments in East Asia had on US security and immigration debates was (and is) an open question.[22] Though there was no shortage of it in the Pacific, histories of Chinese immigration to the Americas rarely mention war at all.[23] That omission is a curious one, given that so much of the expansion of the US security bureaucracy in the twenty-first century has been driven by a desire to police migration. When considered in concert, the War of the Pacific, the Sino-French War, the "New Navy Bills," and debates over Chinese immigration become pieces of a larger question about Pacific threats to the US Empire on the make.

Immigration, sea power, and future ambitions came to a head in California: the "front door to the Pacific."[24] San Francisco's growth reframed the Pacific frontier from a border of continental power into a maritime imaginary full of opportunity – and much else. It represented a site of transition and of the conflicting identities of the United States as both Atlantic and Pacific nation; and by extension a sea power and land power.[25] An early arrival, Mallie Stafford, remembered San Francisco in 1884 as "the Queen of the West ... with her feet in the beautiful sea."[26] Out on the edge, California was served by ships more than overland transport. Its food and architecture reflected that fact. California's Mediterranean climate sustained viniculture more akin to southern Europe (or Chile!) than Cape Cod. "No wonder," Robert Louis Stevenson observed in 1880 from his hotel in Monterey, that "the Pacific coast is a foreign land to visitors from the Eastern states."[27] For the denizens of California and Oregon, as much as those of Valparaiso or Guangdong, the world was a maritime one, and the need for naval power followed as a logical result.

The peculiar security needs of the US Pacific were apparent as early as the 1860s and had grown substantially by the 1880s. CSS *Shenandoah*'s 1865 cruise against the US whaling fleet in the Bering Sea illustrated the point for a generation of residents. As the whaling ships burned, political and commercial interests cried out for protection. They got little or none. Growing settler-colonies in California, Washington, and Oregon – what the Anglo-Saxonist Josiah Strong called the "cradle of the young empire of the West" – exacerbated matters, creating Anglophone outposts at the extreme limits of US force projection.[28] One Republican congressman complained, "we have the great ports of Portland, Oreg., and we have San Francisco, and a dozen or twenty other ports of importance along [the Pacific] coast, and yet not a vessel to defend them."[29] It was a moment all the more fraught because of the gap between US ambitions in the Pacific and what in 1887 Admiral David Dixon Porter called its "especially weak" regional posture. Porter lamented that the Pacific coast, "which forms a part of our great Anglo-Saxon empire is as unprotected as if it belonged to the Fiji Islanders."[30] Two years later, William Sampson echoed the point, noting that with the exception of New York, San Francisco was the "most important port to secure against blockade" given its economic significance and present vulnerability.[31] That tension between opportunity and threat only heightened as a result of the Pacific's wars and the anxious interpretation of their meaning.

5.2 The Rise of Chilean Sea Power (1880–1890)

Much as Japan's victory in 1895 would reshape the global perception and politics of Northeast Asia, Chile's success in the War of the Pacific reordered the hierarchy of naval power in the Americas – with implications from Patagonia to the Puget Sound. Victors at the Battle of Angamos (1879), Chilean warships captured *Huáscar* and with it a newfound position as what its diplomats called "the mistress of all the Bolivian coast, and a very considerable portion of that of Peru."[32] After carving off provinces from Bolivia and Peru, Santiago redoubled on territorial expansion backed by naval power: west into the Pacific basin exploring Tahiti and Easter Island; south toward Patagonia, "pacifying" the region's indigenous peoples and contesting and its unsettled border with Argentina; and north against *yanqui* "Spread-Eagleism."[33] Chilean military performance in the War of the Pacific gave ample justification for optimism about this imperial program. "The trident of Neptune," proclaimed in the inaugural issue of Chile's *Revista de Marina* in 1885 (five years before Mahan's work on sea power), "is the scepter of the world."[34]

That same confidence soon brought Chile into conflict with the United States on several fronts. Chile had defeated its regional rival Peru but in doing so sparked a new race with the United States for security and influence on the Pacific coast. Success bred new challenges, and a sense of threat, in both California and Chile, was mutual. The Chilean military could not stand by, the diplomat and perhaps Santiago's foremost man of letters Benjamin Vicuña Mackenna warned in 1885, while US imperialists eyed a "gigantic belt of islands" from the Aleutians to Midway to the Islas de Lobos. Where would it end, he asked? Was Santiago "to remain without a piece of stone" in this "incessant and little equitable division of the Pacific"?[35] When Vicuña Mackenna alighted triumphant in San Francisco in 1884, he predicted that Chile's "splendid vineyards" would soon compete with California.[36] And why not? The Chilean newly made navy already outclassed the US Old Navy on the Pacific coast.

Fresh ideas about Chilean racial identity were potent fuel for this competition. Chile's war of "national consolidation" against Peru and Bolivia had also been a war of racial remaking, popularizing the concept of a mestizo *Raza Chilena* as the core of the Chilean nation.[37] This neo-race was *not* a product of European settler colonialism in South America (a la Australia or California) but of racial amalgamation: the "mix of the blood of Europe and the Indians," as *El Mercurio* proudly explained.[38] Because, the argument went, Chile's indigenous peoples were especially bellicose, genetic hybridity made Chileans good soldiers. Incredibly, this race was not particularly a "Latin" one. Rather, it claimed derivation from the Germanic peoples, absorbing and adapting the hierarchies of North Atlantic Social Darwinism. It seemed relevant enough to Horace N. Fisher – a merchant and diplomat in Chile – to detail the racial character of the Chilean "Castilian-Gothic line" to the US Secretary of the Navy.[39] The racial theorist Nicolas Palacios posited that Chile was exceptional among Latin American nations because Basque *conquistadors* "of pure Teutonic blood" had reproduced with the Araucanian Indians – "not only heroic, but also capable warriors" – absorbing their genetic traits and creating a unique form of racial-supremacism on the Pacific slope.[40] In 1890, the British naval attaché in Chile regurgitated the same theme. The officers in Chile were "much more like Europeans than those on the eastern side of South America," while the Chilean enlisted men were "strong and hardy, having a strong Indian strain in their blood."[41]

As with other empires in the late nineteenth century, racial superiority offered Chilean aggression a fig-leaf legitimacy. Relative to Peru, proponents argued, the *Raza Chilena*'s "grand virtues" were (supposedly) many, not least "industriousness in times of peace, and heroism in war."[42] Apparently, its only "defect," claimed Minister of the Marine Carlos Condell, was *"confidence."*[43] The War of the Pacific was tautological proof. "The Chileans had won," a correspondent of *El Mercurio* argued, primarily because compared to the Peruvians and Bolivians they were "a superior race, more sober, industrious and intelligent."[44] "Why is Chile Stronger than Peru?" asked another *El Mercurio* headline in 1881: because the "aborigines of Chile … were a robust and warlike race, very distinct morally and physically from those Indians in Peru and Bolivia."[45] La Paz papers sneered during the war at the "cowardly

Araucanos" (a reference to Chile's indigenous people) even as they reinforced the notion that the Chilean soldiers marching on Lima and the native peoples of Patagonia were interrelated.[46] Grotesquely, at the very time "pacification" virtually annihilated the Mapuche people, racialized myths about the genetic legacy of Patagonia's indigenous peoples served to justify Chile's aggression against Peru and Bolivia.[47] In 1883, a Spanish historian even suggested that the *raza*'s amalgamation of characteristics made it not "the daughter of England" but rather a pound-for-pound "powerful rival to Great Britain."[48] If so, why not the US as well?

It was heady stuff, soon augmented by new forms of material power designed to maintain Chilean "supremacy of maritime power over the other American nations."[49] Whole periodicals, such as *El Nuevo Ferrocarril* ("The New Railroad"), appeared after the war with the express purpose of celebrating the Chilean nation's "technical prowess."[50] At sea, this spirit was best captured by the *Esmeralda*: a precedent-setting cruiser built at Newcastle upon Tyne in 1884 according to specifications from the British engineer George Rendel.[51] At the time it was the "fastest ship in the world," and one which, Chilean officials promised, would "threaten convoys and introduce dispiritedness in enemy ports."[52] Indeed, so promising was the *Esmeralda* that it became the first in a series of protected cruisers built for Italy, Japan, China, Argentina, Austria, and the United States.[53] "The *Esmeraldas*" even briefly stood in as shorthand for a class of lightly protected, fast cruisers in general.[54] In Britain, engineers feuded for credit or the ships invention.[55] In the United States, *Esmeralda* provoked spasms of envy – as it should have. As Congress appropriated the first funds for the New Navy, the US Secretary of the Navy William Chandler had stressed the need to acquire "the best which human ingenuity can devise and modern artificers can construct."[56] The 1884 delivery of *Esmeralda* – what the Admiral of the Navy D. D. Porter called "the most perfect ship of her class ever built" – laid down a marker of just how far the Old Navy had fallen behind a regional rival and how far the US "New Navy" had to catch up.[57] In this respect the Chilean Navy was not just a rhetorical prop but a measuring stick for US naval advocates.

Deepening US–Chilean tensions soon provided an opportunity to test *Esmeralda*'s capabilities. Only months after its arrival in Valparaiso, *Esmeralda* deployed to Panama in response to an 1885 US expedition to the isthmus; a mutual display of naval "presence" over a key node of communication in Central America for the United States and Chile alike.[58] US observers saw the Panama Railway as an east–west connection, but for the Chileans the isthmus was a link to the North Atlantic

5.2 The Rise of Chilean Sea Power (1880–1890)

world.[59] That April, a Panamanian political faction revolted against the Colombian central government and imprisoned several US officials in Colon.[60] The United States reacted in what the historian Daniel Wicks called "proto-Rooseveltian" fashion, deploying a force to occupy the city and briefly assuming responsibility for public order there.[61] It was a rare occasion in which A. T. Mahan actually participated in hostilities.[62] William Sims (the future commander of USN forces in Europe during World War I) was there as well, running armored train cars – what he sarcastically called "new iron clads" – on the railroad between Panama City and Aspinwall.[63] Without battleships, armored train cars were the best the USN could muster.

Like the abortive designs over Chimbote, US intervention in Panama sparked worries in Santiago about the possibility of territorial annexation. Encouraged by recent history, Chilean leaders responded with an act of reciprocal gunboat diplomacy. *Esmeralda*'s commander, Juan Lopez, predicted that Washington would act soon, given that an isthmian canal was a "necessity of the first order for the United States."[64] That same July, Vicuña Mackenna – in a polemic echoed by the Chilean Minister of the Marine – argued that Chile could not remain idle while the US demonstrated in Panama the same "forwardness of Fremont and Kearney in California."[65] *Esmeralda* arrived in Panamanian waters on April 28, 1885 and loitered into May, showing the flag as an exercise in deterrence.[66] Vicuña Mackenna compared the "opportune protest" of "our sailors on board the *Esmeralda*" to the Chilean success at Chimbote in 1882.[67] That was likely an exaggeration, but at a minimum, as the ship's commander noted, *Esmeralda*'s "morale effects" were considerable: It left "with its presence a positive idea of naval power and of the importance of the country which possesses it."[68] *El Telégrafo de Guayaquil* concurred, writing that *Esmeralda*'s deployment challenged "*los Yankees*" and their "reckless pretension of preponderance."[69]

"Presence" in Central America went hand in hand with Santiago's steady accumulation of an insular empire in the southern Pacific. While US expeditions to Pacific islands were increasingly "held in abeyance" as a result of mechanical failures and financial limitations, the Chilean Navy organized a series of expeditions in the 1870s and 1880s to Oceania.[70] By the close of the decade, Chile had acquired an archipelagic chain extending, ONI reported, from "the islands in the Straits of Magellan and those contiguous to the west coast of Patagonia [to] Juan Fernandez, Mas Afuera, St. Ambrose [and] St. Felix [*Islas Desventuradas*]."[71] Most notably, in 1888 Chile annexed Easter Island as what *El Mercurio* called a "very important strategic point, and an advanced sentinel in Oceania."[72] Chile, in other words, had joined the race for empire, colliding with the ambitions of US expansionists in the process. The results for the people of Easter Island were (not unexpectedly) pitiful.[73] Looking outward, leaders in Washington, Newport, and San Francisco began to reckon with Chilean sea power in the Pacific.[74]

5.3 Who's Afraid of "Little Chili"?

In the 1880s, a growing set of US military officers, journalists, and politicians eyed Chilean naval capabilities, sensing a threat to US hemispheric primacy, technological prowess, and perhaps more dangerously the assumptions of Anglo-Saxonism. The citizens of San Francisco and Los Angeles voiced "legitimate indignation" about their "very vulnerable position" to attack and bombardment by Chilean warships while journalists in St. Louis fretted over lost "national pride," complaining that "even little Chili has felt safe in treating us contemptuously."[75] If such language was hyperbolic, it was not restricted to the United States. In 1881, the *London Standard* noted (smugly) that "the American Navy, if not a phantom fleet, would certainly find it difficult to compete successfully with the Chilean fleet."[76] Four years later, Vicuña Mackenna took evident satisfaction in the knowledge that Chile "maintains a navy powerful enough to inspire jealousy in the defenseless California coasts."[77] He had a sense of the moment and of the "jealousy" which would drive US naval chasing throughout the 1880s.

Thinking holistically, "Little Chili's" influence on the making of the US New Navy can be ordered into three components: its concrete threat to the US naval power in the Pacific, its cultural challenge to the ideology of Anglo-Saxon racial superiority, and finally – and only as a result of those threats – the rhetorical opportunity it provided to US navalists and politicians to advocate for more resources. These themes, not coincidentally, repeat in the cases of China and Japan, discussed in Section 5.4 and Chapter 7.

To start, there was the hard-power, material challenge to the United States (Figure 5.1).[78] Chile, the consensus held, would never be able to conquer the United States (then again neither would Germany or Britain) but it could inflict serious harm by bombarding its Pacific ports or attacking maritime traffic.[79] In 1883, Porter predicted that in the event of war, the US would eventually "get the better of our antagonists," but at a cost of "ravaged coasts and burned cities" delivered by "the least formidable of maritime nations."[80] In 1884, Senators George Hoar and Eugene Hale shared a sense of "shame and mortification" that Chilean warships could steam along, "laying our towns under contribution, and burning and destroying, if so it seems proper and right in their

5.3 Who's Afraid of "Little Chili"?

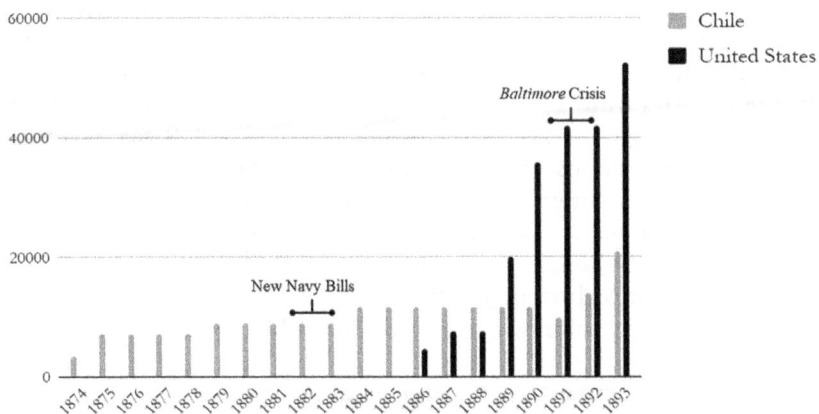

Figure 5.1 US vs Chilean steel and armored warships
Source: *Navy Yearbook, Memoria de Marina* (1886–1897).

will, the metropolis of the Pacific coast."[81] The next year, the USNI's prize-winning essay carried a similar warning about Chile.[82] Royal Navy estimates were more sanguine about the Pacific coast but nonetheless stressed California's vulnerability to a short, sharp assault.[83]

While too often discounted by teleological histories of US ascendancy in the Pacific (toward victory at Manila in 1898 or Tokyo Bay in 1945), the threat of a sporadic attack on US cities or sea routes was a meaningful one – so meaningful it justified outsized investment.[84] After all, British steamships in the Opium War seemed to the Qing, as the historian Odd Arne Westad argued, more like "pirate vessels" or "terrorists" than an existential challenge to dynastic rule but were nonetheless a key motivation for Qing naval expansion.[85] What of a similar attack by Chile? Many scoffed that US size and population made any suggestion of Chilean aggression absurd, but others were equally convinced that raw territory or population offered no protection from a raid. As the 1885 Naval War College graduation address warned: "To suppose that other Nations regard our latent power with fear or even with respect is as ridiculous as were the devices of the Chinese nearly fifty years ago."[86] Raising apprehensions, in the 1880s USN intelligence chronicled several examples of what might be called "terror-shelling" made possible by new explosive projectiles: the Spanish attack on Valparaiso (1866), the Chilean siege of Callao (1879–1881), and the Royal Navy's bombardment of Alexandria (1882).[87] Perhaps California would be next? In 1865, the mere presence of CSS *Shenandoah* in the Pacific caused a low-grade panic in San Francisco.[88] In the 1880s, Chilean ships such as *Esmeralda* – a "modern day *Alabama*" – constituted a reminiscent threat; one for which the USN had no answer in the Pacific until the Union Iron Works built one from the keel up in San Francisco in 1889.[89] All this to say nothing about Chile's ability to interrupt US sea lines through the Straits of Magellan or check US force projection in South America. As late as 1928, ONI would note that Chile's "command of the Strait of Magellan and her possession of a small but efficient naval force are guarantees of her ability to protect this interest against any other South American naval force."[90] To dismiss Chile's accumulation of real naval power is to miss out on a moment of contingency and vulnerability; a sense keenly felt by officials and residents on the US Pacific coast.

More consequential still, Chilean weapon systems – cruisers, torpedo boats, and even a battleship – served as a benchmark illustrating the technological shortcomings of the USN; what Chilean naval officers could (and until the 1890s did) dismiss out of hand as "old and rudimentary."[91] Such comparisons may appear hyperbolic, but at the time they were less akin to Cold War missile-gap fallacies than genuine "Sputnik Moments": a set of realizations about the need to "catch up" with foreign technical capabilities. At the very least, the drive to close the "cruiser gap" between the United States and Chile made the case for naval expansion a realistic goal for the first rounds of New Navy funding. In the 1880s, few deluded themselves with aspirations to compete with a European great power in the near term (witness the incredulous and hostile reactions to the Secretary of the Navy 1889 report calling for a battlefleet), but catching up with regional newly made navies seemed both productive (not least for US industrialists) and doable. In other words, because there was no hope in catching up with Britain in the next decade, Chilean *materiel* was routinely cited as the pacing threat against which US New Navy construction raced in the 1880s.

Consider anxieties about *Esmeralda*. In 1884, Porter identified the vessel as one that would "prove a more formidable vessel than either" of the first two New Navy cruisers then under development.[92] Closing the cruiser gap with Chile by matching the "superiority of the *Esmeralda*" appeared in the *Congressional Record* as a national priority.[93] Things were gloomier still in 1885 after USN officials had an opportunity to make "repeated visits" to *Esmeralda* during its deployment to Panama.[94] For the *New York Times*, the relative capabilities of the "Peerless *Esmeralda*" bordered on outrageous.[95] In 1884, it printed a scathing indictment, observing that while the first New Navy ships "may prove to be great advances on anything we now have ... they are not *Esmeraldas*."[96]

5.3 Who's Afraid of "Little Chili"?

True enough. In 1885, *Esmeralda* was better armed and faster than any of the four steel warships in the United States. It could make eighteen knots to USS *Boston's* sixteen knots and yet carried a heavier armament. British Admiralty intelligence surveyed new US warship construction in 1886, reporting that "none of these ships are completed and when finished they will be inferior to vessels of similar size."[97] At least *Esmeralda* was recognized globally as a worthy competitor. Even at the height of what Paul Kennedy called "British Naval Mastery," Royal Navy observers such as RADM John Wilson found the international proliferation of "the *Esmeraldas*" unsettling.[98] In 1884, he wrote to the industrialist William Armstrong directly, warning an *Esmeralda* class cruiser could "destroy with impunity" the city of Liverpool.[99] Surely, he continued, the Royal Navy should acquire similar capabilities. In the United States, inferiority spurred USN technical investments and imitations, in this case literally. The first ship with capabilities on-par with *Esmeralda* was USS *Charleston* (1889), a vessel built in San Francisco from plans purchased from Armstrong and originally used on the Japanese cruiser *Naniwa*, itself a derivative of the *Esmeralda*.[100] The best way to catch up was simply to copy the stuff Chile already had.

Torpedo warfare proved an additional deficiency relative to Santiago. Like their Qing and Confederate counterparts, Chilean officers saw the torpedo as an economical means of defending a long coastline.[101] Following the War of the Pacific, Santiago dispatched Chilean junior officers to Fiume, Austria – the center of European torpedo development – with the aim of acquiring Whitehead torpedoes and expertise.[102] The results were good. By 1888, there were ten *torpederas* in Chilean ports armed with effective torpedoes when the USN possessed only one such ship (notionally).[103] A year later, the *New York Times* complained "the United States foots the list of nations," behind European countries, Japan, China, "and finally Chili," leaving the USN "wholly un-adapted for modern warfare."[104] Porter was, as usual, scandalized by the relative inferiority of the United States to Chilean torpedo forces.[105]

Chile's 1891 acquisition of two experimental "torpedo cruisers" made this qualitative gap still more stark.[106] Built by Laird Brothers (the same firm responsible for the troublemaking *Huáscar* and *Alabama*), *Almirante Lynch* and *Condell* were "sea-going torpedo-ships," or what Armstrong's maritime engineer George Rendel called "small *Esmeraldas*" designed to conduct offensive torpedo warfare against enemy commerce and fleets.[107] The outbreak of the Chilean Civil War (1891) provided an opportunity to demonstrate the ships' utility. On April 23, 1891, the *Lynch* and *Condell* set a precedent (yet another on the Pacific slope) in the history of naval war: the first use of an automobile torpedo to sink an armored warship. Entering Caldera Bay under cover of darkness, the ships attacked and sank the ironclad *Blanco Encalada* – long a mainstay of the Chilean naval order of battle.[108] It was a remarkable achievement, celebrated with worried undertones by US newspapers. *New York Times* coverage described Chile's "Sea-Going David" in a metaphor more literal than most realized; not only was it a "David and goliath" story, it was a step beyond the Confederate *Davids* launched against Union ships in the Civil War.[109] And just as Union officers copied the concept of CSN torpedo boats in 1863, so too did USN officers argue for adopting the weapons proven by Chile in combat.[110] That same year, Secretary of the Navy Tracy (and his successors) made acquiring torpedo cruisers a priority.[111] Like the actual *Esmeralda* before it, Chile's "small *Esmeralda*'s" represented a technological deficiency vis-à-vis the budding US New Navy, setting anxieties on edge.[112]

Finally, there was *Capitan Prat*: a 7,000-ton battleship ordered in France in 1888 (twice the size of Chile's first ironclads from 1872).[113] Just as *Esmeralda* was a yardstick against which USN cruisers fell short in the early 1880s, *Prat* revealed the limitation of US battleship construction c. 1890.[114] *Capitan Prat*, as Chile's Ministry of the Marine advertised, was "one of the most formidable" battleships constructed to date.[115] The *Revista de Marina* as well as foreign intelligence services highlighted the ship's electrical features and systems – a sure sign of its technological sophistication.[116] In the press, superlatives flew, encouraged by the support of the British engineer Edward Reed.[117] As late as 1894, the *New York Times* enviously described the vessel as "better than anything the United States has at present."[118] It was a sentiment shared in the private writings of USN leaders – Mahan and Roosevelt among them.[119] The US would not commission a comparable battleship until the USS *Indiana* in 1895. As battleships became avatars of state power, the only thing worse than a cruiser gap was a battleship gap.

On a smaller scale, US-built munitions such as the machine-gun also proliferated to Chile, raising concerns about the appropriation of "Yankee ingenuity" as a tool against the *yanqui* primacy in the Americas.[120] In 1885, the Pacific Squadron commander complained that while US designed Gatling guns were common in South America, the USN Pacific Squadron had none.[121] "It does seem strange," he noted acerbically, "that while the foreign men-of-war are fitted with these rapid firing Gatling-guns our own service should be un-supplied with this most useful product of the ingenuity and skill of our own citizens."[122] That same year the Secretary of the Navy complained that inventors such as Ericsson were "receiving more attention and greater encouragement from other Governments [in this case Peru] than from our own."[123]

In the 1860s, the British naval architect Cowper Coles lobbed nearly identical criticisms, contrasting Royal Navy indifference to his innovations with demand from Peru for ships such as *Huáscar*.[124]

The dilution of technical superiority carried with it a still greater menace to the ideology of Anglo-Saxonism.[125] In an age that reified military performance into civilizational rankings, Chile's possession of cutting-edge weapons had worrying implications. Chilean navalists certainly saw maritime power as an index of what *Revista de Marina* called the national "level of progress and science."[126] So too did their counterparts in the United States.[127] Access to "gee-whiz technology," the historian Mark Shulman argued, was fundamental to publicly legitimizing investments in the US New Navy.[128] But what did it mean if the ships of this incipient force consistently and qualitatively lagged behind the Chilean fleet?

Attempts to rationalize Chilean naval progress by recasting the Chilean people as the "Yankees" or the "Prussians of the Pacific" did little to calm racial anxieties.[129] By and large, USN officers, in the words of the historian Peter Karsten, possessed "a fine sense of racial discrimination" against the "inferior peoples" of the world – the Chileans included.[130] For celebrants of what A. T. Mahan and his British pen-pals called Anglo-Saxon "Race Patriotism" the Chileans were decidedly "other."[131] Throughout the 1880s the Chilean nation came to resemble less an outpost of European civilization or "the 'model republic of South America'" and evermore that of an alien menace.[132] US prejudices, in other words, took arguments about the uniqueness of the *Raza Chilena* and reframed them in a pejorative light. Myriad, wrote William Henry Seward in 1853, were the defects in South America "inherited from aboriginal and Spanish parentage."[133] That opinion held a generation later when, in 1881, George Belknap sounded the alarm over the racial contamination of Anglo-Saxon Americans in Chile. There he found that US-Chilean "'half-breeds' are more indolent and unreasonable than the Chilians of pure blood."[134] Three years later, a lecturer at the American Geographical Society described how in Chile Spanish colonists had "smelted with the vigorous Indians and developed a new race," destined for a bellicose future "of which its recent military and naval successes against Peru and Bolivia are only the prelude."[135] The Chileans, warned the *Seattle Post-Intelligencer*, were "the fighting race of South America": "passionate, ignorant and warlike."[136] Mahan, notably, believed those pejorative characteristics were "inbred and ineradicable."[137] In 1891, as Chile descended into Civil War, he wrote to the British navalist Bouverie Clark that the Chileans, whatever their attempts at republican government, "have disappointed everyone ... the blood was too strong."[138]

Judging by public discourse and cultural products, in the 1880s US naval inferiority and racism combined to produce a sense of incredulous humiliation. "Little Chili's" incongruous position as the predominant naval force in South America *and* a nation outside the North Atlantic's racial color-lines undercut the pretensions of Anglo-Saxonism in a way many found difficult to understand. In 1881, the *Dallas Herald* found it "humiliating to admit" that "even little Chili" would defeat the USN in the event of war in the Pacific.[139] Park Benjamin's 1881 "The End of New York" explored the same theme in one of the period's finest examples of "future war stories." It described an attack by Spanish ironclads and airships on New York until "little Chili" intervenes on behalf of the USN. The real "humiliation," Benjamin warned, was not defeat but that US "preservation from utter destruction" was achieved by "the guns of an insignificant Republic of South America."[140] Mahan certainly found touring South American waters in "ships which are a laughingstock" hard to stomach.[141]

The possibility of naval and therefore racial humiliation was most real in California; what Mahan called "the last of the temperate productive seaboards of the earth to be possessed by white men."[142] Press coverage used words such as "mortifying" and "defenseless" to describe the condition of Pacific states relative to Chile.[143] "Even little Chile" became a refrain meant to evoke a sense of shame and scandal. Though it "sounds very ridiculous," the *Sacramento Daily Record Union* warned in 1880, the United States was "incapable of taking the conceit out of even belligerent little Chile."[144] That sense of humiliation courtesy of "little Chili" was a powerful impetus. Similar anxieties had motivated Qing leaders in 1874 confronted with the discordant naval power of the Japanese "dwarf pirates."[145] Small but powerful naval weapons in the hands of perceived inferiors could provoke big responses from continental powers. Perhaps it contributed to the distressingly common and racially motivated lynching of Chileans by Californians.[146]

Some of the foremost leaders of the turn to US navalism took humiliation by the Chilean newly made navy personally. In 1880, a 22-year-old Theodore Roosevelt argued to his friend Henry Cabot Lodge that it was "a disgrace to us ... that our rich seaboard cities should lie at the mercy of any piratical descent from a hostile power. We are actually at the mercy of a tenth-rate country like Chili."[147] On the scene in 1879, the USN commander in the Pacific complained that the US lagged behind "French, English, German, Chilian and Peruvian [ships]."[148] Things were little better six years later, as Mahan confirmed while stationed in South America. In 1885, he took a moment to survey Callao Harbor from his command USS *Wachusett*, reporting to his friend

5.3 Who's Afraid of "Little Chili?"

Samuel Ashe: "There were three foreign ships – a Chilean – an Italian – a German. The former a powerful, though 2d rate, ironclad of a nation of 2,000,000 souls ... The *Wachusett* can make *8* knots. Her guns ... are absolutely obsolete ... The worst of it is, however, that it cannot be said that she is an unfair specimen of the US Navy."[149] The ship was condemned and sold off two years later.[150] Contemporaneously, Mahan was hard at work conducting the exploratory research for his magnum opus on sea power in the library of the English Club of Lima.[151] Gazing out on Chilean warships in the harbor – onboard what he called an "old war horse not yet turned out to grass or slaughter" – he was well motivated and perhaps even inspired.[152]

Here then was a crisis of confidence *and* security. Like all crises, it was also an opportunity, in this case to advocate for naval expansion. Naval officers who complained about Chilean power in private letters took up "little Chili" as a cudgel in public fora.[153] Beyond the USN bureaucracy, politicians – most notably Californian congressional representatives – also used Chile's position to good effect. Consider Senator Leland Stanford. In 1886, he argued that it was pure "Congressional stupidity" that without investment in California's defense the *Esmeralda* "could stand outside of San Francisco [and] force the city to be surrendered."[154] Senator John Franklin Miller made a similar ploy in 1884, recalling the "humiliation" of the United States at the hands of Chile which "might have bombarded or laid San Francisco under contribution."[155] One month later, Miller led a Senate commission to Mare Island Naval Base in San Francisco in an effort to convince his colleagues of its importance.[156] For these men, the menace of "little Chili" was a political tool, but it was a useful one only because of the substantive material and cultural threats the Chilean Navy posed to US ambitions in the Pacific. Chilean navalism and insular acquisitions laid bare the limits of US authority in the Pacific just as officials came to see the "search for opportunity" in Latin America and East Asia as an imperative of the US industrial economy.[157] Real anxieties about technological atrophy and racialized threats explain why Chile became a font of rhetorical invention.

That rhetoric – as rhetoric often does – had consequences. Comparisons to Chile in the 1880s actually *did* result in a fleet of cruisers designed (often explicitly) to compete with smaller, Pacific newly made navies. Initial naval appropriation bills passed in 1882–1883 (during the War of the Pacific) were justified not for the "remote contingency" of a conflict with the Europe but, as the Secretary of the Navy argued, "to assert at all times our natural, justifiable, and necessary ascendancy in the affairs of the American hemisphere."[158] Print journalists echoed the sentiment. In 1882, the *Los Angeles Daily Herald* urged that although the USN need not compete with the great powers, it "should be large enough to enable us to hold our own with any of the second and third rate nations."[159] In 1884, Porter wrote that the US New Navy could not and should not compare with the "greatest naval power" ship-for-ship but rather could gain efficiency by "taking care to adopt no designs in ships or guns that are not superior to those of any navy afloat."[160] *Esmeralda* was a useful yardstick toward that end. Even critics (and there were many) could agree on the need for "a few swift-sailing cruisers as a nucleus for a navy in case of war."[161] Looking out from California and Oregon, the crucial outstanding question was how well the New Navy's "nucleus" of steel cruisers would hold up in the Pacific against peer newly made navies.

5.4   Big China and the "Yellow Peril"

Much as Santiago's victory in the War of the Pacific transformed "little Chili" into a rival, Qing naval performance in the 1870s and 1880s shaped US impressions of the Chinese. Perceptions of the Qing Navy in the Sino-French War fed arguments for restricting immigration by "refracting" (to borrow a term) naval defeats into civilizational and/or racialized shortcomings.[162] Naval failure "proved" racist assessments about the backwardness of China and the Chinese. Paradoxically, however, Qing self-strengthening efforts after 1885 also generated worries about the vast, latent potential of the Qing Empire hanging, one Oregon senator warned, "like a threatening cloud over the virgin States of the Pacific."[163] The Qing newly made navy failed in the Sino-French War, but what if the Chinese could one day make "strong ships and powerful cannon" work? The historian Erica Lee argued that the period coincident with the formation of the New Navy was also one of "closing America's gate to various 'alien invasions.'"[164] Qing naval self-strengthening made metaphorical language about "alien invasions" all too real. The Chinese Exclusion Act (1882) and the New Navy's first appropriations (1882, 1883) were distinct but related responses to that threat.

Objections to Chinese migration were (and in the existing scholarly literature are) usually tied to labor conditions or base racial resentments. Californian "nativists" certainly appealed to both in ugly campaigns against the Chinese – even as 100,000 of the latter transformed the Pacific slope through backbreaking and often lethal toil. Anti-Chinese resentments grew throughout the 1870s, culminating in the passage of the 1882 Chinese Exclusion Act: an absolute ten-year moratorium on Chinese immigration and the first major attempt to proscribe entry to the United States on the basis of race.[165]

5.4 Big China and the "Yellow Peril"

That said, the "threat" of Chinese immigration was also influenced by perceptions of Qing military modernization. While missionaries extolled the dubious need to "civilize" China by Christianizing it, US (and other) military officials tended to view performance in war as the more relevant barometer of civilizational standing. Because, as Stephen B. Luce argued in 1883, "war led the way to civilization," Qing naval capacity said a great deal about the nature of the Chinese people more broadly.[166] How the Qing Empire performed in the Sino-French War had meaning for how Americans – and especially naval officers – understood China and the Chinese. Take, for example, the 1882 "open" letter from Commodore R. W. Shufeldt to the ex-California Senator Aaron A. Sargent – a close friend of President Garfield and a leading advocate of Chinese immigration restrictions.[167] Throughout 1881, Shufeldt spent months in China negotiating the "opening" of Korea and advocating for the reorganization of the Qing Navy. He left deeply frustrated with the Qing leadership, in part reflecting confusion he encountered over an offer of command in the Beiyang Navy.[168] Shufeldt took the lesson that there "never can be any intimate political or commercial relations" between the United States and China. The civilizational differences were simply too stark. It followed, Shufeldt urged, that the United States "should regulate and limit the supply" of Chinese immigration in both California and "its mere outlying county" Hawaii.[169] In 1882, what Shufeldt called his "now somewhat famous little letter" was printed verbatim coast to coast, and eventually in China – prompting controversy.[170] For the *New York Times*, Shufeldt clearly demonstrated that an "intractable hatred" between the Americans and Chinese made immigration undesirable.[171] The San Francisco *Evening Bulletin* was equally credulous, observing that "between the two people so diametrically opposite our naval officer wisely concludes that there never can be here any assimilation."[172]

One year into the exclusionary era, Chinese performance in the Sino-French War seemed to confirm Shufeldt's recommendations. Localized exceptions aside (the defense of Zhenhai and Taiwan), years of Qing preparation appeared to crumble in the face of European opposition. The French, as Zeng Guoquan said, "depended on their strong ships and power cannon to run totally roughshod" over China.[173] Most US observers held the character of the Chinese people responsible for defeat.[174] The American naval adviser L. C. Arlington bemoaned the Chinese "quasi-feminine instinct."[175] Defeat was symptomatic of the fact that in China, as Shufeldt wrote, "there is no military spirit."[176] "There is even less glory," the *New York Times* warned French readers in 1883, "to be got by slaughtering Chinamen than by fighting Arabs."[177] The Chinese "semi-barbarians," the San Francisco *Daily Evening Bulletin* argued, were "pretty much like the Indians": uncivilized and undisciplined.[178] Chilean victory at sea in 1879–1880 signaled the breakout of a progressive and sophisticated state. Chinese defeat in the Sino-French War was equally an indictment of Chinese civilization.

These prejudices, however, did not imply that the Chinese were *un*threatening to the United States in a military sense. To the contrary, a steady series of reports from USN leaders stressed the security (not merely social or economic) implications of Chinese immigration.[179] This "Yellow Peril" existed on intersecting levels: demographic and actualized naval power. China's vast population was an inherent risk. Shufeldt warned as early as 1882 that given the "enormous power" of the 400 million Chinese, Qing "progress in the arts of war is a thing to be checked rather than accelerated by Western nations."[180] In this conclusion he had company among US officials.[181] As early as 1870, Mahan mused with his school friend Samuel Ashe about the "Chinese question" and the coming "conflict of the races."[182] By 1880, war novellas, such as *Last Days of the Republic,* portrayed Chinese immigrants in California as a fifth column engaged in "Trans-Pacific Cooperation" ahead of a Chinese amphibious invasion of the Americas.[183] An "invasion" of Chinese immigrants was a term of art more literal than usually given credit. The diplomat John Young saw the Chinese military as "a human machine" of "infinite possibilities," capable of multiplying with the "infinite resources of this prodigious empire."[184] With that same potential in mind, in 1893 Mahan argued for a robust naval presence in the Pacific, warning that "while China remains as she is, nothing more disastrous for the future can be imagined" than US disarmament.[185] Theodore Roosevelt even worried that Russia might become a more "formidable power" by drilling the Chinese into an efficient army – a Mackinderist threat alongside a Mahanian one.[186]

The vulnerability of Hawaii to Chinese immigration was a particular worry, one which united the fears of naval officials and anti-immigration zealots.[187] In his 1882 letter, Shufeldt warned against Chinese "flooding the Sandwich Islands" and weakening a vital node of US naval operations.[188] A decade later, Mahan still saw Chinese immigration (not Japan or Britain) as the chief threat to Hawaii. He wrote that as Chinese spread across the Pacific it was "impossible to exaggerate the momentous issue dependent upon a firm hold of the Sandwich Islands by a great, civilized maritime power."[189] That same year, ONI officers reported that there was one Chinese resident on the archipelago for every two native born Hawaiians.[190] In 1894, William Sims reckoned the population of Hawaii was already 25 percent Chinese, who were "crowding out the lower classes of the whites."[191] All this to say that while nativists made

5.4 Big China and the "Yellow Peril"

their objections on racial and economic grounds, Chinese immigration had an equally worrying meaning to New Navy leaders, who tracked it in some detail as a matter of military necessity.

The dramatic expansion of Qing naval power after the Sino-French War made this human potential still more ominous. Defeat by France did not so much diminish Chinese sea power as prompt a recommitment to it, ushering in a wave of foreign acquisitions for which US forces in the Pacific had no answer. The onetime minister to China, George Seward, acknowledged in 1882 in the pages of the *North American Review* that Chinese "gun-boats are in fact rather better than ours."[192] USN ships, one congressman whined, "could not stand one hour in front of one of the gunboats of which the Chinese Navy is now composed."[193] Falling behind Chile was bad, but the prospect of naval inferiority to the Qing was a powerful psychic threat and rhetorical opportunity.

Chinese acquisitions soon made Old Navy inferiority manifestly real. In Europe, US observers watched nervously as the Chinese agent Li Fengbao (李凤苞) went on a buying spree, "investigating all the newest styles of every country's steel plated armored ships," along with torpedoes and electrical apparatuses.[194] The ambitions of the Imperial Chinese Navy (ICN), ONI estimated, were to form ten squadrons, "each to be composed of several battleships and sufficient complementary force of the other classes."[195] This was not so far off the mark, the goal proposed by Xue Fucheng.[196] By 1887, the USN reckoned there were ninety-five warships and twenty-five torpedo boats in China, including twenty-two protected vessels (over double the contemporary estimates for Japan).[197] Most important were the German-built battleships *Dingyuan* and *Zhenyuan*, which arrived in 1885 after the Sino-French War and constituted the prestige pieces of the Beiyang.[198] "First rate naval weapons!" pronounced *Shenbao* with justifiable self-regard – no less than fourteen years before the United States would commission a comparable battleship.[199] Complementing the *Dingyuan* and *Zhenyuan* were what ONI in 1887 called "high-powered steel cruisers, somewhat similar to the *Baltimore*": the *Zhiyuan* and *Jingyuan*.[200] They joined the German-made *Jingyuan* and *Laiyuan* as well as smaller Newcastle-built protected cruisers.[201] Thinking asymmetrically, Qing officials also imported what Admiralty intelligence called "the nucleus of a powerful torpedo flotilla."[202] Technical expertise (most often from Britain) came in support of this hardware, building human capital in China.[203] By the end of the decade, China's vast population was matched by a growing navy. As in Chile, dangerous aliens appeared armed with lethally advanced weapons.

Back in California, naval technology and human potential made for a combustible mix. A delta in naval power between the United States and a China sparked worries about racial and civilizational hierarchies – much to the benefit of US naval expansionists. Most often, advocates of USN expansion cited friction over immigration as a plausible motive for Sino-US naval conflict. In 1868, Shufeldt worried that as a (just) consequence of the indignities suffered by "coolies" in the Americas, "the day is bound to come when, with a bloody hand, [China] will free itself at the cost of humiliation and obloquy, or life and treasure to Western Republics."[204] An 1885 cover image on the satirical magazine *Puck* depicted Uncle Sam and a Chinese mandarin comparing lists of murdered citizens and subjects overseas – nor did they want for examples.[205] Among many US "motives for naval power," Mahan cited (as late as 1911) "the Pacific Coast, with its meager population, insufficient resources and somewhat turbulent attitude towards the Asiatic."[206]

Qing technical acquisitions after 1885 provided a means to match that motive. Two years after the exclusion act, a Democratic congressman warned that China had warships that would "easily pass all our land defenses and take their ransom … what a humiliation there would be."[207] In 1886, the Republican Senator Orville Platt noted that the United States had done some "very wicked things with regard to Chinamen in this country" and warned that in response China might send its ironclads to "mow a double swath" through the USN.[208] When reviewing *Modern Ships of War*, the US navalist J. D. Kelley called attention (without irony) to the danger of "modern cruisers and armored battleships" in the hands of "that outer barbarian whom our mobs murder just for a lark!"[209] As the decade turned, one Congressman argued that if US citizens continued to abuse the Chinese like no "other race on this continent," it was an "ordinary precaution" to "build ships equal in power to the ships of the nation which we treat with such contumely."[210] Writers caught the spirit as well. Pierton Dooner's *Last Days of the Republic* (1880) and Robert Woltor's *A Short and Truthful History of the Taking of California and Oregon by the Chinese* (1882) flogged the military threat of the Qing Empire.[211] Looking back from 2013, the film *1894: The Battle of the Yalu* (甲午大海战) made the comparison of naval power explicit. Depicting the apex (in absolute terms) of the Qing naval building in 1890, the narrator intones gravely to impress the audience that the Beiyang Fleet was "even larger than the American Navy."[212] Altogether this meant that the Chinese people may have been "inferior" but they were also dangerous and in possession of a navy that was actually superior to that of the United States in quantitative and key qualitative terms.

Curiously enough, though, concerns over immigration and the racialized threat of the Chinese Navy did little to stop Chinese from serving on US warships in the Pacific during the "gate keeping" period – or dying for that matter.²¹³ Only a handful of stories filter down through the official record but they almost certainly reflect a wider trend. In 1884, a US commander welcomed onboard the Chinese minister in Peru, months after burying the Chinese servant Ah Lam of USS *Iroquois* on San Lorenzo Island; he had contracted Yellow Fever while sleeping ashore in Callao.²¹⁴ Four years later, several "unfortunate Chinamen" on USS *Thetis* and USS *Pinta* drowned and were buried with military honors in the government cemetery in Sitka, Alaska.²¹⁵ As a junior officer, William Sims relied on conversations with his Chinese servant "my boy Ting" for insights into China as well as translations of vernacular newspapers; a contribution of some magnitude.²¹⁶ The Qing Navy may have depended on foreign technical advice, but the USN (especially in the Pacific) had a dependency on Chinese labor all its own.

Shufeldt personified both the nativist and navalist response to China. Months after his China letter hit the US press, he assumed the presidency of the Naval Advisory Board, recommending plans for the first phase of reform and expansion.²¹⁷ Historians have long seen Shufeldt as "the key diplomatic and naval link between Perry and Mahan," but his legacy also speaks to the connections between the New Navy and US immigration policy.²¹⁸ Perceptions of China's immense population and its emerging naval capabilities made for a worrying combination. Fresh from Chinese waters, he had a prescription for naval expansion. As with the case of "even little Chile," the proliferation of hard, material power, racialized threat perceptions, and political opportunism transformed Qing China into an argument for US naval building.

Much the same was true, unsurprisingly, for the Qing's regional competitor, Japan. The Beiyang Fleet's dramatic expansion after 1885 certainly left an impression on the residents of Kobe, Yokohama, and Nagasaki during a series of Qing port visits, the largest of which arrived in 1891. The Beiyang Fleet sailed into Japanese home waters, apparently "ruling the roost" (称雄) among western Pacific navies.²¹⁹ Here, the *North China Herald* reported, were the Qing, six years after defeat in the Sino-French War, in possession of a "fine fleet, with which [Japan] has nothing that can cope."²²⁰ Like their US counterparts, alarmed Meiji naval leaders would soon respond with another twist in the western Pacific's spiraling naval race.

5.5 Racism, Races, and California's Argument for a New Navy

Neglect in the 1860s and 1870s reduced the USN to a point of chronic and almost incredible weakness relative to both its North Atlantic peers and US economic productivity. In 1881, the Qing diplomat Li Boxiang identified the basic irony facing the United States: "America's naval forces are smaller than every country in Europe," and yet, because of its enormous resources, "during the Civil War the United States suddenly achieved maritime effectiveness."[221] Transforming latent power into capacity preoccupied US naval officials throughout the 1880s. The Pacific offered a powerful motivation and emotive rationale for doing so.

In the absence of an existential threat, the Pacific's wars and the newly made navies that participated in them took on disproportionate meaning(s) to US navalists advocating for a peacetime transformation. Chilean naval power during and after the War of the Pacific was an especially sharp contrast to Old Navy weakness. The Old and New Navy alike lagged behind "even little Chili" in a race for regional primacy on the Pacific slope until at least 1890. Highlighting this fact was less a case of selling "fear" to the US public than perceiving real threats against remote California and to the civilizational standing of the United States.[222] In the western Pacific, Qing failure to resist France confirmed China's place in the taxonomy of "inferior" civilizations and bolstered arguments for restricting Chinese immigration to the United States. That said, Chinese naval expansion after 1885 seemed to arm those same dangerous aliens with a formidable navy – a volatile combination.

Such material threats were real enough, but when filtered through racial and cultural prejudices, little Chile and big China became an emotive argument for peacetime naval investment. If, as Kristin Hoganson and Richard Hofstadter argued, psychic attitudes and anxieties could provoke war in 1898, then surely anxiety and "humiliation" about material threats posed by racially alien states could goad the US toward naval expansion in the 1880s.[223] This case for a New Navy in the 1880s was different from the coming Mahanian force at the turn of the century. It was not a weapon of imperial war or great power defense but rather a reactive tool for securing regional power and prestige. Put another way, before the making of the US as an empire "among empires" came the creation of a small, New Navy among newly made navies in the Pacific. How this latest arrival in the race to build an industrial navy would perform is the subject of Chapter 6.[224]

6   The US New Navy Wins a Race – Finally

Bar Harbor, Maine, August 1891. The town was, and is, small, but the season found it cluttered with the Washington well-to-do, including Secretary of State James Blaine and Secretary of the Navy Benjamin F. Tracy. Blaine, perhaps the most important gilded-era politician never elected president, was there convalescing from an illness. Tracy, a peerless advocate for naval funding (the "father of the modern American fighting navy" even) had come to escape the Washington DC summer and to pry loose a few tidbits about Blaine's political ambitions.[1] But besides the weather, Bar Harbor boasted another attraction: a review of the budding US New Navy. Gathered beneath Mt. Desert, the Squadron of Evolution, or "White Squadron," displayed the first results of domestic naval modernization: a group of freshly built steel cruisers and gunboats that could compare fairly on an individual ship-to-ship basis to their counterparts in the North Atlantic. With the Senate Naval Committee in tow to see the product of its funding, Tracy begged President Benjamin Harrison to make the trip over the mountains from his vacation in Vermont and see the "fleet."[2] Harrison sent his regrets but that did little to dampen the festivities.[3] Tracy claimed the Bar Harbor review would "eclipse anything of its kind ever seen in this country."[4] True enough. In 1889, British naval intelligence noted that the "energetic steps to resuscitate its navy" had at last earned the United States a place among the world's "Principal Maritime Nations."[5] More ships were being built all the time, in yards from Philadelphia to San Francisco. The "White Squadron" at Bar Harbor was a modest beginning – and as a fleet remained categorically inferior to any of the European powers – but it was also a "nucleus" for the future: a first step to Roosevelt's "Great White Fleet" seventeen years later.[6] When seen as a reaction to other small, newly made navies in the Pacific, the ships of the White Squadron looked still more promising – proof that the process of catching up was going well.

For Tracy, having secured funding (though much less than he wanted), some demonstration of the New Navy's usefulness seemed politically imperative. The ships gathered in Bar Harbor were, on paper, an achievement, but as the decade turned the New Navy still struggled for credibility amid a chorus of doubters about what an 1888 *New York Herald* story called "Uncle Sam's Toy Navy."[7] A hodgepodge of interests groups campaigned against the very idea of naval expansion on moral and budgetary grounds.[8] Writers in the Chilean *Revista de Marina* were equally skeptical about the US *Flota Nueva*, which as of 1889 was still "good only for a mediocre defense of its coasts."[9] That same year, even Tracy complained that despite progress, "it must not be forgotten that the fleet has still only a nominal existence."[10] As late as 1891, the *Times* of London sniffed that the United States "is on the way to create a formidable navy, but she has not yet done so."[11] Small and underpowered, the White Squadron was unlikely to make a splash against great power navies.

What then to do with it? Perhaps, Tracy suggested to President Harrison, the New Navy would do well to visit Germany, celebrating an agreement on American pork imports.[12] Perhaps not, Harrison demurred, lest it antagonize France. Perhaps if the controversy over sealing in the northern Pacific continued, a naval demonstration might be warranted off Canada? Or in China, Harrison suggested, to signal US intentions and ability to protect its citizens during a moment of periodic unrest?[13] What was really needed, as A. T. Mahan groused in May 1891 to a British counterpart, was something to "tickle the national vanity" and raise US interest in "army and navy affairs."[14] As it turned out, that something – an opportunity to test US naval building – was in the Pacific, where the small New Navy could actually make a difference c. 1890.

Chapters 1–5 explained how transwar developments and newly made navies in the Pacific helped goad the US New Navy into existence during the 1880s. This chapter turns to regional crises in the 1890s as opportunities to showcase USN capabilities in action. After a decade-long effort at "catching up" with Pacific newly made navies, crises from Valparaiso to Hawaii were a chance for the New Navy to justify its fantastic expense. Two war scares with Chile – a familiar irritant – stand out: the Chase of the *Itata* (1891) and the *Baltimore* Incident (1891–1892). The US deployment of naval power in both cases marked the New Navy's first acts of gunboat or "cruiser diplomacy" against a near peer.[15] By comparison, the USN-backed coup in Hawaii (1893) – conventionally the US New Navy's first "overtly imperialist" action – was a relatively minor question insofar as naval assets were concerned.[16] Fast in the wake of these demonstrations, the New Navy took time to celebrate at the New York Naval Review (1893) and smaller reviews on the Pacific coast. The New Navy's record of achievement in Chile and Hawaii gave attendees something tangible to commemorate. Only months later, US intervention in the 1893 Brazilian Civil War built on these earlier actions, mostly by following precedent. Rather than a staccato list of isolated crises, a transwar perspective on this period makes for a connected story of inspiration and demonstration. In the 1870s and 1880s, wars and naval races in the Pacific helped motivate the building of a small, cruiser-dominated US New Navy, while in the 1890s the region also provided chances to demonstrate that same Navy's worth.

6.1 The Best Defense

A stubborn oversimplification too often characterizes the publication of Alfred Thayer Mahan's *Influence of Sea Power upon History* (1890) as the key inflection point in the New Navy's rise.[17] In the bumper sticker telling, Mahan articulated a theory of national prosperity and security through "sea power": the nexus of national production, shipping, and colonies, protected by an oceangoing battlefleet.[18] His book captured the attention of political elites, underwriting the transformation of the US Old Navy (a "navy to construct") into *the* New Navy (a modern, battleship-dominated force capable of offensive action) in the 1890s. With the backing of ever more influential navalists in the US government and commercial circles the "Mahanian Navy" grew steadily until its first test in the War of 1898. Antecedent crises in Chile (1891), Samoa (1889), or Hawaii (1893) were all signposts, running toward the "Splendid Little War" in which US economic and industrial potential was actualized into victory at sea. The interim between Mahan's *Sea Power* and the War of 1898, in this view, was one of "imperial preparation" prior to the breakout of the United States into the great power system, complete with a maritime empire and battlefleet to prove it.

This "imperial preparation" thesis – as several historians have noted – misreads the period in important respects. As early as 1978, James Field argued that the New Navy was not so much an offensive preparation for overt empire as a "defensive answer" to European developments.[19] A centralized battlefleet – Mahan's core prescription – was actually *less* "imperial" than the Old Navy cruisers sent out to protect missionaries and merchants around the world. As Scott Mobley elaborated, between 1886 and 1896, US leaders "reconfigured the US Fleet into an instrument for hemispheric defense and designed contingency plans to defend a hemispheric perimeter – not to extend the nation's imperial reach."[20] Centralized in New York or Norfolk, a concentrated battlefleet was of little use for patrolling ports and coaling stations on the frontiers of US economic expansion. The US New Navy, this Atlantic-facing consensus holds, was a defensive precaution against European developments and in particular a bulwark to defend the Atlantic Coast and Caribbean Basin from a British fleet.

Defensive readiness is certainly the sense that comes through in Secretary Tracy's 1889 report to Congress – which predated Mahan's *Influence* by a year and yet traded in many of the same assumptions about naval power. Tracy opened by measuring the US order of battle against potential rivals: ten in the Atlantic and only China (in a revealing detail of the potential attributed to its naval program) in the Pacific. The threat of raiders striking for ransom along the US coast "without serious difficulty" was a distressing possibility. To defend against it, the US needed a "fighting force" of armored battleships. Without it, the US might just as well "abandon all claim to influence and control on the sea." Before Congress had authorized even one armored combatant, he proposed two fleets of battleships, eight on the Pacific and twelve on the Gulf and Atlantic coasts. Adopted as a statement of principle among navalists in the House and Senate, the report was mostly aspirational, but it set a maker for naval expansion. Tracy's throughline – echoed by the Naval Policy Board he convened to study the question – was one of defensive response to Atlantic Power lest "wholly unprotected" US cities offer "inviting object of attack."[21] In part at least, Tracy got his way a year later. The same year Mahan published his work on sea power, Congress authorized funding for the first of three modern battleships; something that could stand up to Europe.

The "defensive" character of the New Navy looks quite different from the Pacific. For a start, Tracy's and Mahan's arguments trailed the launching of the New Navy's first ships: steel-hulled cruisers built (as noted in Chapter 5) to out-compete Pacific newly made navies. More importantly, as a consequence of the New Navy's reactivity, by the 1890s the USN in the Pacific had a strategic orientation that was as much offensive (driven by the need to prove hemispheric primacy and cultural superiority) as defensive (the protection of West Coast port cities from attack). Far removed from Portsmouth or Cherbourg, the New Navy in the Pacific was geared toward readjusting "a hemispheric naval imbalance" rather than defeating a European power.[22] Moreover, because of the relative weakness of Pacific states vis-à-vis the North Atlantic, small investments created offensively credible forces a decade before the USN would threaten the European balance of power (c. 1898).[23] Cruisers such as USS *Charleston* (commissioned 1889) offered no defensive protection from or offensive threat to North Atlantic battlefleets but they did provide psychic reassurance and a credible form of deployable force against the newly made navies in Chile, China, or Japan.[24] The imperative to test that notional power concretely against a regional rival drove the US New Navy to action in 1890–1893 after a decade of reacting to Pacific newly made navies in the 1880s.

6.2 San Francisco Builds Strong Ships and Power Cannon

The beating heart of this transformation – from humiliation to hemispheric primacy – was the Union Iron Works in South San Francisco (Figure 6.1). Much in the way that the creation of the US New Navy writ

Figure 6.1 The Union Iron Works
Source: *Scientific American* (1892), NMRC/SF.

large was bound up with growing industrial capacity at shipyards such as Bath Ironworks and Cramp and Sons, so too did industrialization on the Pacific coast provide a supply "push" to the "demand" for security and prestige. Union Iron Works – the "Naval Nursery of the Pacific" – would eventually build the cruiser USS *Charleston* (1889), the armored monitor USS *Monterey* (1893), the torpedo boat USS *Farragut* (1899, then the fastest torpedo boat destroyer afloat), and most importantly the battleship USS *Oregon* (1896) – all firsts on the Pacific coast.[25] The continental Qing Empire had dockyards in Fuzhou. The US Empire had the Union Iron Works: the engine of self-strengthening as the "navy to construct" made its first steps toward realization in the Pacific.

The Union Iron Works had humble origins as a blacksmith's shop set up during the 1849 Gold Rush. Operations expanded steadily. In 1880, its general manager, Irving Scott, made a worldwide tour of foreign shipyards – like so many self-strengtheners – before returning to South San Francisco with ambitions to compete with the Atlantic World.[26] The shipyard cut its teeth on the production of civilian steamships until, in 1886, Union Iron Works received a contract to build the cruiser USS *Charleston*; what newspaper editors could look back on in 1901 as "a most portentous and important event in the maritime history of the Pacific Coast."[27] Here was a "revolutionary" concept – one company history noted – to build steel ships on the Pacific coast as an answer to Pacific vulnerability.[28] Scott was proud to have forged much of the steel for this vessel on the West Coast, though some of the larger plates (he lamented) still came from the East; a fact which "hurts my feelings very much."[29] The intellectual property was borrowed as well; a derivative of blueprints produced in Britain for Chilean and Japanese cruisers.[30] Dependency on foreign hardware and expertise was a familiar necessity in self-strengthening movements around the Pacific, including in the building of the US New Navy. Launched in 1888 and commissioned in 1890, the 4,000 ton protected cruiser was "a perfect success" seen by thousands of "enthusiastic spectators" who flocked to see the first USN vessel built on the West Coast.[31] That same year, as Congress authorized cruiser No. 5, advocates called for it to be named for a California landmark – in this case USS *San Francisco*.[32]

These were the sorts of ships available to US naval leaders at the time of *Influence*'s publication in 1890 – and in the Pacific they remained precious few in quantity. USS *Charleston* served as the Pacific flagship, but all the other assets in the Pacific Squadron remained holdovers from the Old Navy.[33] Battleships, let alone the battlefleets advocated by Mahan and Tracy, were still years in the making. Orders for the first battleship produced on the West Coast, USS *Oregon*, came to the Union Iron

Works in 1890, but that vessel was not completed until 1896. With limitations in mind, the first task of New Navy leaders and their industrialist allies was to show conclusively that the doldrums and humiliations of the Civil War-era Old Steam Navy were a thing of the past. Spurred on by comparisons to "even little Chili" for a generation, the US self-strengthening movement seized a chance to test the New Navy's capabilities and settle the festering irritation of the inter-American naval race. The first years of the 1890s offered chances to do both.

6.3 The Chase of the *Itata*

Two hard tests of US New Navy capabilities stemmed from the outbreak of the Chilean Civil War (1891): a yearlong conflict fought by Chilean "Congressionalists" and the sitting President Jose Manuel Balmaceda.[34] In January 1891, the Congressional party commandeered the fleet in Valparaiso and rebelled against Balmaceda, who retained control of Santiago and with it the Chilean Army. Caught in a stalemate, the rebels looked abroad for munitions with which to build an army of their own. Alongside the usual suspects in Europe, "insurgent" agents arrived in the United States, provoking "tangled and important questions of international law" everywhere they went.[35] Over Balmaceda's objections, the US shipping agent Grace and Co. organized a shipment of small arms to Chile aboard the rebel-held steamer *Itata*.[36] A diplomatic crisis ensued, rooted in precedents dating to the US Civil War. Should *Itata* land in Chile, the *New York Times* argued, the US position would be "precisely analogous to that of Great Britain in the matter of the *Alabama*."[37]

The crisis was a legal question but it was quickly turned over to the Navy for practical reasons. The issue came at a tricky moment, just as Benjamin Harrison toured the US Pacific coast – making him a moving target for telegraph operators.[38] After *Itata* evaded a detention notice and slipped out to sea, Attorney General William Miller threw up his hands, cabling Harrison as he traveled up the Columbia River in Oregon: "there is nothing to do but for the navy to pursue."[39] Whatever the risks, Miller stressed a day later, "public sentiment and national self-respect seem to us to call for vigorous action."[40] The Secretary of the Navy Tracy agreed with an eagerness that reflected his hopes for proving the New Navy's worth. Tracy directed USS *Charleston* out to sea to overtake *Itata*. If not, then another US New Navy ship, USS *San Francisco* could intercept it in South American waters.[41] The deployment of advanced ships was necessary because all the while, the insurgent *Esmeralda* – long an inspiration for the USN – loitered along the Mexican coast, waiting to rendezvous with *Itata*. Happily, for Tracy, New Navy ships that had been in commission for months suddenly had purpose: to capture a ship, certainly, but more importantly to act out the sort of "national self-respect" that the Old Navy had been unable to achieve.

Correspondents around the world documented the Chase of the *Itata* that followed in detail, both for its intrinsic value and as a test of US naval expansion to date.[42] *Esmeralda*'s and *Charleston*'s respective capabilities were laid out in the press like the statistics of opposing sports teams.[43] A decade of disparaging comparisons between aging US ships and the "peerless" *Esmeralda* in the 1880s took on new meaning in anticipation of "a fight."[44] By mid-May, tensions built into a "fever of excitement" as more than a few looked forward to a conflict over the "Chilean Corsair."[45] None more so, it seems, than the US navalists who saw USS *Charleston*'s superiority (on paper) as proof of the New Navy's advances relative to Chile. "Let Them Fight," urged the *Los Angeles Herald* anticipating "a Big Naval Battle."[46] After decades of lagging behind, the New Navy seemed to have caught up. But there was only one way to find out for sure.

Though the ships met in Acapulco, the controversy over *Itata* was resolved by diplomatic concessions – a very literal example of gunboat diplomacy.[47] Already engaged in a civil war, the insurgent Chilean government sought to avoid an international one. The Congressional Foreign Minister Isidoro Errázuriz made good on a pledge to turn the *Itata* over to the United States once it reached Chile.[48] On July 4, 1891, USS *Charleston* escorted the *Itata* back into San Diego Harbor, two months after it had escaped. *Esmeralda*'s crew still made the best of the deployment. En route home from Californian waters, the ship attacked a guano mine on the Islas de Lobos, denying Balmaceda's government revenue.[49]

It is possible to skip over this incident as a study in anti-climax – many histories do just that. From a transwar perspective, however, the chase appears as a milestone in a US program of "cruiser diplomacy" and a positive legitimization of the New Navy to date.[50] Nine years after the first US appropriation bills, a New Navy ship had been deployed to coerce a foreign government into accepting US policy objectives. The Pacific Squadron commander reported with some satisfaction that USS *Charleston*'s deployment "had much to do with compelling the compliance ... [of] the insurgent leaders."[51] The presence of two additional steel cruisers, USS *Baltimore* and USS *San Francisco*, on the Pacific slope had a coercive effect as well, Royal Navy officials believed.[52] A disorienting ten years before, one US commander worried that Secretary of State Blaine's interventionist diplomacy during the War of the Pacific might get the Old Steam Navy into an unwinnable war with Chile.[53] In

1891, that same officer traveled around the horn in the wooden-steam frigate USS *Pensacola*. Once in the Pacific, he transferred promptly to the steel cruiser, USS *Baltimore* ready to pursue US policy objectives.[54] A very literal transition from Old to New Navy.

That said, it was not a wholly triumphant moment. The *Itata* incident also illustrated limitations and the enduring vulnerability of California, echoing long-standing concerns over Chilean "presence" operations and their "morale effects."[55] Harrison personally cabled Tracy to keep USS *Charleston* ready for service in the region.[56] That the president expressed interest in the movement of specific ships – the way today the executive might a whole aircraft carrier battlegroup – testifies to the limited number of assets at his disposal and the competition over them.[57] In 1891, Tracy could still complain to Congress that the US Pacific coast was open to sudden raids by a "third-rate power." He continued, resurrecting arguments from the 1880s, that "if anyone believes that such rapidity of movement is impossible, let him recall the circumstances under which the *Esmeralda* appeared in April last, without warning close to the California Coast."[58] The specter of Chile's naval power remained. The second crisis of 1891, the *Baltimore* Incident, would settle matters more definitely.

6.4 The *Baltimore* Incident

As with the Chase of the *Itata*, the progress of the Chilean Civil War set the context for the *Baltimore* Crisis. In September 1891, the insurgent Congressionalists seized control of Santiago and with it victory in the Civil War. Peace came as a welcome respite to US forces who had patrolled along the Chilean coast for months, protecting US interests. USS *Baltimore*'s commander, Winfield Scott Schley – a future hero of the War of 1898 – took advantage of the comparative stability to give his crew liberty in Valparaiso. It was a fateful decision. Once ashore, two US sailors fell into a shoving match with a Chilean. Rumors of the scuffle spread resulting in widespread (if not always serious) violence against US personnel.[59] In the end, two US sailors were dead, seventeen injured and near-as-makes-no-difference two score incarcerated in the city's jail. From these humble sparks came a crisis over hemispheric leadership and the power of the US New Navy.[60]

How to assess the historical significance of the *Baltimore* Incident (1891–1892) depends a great deal on perspective. Through a primarily Atlantic-facing lens, it was a "minor" incident turned war scare in which "the only issue was a point of honor."[61] Contextualized within the transwar history of anxiety and naval racing in the Pacific it becomes something more: a meaningful test of the US New Navy as a collective force against a peer or near-peer antagonist. The *Itata* incident pitted two ships (*Charleston* and *Esmeralda*) against each other, but the *Baltimore* Crisis was a wider challenge of US self-strengthening and hemispheric pretensions. Five New Navy ships surged into the Pacific, representing the bulk of the modern USN. These steel cruisers and gunboats remained of little account to the North Atlantic world but they mattered a great deal to the balance of power in the Pacific. After a decade of naval anxiety about "little Chili" and its newly made navy, the *Baltimore* Incident gave US New Navy leaders a chance to demonstrate the worth of their reforms.

It all could have remained a legal question, but matters soon metastasized into a full-blown war scare, fanned by a toxic mix of nationalist posturing and domestic politics. There was – dubious – testimony as to the "sobriety, good behavior and politeness" of USS *Baltimore*'s crew, and an assertion the riot had been "instigated by discharged Chilian sailors" (they started it!).[62] The Chilean diplomat Agustin Ross argued (skeptically but astutely) that domestic forces would "propel the United States toward an unjust and cowardly" war for the sake of "the political game of [President] Harrison" and the interests of the USN leadership in securing "prestige and an increase to the fleet."[63] Chilean politicians had a great deal at risk as well; namely Chile's political cohesion and credibility so soon after the Civil War. This to say nothing of Santiago's self-image in the Americas standing against *yanqui* arrogance. Confrontation with the United States was at least in part a rational government strategy to establish popular support; or as one reporter put it, to regain "the popular affections by some dashing coup."[64] One US officer noted his sense that the Chilean "mob is all for war with the United States."[65]

By December 1891, domestic and institutional incentives had pushed the would-be belligerents to the edge. "Looks like a Chilean War" ran the *New York Times* on Christmas Eve, 1891, "Little Hope Now of a Peaceful Settlement."[66] On the Pacific slope, the commander of the recently arrived steel gunboat USS *Yorktown*, Robley "Fighting Bob" Evans (a future commander of the Great White Fleet), was equally fatalistic: "I don't see how war can now be avoided."[67] Mahan suddenly had his wish: a real-world crisis with which to "tickle the national vanity" by testing the New Navy's capabilities.[68] A war fever of a sort swept over the United States. The prospect of a racially inferior state "south of the line" heaping resistance on top of insult was a powerful motivator.[69] The Department of the Navy saw applications for service at sea "pour in" faster than they could be processed – a war with Chile looked too good to pass up.[70] Harrison even fielded correspondence from his cousin in

6.4 The *Baltimore* Incident

Mound City, KA, who hoped that Harrison would reserve some opportunities for his "kin folk"; after all, Kansas was "full of boys *longing* for a chance" at the action.[71] Schley's post-1898 biography trades in this same blustering overconfidence. In it, Schley strides into the offices of the Intendente of Valparaiso and demands the release of his sailors – or else![72] Looking back, it was all a foregone conclusion: US latent power so manifestly outclassed "little Chili" that serious resistance was never possible.

That said, at the time the experts tasked with actually planning a campaign against Chile acknowledged much more ambivalence about US prospects.[73] As in earlier engagements with North Atlantic powers (Callao [1866], Pacocha [1877], Zhenhai [1885]), how the US New Navy would perform against a Pacific newly made navy remained highly contingent. Calculations of force were complicated by geography, novel technologies, and the New Navy's own rhetoric – which ran consistently ahead of its demonstrated capabilities.[74] In 1891, most British commentators still believed the Chileans were "better prepared for fighting than are the Americans of the North."[75] Some Chileans officials agreed.[76] The commander of the US Pacific Squadron, RADM George Brown, acknowledged at least a sense of US–Chilean parity when wrote to the Secretary of the Navy that in the event of war, "our whole available force of modern ships and high powered guns supplemented by a fleet of steam coal vessels would be necessary to insure success."[77] The sum of US naval tonnage may have surpassed Chile's by a considerable margin in 1891, but because the United States faced the challenge of a two-ocean defense, not all of these vessels could be dedicated to the Pacific.

Operational commitments complicated the story. At the same time as the Chase of the *Itata* stole headlines, Harrison directed Tracy to send naval assets to the Bering Sea to police the killing of seals.[78] New Navy ships were in high demand across the Pacific, even as obsolete vessels continued to soak up resources.[79] In August 1891, the aging USS *Iroquois* – on which Mahan had served in Japan in the 1860s – made its way from Hawaii to Samoa pathetically and "principally under sail." In October that same year, Schley reported (all the way up to the Whitehouse eventually) that he would need another ten days to clean the bottom of USS *Baltimore* with divers before it could be ready for duty.[80]

When an ONI strategy board convened to contemplate naval operations against Chile, Mahan and other officers expressed particular concern about weapons contracts with Europe.[81] The US military attaché in Austria reported on the millions of cartridges of ammunition and 40,000 rifles purchased by the new government.[82] As the Chilean battleship *Prat* neared completion in France, worries grew that it could threaten US lines of communication to South America. When the crisis reached its climax in January 1892, Mahan complained bitterly that "so formidable a vessel as the *Prat*" was "getting trim to escape."[83] Efforts by Elswick to sell Chile what it advertised as improved *Esmeraldas* complicated matters further.[84] New gun emplacements ringed Valparaiso as well – as Argentine diplomats helpfully pointed out to transiting USN forces in January 1892.[85] US weapons had already leaked out to Chile as well. As late as 1892, Bradley Fiske, one of the US New Navy's key innovators, learned to his chagrin that his newly designed Fiske Range-Finder had been installed on the Chilean *Prat* in advance of its adoption by commanders in his own service.[86] How to value new and advanced weapons in Chile was a source of controversy the world over.[87]

A still more fundamental challenge was brute geographical separation. Chile's distance from US logistical hubs and coaling depots eroded US power, perhaps critically.[88] As Mahan wrote to Luce, "we are so confident in our bigness and so little realize the great extra load entailed by the distance of Chili, in case of war."[89] Scanning the region's geography in 1888, Mahan wrote that the lack of US coaling stations "would be amusing, were it not painful."[90] Matters were no better in 1891. At the height of the *Baltimore* Crisis, Harrison wrote Blaine about "the importance not to say necessity of securing coaling stations for our Navy." The South Pacific was a prime concern. Recent experience, Harrison argued, had shown "how serious an embarrassment we suffer" having to deploy ships south of the line and then steam then north to San Francisco to be serviced.[91] That deficiency in mind, the Peruvian minister in Washington, Jose Yrigoyen, anticipated that the chief challenge for (and vulnerability of) the USN in a war with Chile would be the task of ferrying coal thousands of miles from San Francisco.[92] This deficiency was so obvious that Blaine warned against leasing a coaling base in Peru for fear the Peruvians would gouge the United States.[93] As it had since the cruise of CSS *Shenandoah*, the bi-coastal nature of the United States remained a problem distorting calculations of strategy and power. Even simple things were difficult in the Pacific.

As war looked increasingly likely, jingoistic bellicosity gave way to concern. Writers at the *New York Times* changed tone, warning readers about how "keenly" the Navy Department felt its "lack of armored vessels available for service in Chilean waters."[94] Sensing the city's vulnerability to retaliation, the *Seattle Post-Intelligencer* protested that the "United States is not in a condition to meet the Chileans in a naval conflict."[95] Throughout the winter of 1891–1892, Mahan himself waited "impatiently and somewhat anxiously the outcome of the Chilian trouble," predicting "we may first get some eye openers."[96] Why not? After all, as the *Times* noted, "all things are possible in South America."[97] European defeats at Callao (1866) and Pacocha (1877) illustrated as much. Qing China (1894–1895) and Tsarist Russia (1904–1905) awaited similar "eye openers" in the coming decades against Japan – another small, maritime state with an efficient newly made navy.

Fortunately, like the Chase of the *Itata* before it, the *Baltimore* Crisis ended in diplomatic concessions extracted through naval pressure.[98] New officials shuffled into power in Chile, suggesting, the US Ambassador there noted, a "kindlier feeling toward the United States."[99] Exhausted by the Civil War and having failed to secure diplomatic backing in Europe, Chilean leaders eventually balked at hostilities with the United States.[100] Luis Pereira cabled on January 25, 1892 to apologize and condemn the violence against US sailors "in vigorous terms."[101] After wending its way through various departments and translations at the US State Department, Harrison notified Congress that it was his intent to accept the apology. Blaine celebrated a "full and honorable adjustment" of the issue, and encouraged a return of the "two Republics to a basis of ~~friendship and~~ cordiality."[102] Apparently "friendship" was still a bridge too far. William H. Seward – a distant architect of US primacy in the Pacific – wrote to Harrison with his opinion. Surely, Harrison replied, "the general peace of this Hemisphere would be promoted by giving it to understand that the most peace loving nation of the world – the United States – would defend its honor."[103] Put more cynically, a willingness to engage in cruiser diplomacy was a boon to hemispheric domination and the New Navy that achieved it.

The results seemed to validate Harrison's conviction, and so too investments in the New Navy. The crisis was a material test for this force after a decade of disparaging comparisons to Chile. In 1891, the Pacific Squadron had one New Navy ship. In 1892, the prospect of war surged the New Navy cruisers *San Francisco*, *Charleston*, *Boston*, and *Baltimore*, and the gunboat *Yorktown*, to the region.[104] Even this augmented fleet would have scarcely raised eyebrows in Europe, but it made an impression in South America. US navalists rushed to claim success. Here was "a victory, of sorts" that displayed both the benefits of naval power and its almost tautological necessity.[105] As late as 1889, Tracy warned, US investments had created as of yet "a fleet that has still only a nominal existence."[106] The *Baltimore* Crisis transformed that "nominal existence" into hard power. Key leaders such as Luce, Roosevelt, and Mahan all argued that "the nucleus of the new navy" had demonstrated its worth by compelling Chilean acquiescence.[107] No longer a laughingstock, US diplomats in Argentina wondered if it would be possible to send a few warships to Buenos Aries as long as they were in South America? The naval power of the United States had only been theretofore represented by an "inferior class of vessels" that made for a "sorry appearance beside the war craft of other powers" and had "long been a butt for laughter here."[108] The ships of the New Navy now assembled off Chile were another matter and something of which to be proud.

On a slightly longer timeline, the scare also clarified the relative standing of the United States and Chile in the hemisphere.[109] The Chase of the *Itata* suggested the ascendancy of the USN vis-à-vis Chile; the *Baltimore* Crisis made that shift demonstrably clear at several times the scale. In 1892, with the crisis safely behind them, students at the Naval War College could enjoy lectures on "Naval Lessons in the Recent Civil War in Chile" sure of their standing in the Pacific order.[110] This shift was not lost on Chilean military officials who after 1891 began to chronicle the "Progress of the North American Navy," noting an ever widening capabilities gap.[111] The 1892 cover of the satirical magazine *Puck* distilled the spirit of the moment: Uncle Sam, backed by an industrial navy, chastises a dark-skinned, Chilean toddler with impunity (Figure 6.2).

Thinking in transwar perspective, the contrast to the 1881 *Harper's* cartoon "*Even* Chili could warm US" a decade earlier is stunning (Figure 4.1). Chile's ephemeral preponderance in the Pacific was at an end; a victim, in many ways, of its success in challenging US pretension and power.

As for USS *Baltimore* itself, the ship went on to service in Asia and in the Philippine Insurrection. So too the San Francisco-built USS *Charleston*, which foundered on a reef in the Philippines in 1899. The aging USS *Baltimore* slumped into a second career as a minelayer until its decommissioning at Pearl Harbor in 1922. Fifty years after the war scare in Chile, USS *Baltimore* went up for sale in October 1941. Another USS *Baltimore* was already in the works, slated for commissioning in December 1941. This was good timing, as the USN shook off the constraints of the Washington Naval Treaty and geared up to fight the Japanese Empire.[112] That story – of estrangement between the United States and Japan – had roots in the crises of the 1890s as well.

6.5 The New Navy's New Frontier in Hawaii

As Secretary of the Navy Tracy rested on his laurels, Secretary of State James Blaine harbored his own plans for US Empire in the Pacific. In his more ambitious moments, Blaine envisioned a Conference of the Americas for the adjudication of disputes and a railway network linking California with Chile, down the spine of the Pacific Rim from the Sierra Nevada to the Andes.[113] Complimenting that north–south axis, Hawaii

Figure 6.2 "A Warning," *Puck* (1892)
Source: *Puck*, Library of Congress.

anchored his image of east–west influence across the Pacific. Writing to Harrison in the months before the *Baltimore* Crisis, Blaine described three territories that were "not continental" and yet strategically vital to the United States. Blaine reckoned that two – Cuba and Puerto

Rico – were not immediately in question. The third, Hawaii, "may come up for a decision at any unexpected hour and I hope we shall be prepared to decide it in the affirmative."[114] Blaine died in 1893, but his advice to Harrison (as though echoing Seward a generation earlier) stressed the Pacific as the proximate challenge for US policymakers – competition in the Atlantic could wait. Straddling the 1891–1892 crises in Chile, the American Consul in Hawaii John Stevens sharpened Blaine's sentiments about Hawaii and the North Pacific, "whose dominance fairly belongs to the United States" as "Malta and Cyprus are to Great Britain." A "hesitating, and drifting policy towards them," Stevens warned Blaine, "would be as unwise and unsafe as unstatesmanlike."[115]

As the naval race with "little Chili" ebbed in the wake of the 1891–1892 *Baltimore* Crisis, Hawaii took on still greater significance as a future nerve center of empire in the Pacific. Fittingly, in 1893, a year after the *Baltimore* Incident and a year before the outbreak of the Sino-Japanese War, the US New Navy engaged in what the historian Mark Russell Shulman called its first "overtly imperialist" action: the 1893 intervention by sailors and marines from USS *Boston* (one of the original ships from 1882) in support of the Hawaiian planter-class coup against Queen Liliʻuokalani.[116] In the harbor, USS *Boston* met no symmetrical opposition – at least at first. USS *Boston*'s commander, Gilbert Wilste, obligingly landed his forces to back what he saw as a bloodless revolution ahead of a negotiated annexation to the United States.[117]

The real question for New Navy leaders was not whether the US could land forces in Hawaii but what to do once they had. The navalist set argued that Hawaii should be annexed to support power projection across the region. Having built a small fleet of New Navy ships, the acquisition of territorial infrastructure for coaling and maintenance was a necessary corollary. In the spring of 1893, with US forces in de facto control of Honolulu, navalists from Newport to Mare Island advocated for Hawaiian annexation. Mahan took to the pages of the *Forum* and the *New York Times* to extoll Hawaii's "unique importance" to the US future in the Pacific – not least as a barrier against "an invasion of Chinese Barbarism."[118] ONI assembled a chorus of opinions from "Leading Newspapers on the Hawaiian Question" in support of Secretary of the Navy Benjamin Tracy's campaign within the Harrison administration.[119] They had ample fodder. The *Philadelphia Inquirer* urged the US to "become the spider" at the center of Hawaii's web of Pacific trade routes.[120] The *Chicago Inter-Ocean* reckoned annexation would rank the Harrison administration "second only to Jefferson's with its achievement of the Louisiana Purchase": the one had secured a continental empire, the other would guarantee the territorial infrastructure of a maritime one.[121] A copy of the *New York Daily Tribune* made its way to Harrison's desk, describing Hawaii as not only a lynchpin in US commercial aspirations in the Pacific but also a potential link in "England's Remarkable Chain of Offensive Fortifications around the Coasts of the United States."[122] San Francisco's businessmen pursued annexation as a sort of patriotic duty, becoming what the historian Ernest May called "the first identifiable imperialist group in the country."[123] As usual, the geopolitical and security imperatives of the United States looked different along the Pacific Rim.

Unfortunately for the navalists, the benefits of annexation were not universally self-evident – certainly not to the newly elected Democratic President Grover Cleveland. Even as the Republican appointees Tracy and Blaine made their case, Cleveland prepared to take control of the federal government, bringing with him a more skeptical view toward the islands and the "revolution" there. He had considerable company. A lecturer at the Iowa Agricultural College made clear that he had defected to the Democratic party after witnessing the Republican "filibustering scheme" in Hawaii and that it was "to the credit of President Cleveland that he refused to join these men."[124] Californians, too, had mixed opinions. At the height of the debate, the Democratic leader, John P. Irish, wrote to Cleveland stressing that a silent majority in California was against annexation.[125] Taking Hawaii, he argued, would make a sham of American values. Rather than seize the islands as a US Gibraltar, he concluded, the United States should protect them as a neutral "Switzerland of the seas."[126]

These views in mind, the newly (re)installed Grover Cleveland rejected "jingo" arguments on moral and political grounds, leaving the Hawaiian planter class to establish a short-lived, notionally independent Hawaiian Republic.[127] Few were satisfied. On the one hand, the dispossessed Queen Lili'uokalani bitterly protested the loss of her kingdom – and would continue to do so for years.[128] On the other, US navalists lamented a wasted opportunity, or what the *New York Tribune* called the "crowning shame of the Hawaiian business."[129] Mahan claimed Cleveland's failure to annex the islands in 1893 led him "finally" to the Republican Party.[130] Roosevelt, too, stewed, writing to Lodge, Mahan, and others that Cleveland's decision was "a colossal crime" and "a most horrible failure" of US diplomacy.[131] Addressing that failure became a political object for both men in the coming years.

In its sensitivity toward Hawaii, the US New Navy shared a great deal with another newly made navy in the Pacific: Japan. Even as USS *Boston* landed its marines and sailors in Honolulu, the Japanese cruiser *Naniwa* was en route to Hawaii: an "enlarged and perfected" version of the *Esmeralda*, built by the same shipyard.[132] William Sims – perhaps the interwar USN's most successful innovator – took stock of an evolving security environment, anchored alongside the Japanese cruisers *Naniwa* and *Takachiho*: two Elswick-built "improved *Esmeraldas*," which Sims considered "quite as powerful as we are."[133] Next to these new Japanese ships, the original Chilean *Esmeralda* that had inspired so much commentary in the US during the 1880s was, Sims reckoned, just a "tub."[134] Through its cruiser diplomacy, the US New Navy created a novel source of friction: "Maritime Japan" and its frontier in the eastern Pacific. Like Chile and China before it, those tensions entangled questions of naval power, immigration, and civilizational standing.[135] In all these respects, Japan's role in the 1893 Hawaiian Coup was a useful primer for the coming perspectival revolution wrought by the Sino-Japanese War.

6.6 Something to Celebrate

The failure to annex Hawaii smarted, but for the architects of the New Navy there was still a great deal of achievement to celebrate by 1893. Conveniently enough, the conclusion of the *Baltimore* Crisis coincided with two naval demonstrations, commemorating centennials in the history of North America exploration: Columbus' landing in the New World (1492) and the European discovery of the Columbia River (1792). From coast to coast these festivals provided a chance to at once stage the New Navy for the American public and reflect on its tangible achievements in the Pacific. In the aggregate, US steel cruisers and gunboats still lagged behind the fleets of the North Atlantic industrial powers, but the New Navy's record of cruiser diplomacy in the Pacific made it a tool and symbol of US prestige worth celebrating.

The denizens of the Pacific coast did not have long to wait. The organizers of the 1892 Columbia River Centennial featured the New Navy's ships as their central attractions. In 1891, shortly after the Chase of the *Itata*, the secretary of the Portland Industrial Exposition wrote to Tracy, entreating him to loan out ships: "the sight of a modern war ship … with permission to board her and see the wonderful advances that have been made in naval architecture and equipment, would be attended by thousands and would go down to your credit."[136] The following spring, USS *Baltimore* and USS *Charleston* steamed north from California to Astoria and Portland as the Centennial's "chief features of interest."[137] From San Francisco, USS *Baltimore* traveled as far north as Portland and was the first US New Navy ship to negotiate the perilous sand bar at the mouth of the Columbia River – 100 years after the American Robert Gray's *Columbia Redivia* accomplished the same.[138] In Astoria, sightseers

6.6 Something to Celebrate

at the 1892 Columbia River Centennial crowded around, the *Dalles Daily Chronicle* reported, to see, "especially the *Baltimore*, which came so near to having to teach the Chilians a lesson."[139] The celebrations were a capstone to the regional naval race with Chile but they also whetted appetites for more. Oregonian journalists would see in the New Navy's cruisers a mere prelude to the launching of the battleship USS *Oregon*, then being built at San Francisco's Union Iron Works.[140]

For the growing cities of the Pacific Northwest, it was a considerable display, but it paled next to what was in store in New York a year later. Plans to hold a "Columbian Navy Rendezvous" in New York were laid in 1890 as a compliment to the World's Fair Exhibition in Chicago but gained a new raison d'être after the *Baltimore* Crisis.[141] In 1893, warships from Spain, Germany, Russia, the Netherlands, France, Italy, Great Britain, Argentina, and Brazil arrived in New York.[142] Among the US participants were USS *Yorktown* and USS *Baltimore*, both fresh from Chilean waters. As the fleets formed into lines, USS *Baltimore* took its position at the lead.

The New Navy's record of achievement in the Pacific made all this pomp and circumstance relevant. In August of 1892, thousands of mourners had gathered to watch the funeral procession of one of the US sailors killed in Valparaiso.[143] The crowds of 1893 enjoyed something these mourners did not: a sense of vengeance against Chile courtesy of the New Navy. USS *Yorktown* and USS *Baltimore* arrived in New York in February 1893, after mammoth voyages. USS *Yorktown* was still encrusted with barnacles from the Pacific. The flagship USS *Baltimore* had a still more epic journey. It began in August of 1890 when the ship carried the body of John Ericsson – the inventor of the *Monitor* – back to his native Sweden. USS *Baltimore* traversed nearly 60,000 miles, visited seventy ports, and nearly precipitated a war with Chile.[144] Now the flagship of the review, the ship's commander Schley had a final order of business. Having transported the remains of the inventor of the Civil War-era *Monitor* onboard USS *Baltimore* back to Stockholm, he carried onboard a photograph of the exchange, personally delivering it back to Harrison – too precious to be trusted to a courier.[145] Ericsson's inventions marked an inflection point in US naval history in 1862. His death, and transport onboard a leading ship of the New Navy, was a symbol of another, ongoing transformation.

The scale and significance of the proceedings was obvious to all those in attendance (Figure 6.3). "The ships from our Navy which will appear in the great naval parade [April 1893] in the harbor of New York," Harrison promised Congress, "will be a convincing demonstration to the world that the United States is again a naval power."[146] The *Providence*

Figure 6.3 Fred Cozzens, *New York Naval Parade*
Source: J. D. Kelley, *Our Navy: Its Growth and Achievements* (1893), front materials.

News caught the spirit with the headline, "How the United States Representation Will Compare with That of Other Nations – Americans Will Have No Reason to Feel Ashamed. In 1886 we were nineteenth among naval powers, now we stand fifth."[147] It was, the San Francisco *Morning Call* reported, "the grandest marine spectacle ever presented in American waters, if not the world" – at least before rain dampened the mood.[148] "Immense crowds" thronged the riverways of New York City and the "spectacle of rare enthusiasm" left the domestic press universally impressed.[149] As the assembled ships steamed past and "rendered him the honors due his office," the newly elected President Grover Cleveland stood onboard a dispatch ship, *Dolphin*, looking every bit the part of a great power leader.[150] Fresh from disappointing the navalists by rejecting Hawaiian annexation, his inclusion in the review represented a growing bipartisan consensus around naval rejuvenation.

In contrast to this jubilation, many North Atlantic observers remained underwhelmed. Conditioned to the massive Royal Navy reviews at Spithead (1887, 1897), the *Times* of London had no superlatives for the USN or its review.[151] The lead from *Reuters* began with an account not of the ships but of the disappointing drizzle and mist. The US New Navy was worth a party but not yet serious consideration from the dominant states in the North Atlantic.[152] The protected cruisers assembled by the United States were, in most respects, artifacts of a "second class navy" cosplaying "as prestigious front-line" capital ships.[153] An article in the *Times* a month after the New York parade noted feverish activity in Europe but made no mention of the United States.[154] No battleships, yet, and no battlefleet either, but the New Navy still mattered, if only against the newly made navies in the Pacific.

That naval parade was notable for its absences as well. Despite invitations to Chile's "splendid Navy," Santiago declined, citing "measures of economy."[155] So too Japan, as the naval race between the Qing and Meiji entered its last sprint before the Sino-Japanese War. No matter. US New Navy officers had an intimate view into Japanese naval diplomacy and advancement in Hawaii. Comparing cruisers to cruisers in Honolulu, many of the old doubts and rhetorical ticks about inferiority crept back into correspondence. Those doubts became all the more pronounced as US officers reckoned with the results of the Sino-Japanese War a year later. But first the New Navy (and another curious sort of newly made navy) took a victory lap, deploying forces to intervene in the Brazilian Civil War.

6.7 New Navies in Brazil (1893–1894)

On September 6, 1893, just months after the New York Naval parade, Admiral Custódio de Melo sized control of Brazil's fleet – one of the most sophisticated in the hemisphere – and demanded the resignation of the sitting President Floriano Peixoto.[156] The result was a curious mirror of the Chilean Civil War in 1891: a standoff between rebels with a navy and a government in control of the army ashore. The revolt quickly ensnared the United States when the rebels moved to cut off shipping into Rio.[157] For the Cleveland administration, the Brazilian Naval Revolt raised questions about the safety of US merchants and, more broadly, the political orientation of what had been a reliable partner in Latin America. For the leaders of the US New Navy, it was a fresh test of capabilities just on display in Chilean waters and New York.

The US response got off to an uneven start. No US warship had been present at the time of the rising in Rio. When two cruisers did arrive, the commander in charge committed the diplomatic faux pas of saluting (and therefore giving a form of legitimacy to) the rebel fleet.[158] Months of inaction and diplomatic prevarications followed until January 1894, when Admiral Andrew Benham assumed command of the US operation. Arriving with a force of five New Navy warships (now the most powerful foreign fleet off Brazil), he declared his intention to escort US commercial ships into Rio Harbor. On January 29, 1894, Benham dispatched the smallest ship in his arsenal, the gunboat USS *Detroit*, to run the blockading gauntlet. Challenged by the rebel forces, USS *Detroit* traded warning shots with the Brazilians, crossing their lines and escorting commercial vessels to shore.[159] Magnified through a navalist lens, the intervention took on an exaggerated significance. The "gallant fight" showed American merchantmen protected by force.[160] The New Navy, as the papers reported back home, had won respect for "the Old Flag."[161]

After Benham's actions, Rio was open, but the rebels retained control over the Brazilian fleet. The standoff between a maritime force in revolt and a government ashore dragged on with no resolution in sight; the army could do little to the navy at sea, and the navy could not bring the fight to the army ashore. To end it, the "navyless" Floriano turned, like so many before him, to private contractors who promised a ready-built navy.[162] Enter Charles Flint: an American shipping agent and entrepreneur who had sold weapons to Latin America for the most of his adult life.[163] Flint's response was to purchase merchant ships in the United States and modify them for military purposes. Floriano (echoing men such as Bulloch and Mallory in the US Civil War) hoped that this mercenary fleet might compensate for its small size with technical surprise ("exotic weapons of destruction").[164] In this sense, the war had a reciprocal benefit for Flint: like earlier wars, it was a testing ground for novel technologies. When Flint sold arms during the War of the Pacific, he also tested various forms of the torpedo. In Brazil a decade later, Flint wanted information on the "dynamite gun": a newfangled device meant to hurl an explosive charge at enemy vessels. Flint cobbled together a small flotilla of merchant steamers equipped with dynamite guns, torpedoes, and even dirigibles.[165] A reporter visiting Flint's office found catalogs from Krupp and other firms carefully displayed for his benefit – stage props showing how seriously Flint took the task of arming Brazil.[166] Private inventors volunteered submarines.[167] The torpedo boat *Destroyer*, built by Ericsson but rejected by the USN, found use as well.

It all worked up to a point. By the time Flint's "new navy" (his term) it arrived in Rio in March, 1894, much of the revolt had already collapsed.[168] Nonetheless, Flint's fleet broke any prospect of further resistance. The foremost historian of the crisis credits Flint as the "decisive factor in saving Floriano's government and cementing US–Brazilian friendship."[169] Flint was typically quick to claim the victory for himself as Rio's society gleefully feted the new navy, triumphant in the harbor.[170]

Other Americans found their way to Brazil as well, promising to upset the rebel's armored fleet on the cheap. The Civil War veteran George Boynton won a contract from the Floriano government to construct a "remarkable torpedo" and attack the Brazilian navy's primary armored

6.7 New Navies in Brazil (1893–1894)

vessel, the battleship *Aquidaban*.[171] Without the ability to produce an armored warship or acquire one abroad, attacking the *Aquidaban* with an asymmetric torpedo appealed for the same reasons the tactic was popular among the Confederates, Peruvians, Chileans, and Chinese. Boynton gave it a go but was captured by a British warship and handed over to the Americans onboard USS *Charleston*.[172] Even in failure his logic was sound. Government torpedo boats eventually sank *Aquidaban*, another echo of the Chilean Civil War.[173] Still more inventively, the American John Wilde had the inklings of a scheme to use poison gas wafting over the water to asphyxiate the sailors of the rebel fleet. Floriano rejected the idea as "unsoldierlike," but Wilde was undeterred. He soon hawked the plan in the Sino-Japanese War.[174] Unsurprisingly, when considered in a transwar lens, Floriano looked to the same template used by the CSN. Like the Confederates and, indeed, other "navyless" self-strengtheners, he found private inventors armed with novel weapons willing to fill the gap.

There is a good case to be made – and historians interested in US–Brazil bilateral relations have made it – that this drama in the South Atlantic was the first real demonstration of the US New Navy as an instrument of hemispheric domination (including vis-à-vis the Europeans).[175] And in a sense, it was. Practically, the expedition served as a dress rehearsal for the sort of projection needed to defend the Caribbean Basin from a European expedition (the strategic purpose most often cited by historians of the US New Navy). At Rio, the gunboat USS *Detroit* even fired warning shots against Brazilian craft running interference. That act was exaggerated ludicrously in newspapers of the day into a full-blown shoot-out by the "Not Toy Gunners" of the USN.[176] If one believes that the New Navy was a battlefleet driven by great power naval racing and the need to secure the future Panama Canal, then the US response to the Brazilian Naval Revolt was a test bed for aspirational capabilities.

Stipulating all that, the crisis in Brazil posed a less serious challenge than its antecedents in the Pacific World; a fact not lost on contemporary US and international observers. For a start there was the general political context. Where Brazil and the United States found ample ground for collaboration (especially by the 1880s), Chilean leaders had long been suspicious of the United States – and the feeling was mutual. The titles of the two standard accounts of US–Brazil and US–Chile relations capture the difference. The US and Brazil were "Unequal Giants" ("Sister Republics" even).[177] Chile and the United States were "Empires in Conflict."[178] More particularly, unlike the gunboat diplomacy of the *Baltimore* Crisis, US intervention in Brazil actually *helped* the government in power.[179] Recognizing as much, Floriano Peixoto declared

July 4, 1894 a national holiday in an unsubtle expression of gratitude to the United States.[180] There is still a city called "Clevelandia" in Brazil named in honor of the US president who helped put down the revolt.[181]

Beyond the political climate, there was the Chilean Navy's deadly real experience in the War of the Pacific and Civil War. The Brazilian Naval Revolt was, by contrast, more a political maneuver than a naval one. Comparing and contrasting the world's "modern naval campaigns" in 1902, the historian William Laird Clowes noted that while, "the Chilian revolution presents us with a picture of a very well-managed and thoroughly successful revolt, the rising in Brazil affords us an illustration of exactly the opposite character."[182] Herbert Wilson's 1896 account was even more dismissive, describing "a struggle so feebly and fatuously conducted that it seems almost absurd to call it a war."[183] For the American mercenary Boynton, the revolt was a "comic opera duel."[184] While US rhetoric and war planning after Chilean victory in the War of the Pacific suggested genuine worries, the threat posed by the Brazilian Naval Revolt could be, and often was, dismissed as parody.[185]

Finally, the geography was less of an issue in Brazil than in the Pacific. Projecting force into the South Atlantic from East Coast shipyards was relatively straightforward. Sustaining operations in the South Pacific from a base in distant San Francisco was another matter.[186] The arrival of Benham and his five ships suggested the growing ability of the United States to defend the Atlantic Coast and its outlying periphery. The operational and geostrategic challenge of deploying to (let alone sustaining them across) the Pacific remained unanswered. That deficiency looked more worrying as the decade wore on and another Pacific newly made navy rose up the international rankings.

6.8 One Race Ends, Another Begins

Predictability, given a generation of anxiety about physical threats and hemispheric prestige, the New Navy's first serious tests took place in the Pacific. During the 1891 Chase of the *Itata*, USS *Charleston* outmatched the Chilean *Esmeralda*, a ship evoked as a threat to US maritime prowess for years, like the CSS *Alabama* before it. Just months later, the *Baltimore* Crisis offered a wider proving ground of the New Navy's capacity for power projection in the Pacific. US "victory" (or more properly coercion) marked the end of US–Chilean regional naval racing and the beginning of what the historian William Sater called Santiago's "long descent" relative to the United States.[187]

At the time, US success in these tests represented less preparation for the War of 1898 or posturing against European powers than an end

6.8 One Race Ends, Another Begins

to regional racing and (physical and psychic) insecurity in the Pacific. Demonstrating the ability to project naval forces offensively in the hemisphere was a meaningful end in and of itself. Ernest May was right to note that nothing the US and its New Navy did as of 1891–1892 convinced "the world that America had become a great power."[188] But then again, the "great power" standard was an almost impossibly high one after just a decade of what might fairly be called US self-strengthening. There remained a long way to go, but by 1892 the US record of cruiser diplomacy did settle the old question of humiliation and deterioration behind newly made Pacific navies. In this context, US intervention in the Hawaiian Revolution was a logical extension of the US commitment to Pacific threats and the performance of regional naval superiority. When the New Navy deployed as a fleet to Brazil in 1893–1894 to protect US commercial interests, it did so with confidence from its experience in the more challenging environment of the South American Pacific.

All of this was a major departure, but the "American Naval Revolution" (the eventual making of a great power battlefleet that could defeat Spain and/or defend the Caribbean) was an incomplete project at best. Even as New Navy ships triumphantly piloted the Hudson and Columbia rivers, much of the USN order of battle remained of Old Navy vintage.[189] As late as 1889, William Sampson (hero of the Battle of Santiago de Cuba, 1898) complained, "this nation has been for thirty years at a standstill, while others have been steadily advancing, so that now we find ourselves far in the rear."[190] Alongside the new cruisers, Civil War-era steamers wearily chugged along, doing the same tasks that they had been assigned for generations. The venerable USS *Kearsarge* – which had ended CSS *Alabama*'s infamous campaign at the Battle of Cherbourg in 1864 – still cruised the Caribbean, as it had for thirty years, until it wrecked in 1894 off the coast of Venezuela.[191] Still in the process of remaking, and still saddled by sunk costs and graying officers, any confidence gleaned from the US New Navy's triumphs in the Pacific was fragile and, as will be seen, ephemeral. At the same moment as US–Chilean naval competition tapered off, the intra-regional naval race in the western Pacific between Qing China and Meiji Japan accelerated. A fresh wave of anxiety about newly made navies followed, further legitimizing the transformation of the USN from Old to New.

7   The Sino-Japanese War and New "Yankees" in the Pacific

The American naval adviser Philo Norton McGiffin found sea power the hard way: via a Pacific war that would eventually kill him. Caught in the eddy of post-Civil War stagnation, he left the US Old Navy in 1885 for a newly made one under construction in China. His timing was good. Defeat in the Sino-French War (1883–1885) accelerated Qing naval expansion, creating demand for expertise. McGiffin taught cadets in Tianjin, directed the Qing Naval Academy at Weihaiwei, and shepherded cruisers back to China from British shipyards. By 1891, McGiffin could survey his contributions and find many reasons for optimism about the future of Chinese power. Even as Mahan's *Influence* made its debut in the United States, the Qing newly made navy already had battleships, steel cruisers, and torpedo boats; all the markers of an ascendant great power force.[1] When the Qing Beiyang Fleet finally went to war in 1894, McGiffin went with it, both as a "point of honor" and out of a sense that he might well win.[2]

All that promise came crashing down in the First Sino-Japanese War (甲午战争) (1894–1895), which was another test of self-strengthening that upset military and cultural assumptions about the Pacific.[3] This chapter describes the Sino-Japanese naval race (1885–1894), before turning to the war itself and its implications for regional standing in the Pacific. Adopting a transwar approach, it contends that the War of the Pacific (1879–1884) was to the Pacific slope of South America what the Sino-Japanese War was to Northeast Asia. Note three similarities. Like the War of the Pacific, the Sino-Japanese War broke out after a generation of intra-regional naval racing. Like the War of the Pacific, the Sino-Japanese War's military results not only redrew territorial boundaries but reordered international perceptions of the Qing and Japanese Empires. Finally, like the War of the Pacific, Japan's victory in the war created another Pacific rival for US navalists to posture against.

With so many points of comparison, the Sino-Japanese War's implications were at once unsettling and reassuringly familiar for USN officers and their political backers. As the threat from Chile receded after the *Baltimore* Crisis (1891–1892), Tokyo took Santiago's place, almost as if by institutional necessity; the waning "Yankees of South America" were eclipsed by the ascendant "Yankees of the East."[4] Familiar themes characterized both rivalries: notably, hard-power competition, racial antipathy, and the opportunism of North American Yankees eager to highlight novel threats in the Pacific. Largely because of their comparability, the "little" Japanese replaced "little Chili" with a near seamless ease in transwar navalist debates – a transition most obvious in the sale of the Chilean cruiser *Esmeralda* to Japan in 1895.[5]

Beginning in the 1890s, Hawaii served as the primary site of competition between Japanese and US imperialism; a point of exchange and threat, playing much the same role the California coast had during US–Chilean competition in the 1880s. Descriptions of Honolulu's vulnerability echoed rhetoric about "defenseless" San Francisco almost word for word. Japanese cruiser deployments to the archipelago (1893, 1897) evoked retrospectives about Chilean operations off Central America (1885, 1891) even as they anticipated the rise of Japanese naval power during and after the Sino-Japanese War. As with earlier rivalries, technical power and transoceanic migration interacted to produce volatile threat perceptions in the western Pacific. Those threats not only underwrote a drive by US naval advocates to annex the Hawaiian archipelago in the 1890s but an emphasis on the deployment of oceangoing battleships in the Pacific as an explicit answer to Japanese naval capabilities. Once again, the mastery of modern naval violence by an *ersatz* white empire in the Pacific seemed to compel US naval expansion. After the Sino-Japanese War, the US New Navy had another pacing threat, and one that influential US observers could not help but compare to their earlier rivalry with Chile for primacy on the Pacific slope.

7.1 The Sino-Japanese Naval Race (1885–1894)

The naval race between China and Japan played out for a generation as a defining feature of the western Pacific's geopolitics. North Atlantic naval power – be it the Opium Wars or Perry's Black Ships – motivated Chinese and Japanese self-strengthening initially, but mutually exacerbating threat perceptions were the main engine of Japanese and especially Qing naval expansion.[6] The Japanese invasion of Taiwan (1874) and annexation of the Ryukyus (1879) convinced Qing officials that the Imperial Japanese Navy's (IJN) proximity to China and access to "strong ships and powerful cannon" made "defending against Japan more important than guarding against the Westerners."[7] The race accelerated from there. Qing leaders worked to graft naval power onto the

Chinese continental empire, while Meiji reforms embraced the identity of "Maritime Japan."[8] The catalytic interaction of those efforts was obvious to outsiders such as Commodore Shufeldt, who in 1882 advised Li Hongzhang to expand the Chinese Navy as a response to the "enormous menace" of Japan.[9] By 1894, *Shenbao* would look back on the origins of the Sino-Japanese War and see a pattern of aggression from 1874 when Japanese leaders began to "drool" over the possibility of annexing Taiwan.[10]

To most of the world, the Qing seemed to dominate this intra-regional competition for naval primacy. Chinese reforms and acquisitions after the Sino-French War transformed the Qing Empire into the preponderant maritime power in East Asia – albeit briefly. In the same way that "little Chili" drove navalist rhetoric in the United States, the threat of what Li Hongzhang called "that little country" (Japan) was a cultural *and* strategic challenge to which the Qing mustered an impressive response, from "navy to construct" to the largest newly made navy in Asia.[11] Top-line assessments invariably listed the German-built battleships *Dingyuan* and *Zhenyuan*: 7,000-ton warships which conferred a notional advantage to the Qing over the cruiser-dominated IJN.[12] Li Hongzhang predicted that although Japan was "stubbornly strong in the Eastern Sea at present," the IJN was limited by an inability to acquire "true ironclads" (真铁甲) capable of competing with these Chinese battleships.[13] The ships arrived in China after the Sino-French War, too late for combat but in time to serve as the nucleus of postwar acquisitions. In the 1860s, Peru had the two ironclads *Huáscar* and *Independencia* as the core of its newly made navy. In the 1870s, Chile had the *Cochrane* and *Blanco Encalada*. By the late 1880s, the Qing had the *Dingyuan* and *Zhenyuan*, again two armored capital ships surrounded by a small fleet of advanced cruisers and gunboats. At the time, most (including ONI and Royal Navy intelligence) saw the Qing as the principal naval force in the western Pacific.[14] In contrast to the Qing, British naval intelligence estimated that as of 1885 the IJN consisted of a mere seven "really effective vessels," the remainder "being old, half worn-out vessels purchased at different times by Daimios [sic]."[15]

There were apparent qualitative advantages as well. For a start, a centralization of command, ONI argued in 1886, transformed the Qing into a more "efficient naval force."[16] No longer could an adversary count on regional loyalties to frustrate concentrated Qing action (as they had in the Sino-French War). Years of foreign advisory relationships paid dividends as well. William Lang – the onetime British adviser to the Qing Navy – claimed in 1894 that the Beiyang Navy was "very strong" and a "splendid force" relative to the IJN, not least because it was the

7.1 The Sino-Japanese Naval Race (1885–1894)

beneficiary of nearly a decade of his advice.[17] New naval colleges, such as the one at Weihaiwei overseen by the American Philo McGiffin, continued to support the cultivation of human talent.[18]

In all, as of 1890 the Qing appeared well on their way to winning the naval race in the western Pacific. Japan's victory in the Sino-Japanese War tends to *ex post facto* obscure this conventional wisdom. In 1891, *Shenbao* celebrated the Qing's "glorious" military as the leading maritime power in the "Eastern Sea."[19] Just weeks before the decisive Battle of the Yalu, the *North China Herald* still serenely maintained that China was the "only great Asiatic State that really commands the respect of the Great Powers of the World."[20]

There were, however, reasons for skepticism. In a mirror of Chilean/Peruvian naval competition during the 1870s, Meiji reformers seized on Qing military development to justify a program of naval and infrastructure development designed to make Japan "the key of the Pacific."[21] In 1887, the Meiji emperor stressed that "strengthening maritime defense is a matter in which we cannot let up for even a single day."[22] That same year, ONI reported that Japanese policy was to maintain "a small compact squadron of vessels of the highest modern type," relying on British shipyards for protected cruisers, headlined by the Elswick-built *Naniwa*.[23] Chinese battleships visiting (or menacing) Japan in 1891 precipitated further investment.[24] In 1891, the Japanese minister of the Navy proposed doubling the IJN's tonnage, including the acquisition of two "armor-clads" built to out-class the *Dingyuan* and *Zhenyuan*.[25] Chilean officials had similar motivations in the 1870s, hoping the *Cochrane* and *Blanco Encalada* would eclipse the Peruvian *Huáscar* and *Independencia*. In the years before the Sino-Japanese War, Japanese schoolchildren played the "Sink the *Dingyuan* and *Zhenyuan* Game," aiming for the Beiyang Navy's center of gravity.[26] Comparatively, during the same period, Li Hongzhang complained that China "had not added even one ship," allowing the naval race with "that little country" to tighten into a quantitative dead heat (Figure 7.1).[27] Qualitatively, China's reliance on "relatively old style" weapons and foreign technical advice meant a shift was afoot.[28]

By the summer of 1894, as Chinese officials watched Japan "stir up trouble in Korea," the theoretical efficacy of the Qing and Meiji navies faced a concrete test.[29] As they had in other naval races in the Pacific, officials balanced imponderable questions of tonnage, technological change, and civilizational character as they attempted to forecast the impending war's outcome.[30] The author of the best English-language history of the war, S. C. M. Paine (and others), argue that in the run-up to the Sino-Japanese War foreign observers continued to see China as the stronger

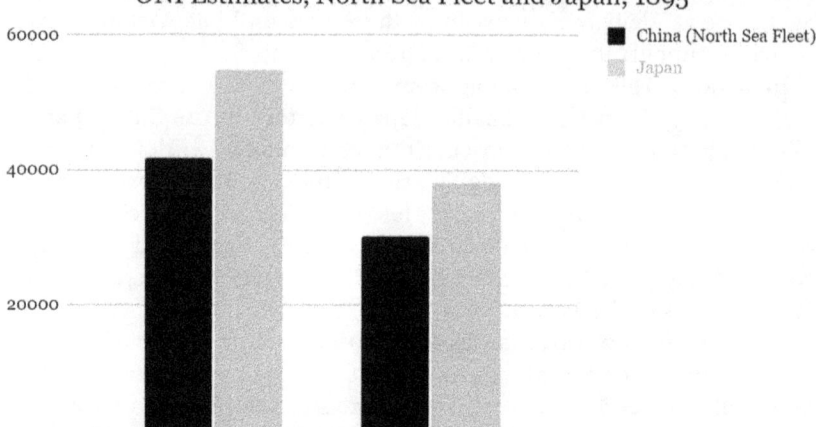

Figure 7.1 ONI data comparing Qing and Japanese naval power (1895)

of the two empires.[31] In fact, ambivalence was widespread.[32] In 1894, just weeks before the Battle of the Yalu, one British diplomat reported, "notwithstanding the greater figures of the Chinese tonnage and guns the Japanese organization, discipline, and training are so superior that Japan may reasonably be considered the stronger Power on the sea."[33] Li Hongzhang, for his part, believed that Chinese success against Japan and its small but efficient newly made navy was "extremely doubtful."[34] Further afield, similar anxiety about Japanese naval power afflicted USN officers as they confronted the technical sophistication and cultural meaning of IJN steel cruisers in Hawaii. As the Sino-Japanese naval race reached its climax, another waited in the wings.

7.2 US and Japanese "*Esmeraldas*" in Hawaii

US New Navy officers had their own lens onto the western Pacific naval race, via Japanese deployments to Hawaii. Even as it shifted the frontiers of US imperialism, the US overthrow of Queen Liliʻuokalani prompted reciprocal questions about what the historian Hilary Conroy called the "Japanese frontier in Hawaii."[35] In the same way that US intervention in Panama in 1885 stirred worries in Chile about the rise of American power in the Pacific, so too were the 1893 US landings a threat to Japanese priorities.[36] The safety and political rights of Japanese laborers in the wake of the coup became an immediate point of contention with

7.2 US and Japanese "*Esmeraldas*" in Hawaii

the United States.[37] Just as Chinese immigration to California in the 1880s had military implications, so too was the status of Japanese immigrants in Hawaii integrally tied to Japan's maturing naval capabilities; not for nothing did ONI keep tabs on Japanese demographics in Hawaii.[38] California, the maritime frontier of US expansion in the 1880s, seemed menaced by Chilean sea power and Chinese migrants. As the US frontier expanded to Hawaii in the 1890s, another technologically sophisticated, racially alien newly made navy appeared on the horizon.

Japanese cruiser diplomacy in Hawaii brought home this inter-imperial friction in hard-power terms. In 1893, Tokyo responded to the USS *Boston* in kind, dispatching the IJN cruiser *Naniwa* to Honolulu under the command of Tōgō Heihachirō (later the architect of Japanese victory in the Russo-Japanese War). Chilean leaders did much the same in 1885 with *Esmeralda* – a literal forerunner of *Naniwa* – in Panama.[39] In Hawaii, *Naniwa*'s arrival sparked "fevered excitement" and "Rumors of War," mixing worries about Japanese warships with the latent threat of Japanese immigration.[40] "The story goes," the *Daily Pacific Commercial Advertiser* recorded, that Tōgō intended to arm resident Japanese, precipitate an insurrection, and ultimately "hoist the Mikado's flag over this country."[41] The *Hawaiian Star* carried news that Japan might cooperate with the deposed Lili'uokalani' and that *Naniwa*'s commander had "declared his ability and hinted his inclination, to blow the United States vessels out of water."[42] Tōgō's instructions were more modest, but apprehensions about "Japanese ambitions as to the future control of the islands" lingered.[43] All the while, residents in Waikiki could hear *Naniwa* conducting gun practice at sea.[44]

Often dismissed as self-serving "exaggerated vulnerabilities," fears expressed by the *Daily Pacific Commercial Advertiser* – like those aired about Chile in the 1880s – were grounded in the self-evident parity of the US New Navy and IJN assets in the Pacific.[45] In the same way US constructors and commanders sincerely envied the technical capabilities of the Chilean *Esmeralda* in the 1880s, *Naniwa* represented a symmetrical threat to US warships deployed to Hawaii.[46] In fact, *Naniwa* was an Elswick-built "enlarged and perfected" version of the Chilean *Esmeralda* and a near mirror of USS *Charleston*. US officials sheepishly admitted that USS *Charleston* was built on the same set of plans as the *Naniwa*.[47] And like its Chilean forerunner, the proliferation of what ONI called "improved *Esmeraldas*" to Japan raised questions about the relative power of the United States and the security of its expanding oceanic frontier.[48] The March 1894 arrival of *Naniwa*'s sistership IJN *Takachiho* in Honolulu reinforced (literally and figuratively) perceptions of "Maritime Japan" as a near-peer competitor to US capabilities.[49]

Racing against Qing China, the newly made IJN began to take up a position as a pacing threat for the US New Navy in the Pacific. One transwar result was that much of the rhetoric used for Chile was repurposed in US navalist discourse in an effort to understand Japan.

None of this was lost on William Sims, the future leader of USN forces in Europe during World War I and (rivaling Mahan) one of the main intellectual architects of US maritime power in the twentieth century.[50] In 1894, he arrived in Honolulu as a junior officer on the New Navy cruiser USS *Philadelphia* (1890) to find both IJN *Naniwa* and IJN *Takachiho* at anchor and the political unrest in Hawaii "boiling away merrily."[51] Technical parity between the US and Japanese vessels was obvious to Sims. He recognized the IJN ships as both "quite as powerful as we are," and common derivatives of the onetime Chilean "wonder" *Esmeralda*.[52] With technical parity came shifts in cultural attitudes – and anxieties. Months ahead of the Sino-Japanese War, what Paine called a "revolution in perceptions" was already well underway in Hawaii.[53] Naval power – standing in as it so often did as a marker of civilizational attainment – encouraged the social acceptance of Japanese officers by their Anglophone counterparts in Hawaii. In 1894, military detachments from USS *Adams* and USS *Philadelphia* as well as HMS *Champion* participated in the funeral of a Japanese midshipman from IJN *Takachiho*. USN bluejackets paraded through the streets of Honolulu alongside British and Japanese sailors, looking to all the world as peer members of an "imperialists' club."[54] That same spring, as tensions over the islands ebbed, Sims attended "the great social event of the season" onboard the IJN *Takachiho*, a reception he later remembered "as the most beautifully gotten up affair that I ever saw."[55] In a private letter to family he wrote: "[The *Takachiho*] was covered with vines and flowers made of papers by the sailors ... In odd corners were all sorts of gin cracks, a glass jar containing fish and having an electric light in the center ... a large paper lantern with moving panorama of shadows, representations of the vessels of the fleet, etc, etc."[56] The *Hawaiian Gazette* was just as effusive about this orientalist fantasy of Japanese gunboat imperialism.[57] The IJN may have missed the contemporaneous New York Naval Review, but it nonetheless made a substantial impression on Sims as it pledged the fraternity of "civilized" empires in Hawaii.

Of course, as with the Chilean Navy a decade earlier, there were caveats. Neither technical parity with the USN nor Japanese stagecraft could shake Sims' ethnic chauvinism about the "little Japs." *Materiel* aside, his chief impression of the Japanese crew was that they "were not really in 'it,'" even if they did see "that everyone was well supplied and played host to perfection while the Caucasians danced."[58] The Japanese were good for origami and drinks – and even as classmates at the United States Naval Academy – but war?[59] Sims' skepticism spoke for many, reproducing in miniature an assumed hierarchy of civilizations which would (imminently) be challenged by Japan's military operations in the western Pacific. IJN *Takachiho* left Honolulu just weeks after that florid reception en route to its part in the Sino-Japanese War.[60] Sims soon followed onboard USS *Charleston*, tasked with observing the capabilities of Japanese and Qing hardware in person. Like the rest of the Pacific World, he was in for a shock.[61]

7.3 Testing the East Asian Naval Race (1894–1895)

Fought ostensibly over the status of Korea, the naval phase of the Sino-Japanese War began in earnest in the summer of 1894.[62] On July 25, 1894, IJN *Naniwa* – still under the command of Tōgō Heihachirō – torpedoed and shelled the British-operated Qing troopship *Gaosheng*, sinking the vessel and killing nearly a thousand Chinese soldiers.[63] The torpedo missed but nonetheless (like a proto-*Lusitania*) inspired lurid reports about the weapon's "earth-shaking explosion" and the "unimaginable brutality of the Japanese in launching a torpedo against a defenseless merchant-vessel."[64] Lawyers and diplomats exchanged notes, but it was clear, one British diplomat noted, that matters would invariably be settled by the "arbitrament of arms."[65]

The operational details are fascinating, but for purposes here it is sufficient to say the Sino-Japanese War at sea was decided by a pair of decisive Japanese naval victories: the Battle of the Yalu (September 17, 1894) and the subsequent Japanese amphibious assault on Weihaiwei (January–February 1895).[66] At the Yalu, a half-dozen lead-colored Japanese cruisers attacked in a sweeping arc, sinking or disabling five of the twelve Beiyang Navy ships they engaged.[67] The battleships *Dingyuan* and *Zhenyuan* escaped but only after enduring a volume of shellfire that staggered observers.[68] Recently designed "quick-firing guns" aboard cruisers such as IJN *Yoshino* (the latest iteration of *Esmeralda* concept) devastated the unprotected superstructure of the Chinese ironclads, leaving, as one military observer wrote to Theodore Roosevelt, "everything above the waterline in unprotected parts riddled with shells and splinters."[69] The lightly armored Beiyang cruisers were considerably less resilient against the "heavy and continuous" Japanese fire.[70] Japan's Armstrong-built cruisers proved better armed, "more modern, larger and speedier" than their Chinese counterparts – even those constructed at the same Newcastle shipyard.[71] Li Hongzhang had foreseen the possibilities of quick-firing guns in 1894 but his last-minute attempts to acquire the weapons came too late for the Beiyang Navy.[72] Novel technologies, employed with tactical skill, confounded a decade's worth of assessments. Like the Battle of Angamos during the War of the Pacific (1879), the Yalu reduced the Beiyang Navy to a handful of seaworthy vessels and left the IJN, British naval officers noted, "practically in full command of the sea."[73]

Sea control in hand, Japanese commanders next turned to the substantial task of reducing Qing coastal defenses and eliminating the Chinese "fleet-in-being": the credible threat represented by the surviving Beiyang warships. The remnants of the Beiyang Navy retreated to bases in the Bohai Gulf, sheltering behind coastal defenses hardened since the 1870s.[74] The *North China Herald* contended that although the Beiyang Navy was "weakened" by its defeat at the Yalu, it would still "take a great deal of beating."[75] Port Arthur – what Sims called "the Gibraltar of the North" – sprouted fortifications and obstacles which rendered it, the ranking British officer on the China Station noted, "absolutely safe from shellfire and torpedo attack."[76] By the winter of 1894, the "impregnable" Weihaiwei appeared still better defended.[77] Such assessments followed a tradition of overestimating Qing military power. Port Arthur fell in November of 1894 to an overland invasion under the command of Ōyama Iwao. The subsequent capture of Weihaiwei two months later left little to doubt about the IJN's mastery of the maritime domain, and with it the practice of modern naval and littoral warfare.

While the Yalu dominated (and continues to dominate) discussions of the war, the Japanese capture of Weihaiwei was in many ways more significant in transwar perspective.[78] It was at Weihaiwei – in still another of the Pacific's firsts – that a series of "terribly efficient" nocturnal torpedo attacks first achieved a tactical success over a conventional fleet – a Caldera (1891) at several times the scale.[79] As early as October 1894, Japanese forces explored a torpedo attack on Weihaiwei and "confidently expected that the attack of the torpedo boats would be successful and that the Chinese men-of-war, being totally unprepared, would be destroyed."[80] After repeated nights of reconnaissance, on February 5 and 6, Japanese torpedo boats skirted Chinese obstacles and launched coordinated attacks that functionally destroyed the Beiyang Navy.[81] In a spectacular reversal, the weapons in which Li Hongzhang had placed such faith for twenty years as a means of defense actually delivered the coup de grace to the Beiyang Fleet. The battleship *Dingyuan* was torpedoed and then scuttled, leaving a colossal wreck of "shattered wood and twisted iron" in the harbor.[82] Japanese torpedo boats sunk or wrecked three other ICN warships as well. Days later – while the vernacular newspaper *Shenbao* still feebly celebrated accounts of Qing

7.3 Testing the East Asian Naval Race (1894–1895)

resistance to the "crafty Japanese" – fleeing ICN torpedo boats were pursued and destroyed by the Japanese fleet.[83] Worse still, the IJN captured (as did Chile the Peruvian *Huáscar*) the remaining Qing battleship *Zhenyuan* intact. The Qing official Zhang Zhidong reported laconically, "Weihai[wei] has fallen and the Beiyang ships have been completely lost."[84] Weihaiwei, what Xue Fucheng had hoped would be the Beiyang Navy's "primary base," was in practice the site of its unraveling.[85] The Chinese officer in charge, Admiral Ding, committed suicide.

In terms of technical development, the war was a tantalizing display of modern naval weapons. Not just of ships and armor, but of what one US adviser to the Qing called the "dark horse of modern naval warfare: the dreaded and much discussed torpedo."[86] The conflict began with an attempt by IJN *Naniwa* to torpedo the *Gaosheng* in the summer 1894 and ended with a flurry of offensive torpedo boat attacks against the Chinese fleet at Weihaiwei in the winter of 1895. A decade earlier, British naval intelligence noted that Japan had recognized the "value and importance of torpedoes" and built a depot that "bids fair to rival many European torpedo establishments."[87] Those investments paid off decisively at Weihaiwei, building on decades of experience in the Pacific's wars.

The Qing too, as a coda, made still more ambitious if inchoate progress toward modern war in a manner reminiscent of Peruvian experiments after Angamos. Just as the loss of the *Huáscar* encouraged experiments with torpedoes and improvised explosive devices, defeat at the Yalu and Weihaiwei spurred the Qing toward asymmetric weapons and other *outré* technologies. Imitation (and a begrudging admiration) of the Japanese torpedo boat's ability to "achieve victory over the great ironclads" was one manifestation of that trend.[88] "If we wish to be saved from today's emergency," Li Mingyu advocated, "nothing would be better than to order the manufacturing centers to stop production and specialize in torpedoes with all their energies."[89] Scheliha's theories on coastal defense seemed newly relevant – and indeed are a striking echo of language about Taiwan's need in the 2020s to shift away from symmetrical competition with "prestige" weapons such as fighter jets to an asymmetric strategy using "a great quantity of mobile, distributable, accurate, and lethal little things."[90] More striking, and again echoing the War of the Pacific, was Qing interest in prototypes sold by experts and mercenaries. One US engineer, John Wilde, secured qualified support from Qing diplomats to "asphyxiate" the Japanese fleet with poison gasses – the same offer he made the Brazilian army a year earlier during Brazil's Naval Revolt. It was an "awful scheme," the *New York Times* judged, and an unhappy harbinger of chemical weapons used during World War I.[91] It also reflected an enduring logic of naval racing in the Pacific: an attempt to gamble on new technologies as a means of overcoming power asymmetries. Following in the steps of fellow American inventors such as John Lay in Peru (c. 1880), Wilde and his Qing backers pointed toward the future of modern war. Defeat, as was the case in the Confederacy and Peru, spurred the Qing to transnational innovation.

7.4 The Curious Case of the *Esmeralda*/*Izumi* (1894–1895)

The Sino-Japanese War – like all the Pacific's wars before it – was a regional one with a great number of international articulations. There were links to western Europe, Russia, and the United States, certainly, but also underappreciated transnational connections to Chile. That is to say, in addition to the comparative similarities between the War of the Pacific and the Sino-Japanese War that were obvious to contemporary US observers (a regional naval race leading to naval war in which a more capable but less populous state achieved victory), there were also transoceanic links between the newly made navies. As with the proliferation of Confederate tactics and *materiel* in the Pacific after 1865, structural similarities between Japan and Chile encouraged transnational connections.

Most notable by far was the Japanese acquisition of the ex-Chilean *Esmeralda*: the very same ship that had provoked anxiety and racing on the Pacific slope since 1885. On February 5, 1895, as Japanese torpedo boats began their assault on Weihaiwei, the Chilean cruiser *Esmeralda* steamed into Yokosuka Harbor under the command of the "noted" Chilean officer Emilio Garin and a handful of cadets from the Chilean Naval Academy.[92] Officials wasted little time in recommissioning the vessel as IJN *Izumi*.[93] How the forerunner of the IJN *Naniwa*, ICN *Zhiyuan*, and USS *Charleston* (all of which were contemporaneously active in the western Pacific) wended its way from Newcastle, to Valparaiso, to Yokosuka spoke to the far-ranging proliferation of industrial naval technologies in the Pacific at the *fin-de-siècle*. It was the CSS *Stonewall*/*Kōtetsu* of its generation. For US navalists, the ship's path also provided an explicit symbol of shifting threat perceptions from Chile to Japan.

Tokyo's interest in *Esmeralda* (and Chilean cruisers generally) dated to the 1880s but found a fresh impetus in 1894 as neutrality concerns interrupted supply chains and weapons contracts.[94] After the Japanese cruiser/gunboat *Tatsuta* was detained en route to the Pacific by British authorities in Aden, officials in Tokyo (and to an extent Beijing) looked abroad for weapons and private agents who could supply them.[95] The New York-based Charles Flint seemed like an eligible candidate, given his morally dubious history selling arms in the Pacific and the Americas.[96] In 1894, Flint brokered a deal between Japanese and Chilean diplomats

7.4 The Curious Case of the *Esmeralda/Izumi*

Figure 7.2 *Esmeralda, Diario de la Unión* (1894)

to purchase the cruiser *Esmeralda* – a ship he still advertised as "one of the best" in the world.[97] He proposed to skirt the neutrality concerns which had stymied the *Tatsuta*'s sale by using the Ecuadorian government (or at least a handful of its representatives) as an intermediary. Ecuador would "purchase" the *Esmeralda* and then sell it to Japan, changing flags in the titular sovereign Republic of Hawaii (Figure 7.2).[98] Chile would thus avoid connections with a belligerent state. The money moved through a dizzying chain of custody via banks in New York, London, and Paris, further obscuring matters.[99]

The ruse was a technical success, even if it failed to deceive interested parties for very long.[100] Shortly after *Esmeralda* arrived in Yokosuka, deadly protests broke out in Ecuador over the so-called sale of the flag.[101] Crowds in Guayaquil hoisted a Japanese flag over the mansion of the provincial governor – one of several alleged conspirators in the plot against Ecuador's "national honor."[102] Not long after, revolutionaries toppled the government of President Luis Cordero, using his complicity in the "impudent sale of the *Esmeralda*" as a pretextual justification.[103]

Across the Pacific, the *Esmeralda*'s sale came as a sharp disappointment to Li Hongzhang.[104] After the Yalu, Li expressed interest in the *Esmeralda* as one of seven "first-class" warships in Chile that could be purchased and instantly "transformed into a fleet," replacing the one lost to the Japanese.[105] In the 1880s, the *Esmeralda* had served as a barometer (as in the US) of the capabilities of Qing cruisers such as the Elswick-built *Zhiyuan* and the *Jingyuan*.[106] After Weihaiwei, reports in *Shenbao* sounded optimistic notes about the purchase of "several ironclad warships" from Chile, at least one of which (*Esmeralda*) was a known quantity.[107] In the same way Mallory and his Confederate agents in Europe, or Flint in Brazil, hoped to extemporize a fleet by buying it overseas, so too did the acquisition of Chile's warships offer the possibility of immediate resistance. How aggravating it must have been that, in the end, Japanese officials beat Li to the punch. *Shenbao* protested caustically, but to little effect, that "in violation of precedent" Japan had sent officials to Chile "to secretly purchase ships and weapons."[108] If Flint was troubled by any of this it did not show. In 1904, he attempted to sell the Chilean battleship *Capitan Prat* (the same warship Mahan and Roosevelt discussed as a threat during the *Baltimore* Crisis) to Korea.[109]

More immediately, fallout from the sale of the *Esmeralda* reached the United States, where the ship doubled as a warning about Japanese interests in the Pacific. As the *Esmeralda* coaled in Honolulu en route Japan, Henry Cabot Lodge took to the floor of the US Senate to warn his colleagues that "the *Esmeralda* [is in Hawaii] representing Japan," and threatening to whip up the "dangerous" Japanese population.[110] Supported by what he called the "Japanese cruiser *Esmeralda*," it was easy for Lodge to imagine "an uprising" of Japanese migrants against the white planters; a direct echo of fears in 1894 about IJN *Naniwa*.[111] Long conjured as a symbol of the Chilean threat against California, in 1895 the ship was transmuted into a harbinger of a rising Japanese peril.[112] Weeks later, the *New York Times* wondered about the "possibility of a compact between Chile, Ecuador, and Japan" balancing against US expansion in the Pacific.[113] It was a concern with some precedent. In December 1883, the IJN *Ryūjō* had traveled to Valparaiso on a "voyage of instruction"; the first of its kind to South America by a Japanese warship and one rewarded by an audience with the Chilean president.[114] Reports of a Japanese–Chilean alliance at the time had been treated as "a mere freak of some wild imagination," but the *Esmeralda* fueled speculation about a nexus between Chilean decline and the novel threat of "Maritime Japan."[115] It was a moment of transition and one with which US navalists now openly wrestled.

7.5 The Sino-Japanese War, the United States, and the Pacific

The Sino-Japanese War has long figured as an inflection point in the history of the western Pacific. For many, it marked Qing "failure" and Meiji "success" in military modernization. For others it was a step on

7.5 The Sino-Japanese War, the US, and the Pacific

the road to *the* "Pacific War" (1931–1945 or 1937–1945 or 1941–1945, depending on your politics).[116] At the time, and as importantly, Japanese performance upended regional perceptions. S. C. M. Paine's standard-setting *The Sino-Japanese War*, for example, noted that the conflict "shattered Chinese hegemony and demonstrated to an astonished West that Japan had become a modern great power."[117] In doing so, Paine continued, Japan proved "that industrialization was not the cultural monopoly of the West" – a theme that should have already been in doubt given precedents in earlier Pacific wars.[118]

What influence the war had on US and inter-American security politics is comparatively nebulous. The first history of the US and the "Pigtail War" concluded that the Sino-Japanese War was only "a minor incident in the late [US] nineteenth-century diplomacy and politics."[119] That interpretation has good company in standard surveys of US foreign relations, emphasizing (most often) insurgency in Cuba, the Venezuelan Crisis, and the eventual War of 1898 as the prime US security challenges in the 1890s.[120] Bilateral histories of US–Japanese relations likewise tend to subordinate the Sino-Japanese War as a waypoint to the Russo-Japanese War (1904–1905) and War Plan Orange (preparations for a general war with Japan began in the early 1900s).[121] Only narrowly focused works, such as those by Akira Iriye and William Morgan, develop links between what Iriye called the "Japanese variable" (if not always the Sino-Japanese War) and US military policy in the 1890s.[122]

That said, by concentrating on US–Japanese relations even a historian as subtle as Akira Iriye marginalized the war's articulations with other relevant states and empires in the Pacific – in this case Chile and China.[123] Opening a transwar aperture reveals that tensions between the United States and Japan were not sui generis but rather mirrored and at times concretely linked to earlier conflicts with Pacific newly made navies in the 1880 and 1890s. Iriye noted that the US–Japanese "Estrangement" was characterized by "racial antagonism, jingoism, struggle for influence and power away from the home-base [i.e., Honshu and the continental United States, respectively]."[124] The same could be said about the antecedent conflict between the US and Chile; nineteenth-century US navalists were quick to make the comparison.

The threat of Japan, like that of the Chilean newly made navy before it, hinged on more than tonnage and guns. Japan after 1895 presented a multifaceted set of concerns that can be ordered into three interrelated components: (1) a hard-power, racially alien threat to the territorial infrastructure of the US New Empire (above all Hawaii); (2) a crisis of confidence about what Japan's naval power suggested about civilizational hierarchy in the Pacific; and finally (3) a political campaign emphasizing Hawaii's vulnerability.[125] If California was, in effect, an overseas territory in the 1870s, Hawaii was quite literally one. Japanese success in the Sino-Japanese War, much like Chilean victory in the War of the Pacific, created a new maritime power contending for influence, shaping US threat perceptions along the way.

Those parallels – so apparent at the time – have escaped historical scrutiny chiefly because of bureaucratic and historiographical boundaries which truncate the Pacific into Latin America, North America, East Asia, and Oceania. In the 1880s and 1890s, such divisions were not necessarily meaningful or even evident as trade routes, steamships, and telegraph lines knit a web across the ocean, forming what Mahan called a global "articulated system."[126] For example, in 1882, George Balch, the commander of the US Pacific Squadron, politely declined invitations to visit Tokyo, explaining to surprised Japanese diplomats in Washington that "the limits of the Pacific Station do not include Japan."[127] It was a division still less familiar to the Japanese fisherman Balch rescued off the Chilean coast later that year.[128] Chilean officials playing host to the first Japanese warship to visit the Americas in 1883–1884 experienced the Pacific as an equally Braudelian space.[129] Unlike military/academic divisions, it was only natural to see the ocean as a whole and to connect the competition with Chile in the 1880s to the one with Japan in the 1890s.

At their root, US attitudes about Japan were shaped by the IJN's performance in 1894–1895. Victory by Japan's newly made navy solidified its position as what one congressman called a "new first-class power in the world and upon the Pacific."[130] In the US Senate, Henry Cabot Lodge described Japan as both "a great rising naval power" and a "great fighting race at sea."[131] Another senator warned that the "new Empire of Japan" would pursue the "domination or attempted domination of whatever may be brought within their reach."[132] Having "just whipped somebody," Lodge agreed, the Japanese "think they can whip anybody."[133] In China, Li Hongzhang and the British editors at *Shenbao* offered similar assessments.[134] So too did firsthand US military observers such as Daniel Mannix, William Sims, and Philo McGiffin – the latter no doubt embittered by the physical trauma he suffered from Japanese shellfire.[135] In 1895, recalling when "Chile had a stronger naval power upon the Pacific coast than we had," Senator Anthony O'Higgins stressed "the Warning of Wei-Hai-Wei": namely that the Japanese would combine material technology with racial vitality to threaten the "white world."[136] "Occidental methods in Oriental hands," as the *North China Herald* put it in 1894, apparently unironically paraphrasing the strategy prescribed by Wei Yuan two generations earlier (师夷长技以制夷).[137] Japan seemed to have a newly made navy, with aspirations for a "new Empire" to match it.

7.5 The Sino-Japanese War, the US, and the Pacific

Subsequent acquisitions of advanced naval technologies – notably oceangoing battleships and torpedo boats – made matters worse. In 1896 – the same year Mahan's *The Influence of Sea Power upon History* appeared in Japanese – Armstrong launched the battleship *Yashima* in Newcastle, elevating the IJN to what the historians Evans and Peattie called "a strategic status."[138] Supporting that shift, the Japanese Diet passed a "Ten Year Naval Expansion Program" providing for additional battleships, cruisers, and the infrastructure to support them.[139] Contemporaneously, British Intelligence products began listing Japan alongside the United States and "The Principal European Countries," documenting its ascension into the ranks of the Great Powers – rather literally.[140] Writing in 1897, J. D. Kelley estimated that Japan's program of naval acquisitions had launched it from sixteenth position to eighth and that it would soon surpass Spain, coming "very close to the United States and Germany."[141] After traveling back to the United States, the American McGiffin told a hometown audience the Japanese had gotten a "'swelled head,' a swelling which only can be reduced by a good thrashing, received by some other power."[142] He did not say if he believed the New Navy was up to the task.

As in the case of Chile in the 1880s, Japan's naval capabilities illustrated the relative weakness of US naval power in the Pacific. In 1895, Li Hongzhang (allegedly) warned a US translator in Beijing that Japan could send "[h]er ships from [China's] harbors over to your country and would have taken possession of your Pacific states ... She has a larger and better fleet of warships than the United States. She has ten times as many torpedo boats as your government and her sailors know how to use them, while your sailors do not."[143] On the front lines, Sims had a similar impression. He left the Sino-Japanese War firm in his conviction that for the moment the acquisition of territories in the western Pacific would be "a real misfortune" for the US because "we could not possibly hold [them]."[144] Observing foreign fleets along the Chinese coast convinced him (as it did Mahan a decade earlier outside of Chilean-occupied Callao) that "as a military force our navy is not counted as it is not up to date in any way," even when compared to "a second or third-class power" (i.e., Japan).[145] That same year, Mahan complained that the New Navy was still "so small" that it was difficult to conduct realistic maneuvers, let alone an oceanic war.[146] By comparison, Japan, the US industrialist Charles Cramp warned in 1897, was now like a "cyclone in a smooth sea of common-place progress."[147] He stressed that, "in the race for naval supremacy in the Pacific, Japan is gaining, while Russia and the United States are losing ground."[148] In 1903, the IJN invited the surviving veterans of Perry's Black Ships to Tokyo. One, George

Balch, noted an astounding metamorphosis from "some pseudo-forts of dungaree cloth that might have done service in a theater" into a rival of the United States in the Pacific.[149] The sense of confidence US navalists won after the *Baltimore* Crisis in 1892 gave way to a familiar anxiety about falling behind a newly made Pacific navy almost instantly.

The relative parity of Japan's newly made navy and the US New Navy c. 1895 was real enough, but in an age of peak "race patriotism" the erosion of the North Atlantic's monopoly on industrial power set off deeper anxieties in the United States.[150] Japan's apparent position as what Henry Cabot Lodge called a "great fighting race at sea" was an old worry about Chile made fresh.[151] The war may have transformed Japan into what S. C. M. Paine called "the only non-western Great Power," but it would be too much to suggest that Japan became an outpost of European civilization (a la the United States or the British dominions).[152] When US travelogues described the Japanese as the "Yankees of the East" it was not – as Walter LaFeber too sympathetically argued – the "ultimate compliment" but rather an expression of ambivalence about how to sort Japan as an empire among empires.[153] Recall the enduring racial otherness of Chile, despite honorifics such as "Prussians of the Pacific" and "Yankees of South America."[154]

Japan's otherness comes through in the war reporting. For every plaudit about the "dash, nerve and coolness" of the IJN came countervailing examples of Japanese barbarity.[155] Foreign depictions of the Japanese "slaughter of Chinese soldiers at Port Arthur" illustrate the point.[156] Real crimes committed by Japanese troops storming the city took on new meaning as observers wrestled with Japan's place in the community of nations. Sims recoiled at reports from Port Arthur, scoffing that the Japanese "seem to have forgotten what they have read in the European military books and returned to their customary manner of making war." Japan's superficial gloss of civilization obscured a more basic otherness which, Sims noted, was "quite impossible for tall Anglo-Saxons to mistake."[157] In a similar vein, a US mercenary serving in the Qing Navy recorded the Japanese Army's "diabolical orgy of murder and mutilation, rape, lust, and rapine," at Port Arthur in melodramatic detail.[158] Those same atrocities left US congressmen to debate whether to consider Japan "civilized or barbarous."[159] The stakes were considerable. In 1896, Mahan warned a British colleague about "outside barbarians" who would "readily assimilate our material advances" without the tempering virtues of Christian (which is to say white) civilization.[160] Months after the sack of Port Arthur, Mahan's target was obvious enough. The satirical magazine *Punch* waxed poetic, writing that the Japanese would blend the "wild savagery of Vandals, Goths or Huns" with "the Scientific

7.5 The Sino-Japanese War, the US, and the Pacific 169

slaughter of the Blood-and-Iron Teuton."[161] The "little Japs" like "little Chili" took on a new standing as a result of their naval victories, but a pervasive sense of racial condescension remained.

The proliferation of industrial power to this culturally alien "new Empire of Japan" prompted hand wringing in the US naval bureaucracy, not least about the strategic similarities between the United States and the Qing Empire.[162] US continental power might win-out in the end, the consensus held, but the Sino-Japanese War emphasized the threat of "the sudden, sharp, and short warfare of modern times."[163] Writing in 1894, Secretary of the Navy Hilary Herbert noted that "one of the most impressive lessons in all history" was taught by the Sino-Japanese War: China had "relied upon its numbers" and was now victim to "the assaults of a nation vastly its inferior in numbers," but which was technically more sophisticated.[164] Echoing Herbert a year later, William McAdoo, the assistant Secretary of the Navy and former chair of the House Naval Affairs Committee, wrote that the Sino-Japanese War proved "that mere territory and vastness of numbers are not of themselves a national defense."[165] He redoubled that argument in 1896.[166] Roosevelt, too, observed that the Qing collapse was an object lesson to continental empires "full of an ignorant self-confidence."[167] From the front lines of the war in Asia, Sims was more invested than most, writing to his parents that while US continental resources would eventually be decisive against Japan, that "knowledge would perhaps not bring sufficient conciliation to those who were keeping my New Grave while they were building a New Navy."[168] Deterministic tabulations of industrial power – this much iron and that much coal – fail to capture this sense of contingent foreboding which, incredibly enough, recast the United States in the mold of the Qing Empire. In much the same way the United States could lose out to Chile in a short war, so too was it vulnerable to Japan; Qing defeat proved as much.

Here then was yet another crisis of confidence in the Pacific, and one that once again highlighted the imperative of USN expansion. Like the menace of Tucker's ex-Confederates in Peru in the 1860s, or the ironclads of "little Chili" in the 1880s, after 1895 maritime Japan provided an opportunity for US navalists to advocate for resources in the Pacific. Most clearly, the war was an argument for increased battleship production – the avatar of navalist development – as a practical and symbolic answer to Japanese capabilities.[169] Sims wrote, a touch acerbically, that Japan's naval expansion would be a "boon for our navy," because "the jingoists will of course tear their hair and howl a dozen new ironclads."[170] Obligingly, Roosevelt was already a step ahead, arguing that the war's key lesson was that "the most powerful cruisers cannot successfully fight iron-clads."[171] In 1896, as *Yashima* left its dry-dock, Herbert (originally a skeptic) agreed about the "inefficiency of cruisers when operating against battleships."[172] In the spring of 1896, Roosevelt wrote to Lodge that groups resisting battleship expansion were "doing their best to bring this country down to the Chinese level" – an especially damning critique after 1894.[173] Worryingly, British observers at the Yalu explicitly compared Japanese cruisers to the existing cruisers of the US New Navy, "on a smaller scale."[174] As late as the spring of 1894, the *New York Times* had fawned over the Chilean battleship *Capitan Prat*, describing it (accurately) as "better than anything the United States has at Present" and a standard to which the New Navy should aspire.[175] By September of that same year, US navalists and their backers shifted perspective across the Pacific. The results of the Yalu provided a still better argument for continued naval expansion.[176] The war, Herbert concluded, showed that if nothing else "we certainly need more battleships."[177] Almost as soon as one Pacific naval race closed, another opened.

The Japanese threat stood larger still because of a coincident shift in US perceptions of Great Britain. While a popular and reflexive Anglophobia was common in the United States, late nineteenth-century naval officers and their political allies were disproportionately Anglophilic.[178] The "Great Rapprochement" underway after 1890 anticipated closer relations between the US and Britain; some prominent US navalists in both countries even proposed a "Naval Union with Great Britain."[179] In 1892 Mahan wrote to the British Secretary of Colonial Defence Committee that he would like to see Anglo–US policy "conjoined" and reflect the fact that the two nations were "kin" by blood and "the rest alien."[180] Naturally, as the threat of confrontation with Great Britain decreased, the capabilities of the IJN grew in relative importance. In 1893, ONI had framed Britain as the leading threat to Hawaii.[181] By 1897, it was clear to Mahan, as he wrote to a friend in the UK, that "in the Pacific [the United States and Britain] are natural allies."[182] "Blood is thicker than water," announced the commander of USS *Philadelphia* that same year, while hosting a joint reception with HMS *Penguin* in Honolulu.[183]

Alongside this Anglophilia, the recent history of US competition with "little Chili" helped frame Japan as a potential transoceanic rival in the minds of Mahan, Roosevelt, and others. Earlier conflict with Chile sensitized US navalists to the possibilities of a challenge from a Pacific power, laying the mental groundwork to understand Japan. After the *Baltimore* Crisis (1891–1892) and Sino-Japanese War (1894–1895), US threat perceptions shifted from a north–south axis, along the Pacific slope, to a transpacific, east–west one that endures today (graduating from Japan to the Soviet Union to the PRC, all while assuming US hegemony in the

Americas). In 1897, Mahan acknowledged to Roosevelt that, "of course Japan is a small and a poor state as compared to ourselves." But, then again, he continued, Chile was also small and there was a time "when the Chilians would have torn out their eyes for us."[184] Days later Mahan again wrote to Roosevelt reminding him of the "anxiety we all felt at the time of the Chili trouble over the progress of the *Prat*, we not then having any battleships." As Japan and the US sparred over Hawaii, he continued, "the same situation recurs; shall two Japanese battleships appear when we have but one and a monitor?"[185] It was a timely observation. Weeks later, Roosevelt, then the assistant Secretary of the Navy, repurposed Mahan's arguments about "our trouble with Chile" in an address to Naval War College students and faculty as he encouraged them to contemplate a war with Japan over the Hawaiian archipelago.[186]

7.6 A War Scare in Hawaii (1897)

As late as 1894, most US observers (Mahan included) saw Chinese immigration as a greater threat to Hawaii than the IJN.[187] After 1895, navalists and politicians increasingly argued that Japan's victory in the Sino-Japanese War and overseas populations made it not only a regional power but a threat to US interests in the Pacific. "They are our nearest neighbor on the Pacific," Lodge gravely intoned, "with Hawaii lying halfway between us."[188] By 1897, a US–Japanese conflict over the islands looked just as inevitable as the 1891 US–Chilean war-that-wasn't, entangling the proliferation of industrial weapons, race, and the collision of US and Japanese expansionism in a toxic stew. Mahan predicted "tears of blood" over the islands.[189]

Tensions came to a head in 1897 in what the *New York Times* called the "Japanese Scare in Hawaii" – in almost all respects a *Baltimore* Crisis redux.[190] As in 1893, the immediate crisis stemmed from concerns over the treatment of Japanese immigrants in Hawaii and with them what the Japanese Foreign Ministry called the "general *status quo* in the Pacific."[191] Flush with confidence from the Sino-Japanese War, the Meiji government responded to a growing US presence in the islands by dispatching the "big cruiser *Naniwa*" to Honolulu, where English-language papers were quick to point out the ship's ambivalent "history with the Hawaiian people."[192] Once there, the articulations of Japanese technical capabilities and racial antipathy seemed to endanger what Roosevelt called "the interests of the White race" in the Pacific.[193] US navalist leaders confronted the uncomfortable possibility, as one senator warned, that "the American navy is absolutely unfit to protect the islands."[194] Roosevelt cautioned President McKinley that while USS

Philadelphia – then deployed to Hawaii – was "just about the strength of the *Naniwa*," it had no torpedoes; a worrying deficiency given the experience at Weihaiwei.[195] In Japan, the vernacular press took "particular pride" in the deployment of the *Naniwa*, "owing to her work in the China–Japan War."[196] Unlike the USN, it had a record of achievement modern combat.

US officials responded to this hybrid threat with a flurry of paper and naval diplomacy. Cruisers and gunboats, headed by USS *Philadelphia*, sortied to Honolulu.[197] Roosevelt ordered strategists and legal experts at the US Naval War College to contemplate a military counteroffensive against the Japanese occupation of Honolulu.[198] Six years earlier, Mahan and others at ONI had wrestled with similar contingencies ahead of a possible naval action against Chile. More bellicose than the professionals, Roosevelt hoped to coerce the IJN by deploying USS *Baltimore* and USS *Charleston* ahead of the newly completed battleship USS *Oregon* to Hawaii where "she would be an overmatch for half the entire Japanese navy."[199] Toward that end, US coercive naval diplomacy against Chile in 1891 offered a positive model, one which Roosevelt explicitly referenced as a guide for engaging Japan.[200] The chief lesson of 1891, he argued to naval officers in 1897, was that "an unmanly desire to avoid a quarrel is often the surest way to precipitate one."[201] The US race with Chile in the 1880s became an imperfect heuristic for understanding the Pacific World and its latest newly made navy.

Fortunately, as with earlier US scares in the Pacific, diplomacy won out. What Akira Iriye called the "first serious crisis" between the United States and Japan ended just as bathetically as the US–Chilean crisis did in 1892. Diplomats eased tensions (or at least delayed them for a generation) and cooler heads prevailed.[202] With the possibility of war fading, the officers of the *Naniwa* astonished Hawaii's white ruling class with a shipboard reception reminiscent of *Takachiho*'s 1894 ball, complete with a garden of origami flowers.[203] In a cooperative spirit, launches from USS *Philadelphia* and USS *Adams* ferried attendees aboard, sensibly unwilling to let a war scare stand in the way of a good party.[204] A month later, USS *Philadelphia* officers responded with a party of their own which "compared favorably with the famous groupings on the Naniwa."[205] By October 1897, matters had abated to the point that Stephen Luce (founder of the Naval War College) could relish the idea of visiting Japan in his retirement, given "the courtesy and affability of the natives" and the "change brought about by that wonderful people in fifty years."[206]

It was a conflict forestalled, but not without consequence. US–Japanese tensions over Hawaii illustrated – certainly for Roosevelt and Mahan – the imperative of rebalancing US policy toward the Pacific. As of 1897, Mahan believed, "in Asia, not in Europe, is now the greatest danger to our proximate interest," urging Roosevelt to shift battleship construction to San Francisco and assign the Navy's "best admiral" to the Pacific Ocean.[207] Roosevelt agreed, responding, "if I had my way we would annex those islands tomorrow ... and in the meantime we should build a dozen new battleships, half of them on the Pacific Coast .... I am fully alive to the danger from Japan."[208] Ships moved accordingly. It was true that before the War of 1898 the USN maintained twenty ships on the North Atlantic Station and only eight in the Pacific. However, when combined with the Asiatic and South Atlantic Station (i.e., the ships needed to protect the sea lanes to the Pacific) that number climbs to nineteen, a rough equivalency with the North Atlantic core.[209] In fact, Roosevelt was so sensitive to the Japanese threat that on the eve of the War of 1898 he still believed that "Japan is a more dangerous opponent than Spain."[210] Perhaps he was right. Secretary of the Navy John Long worried that if things continued, by 1902 Japan would be "the strongest naval power in the Pacific Ocean."[211] Roosevelt concurred, writing privately in 1898 "that in the Pacific we are now inferior to Japan, and we shall continue to be inferior."[212] Responding to that sense of vulnerability (exaggerated or otherwise) became a theme of Roosevelt's presidency and the twentieth century more broadly. If, as a number of historians note, Roosevelt was the first president to see the "United States as both an Atlantic and a Pacific power," he did so as a result of the Sino-Japanese War and its Chilean antecedents.[213] More immediately, having shifted resources and emphasis to the Pacific, US forces were well-positioned to attack Manila in 1898. Decisive victory there confirmed both the rise of the United States into the ranks of the "Principal Maritime Nations" and its turn to overt imperialism in the Pacific.

7.7 From Valparaiso to Manila Bay via the "Pigtail War"

North Atlantic threats to the Caribbean Basin – notably crises in Cuba and Venezuela – loom large in the literature on US foreign relations in the 1890s, leading with almost magnetic force to the War of 1898 and the "Emergence of America as a Great Power."[214] Shifting perspective to the Pacific reveals that what was once dismissed as the "Pigtail War" (1894–1895) had underappreciated implications for US security policy; not unlike the "Ten Cents War" (1879–1884) before it.[215] Much as the War of the Pacific helped inspire a small, cruising navy capable of defending California from "Little Chili," the Sino-Japanese War made a compelling argument for battleships and insular annexations to resist "little" Japan and its threat to Hawaii. Those connections were not lost on US navalists who routinely used Chilean competition (which is to say their own prior experiences) as a transwar lens through which to understand Japanese intentions and capabilities.

Similar forces undergirded both periods. The proliferation of advanced military technologies to Pacific states (and emerging empires) was an enduring anxiety for New Navy leaders, even if the specific targets of that angst shifted – consider the *Esmeralda/Izumi* (1895) or the *Stonewall/Kōtetsu* (1867) as concrete examples. In a transwar context, threat perceptions of Japan were a culmination of earlier experiences. The inter-American (north–south) naval competition was a thematic and material antecedent of the US security conflict in the northern Pacific (east–west). In terms of US New Navy expansion, the Pacific's naval races had an almost fractal geometry. Victorious against Peru, Chile became a threat to the United States (1880–1892) just as Japan challenged the United States only after its victory against the Qing (1894–1895). In this transwar light, the Pacific, rather than the industrial North Atlantic, was the critical inspiration for and proving ground of modern US naval power.

Looking back from 1898 and Dewey's victory at Manila Bay, there was a fitting symmetry to it all. As early as 1866, the ex-Confederate John R. Tucker and his Peruvian colleagues had plotted to cross the Spanish Lake and attack Manila with an ironclad, torpedo-armed fleet. Thirty-two years later, having been shaped by the threat of self-strengthening navies in the Pacific for a generation, George Dewey – the quintessential "Admiral of the New Empire" – put a variation on Tucker's plan into action, sailing across the Pacific and defeating the Spanish force in the Philippines.[216] By doing so, he made good on a three decades of competition with Pacific states and empires, of which Spain was only the latest.

Conclusion

Sundown, liberty barges plod across Manila Bay. Seawater catches the city's neon lights, turning oil slicks iridescent. Dockside, bored-to-death-looking TGI Fridays and Hooters servers pass out coupons for discounted mozzarella sticks and beer. On the horizon, a US aircraft carrier dwarfs the cargo ships anchored nearby, its silhouette so vast the untrained eye wonders for a moment – wait, wait – is that a ship or an island? If today the global network of US military bases and deployments adds up to an empire, it's not one that seems very interested in hiding.[1] San Francisco's Dewey Monument (remember Theodore Roosevelt, Nike, and her trident of sea power?) is still standing in the center of Union Square, but it is here, and so many places like it, where you can find the real, living monument to the New Navy in the Pacific.

Victory at Manila Bay (1898) opened the way to formal empire in the western Pacific. It was a test of the US New Navy (as the Yalu was for the Japanese newly made one in 1894) that confirmed the bluewater fleet as the premier tool of US power projection. Dewey's success pointed toward Roosevelt's Great White Fleet (1907–1909), Woodrow Wilson's "Big Navy Act" (1916), and Ronald Reagan's (aspirational) 600-ships (1980).[2] All the while, assumptions underwriting US maritime power have survived; even after two world wars and the collapse of the Soviet Union. In an age of resurgent "strategic competition," the Mahanian Navy seems likely to endure well into the twenty-first century – if contemporary navalists and military contractors have their say.

How and why this global force came into being in the late nineteenth century is a historical and political question of some magnitude. Existing analyses focus on a cocktail of North Atlantic and domestic influences: US congressional politics, institutional advocacy, industrial development, and inter-imperial competition over the Caribbean Basin. That all stands to reason. Ships are big and naval historians, as one of the best has noted, disproportionately tend to study the big stuff that goes into them: armor, guns, propulsion, etc.[3] In the 1880s and 1890s there was nothing "bigger" than the industrial economies and maritime empires of the

North Atlantic. At the wave top level, these "great powers" appeared to shape US naval policy in one of two ways. Either the United States built a New Navy as preparation to conquer overseas colonies (imitating other North Atlantic powers) or else as a concentrated, battleship-led defense of the western hemisphere against European imperialists. For the purposes of this book, it is less important to adjudicate these two theses than to note that in both interpretations Europe and its dominant empires led the way for the United States. There is sound logic and voluminous evidence behind this regional emphasis. It is undeniable that domestic and intra-Atlantic factors weighed heavily on the minds of US navalists and their backers as they surveyed matters from Washington, Annapolis, New York, and Newport.

But, the United States has never been an exclusively Atlantic-facing nation. Adopting a new regional perspective creates a different set of causal relationships. Looking out from California onto the Pacific after 1865, US military officials, politicians, and merchants witnessed a nearly continuous series of sophisticated industrial wars, fought by Pacific states and empires. Taken together, it was a period of intense (if limited) transwar naval violence that has been too long obscured by the blinders of area studies containers or marginalized by teleologies about "failed" modernizations. At the time, the import of the Pacific's wars was manifestly obvious to USN officials given the relative weakness of "our little Navy."[4] A transwar perspective on the Pacific – one that escapes conventional geographic and temporal boundaries – demonstrates that the region (as a whole) was the site of tremendous activity in the latter half of the nineteenth century, just as the Civil War-era Navy demobilized. US policymakers were forced to react.

The influence of the Pacific's newly made navies can be divided into four categories: demand, testing, threat, and opportunity. First, *demand*. Beginning in the 1860s, the Pacific's wars and naval races generated demand for weapons and expertise in modern naval conflict; most often derived from CSN experiments during the US Civil War (1861–1865). Meiji officials commissioned the ex-Confederate ship *Stonewall* as the first armored combatant in the IJN. The commander of CSN forces at Charleston Harbor secured a position as a flag officer in Peru. Qing reformers adopted a manual on coastal defense written by an adviser to the CSA. It was a pattern for the coming decades as Pacific navy builders from Chile to China sought to capitalize on new technologies and tactics to compete with each other and the world's dominant maritime states.

Such demand was a commercial boon to firms and out-of-work veterans but, more importantly, funding from Pacific states also had the effect of encouraging North Atlantic innovation. Early prototypes of oceangoing battleships, automobile torpedoes, and protected cruisers all found eager and early buyers in the Pacific. Witness the Laird-built ironclad monitor *Huáscar* and Elswick's protected cruiser *Esmeralda* seen up close by USN officers out on patrol. Pacific navies also embraced smaller weapons, notably the automobile torpedo and associated delivery systems, providing feedback on early designs. Often only marginally industrialized states showed the greatest interest in advanced and experimental weapons. As with the Confederacy, a "dearth of defensive resources" drove Pacific "navies to construct" to gamble on technologies.[5] Rather than "failed" modernizers, these newly made navies were leading innovators. "Fail Early, Fail Often" is close to gospel in the modern Silicon Valley innovation "ecosystem." Failure in the Pacific was likewise very useful.

Second, *testing*. Reciprocally, for North Atlantic observers, the Pacific's wars provided an operational laboratory for novel technologies and tactics under the stress of war at sea. At engagements such as Pacocha (1877), Angamos (1879), Caldera (1891), and Weihaiwei (1895), Pacific navies set a host of precedents with some of the defining weapons of modern naval war (Table C.1).

Foreign technicians and intelligence officers mined those conflicts for data; an essential supplement to proving ground tests and "sham" wargames carried out in the North Atlantic.[6] Tellingly, many of the men

Table C.1 *Pacific naval battles and precedents set (1877–1895)*

Battle	Participants	Outcome	Notes
Pacocha (1877)	Peru/Britain	Tactical stalemate	First firing of an automobile torpedo in combat
Angamos (1879)	Chile/Peru	Chilean victory, establishment of sea control in the War of the Pacific	First engagement between modern armored warships
Caldera Bay (1891)	Chilean Political Factions	Tactical victory by government forces	First sinking of an armored warship by an automobile torpedo
Yalu (1894)	China/Japan	Japanese victory, establishment of sea control in the Sino-Japanese War	First fleet engagement between armored cruisers and battleships
Weihaiwei (1895)	China/Japan	Japanese victory, capture and/or destruction of the Beiyang Navy	First systematic use of torpedo boats and automobile torpedoes as an offensive weapon

who would make up the leadership of ONI during its formative years gleaned firsthand lessons from the Pacific about the utility of armor in battleships, the maturation of torpedoes, and the endurance of coal-powered ships. As it built from scratch in an era of technical flux, the "test of war" in the Pacific had considerable value to the US New Navy.[7] Results were debated and distorted through existing biases and institutional cultures – as lessons from foreign wars so often are – but the interest was intense.[8] All the better, it seemed, that such experience came at the expense in lives and resources of Pacific states.

Third, *threat*. Predictably, how well newly made navies used these weapons had a direct bearing on US threat perceptions. Victory or defeat in the Pacific's wars reshuffled indices of civilizational standing and military power. The rapid emergence of newly made industrial navies in Chile, China, and Japan contrasted with the "Old Navy" at the nadir of its post-Civil War demobilization. As early as 1866, a diverse group of US journalists, politicians, and naval officials began to voice anxieties about the distribution of power in the region. Ironically enough, something similar happened in Britain in 1864–1865, when the expansion of the USN's Civil War ironclad fleet motivated an "angry and afraid" British public to pressure the Admiralty for a symmetrical answer.[9] If peripheral threats could shape the behavior of even the world's most powerful navy, why not the United States as well? By the 1870s, US ambitions in California and Oregon exacerbated matters. US commercial and expansionist interests looked out from San Francisco onto a new frontier teeming with opportunities for trade and exchange. Naval officers, though, saw extended sea lines of communication around South America and an undefended coastline at the extreme edge of the North American continent. They had good reasons to be anxious. Until the late 1880s, the USN really *was* inferior to Pacific newly made navies in key measures. That such threats came from outside the North Atlantic's color-lines was all the more concerning in an age of peak Social Darwinism. Like the contemporaneous gendered anxieties explored by Kristin Hoganson, racially alien threats cut to the core of US pretensions about civilizational primacy in the Americas and the Pacific.[10] Little Japan shocked the consciousness of the continental Qing in 1874 much in the same way that small powers such as Chile and Japan provided a disproportionate impetus to US naval modernization.

Fourth, *opportunity*. USN officials and their political allies put this crisis of confidence to good use. Humiliated for a generation by unfavorable comparisons to Peruvian, Chilean, and Chinese warships, the navalist set did not intend to waste the moment. Localized parity or even technical inferiority to Pacific rivals became a rallying cry for investment.

Conclusion

It was especially shrill in the 1880s as New Navy advocates convinced a skeptical public about initial investments in steel cruisers. The historian Charles Schencking has documented the extraordinary lengths Japanese naval leaders went to in their efforts at "selling naval expansion" by massaging Japanese public opinion.[11] So too does "Selling Sea Power" have a long heritage in the United States.[12] Men such as Lodge, Roosevelt, and Mahan sharpened their arguments for funding by highlighting the dissonance between US economic power and the nation's lagging military capabilities relative to Pacific newly made navies. After the War of the Pacific, "even little Chili" filled this role (primarily) until the US *Flota Nueva* surpassed it; a shift made manifest by the New Navy's coercive diplomacy during the *Baltimore* Crisis (1891–1892).[13] Thereafter, naval advocates cast an ascendant Japan as the chief Pacific rival to US expansionist ambitions. It was a swift transition. The Sino-Japanese War transformed Japan (and as importantly perceptions of it) into what Henry Cabot Lodge called "a great rising naval power" in the Pacific.[14] For US policymakers, tensions with Japan formed part of a familiar pattern, echoing back to the Pacific slope in the 1860s. In the case of the Chilean and then Japanese ship *Esmeralda/Izumi*, that transition was a concrete one.

In the aggregate, it all makes for a logical enough story – with some caveats. From the docks of San Francisco or Valparaiso or Yokohama it seems reasonable that war (and so much of it) in the Pacific would have some sort of effect on the decision to build up naval forces capable of operating in the region. No surprise either that as the US New Navy reinvented itself in the 1880s and 1890s, naval leaders focused on competing with smaller, newly made Pacific navies before measuring up against "great power" ones in the North Atlantic. Intra-regional naval races (Peru/Chile and China/Japan) created ascendant maritime powers (notably Chile and Japan) which justified the first investments in the US New Navy. That New Navy – especially the weak and awkward force of the 1880s – was a reaction to war in the Pacific rather than preparation for an imperialistic campaign in 1898 or a defense against a foreign battlefleet.

But now for the caveats and surprises. Each serves as a provocation about power, war, and international history. For a start, in the latter half of the nineteenth century there was a great deal of war in the nominally "Pacific" Ocean. Rebalancing the history of US naval development toward the Pacific reminds us that there was nothing peaceful about the "long peace" between the Conference of Vienna (1814) and the July Crisis (1914). Historians are quick to note examples of violence done *by* North Atlantic empires *to* colonial peoples during this period. That is true, of course, but the Pacific also witnessed a nearly uninterrupted succession of wars waged between relatively minor powers with outsized and unpredictable consequences. Between 1866 and 1898, hot war and the preparation for it was the rule rather than the exception. Area studies containers (East Asia, Latin America) and military demarcations (Indopacific Command, Southern Command, etc.) tend to obscure this fact, but it comes into focus immediately if the Pacific is adopted as a coherent unit of analysis. In particular, the connections linking the US Civil War to the Pacific as well as the parallels between the War of the Pacific (1879–1884) and the Sino-Japanese War (1894–1895) have for too long been hidden behind the borders of regional specialization.

All this Pacific war, in turn, highlights the implicit Eurocentrism (or Atlanticism) in the history of military industrialization and innovation: a focus on production targets, patents, strategic debates, and war-gaming in the North Atlantic. In most respects, naval innovation appeared to emanate exclusively from the "bureaucracies of the Royal Navy, Imperial German Navy and the US Navy," spreading outward to regions such as the Pacific at the sharp end of imperial expansion: the "tentacles of progress" and the "tools of empire" in Daniel Headrick's memorable phrasing.[15] It is a perspective with great coherence in a Q: "why did you rob the bank?" A: "Because that's where the money is" sort of way. This emphasis on Europe, however, marginalizes all the "actual warfare" in the Pacific and its outsized and reciprocal effect(s) on peacetime developments in the core of the North Atlantic world (above all the United States). While the great powers remained at peace, the Pacific's wars mattered as sources of demand and test beds of development. That the nineteenth-century attention devoted to far-away engagements such as Angamos (1879) seems so "disproportionate" today was and is highly instructive; an ipso facto argument for why historians should take small wars and newly made navies as seriously as contemporaries did.[16] The money was in the North Atlantic but the action was in the Pacific.

Connections among people are a further irony. Consider the way in which so many ex-Confederates – men who had dedicated their lives and innovations to the preservation of chattel slavery – made common cause in the 1860s and 1870s with their erstwhile Union adversaries and newly made navy builders in the Pacific. In doing so, Civil War veterans formed a sort of transnational epistemic community, united by the technical mastery of naval violence and the goal of resisting foreign imperial adventurism (though individual motives were often nakedly pecuniary). By extension, that phenomenon points to a historiographical opportunity in the study of what Erez Manela and others call "International Society."[17] Historians have recently shown a great deal of interest in networks of institutions, advocates, and experts who work with and/or outside of national governments. Across this highly productive field, scholars tend to focus on actors and institutions who do (or at least *try* to do) "good" things: alleviating famine, promoting development, protecting human rights, eradicating diseases, etc.[18] Unfortunately, as the post-1865 careers of men such as John Randolph Tucker and John Lay demonstrate, International Society has had more than its share of mercenaries and charlatans hawking violence for profit and dubious fame. Today, transnationally active racial bigots, terrorists, and "private military contractors" are fellow travelers across International Society, as they have been since its origins in the late nineteenth century.

The transnational circulation of *materiel* (as opposed to people) presents still another ironic tension. Consider the internationally entangled histories of warships such as the Peruvian/Chilean *Huáscar* and the Chilean/Japanese *Esmeralda/Izumi*. These were at once symbols of coalescing national identity *and* monuments to an early phase of industrial globalization. Peru's four ironclads – the *Huáscar, Independencia, Manco Capac,* and *Atahualpa* – all referenced Peruvian and/or Inca resistance to Spanish rule but depended on North Atlantic experts to man key technical billets. Likewise, Chilean ironclads may have commemorated leaders from the Chilean War of Independence but nonetheless relied extensively on imported materials, notably Welsh coal. The global aftermarket for surplus weapons further demonstrates the fluidity of the warship-as-national-symbol in this era of nation-making wars. Japan appropriated the CSS *Stonewall* as the *Kōtetsu*; Peru snapped up CSS *Georgia* and renamed it (deliciously) the *Union*; Chile sold its onetime wonder-ship *Esmeralda* to Japan via Ecuador during the Sino-Japanese War. The sentiments of modern nationalism and the globalization of industrial technology made for strange combinations.

More tangibly, as these weapons proliferated around the Pacific, relative military power fluctuated – often radically in the short term – cutting against the conventional wisdom about the period. During the heyday of gunboat imperialism, brute distance and the global circulation of advanced industrial weapons enabled Pacific newly made navies to compete with Euro-US empires. Hence why they were so threatening to the US Old Navy. As the industrial revolution drove a "great divergence" between North Atlantic economies and the rest, the Pacific's wars featured several ironic battlefield reversals.[19] Notice "upsets" such as the Spanish defeat at Callao (1866), the British stalemate at Pacocha (1877), and French frustrations at Zhenhai (1885). All those examples were transformed by nationalist memorialization into dramatic victories. This sort of unpredictability was even more pronounced vis-à-vis the

United States and its incipient New Navy as the deep anxieties voiced by naval officials during crises with Chile (1891) and Japan (1897) suggest. Contemporary war-planners did not have the luxury of hindsight. Had it come to actual war with Chile or Japan, the results may well have been as surprising for the United States as they were for the Qing at the Yalu (1894) or the Russians at Tsushima (1905).

The aggressive adoption and adaptation of advanced technologies by Pacific newly made navies leads to yet another surprise, this time about the development of modern war. Contrary to expectations, states with weak industrial bases and scientific establishments were often at the forefront of military modernization. Unlike the world's dominant militaries, newly made navies had every incentive to assume the risks and rewards of experimental technologies. By embracing the torpedo and submersible weapons alongside armored ships, Pacific states expanded the temporal and spatial boundaries of industrial war. In doing so they became partners in the creation of an inchoate form of naval modernity which would be fully realized during World War I: three-dimensional, nocturnal, and industrial violence at sea.

This prototypical modernity sits uneasily with both the existing literature on naval development and the "punctuated equilibrium" model of military technological progress.[20] Adapted from findings in evolutionary biology, the theory of "punctuated equilibrium" argues that long periods of military stasis are interrupted by short, sharp bursts of technological adaptation; paradigmatically, the "long peace" of the nineteenth century was broken by total industrial war in Europe (1914–1918).[21] It is an elegant theory; perhaps too elegant. Centering the Pacific in the history of military development suggests that modern naval violence emerged incrementally after the US Civil War. Just as the introduction of the "all big-gun" battleship before World War I was a long and uneven evolution competing with other technologies and dating to the 1850s, so too did modern naval war graduate in practice through small steps across the Pacific's wars.[22] Witness the evolution of undersea weapons from Callao (1866), to Pacocha (1877), to Caldera (1891), and finally to Weihaiwei (1895).

Looking forward, a final irony is that present-day interest in disruptive military technologies and multipolar competition is matched by comparative negligence about the long history of both in the Pacific.[23] In most respects, contemporary intra-regional tensions and technological uncertainty are a reversion to a nineteenth-century norm. Policymakers might derive some cold comfort from that fact, along with two "lessons of the past."[24] The first pertains to the frequency of paradigmatic shifts in military technology: that is, innovations that render earlier classes of weapons obsolete. The pace of technological change in the information age astounds many but the sensation would be familiar to military leaders in the late nineteenth century. One naval historian writing in 1897 observed that because of "the state of flux unparalleled in the past," what "was yesterday the most formidable of fighting machines may be looked upon tomorrow as little better than lumber."[25] Military and industry leaders confronting hypersonic and digital weapons might empathize. Each generation tends to be surprised by technological acceleration, but the feeling of disorientation induced by change is at least as old as the industrial revolution. Today, even nineteenth-century-style "future war stories" have enjoyed a renaissance as officials ponder vast and untried technologies.[26] It seems dubious we are any better now at guessing the future of warfare than were practitioners who first tried their hands at this in the nineteenth century.

A second lesson is to appreciate the place of the United States and Latin America as members of the Pacific community with roots deep in the nineteenth century. A walk around the Chinatowns of Lima or San Francisco today confirms as much. Better yet, one can appreciate the depth of Latin America's connections to the western Pacific by sampling a plate of *lomo saltado*, the Peruvian national dish: essentially stir-fried beef with peppers served with French fries and rice in an almost perfect amalgam of transpacific culinary influences. US connections are equally deep. Allegedly, the Chinese-American classic General Tso's chicken is named for the very same Zuo Zongtang who founded China's first modern naval shipyard in Fuzhou. As such, the cultural and strategic US "turn" to the Pacific is a very old one.

The political implications of appreciating all this, of escaping "the specter of the short term," bears most directly on debates over the future of Sino-US relations.[27] The European empires and their great power navies are long gone, but transpacific competition and inter-American security politics remain. Contemporary advocates of a "pivot to Asia" or the "free and open Indo-Pacific" could scarcely find better spokesmen than Herman Melville or William H. Seward.[28] China's nineteenth century looks newly relevant too. Since 1949, the "China threat" in US debates has historically been contextualized within the framework of the Cold War: as either the junior partner to the Soviet Union or the radical leader of Third World nationalism. Today, these categories have little explanatory value. On a longer timeline, the waning days of the Qing Empire and its sensitivities to Xinjiang and Taiwan are a better model for Chinese Communist Party behavior, ambitions, and vulnerabilities. Geographically, the United States and China exist today much as they did in the nineteenth century: two continental powers on either side of the North Pacific, bound by maritime trade and exchange. Likewise, how to balance the PRC's position between a continental frontier – even empire – and a maritime one remains a central dilemma for Beijing.

The Qing past speaks to controversies over technological transfers and military power as well. As in the 1880s and 1890s, the potential of the Chinese military to appropriate foreign technology and combine it with the immense human and environmental resources of the PRC figures titanically in the US strategic imagination. Wei Yuan's prescription for resisting maritime aggression – adopt the tools of the foreigners in order to control them – has held up remarkably well. The drive to transform the People's Liberation Army Navy's into a force capable of fighting "limited wars under high-tech conditions" (and subsequent iterations of this military-strategic guideline) is a distant but clear echo of China's first naval modernization c. 1874–1895.[29]

Incredibly, the United States reacted in a similar manner to both periods: with the extension of military technical assistance and then a reverse course to enmity. In 1881, Commodore Robert W. Shufeldt loaned out US torpedo advisers to Li Hongzhang and the Tianjin Torpedo School but soon regretted it, citing the danger of arming alien China with modern weapons. A century later, during the George H. W. Bush administration, Chinese engineers traveled to aerospace plants in New York, hoping to modernize legacy fighter aircraft and, perhaps, build more enduring connections with the United States.[30] Bush abandoned the program after Tiananmen Square (1989) upset perceptions of Deng Xiaoping's regime, transforming an ally against the Soviet Union into a potential threat. Li Hongzhang and Robert W. Shufeldt would have recognized the script: the ephemeral promise of cooperation between two geographically similar empires giving way to suspicion. What was old is new in the Pacific, as once again the region looks poised to drive US security politics and behavior.

Notes

Introduction

1 "President Roosevelt Dedicates Column that Blazons Glory of Dewey's Fleet," *The Call* (San Francisco, CA) May 15, 1903.
2 A. T. Mahan, "The United States Looking Outward," in *The Interest of America in Sea Power* (Boston: Little Brown and Company, 1897), 3.
3 William A. Williams, *The Roots of the Modern American Empire* (New York: Random House, 1969), 236; Walter LaFeber, *The New Empire* (Ithaca, NY: Cornell University Press, 1963), vii; David Healy, *U.S. Expansionism: The Imperialist Urge in the 1890s* (Madison: University of Wisconsin Press, 1970), 112; Ernest Paolino, *The Foundations of the American Empire: William Henry Seward and U.S. Foreign Policy* (Ithaca, NY: Cornell University Press, 1973), 209.
4 James Field, "American Imperialism: The Worst Chapter in Almost Any Book," *The American Historical Review*, Vol. 83, No. 3 (June, 1978), 647; Scott Mobley, *Progressives in Navy Blue: Maritime Strategy, American Empire and the Transformation of U.S. Naval Identity, 1873–1897* (Annapolis: Naval Institute Press, 2018), 12.
5 Niels Eichhorn, "A 'Century of Peace' That Was Not: War in the Nineteenth Century," *Journal of Military History*, Vol. 84, No. 4 (2020): 1051–1077.
6 Paul Kennedy, "The Sea and Sea Power within the International System," in *The Sea in History: The Modern World*, ed. N. A. M Rodger (Woodbridge, UK: The Boydell Press, 2017), 7. This list includes all naval conflicts in the Pacific fought with industrial weapons between the conclusion of the Taiping War and the War of 1898. It excludes wars fought between nonindustrial and industrially armed forces, namely US expeditions against the indigenous people of Taiwan (1867) or Korea (1871).
7 For surveys: Jeremy Black, *Naval War: A Global History Since 1860* (Lanham, MD: Rowman & Littlefield, 2017); Lisle A. Rose, *Power at Sea: The Age of Navalism, 1890–1918* (Columbia: University of Missouri Press, 2007); Lawrence Sondhaus, *Naval War 1815–1914* (New York: Routledge, 2001); John Keegan, *The Price of Admiralty: The Evolution of Naval Warfare* (New York: Viking, 1988).
8 Mark Shulman, *Navalism and the Emergence of American Sea Power* (Annapolis: Naval Institute Press, 1995), 1.
9 William Seward, "The Physical, Moral and Intellectual Development of the American People" (1854), in *The Works of William H. Seward*, Vol. 4, ed.

George Baker (Boston: Houghton and Mifflin, 1884), 165. See also: Andrew Preston "America's Pacific Power in Global Age," in *The Sea in History*, 316–317; Michael Green, *By More than Providence* (New York: Columbia University Press, 2017); Bruce Cumings, *Dominion from Sea to Sea: Pacific Ascendency and American Power* (New Haven: Yale University Press, 2009); Walter McDougall, *Let the Sea Make a Noise* (New York: Harper, 2004); Arthur Power Dudden, *The American Pacific* (New York: Oxford University Press, 1992). For naval historians: Jason W. Smith, *To Master the Boundless Sea: The U.S. Navy, the Marine Environment, and the Cartography of Empire* (Chapel Hill: University of North Carolina Press, 2018); Brian Rouleau, *With Sails Whitening Every Sea* (Ithaca, NY: Cornell University Press, 2014); Claude Berube, *On Wide Seas: The U.S. Navy in the Jacksonian Era* (Tuscaloosa: University of Alabama Press, 2021); Michael Verney, *A Great and Rising Nation: Naval Exploration and Global Empire in the Early US Republic* (Chicago: University of Chicago Press, July 2022); Shulman, *Navalism*, chapters 4 and 5.
10 Herman Melville, *Moby Dick* (London: Wordsworth Classics, 1993), 397. For the case to "recenter" domestic power in the history of US foreign relations, see: Daniel Bessner and Fredrik Logevall, "Recentering the United States in the Historiography of American Foreign Relations," *Texas National Security Review*, Vol. 3, No. 2 (Spring, 2020): 39–55.
11 George Davis, *A Navy Second to None: The Development of Modern American Naval Policy* (New York: Harcourt, Brace and Company, 1940); Paolo E. Coletta, *A Survey of U.S. Naval Affairs* (London: University Press of America, 1987), 9.
12 "Present and Prospective Ship-Building Policy of Foreign Nations" (1886) The National Archives, Admiralty Files [hereafter TNA/ADM] 231/10, Kew, UK; Stephen Howarth, *To Shining Sea: A History of the United States Navy, 1775–1991* (New York: Random House, 1991), 216.
13 "Cronica," *Revista de Marina*, November 1887, No. 30, 580.
14 LaFeber, *The New Empire*; Thomas J. McCormick, *China Market: America's Quest for Informal Empire 1893–1901* (Chicago: Quadrangle Books, 1967); Cumings, *Dominion from Sea to Sea*, 131.
15 William H. Seward, "Survey of the Arctic and Pacific Oceans" (1852), *The Works of William H. Seward*, Vol. 1, 250; Norman Graebner, *Empire on the Pacific: A Study in American Continental Expansion* (New York: Ronald Press, 1955); Thomas R. Hietala, *Manifest Design: American Exceptionalism and Empire* (Ithaca, NY: Cornell University Press, 2003).
16 Matthew Karp, *This Vast Southern Empire: Slaveholders at the Helm of American Foreign Policy* (Cambridge, MA: Harvard University Press, 2016), 2.
17 *Letters and Papers of Alfred Thayer Mahan* [hereafter *LPATM*], ed. Robert Seager II and Doris Maguire (Annapolis: Naval Institute Press, 1975), Vol. 1, 341, 559–605; Robert Seager, *Alfred Thayer Mahan: The Man and His Letters* (Annapolis: Naval Institute Press, 1977).
18 A. T. Mahan, *From Sail to Steam* (New York: Harper Brothers, 1907), 277; A. T. Mahan to Roy Marston, February 19, 1897, *LPATM*, Vol. 2, 441; A. T. Mahan, *The Influence of Sea Power Upon History* (Boston: Little, Brown & Co., 1890).

19 David Shaw, S*ea Wolf of the Confederacy* (New York: Free Press, 2004); "The Dano-Rebel Ram Sphynx," *New York Herald*, February 15, 1865; Rodgers to Welles, September 9, 1864, Department of the Navy, *Official Records of the Union and Confederate Navies in the War of the Rebellion* [hereafter *ORN*], Series 1, Vol. 3 (Washington, DC: Government Printing Office, 1896), 206–209; 志剛 [Zhi Gang], 1868, 初使泰西記 [Journal of the First Mission to the West] in《洋务运动, 第8册》[*Foreign Affairs Movement*, Vol. 8] (上海: 上海人民出版社, 1961), 260.
20 Odd Arne Westad, *Restless Empire: China and the World Since 1750* (New York: Basic Books, 2012), 91; 两江总督曾国荃总遵旨筹议海防 [Viceroy of Jiangnan and Jiangxi, Zeng Guoquan on the Founding of Maritime Defense], July 3, 1885《清末海軍史料》[*Late Qing Naval Historical Materials*] 张侠 ed. [Zhang Xia, et al] (北京: 海洋出版社, 1982), 42.
21 Pedro Bustamante, July 28, 1878, *Memória del Rama de Guerra*, Vol. 2 (Lima: Imprenta Nacional, 1878), 9; 李宗羲 [Li Zongxi] 奏總理衙門 [Memorial, Zongli Yamen]《洋务运动第1册》[*Foreign Affairs Movement*, Vol. 1], 69.
22 Excepting Lissa (1866). William Laird Clowes, *Four Modern Naval Campaigns: Historical, Strategical and Tactical* (New York: Unit Library, 1902), 1; Wilson, *Ironclads in Action*, Vol. 1, xviii.
23 Clowes, *Four Modern Naval Campaigns*, vii.
24 Mahan, "Introduction," in Wilson, *Ironclads in Action*, xiv–xv.
25 Frederick Rodgers to Secretary of the Navy, October 24, 1879, National Archives and Records Administration [hereafter NARA-1], RG-45, M 89, Roll 67, Folio 102, Washington, DC.
26 William Sims, "Condition of the Chinese Vessels," February 25, 1895, NARA-1, RG-45, Box 460.
27 Mobley, *Progressives in Navy Blue*; *Colonial Crucible: Empire in the Making of the Modern American State*, ed. A. W. McCoy and Francisco A. Scarano (Madison: University of Wisconsin Press, 2009); Warwick Anderson, *Colonial Pathologies: American Tropical Medicine, Race, and Hygiene in the Philippines* (Durham, NC: Duke University Press, 2016).
28 Benjamín Vicuña Mackenna, "El Reparto del Pacífico," *Revista de Marina* (Chile), No. 1, July 1885, 68.
29 John D. Long, "Our Navy," *New York Times*, December 12, 1903. See also: John Long, *The New American Navy* (New York: Outlook Co., 1903).
30 Mahan to Sterling, February 13, 1896, *LPATM*, Vol. 2, 445. See also: A. G. Hopkins, *American Empire: A Global History* (Princeton: Princeton University Press, 2018), 251; Michael Hunt, *Ideology and U.S. Foreign Relations*, 2nd ed. (New Haven, CT: Yale University Press, 2009); Paul Kramer, "Empires, Exceptions, and Anglo-Saxons: Race and Rule between the British and United States Empires, 1880–1910," *Journal of American History*, Vol. 88, No. 4 (2002): 1315–53; Eric Love, *Race over Empire: Racism and U.S. Imperialism, 1865–1900* (Chapel Hill: University of North Carolina Press, 2004); James Belich, *Replenishing the Earth* (Oxford: Oxford University Press, 2009), 5; Frederick Merk, *Manifest Destiny and Mission in American History: A Reinterpretation* (New York: Alfred Knopf, 1963), 237; Frank Ninkovich, *Global Dawn: The Cultural Foundations of American Internationalism, 1865–1890* (Cambridge, MA: Harvard University Press, 2009).

31 John Thompson, "Exaggeration of American Vulnerability," *Diplomatic History*, Vol. 16, No. 1 (January, 1992): 23–43. See also: Michael Sherry, *In the Shadow of War: The United States Since the 1930s* (New Haven, CT: Yale University Press, 1995), 7.
32 Stephen B. Luce, "Christian Ethics an Element of Military Education," *United Service* (January, 1883): 1.
33 Huntington, "Arms Races: Prerequisites and Results," 42.
34 Roger Lotchin, *Fortress California, 1910–1961: From Warfare to Welfare* (New York: Oxford University Press, 1992), 3.
35 For Chile: T. B. Mason, *The War on the Pacific Coast of South America* (Washington, DC: Government Print Office, 1883), 6. For Japan: William Curtis, *Yankees of the East: Sketches of Modern Japan* (New York: Stone and Kimball, 1896), 1.
36 John Henry Palmer, *The Invasion of New York: Or How Hawaii Was Annexed* (New York: F. Tennyson Neely, 1897); Park Benjamin, *The End of New York*, in *Stories by American Authors*, Vol. 5 (New York: Scribner's Sons, 1900), 140; Pierton Dooner, *Last Days of the Republic* (San Francisco: Alta California Publishing House, 1879), 22; Robert Woltor, *A Short and Truthful History of the Taking of Californian and Oregon by the Chinese in the Year AD 1889* (San Francisco: Bancroft, 1882).
37 Mahan to Bouverie Clark, May 22, 1891, *LPATM*, Vol. 2, 47.
38 Notably collections of diplomatic correspondence akin to *Foreign Relations of the United States*. See:《洋务运动》第1–8册 [*Foreign Affairs Movement*, Vols. 1–8];《清末海軍史料》[*Late Qing Naval Historical Materials*];《中法戰爭》第1–8册 [*Sino-French War*, Vols. 1–8] 邵循正, ed. Shao Xunzheng (上海: 新知出版社, 1961);《申報》[*Shenbao*] (Shanghai, China).
39 *Crossing Empires: Taking U.S. History into Transimperial Terrain*, ed. Kristin L. Hoganson and Jay Sexton (Durham, NC: Duke University Press, 2020), 5; Andrew Priest, *Designs on Empire: America's Rise to Power in the Age of European Imperialism* (New York: Columbia University Press, 2021), 1; Gareth Curless, et al., "Editors' Introduction: Networks in Imperial History," *Journal of World History*, Vol. 26, No. 4 (December, 2015), 705–732.
40 *Transwar Asia: Ideology, Practices, and Institutions, 1920–1960*, ed. Reto Hofmann and Max Ward (New York: Bloomsbury Academic, 2022); Andrew Gordon, "Consumption, Leisure and the Middle Class in Transwar Japan," *Social Science Japan Journal*, No. 1 (April, 2007): 1–21.
41 Benedict Anderson, *Imagined Communities* (London: Verso, 1983), 175.
42 Fernand Braudel, *The Mediterranean and the Mediterranean World in the Age of Philip II* (New York: Row, 1972); Sunil Amrith, *Crossing the Bay of Bengal* (Cambridge, MA: Harvard University Press, 2013); *Japan and the Pacific, 1540–1920*, ed. Mark Caprio and Matsuda Koichirō (Burlington, VT: Ashgate, 2006), xiii.
43 Immanuel Wallerstein, *World-Systems Analysis: An Introduction* (Durham, NC: Duke, 2004).
44 Eric Hobsbawm, *The Age of Empire* (New York: Random House, 1987), 59.
45 Kenneth Pomeranz, *The Great Divergence* (Princeton, NJ: Princeton University Press, 2000).

46 Niall Ferguson, *Civilization: The West and the Rest* (New York: Penguin Press, 2011).
47 Mark Peattie, "The Japanese Colonial Empire, 1895–1945," *The Cambridge History of Japan* (Cambridge: Cambridge University Press, 1989), 217.
48 Those economies that were export driven and underpinned by expropriated labor. Daniel Botsman, "Freedom without Slavery? 'Coolies,' Prostitutes, and Outcastes in Meiji Japan's 'Emancipation Moment,'" *The American Historical Review*, Vol. 116, No. 5 (2011): 1323–1347; Aurelio García y García (1873), Caja 217, Carpeta 4, Código 5-17-A, Archive of the Peruvian Ministerio de Relaciones Exteriores [hereafter MREP], Lima, Perú. 张荫桓 [Zhang Yinhuan] 三洲日記 [*Diary of Three Continents*] (上海: 古籍出版社, 1995). See also, C. Harvey Gardiner, *The Japanese and Peru 1873–1973* (Albuquerque: University of New Mexico Press, 1975); "Inmigración de Chinos por el Callao, 1860–1870," *Historia Marítima del Perú*, Tomo VIII, Vol. 3 (Lima, Perú: Estudios Histórico-Marítimos del Perú, 1984), 504; Sven Beckert, *Empire of Cotton: A Global History* (New York: Knopf, 2014), 258; 《花糖近市》 [Cotton Enters the Market] *Shenbao* (Shanghai, China) November 11, 1876.
49 William Endicott Jr. to John Long, November 8, 1897, *Papers of John Davis Long, 1897–1904*, ed. Gardner Weld Allen (Boston: Massachusetts Historical Society, 1939), 32; George Robeson, *Annual Reports of the Secretary of the Navy* [hereafter *ARSN*] *1870*, 4; "A Valuable Witness," *Daily Evening Bulletin* (San Francisco, CA) March 21, 1882. For secondary, see: Kenneth J. Hagan, *American Gunboat Diplomacy and the Old Navy* (Westport, CT: Greenwood Press, 1973), 56.
50 Charles S. Maier, *Among Empires: American Ascendancy and Its Predecessors* (Cambridge, MA: Harvard University Press, 2006).
51 李鸿章 [Li Hongzhang] September 21, 1880, Shufeldt Papers, Box 24, China, Misc., Library of Congress [hereafter LOC] Washington, DC; Commission de Construcción Naval en Inglaterra *Independencia*, Archivo Histórico de la Marina del Perú [hereafter AHMP]; Órdenes, 1872, AHMP, Caja 10 Sobre 17, Folio 9; Legation of Perú and Japan and China, "Memorandum," March 5, 1873, MREP, Caja 216, Carpeta 6, Código 5–11, 42–44.
52 Realists: Davis, *A Navy Second to None*, 27; Paul Kennedy, *The Rise of the Anglo-German Antagonism, 1860–1914* (Boston: Allen & Unwin, 1980); Robert Love Jr., *History of the U.S. Navy*, Vol. 1, *1775–1941* (Harrisburg, PA: Stackpole Books, 1992); George W. Baer, *One Hundred Years of Sea Power: The U.S. Navy, 1890–1990* (Stanford: Stanford University Press, 1993), 12; Howarth, *To Shining Sea*; William Braisted, *The United States Navy in the Pacific* (Austin: University of Texas Press, 1958); Rose, *Power at Sea*; Ernest May, *Imperial Democracy* (New York: Harcourt, 1961); Kenneth Hagan "The U.S. as a New Naval Power, 1890–1919," in *The Sea in History*, 38–49. For economic historians, see: Charles Beard, *The Navy: Defense or Portent?* (New York: Harper & Brothers, 1932); LaFeber, *The New Empire*; Benjamin F. Cooling, *Gray Steel and Blue Water Navy* (Hamden CT: Archon Books, 1979); Williams, *Roots of the Modern American Empire*; Kurt Hackemer, *The U.S. Navy and the Origins of the Military-industrial Complex, 1847–1883* (Annapolis: Naval Institute Press, 2001). For domestic politics: Harold and

Margaret Sprout, *The Rise of American Naval Power* (Princeton: Princeton University Press, 1939/1967); Armin Rappaport, *The Navy League of the United States* (Detroit: WSU Press, 1962); Paul Everett Pedisich, *Congress Buys a Navy: Politics, Economics, and the Rise of American Naval Power, 1881–1921* (Annapolis: Naval Institute Press, 2016); Donald Sexton, "Forging the Sword: Congress and the American Naval Renaissance, 1880–1900" (Ph.D. Diss., University of Tennessee, 1976). For institutions: Peter Karsten, *The Naval Aristocracy: The Golden Age of Annapolis and the Emergence of Modem American Navalism* (New York: Free Press, 1972); Walter Herrick, *The American Naval Revolution* (Baton Rouge: Louisiana State University Press, 1967), 23; Charles O. Paullin, *History of Naval Administration 1775–1911* (Annapolis: Naval Institute Press, 1968); Ronald Spector, *Professors of War: The Naval War College and the Development of the Naval Profession* (Newport, RI: Naval War College Press, 1977); Donald Chisholm, *Waiting for Dead Men's Shoes: Origins and Development of the U.S. Navy's Officer Personnel System, 1793–1941* (Stanford: Stanford University Press, 2001); Laurence Wood Bartlett III, "Not Merely for Defense: The Creation of the New American Navy" (Ph.D. Diss., Texas Christian University, 2011); Robert Seager, "Ten Years before Mahan: The Unofficial Case for the New Navy, 1880–1890," *The Mississippi Valley Historical Review*, Vol. 40, No. 3 (1953): 491–512.

53 Katherine Epstein, *Torpedo: Inventing the Industrial-Military Complex in the United States and Britain* (Cambridge, MA: Harvard University Press, 2014); Elting Morison, *Admiral Sims and the Modern American Navy* (Boston: Houghton Mifflin, 1942); Braisted, *The United States Navy in the Pacific*; Robert Erwin Johnson, *Rear Admiral John Rodgers* (Annapolis: Naval Institute Press, 1967); Seager, *Alfred Thayer Mahan*; Roland Spector, *Admiral of the New Empire: The Life and Career of George Dewey* (Baton Rouge: LSU Press, 1974); Daniel H. Wicks, "New Navy and New Empire: The Life and Times of John Grimes Walker" (Ph.D. Diss., University of California, Berkeley, 1979); Robert Erwin Johnson, *Far China Station: The U.S. Navy in Asian Waters 1800–1898* (Annapolis: Naval Institute Press, 1979); *Captains of the Old Steam Navy: Makers of the American Naval Tradition, 1840–1880*, ed. James C. Bradford (Annapolis: Naval Institute Press, 1986); *Admirals of the New Steel Navy: Makers of the American Naval Tradition, 1880–1930*, ed. James Bradford (Annapolis: Naval Institute Press, 1990); Frederick Drake, *The Empire of the Sea: A Biography of Rear Admiral Robert Wilson Shufeldt, USN* (Honolulu: University of Hawaii Press, 1984); Henry Hendrix, *Theodore Roosevelt's Naval Diplomacy: The U.S. Navy and the Birth of the American Century* (Annapolis: Naval Institute Press, 2009); Richard Sedgwick West, *Admirals of the American Empire: The Combined Story of George Dewey, Alfred Thayer Mahan, Winfield Scott Schley and William Thomas Sampson* (Indianapolis: Bobbs-Merrill Co., 1948); Curtis Henson, *Commissioners and Commodores: The East India Squadron and American Diplomacy in China* (Tuscaloosa: University of Alabama Press, 1982).

54 Mobley, *Progressives in Navy Blue*; William McBride, *Technological Change and the United States Navy 1865–1945* (Baltimore: Johns Hopkins University Press, 2000); Shulman, *Navalism and the Emergence of American Sea Power*;

Kristin Hoganson, *Fighting for American Manhood: How Gender Politics Provoked the Spanish–American and Philippine–American Wars* (New Haven: Yale University Press, 1998); Robert O'Connell, *Sacred Vessels: The Cult of the Battleship and the Rise of the U.S. Navy* (Boulder, CO: Westview Press, 1991); Suzanne Geissler, *God and Sea Power: The Influence of Religion on Alfred Thayer Mahan* (Annapolis: Naval Institute Press, 2015); Daniel Wayne Stewart, "The Greatest Gift to Modern Civilization: Naval Power and Moral Order in the United States and Great Britain, 1880–1918" (Ph.D. Diss., Temple University, 1999).

55 A. T. Mahan, "The Isthmus and Sea Power," *The Interest of America in Sea Power*, 87–88. See also: Thomas Schoonover, *Uncle Sam's War of 1898 and the Origins of Globalization* (Lexington: University Press of Kentucky, 2003).

56 Dirk Bönker, *Militarism in a Global Age: Naval Ambitions in Germany and the United States before World War I* (Ithaca, NY: Cornell University Press, 2012).

57 E. Chouteau, "Introduccion," *Revista de la Marina*, No. 1 (July, 1885): 6–7 (emphasis in original).

58 戚其章 [Qi Qizhang] 北洋舰队覆没的历史反思 [Reflections on the Annihilation of the Beiyang Navy], 《北洋海軍新探北洋海軍成军120周年国际学术研讨会论文集》[*The Beiyang Navy: New Explorations*], ed. 張榮国 [Zhang Rongguo] (北京: 中华书局, 2012), 12.

59 *The Pacific World: Lands, Peoples and History of the Pacific, 1500–1900* (Burlington, VT: Ashgate, 2000); *The Pacific Ocean in History*, ed. H. Morse Stephens and Hebert E. Bolton (New York: Macmillan Company, 1917), 5; Donald B. Freeman, *The Pacific* (New York: Routledge, 2010); Frances Steel, *Oceania under Steam* (New York: Manchester University Press, 2011); *Pacific Histories: Ocean, Land, People*, ed. David Armitage and Alison Bashford (New York: Palgrave Macmillan, 2014); Alison Bashford, "Pacific History," *Oceanic History*, ed. David Armitage, Alison Bashford, Sujit Sivasundaram (Cambridge: Cambridge University Press, 2018); Matt Matsuda, *Pacific Worlds* (New York: Cambridge University Press, 2012); David Igler, *The Great Ocean* (Oxford: Oxford University Press, 2013).

60 W. E. B. DuBois, *The Suppression of the African Slave Trade to the United States of America, 1638–1870* (New York: Oxford University Press, 2007).

61 Commodore Powell to Secretary of the Admiralty, November 27, 1866, No. 248, Enclosure 1, The National Archives, Foreign Office Correspondence [TNA/FO] 498/22; Prado to Tucker, August 17, 1866, MREP, Caja 161, Carpeta 3, Código 5-4-, 1866, Folio 85–86.

62 李鸿章电总理衙门智利出售兵船 [Li Hongzhang Telegram to the Zongli Yamen on Chile's Offer to Export Warships] October 12, 1894,《清末海軍史料》[*Late Qing Navy Historical Materials*], 125.

63 A. T. Mahan to Jane Leigh Mahan, November 7, 1869, *LPATM*, Vol. 1, 341.

64 Arthur Waldron, *From War to Nationalism: China's Turning Point* (London: Cambridge University Press, 2003); Jonathan B. A. Bailey, "The First World War and the Birth of Modern Warfare," in *The Dynamics of Military Revolution*, 132.

65 Black, *Naval Warfare*, 2; *Fighting in the Dark: Naval Combat at Night, 1904–1944*, ed. Vincent P. O'Hara and Trent Hone (Annapolis: Naval Institute

Press, 2023). For "grammar," see: Carol Gluck, "The End of Elsewhere: Writing Modernity Now," *The American Historical Review*, Vol. 116, No. 3 (2011): 676–687.
66 Richard Harding, *Modern Naval History: Debates and Prospects* (New York: Bloomsbury Academic, 2016), 42; Stephen Biddle, *Military Power: Explaining Victory and Defeat in Modern Battle* (Princeton: Princeton University Press, 2004).
67 Karl Marx, *The Portable Karl Marx*, ed. Eugene Kamenka (New York: Penguin Books, 1983), 483; Hobsbawm, *The Age of Empire*, 59; Kennedy, *The Rise and Fall of Great Powers*, 144; Jurgen Osterhammel and Niels Petersen, *Globalization: A Short History* (Princeton, NJ: Princeton University Press, 2005), 66.
68 Jurgen Osterhammel, *The Transformation of the World: A Global History of the Nineteenth Century* (Princeton: Princeton University Press, 2014), 394; Sondhaus, *Naval War*, 27; Black, *Naval Warfare*, 2.
69 Hilarire Belloc, "The Modern Traveler" (1898).
70 Kennedy, *The Rise and Fall of Great Powers*, 150.
71 "List of Vessels Constructed by Cammell Laird Shipbuilders," Wirral Archives [hereafter WA/UK], Birkenhead, UK, No. 28, No. 290, No. 321.
72 For imitation see: Joao Resende-Santos, *Neorealism, States, and the Modern Mass Army* (New York: Cambridge University Press, 2007); for "hybrid" see Meng Yue, "Hybrid Science versus Modernity: The Practice of the Jiangnan Arsenal," *East Asian Science, Technology, and Medicine*, No. 16 (1999): 13–52.
73 Richard White, *The Middle Ground* (New York: Cambridge University Press, 1991); Brian Delay, *War of a Thousand Deserts* (New Haven: Yale University Press, 2008); Pekka Hämäläinen, *The Comanche Empire* (New Haven: Yale University Press, 2008).
74 French Legation, October 29, 1897, *Informes Inéditos de Diplomáticos Extranjeros Durante la Guerra del Pacífico* (Santiago: Andrés Bello, 1980), 270.
75 Akira Iriye, *Pacific Estrangement: Japanese and American Expansion 1897–1911* (Cambridge, MA: Harvard University Press, 1972); Walter LaFeber, *The Clash: U.S. Japanese Relations throughout History* (New York: Norton, 1997).

1 The Confederate "Navy to Construct"

1 James Bulloch, *The Secret Service of the Confederate States in Europe* (New York: Putnam's Sons, 1884), 48, 389–394. See also: David M. Sullivan, "Phantom Fleet: The Confederacy's Unclaimed European-Built Warships," *Warship International*, Vol. 24, No. 1 (1987): 12–32; Warren Spencer, *The Confederate Navy in Europe* (Tuscaloosa: University of Alabama Press, 1983), 2; Frank Merli, *Great Britain and the Confederate Navy, 1861–1865* (Bloomington: Indiana University Press, 1970). For reference: Paul Silverstone, *Civil War Navies 1855–1883* (Annapolis: USNI Press, 2001).
2 Beckert, *Empire of Cotton*, 203.
3 Bulloch, *The Secret Service*, 394.
4 "Specifications," ORN, Series 2, Vol. 2, 193–204.

5 Sarah Goldberger, "An Indissoluble Union," in *Forging the Trident: Theodore Roosevelt and the United States Navy*, ed. John Hattendorf and William Leeman (Annapolis: Naval Institute Press, 2020), 16; for Roosevelt, see: T. Roosevelt to H. C. Lodge, December 16, 1881, *Selections from the Correspondence of Theodore Roosevelt and Henry Cabot Lodge, 1884–1918*, Vol. 1 (New York: Charles Scribner's Sons, 1925), 73.

6 For secondary histories: James McPherson, *War on the Waters: The Union and Confederate Navies, 1861–1865* (Chapel Hill: University of North Carolina Press, 2012); Roberts, *Now for the Contest*, xiv; Raimondo Luraghi, *A History of the Confederate Navy* (Annapolis: Naval Institute Press, 1996), 69; Craig Symonds, *The Civil War at Sea* (Oxford: Oxford University Press, 2012). Veterans' publications include: *Confederate Magazine* and the *Southern Historical Society Papers* (*SHSP*) as well as numerous memoirs. For official records, see: *ORN*. For personal papers see: Duke, University of North Carolina Chapel Hill, Old Dominion University, as well as edited compilations of correspondence, often published by McFarland. For the wider internationalization of the Civil War, see: Don H. Doyle, *The Cause of All Nations: An International History of the American Civil War* (New York: Basic Books, 2015); Joseph Fry, *Dixie Looks Abroad: The South in U.S. Foreign Relations* (Baton Rouge: LSU Press, 2002).

7 David Brion Davis, *Inhuman Bondage: The Rise and Fall of Slavery in the New World* (Oxford: Oxford University Press, 2006); Rebecca Scott, *Degrees of Freedom: Louisiana and Cuba after Slavery* (Cambridge, MA: Harvard University Press, 2008); Beckert, *Empire of Cotton*, 83–136; Samantha Payne, "'A General Insurrection in the Countries with Slaves': The US Civil War and the Origins of an Atlantic Revolution, 1861–1866," *Past & Present*, Vol, 257, No. 1 (2022): 248–279; Walter Johnson, *River of Dark Dreams Slavery and Empire in the Cotton Kingdom* (Cambridge, MA: Belknap Press, 2013), 15; Karp, *This Vast Southern Empire*; Robert May, *Manifest Destiny's Underworld* (Chapel Hill, NC: UNC-CH Press, 2002).

8 Hans Van de Ven, "Introduction," in *The Cambridge History of War: War and the Modern World*, Vol. 4, ed. Roger Chickering, Dennis Showalter, and Hans Van De Ven (Cambridge: Cambridge University Press, 2012), 44; John R. Rawlinson, *China's Struggle for Naval Development, 1839–1895* (Cambridge, MA: Harvard University Press, 1967), 41; Benjamin Schwartz, *In Search of Wealth and Power: Yen Fun and the West* (Cambridge, MA: Harvard University Press, 1964); Orville Schell and John Delury, *Wealth and Power: China's Long March to the Twenty-First Century* (New York: Random House, 2013), 44; 《洋务运动》第1-8册 [*Foreign Affairs Movement*, Vols. 1–8] (上海: 上海人民出版社, 1961); 夏东元 [Xia Dongyuan] 《洋务运动》 [*The Foreign Affairs Movement*] 上海: 华东师范大学出版社, 1992.

9 Van de Ven, "Introduction," *The Cambridge History of War*, 43.

10 McPherson, *War on the Waters*, 8; Frank Merli, *Great Britain and the Confederate Navy, 1861–1865* (Bloomington: Indiana University Press, 1970), xv.

11 Robert Bonner, "The Salt Water Civil War: Thalassological Approaches, Ocean-Centered Opportunities," *Journal of the Civil War Era*, Vol. 6, No. 2 (June, 2016), 243.

12 Wallerstein, *World-Systems Analysis*.
13 Luraghi, *A History of the Confederate Navy*, 34; Harold Woodman, *King Cotton and His Retainers: Financing and Marketing the Cotton Crop of the South, 1800–1925* (Lexington: University of Kentucky Press, 1968), 153; *The United States and world Sea Power*, ed. E. B. Potter (Englewood Cliffs, NJ: Prentice Hall, 1955), 382.
14 David Hollett, *Men of Iron: The Story of Cammell Laird Shipbuilders 1828–1991* (Rock Ferry: Countyvise Limited, 1992), 12; List of Vessels, Laird Brothers, WA/UK; Sullivan, "Phantom Fleet," 12–32.
15 Kennedy, *Rise and Fall of Great Powers*, 180; McPherson, *Battle Cry of Freedom*, 91–92; David G. Surdam, *Northern Naval Superiority and the Economics of the American Civil War* (Columbia: University of South Carolina Press, 2001).
16 Karp, *This Vast Southern Empire*, 203.
17 Thomas Jordan, "Seacoast Defenses of Southern Carolina and Georgia," *SHSP*, Vol. 1 (June, 1876): 404.
18 Mallory to Davis, February 27, 1862, *ORN*, Series 2, Vol. 2, 150–151; see also, Kennedy, *Rise and Fall of Great Powers*, 181.
19 Bulloch, *The Secret Service*, 20.
20 Thomas Campbell, *Academy on the James: The Confederate Naval School* (Shippensburg, PA: Burd Street Press, 1998), 33.
21 Mallory to Davis, February 27, 1862, *ORN*, Series 2, Vol. 2, 151.
22 Covarrubias to Nelson, October 18, 1865, Encl. 1, No. 89, TNA/FO 498/22, Kew, United Kingdom.
23 José Manuel Pinto, *Memória de Marina de Chile, 1865* (Santiago: Imprenta Nacional, 1866), 16.
24 直隸總督李鴻章奏摺 [Memorial of the Viceroy of Zhili Li Hongzhang, 1879],《洋务运动第2册》[*Foreign Affairs Movement*, Vol. 2], 420; 戚其章 [Qi Qizhang] 北洋舰队覆没的历史反思 [Rethinking the Annihilation of the Beiyang Navy] in《北洋海軍: 新探》[*Beiyang Navy: New Explorations …*], 14–15.
25 Mallory to C. M. Conrad, May 8, 1861, *ORN*, Series 2, Vol. 1, 742.
26 李鸿章 [Li Hongzhang] 创建轮船水师条款 [Provisions for Founding a Steam Ship Navy] 1867《清末海军史料》[*Late Qing Naval Historical Materials*], 2
27 Johnson, *River of Dark Dreams*, 4; James M. McPherson, *Battle Cry of Freedom: The Civil War Era* (New York: Oxford University Press, 1988), 392–428. For Jasanoff, see: Maya Jasanoff, "Our Steamboat Imperialism," *New York Review of Books*, October 10, 2013.
28 McPherson, *Battle Cry of Freedom*, 392–427.
29 For Chile, note Chilean minister José Manuel Pinto, *Memória de Marina de Chile 1865* (Santiago: Imprenta Nacional, 1866), 17; Carlos López, *La Guerra Del Pacífico* (Madrid: Ristre Media, 2003), 15.
30 李鸿章 [Li Hongzhang] 创建轮船水师条款 [Provisions for Founding a Steam Ship Navy] December 31, 1867《清末海军史料》[*Late Qing Naval Historical Materials*], 2; 李鸿章 [Li Hongzhang] 为请设海部兼筹海军事务总理雁门 [Requesting the Establishment of a Maritime Bureau and Office in Charge of Naval Affairs] March 3, 1884《清末海军史料》[*Late Qing Naval Historical Materials*], 31.

31 李鴻章 [Li Hongzhang] 式夫脫 [Shufeldt], September 21, 1888, Shufeldt Papers, Box 25, LOC.
32 A David Evans and Mark Peattie, *Kaigun: Strategy, Tactics, and Technology in the Imperial Japanese Navy 1887–1941* (Annapolis: Naval Institute Press, 1997), 1–7. Though ideas on maritime defense dated to Hayashi Shihei, *Military Discussion in a Maritime Country* (海国兵谈) (1787).
33 A. T. Mahan, *The Influence of Sea Power Upon History 1660–1783* (hereafter *Influence*) (Boston: Little Brown, and Company, 1898), 38.
34 Spencer, *The Confederate Navy in Europe*, 2.
35 Mallory to Davis, February 27, 1862, *ORN*, Series 2, Vol. 2, 151.
36 Mallory to Navy Department CSA, May 19, 1861, *ORN*, Series 2, Vol. 2, 69.
37 Roberts, *Now for the Contest*, xiv; Luraghi, *A History of the Confederate Navy*, 69.
38 Beckert, *Empire of Cotton*, 245; Woodman, *King Cotton and His Retainers*, 217; *The United States and World Sea Power*, 301; Silverstone, *Civil War Navies*, 149.
39 Anna Gibson Holloway and Jonathan W. White, *"Our Little Monitor": The Greatest Invention of the Civil War* (Kent, OH: Kent State University Press, 2018); David A. Mindell, *War, Technology and Experience Aboard the USS Monitor* (Baltimore: Johns Hopkins University Press, 2000); William Still, *Iron Afloat: The Story of the Confederate Armorclads* (Nashville: Vanderbilt Press, 1971); Herman Melville, "A Utilitarian View of the Monitor's Fight," in *Battle Pieces and Aspects of the Civil War* (New York: Harper and Brothers, 1866).
40 McPherson, *War on the Waters*, 224; Thomas Campbell, *Confederate Ironclads at War* (Jefferson, NC: McFarland & Company, 2019).
41 Silverstone, *Civil War Era Navies*, 168.
42 Beckert, *Empire of Cotton*, 260; Spencer, *The Confederate Navy in Europe*, 1; Merli, *Great Britain and the Confederate Navy, 1861–1865*, 14.
43 *The Globe* (London, UK), August 12, 1869, CCC/3 1868, National Maritime Museum/United Kingdom [hereafter NMM/UK]; Hollett, *Men of Iron*, 12. See also: R. Semmes, *The Confederate Raider Alabama*, ed. Philip van Doren Stern (Bloomington: University of Indiana Press, 1962).
44 George W. Dalzell, *The Flight from the Flag: The Continuing Effect of the Civil War upon the American Carrying Trade* (Chapel Hill: University of North Carolina Press, 1940), 238. *The United States and World Sea Power*, 310.
45 Merli, *Great Britain and the Confederate Navy*, 54.
46 Frank Merli, *The Alabama, British Neutrality, and the American Civil War* (Bloomington: Indiana University Press, 2004).
47 "License to use Captain Cowper Coles Shield and Patent Apparatuses on No. 294," December 10, 1862, WA/UK.
48 Walter Wilson and Gary McKay, *James D. Bulloch: Secret Agent and Mastermind of the Confederate Navy* (Jefferson, NC: McFarland & Co., 2012), 277.
49 "Details of Contracts," No. 294 and 295, Ref 5/26, WA/UK. "Details of Contracts," No. 294 and 295, Ref 5/26, WA/UK.
50 Mallory to Navy Department CSA, May 19, 1861, *ORN*, Series 2, Vol. 2, 69.
51 "Details of Contracts," Nos. 294 and 295, Ref 5/26, WA/UK. Though European shipyards had produced armored ships before the US Civil War, Hampton Roads provided an impetus for development. See: Baxter, *The Introduction of the Ironclad Warship*.

52 Wilson and McKay, *James D. Bulloch*, 101.
53 Bulloch to Mallory, December 18, 1862, *ORN*, Series 2, Vol. 2, 309.
54 Carter Stevens, "When the Confederates Terrorized Maine: The Battle of Portland Harbor" (Honors Thesis, Colby College, 2013).
55 Scharf, *Confederate States Navy*, 784.
56 Merli, *Great Britain and the Confederate Navy*, 136.
57 McPherson, *Battle Cry of Freedom*, 547.
58 "Laird and Others to the Commissioners for Executing the Office of Lord High Admiral: Agreement," August 8, 1864, WA/UK; Silverstone, *Civil War Navies*, 151.
59 Merli, *Great Britain and the Confederate Navy*, 194.
60 Rawlinson, *China's Struggle for Naval Development*, 41; Details of Contracts for Vessels, No. 296, No. 297, Ref. 5/26, WA/UK.
61 Details of Contracts for Vessels, No. 326, No. 327, Ref. 5/26, WA/UK.
62 Hollett, *Men of Iron*, 43.
63 Mallory, May 19, 1861, *ORN*, Series 2, Vol. 2, 69.
64 Comisión de Construcción Naval en Estados Unidos, May 29, 1862, AHMP, Comisión de Construcción Naval en Estados Unidos CCEEUU (1862) 0382 Caja 1, Sobre 2, Folio 2; "Specifications," Ericsson to Peruvian Construction Commission in New York, August 25, 1862, AHMP, Comisión de Construcción Naval en Estados Unidos (1862) 0382 Caja 1, Sobre 2, Folio 7.
65 Barreda to Ministerio de Relaciones Exteriores, June 7, 1862, AHMP, Comisión de Construcción Naval en Estados Unidos (1862) 0382 Caja 1, Sobre 2.
66 Details of Contracts for Vessels, No. 321, Ref. 5/26, WA/UK.
67 June 3 1864, AHMP, Caja 1 Sobre 4 Comisión de Construcción Naval en Inglaterra (Huáscar) 1864–1865.
68 Details of Contracts for Vessels, No. 321, Ref 5/26, WA/UK.
69 Fernando Romero Pintado, *Historia Marítima del Perú* (Lima: Instituto de Estudios Histórico-Marítimos Del Perú, 1984) Tomo VIII, Vol. 2, 530; López and Ortiz, *Monitor Huáscar: Una Historia Compartida* (Lima: Association de Historia Marítima Y Naval Iberoamericana, 2005), 10.
70 "An Armour-Clad Turret Ship at Sea," *The Standard* (London, UK), January 31, 1866, CCC/1 1862–1866, NMM/UK; "Captain Cowper Coles and the Admiralty" (Portsmouth, UK), February 10, 1866, CCC/1 1862–1866, NMM/UK.
71 Sullivan, *Phantom Fleet*, 17.
72 Aurelio Garcia y Garcia to Ministerio de la Marina, "Commission de Construcción Naval en Inglaterra Para la Fragata *Independencia*," AHMP, Sub-Series Comisiones de Adquirse Buques-b, Folio 9–10.
73 Aurelio Garcia y Garcia to Ministerio de la Marina, AHMP, Series Comisiones, Sub-Series Comisiones de Adquirse Buques-b, Folio 13, 20.
74 "Details of Contracts," 5/26, 289, WA/UK.
75 Cowper P. Coles, *Journal of the Royal United Service Institution*, Vol. 9 (London, 1868), 436.
76 *Army and Navy Gazette* (London, UK), February 10, 1866, CCC/1 1862–1866, NMM/UK.

77 "Our Ironclad Navy," *Times* (London, UK), August 3, 1870.
78 Jose M. Salcedo to Laird Brothers, December 27, 1864, V0321, WA/UK; Salcedo to Ministry of the Marine, July 16 1865, Caja 1, Sobre 4, Comisión de Construcción Naval en Inglaterra (*Huáscar*) 1864–1865, AHMP, Folio 8. As Federico L Barreda – the Peruvian representative plenipotentiary in London and Paris – stressed in January 1865, nothing but another, completed ironclad ready to sail should persuade Peru to disengage "from so important a commission." Barreda to Ministerio de Relaciones Exteriores, January 31, 1865, Box 1, Folder 2, Southern Illinois University, Special Collections Research Center [hereafter SIU/SCRC], Carbondale, Illinois.
79 Coles personally collected several volumes of newspaper reports covering the debates surrounding his design, see CCC/1-CCC/3, NMM/UK, in particular, "An Armour-Clad Turret Ship at Sea," *The Standard* (London, Great Britain), January 31, 1866; *Illustrated London News* (London, Great Britain), February 17, 1866. See also: Barreda to Ministerio de Relaciones Exteriores, January 31, 1865, Box 1, Folder 2, SIU/SCRC; Cowper P. Coles, *Journal of the Royal United Service Institute*, Vol. 11 (London, 1868), 436.
80 Howard Fuller, *Turret versus Broadside: An Anatomy of British Naval Prestige, Revolution and Disaster 1860–1870* (Warwick, UK: Helion & Company, 2020), 186, 211.
81 A standard textbook on naval history confined the contributions of mine warfare in the Civil War to a footnote. *The United States and World Sea Power*, 368.
82 Louis S. Schafer, *Confederate Underwater Warfare* (Jefferson, NC: McFarland & Co., 1996).
83 Scharf, *History of the Confederate Navy*, 750.
84 D. Farragut to Gideon Welles, March 25, 1864, in John Barnes, *Submarine Warfare* (New York: Van Nostrand, 1869), 102.
85 M. C. Butler, "Southern Genius: How War Developed in an Industrial and Military Way," *SHSP*, Vol. 16 (1888).
86 McPherson, *War on the Waters*, 5.
87 G. T. Beauregard, "Torpedo Service in the Harbor and Water Defences of Charleston," *SHSP*, Vol. 5 (1878): 151. Sometimes "Toombs."
88 J. R. Tucker to W. T. Glassell, September 22, 1863, *ORN*, Series 1, Vol. 15, 12.
89 W. T. Glassell, "Reminiscences of the Torpedo Service in Charleston Harbor," *SHSP*, Vol. 4 (1877): 225.
90 Silverstone, *Civil War Navies*, 167.
91 "Work of Submarine Boats of the CSN," *SHSP*, Vol. 30 (1902): 164.
92 Hunter Davidson, "Electrical Torpedoes as a System of Defence," *SHSP* Vol. 2 (1876): 1; Timothy S. Wolters, "Electric Torpedoes in the Confederacy: Reconciling Conflicting Histories," *The Journal of Military History*, Vol. 72, No. 3 (July, 2008): 755–783.
93 Kenneth Hagan argued that the naval component of coastal defense "did not work" because it failed to "disrupt the Union blockade." This should be weighed against the CSN/CSA's limited successes at riverine and port defense, or what might be called area denial. Kenneth Hagan, *This People's Navy: The Making of American Sea Power* (New York: Free Press, 1991), 173.

94 Luraghi, *A History of the Confederate Navy*, 249; McPherson, *War on the Waters*, 5.
95 Sherman to Dahlgren, February 14, 1866, LOC Dahlgren Papers [hereafter LOC/DP], Box 18, Vol. 1, No. 283.
96 Mallory to Bulloch May 7, 1863, *ORN*, Series 2, Vol. 2, 418.
97 M. C. Butler, "Southern Genius: How War Developed in an Industrial and Military Way," *SHSP*, Vol. 16 (1888): 285.
98 John Schneller and Robert Schneller, *Quest for Glory: A Biography of Rear Admiral John A. Dahlgren* (Annapolis: Naval Institute Press, 1996); Rear Admiral Dahlgren, Report on the *David*, October 7, 1863, *ORN*, Series 1, Vol. 15, 14.
99 Rear Admiral Dahlgren, Report on the *David*, October 7, 1863, *ORN*, Series 1, Vol. 15, 13–14; Line Drawing, Spar Torpedo-Boat, J. H. Tomb Papers, Folder 1, Correspondence 1855–1899, Wilson Special Collections, University of North Carolina [hereafter UNC-CH/WL].
100 S. P. Lee to Gideon Welles, August 25, 1863, *ORN*, Series 1, Vol. 9, 181; Julian McQuiston, *William B. Cushing in the Far East: A Civil War Naval Hero Abroad, 1865–1869* (Jefferson, NC: Mcfarland & Co., 2013), 44.
101 Kennedy, *The Rise and Fall of British Naval Mastery* (New York: Scribner, 1976), 249; Keegan, *The Price of Admiralty*, 7.
102 W. S. Wells to Tomb, December 20, 1916, Folder 2, UNC-CH/WL; W.S. Wells to Tomb, February 15, 1916, Folder 2, UNC-CH/WL.
103 Vicuña Mackenna, *Diez Meses de Misión a los Estados Unidos de Norte América*, 326; Vicuña Mackenna, "Torpedos," *Memória de Marina de Chile*, 1866, 61.
104 志剛 [Zhi Gan], July 14, 1868, 初使泰西記 [Journal of the First Mission to the West] in 《洋务运动, 第8册》 [*Foreign Affairs Movement*, Vol. 8], 260.
105 Kenneth Boulding, *Conflict and Defense* (New York and London: Harper & Row, 1963), 262.
106 Hampton Sides, *Blood and Thunder* (New York: Knopf, 2007), 162.
107 Megan Kate Nelson, *The Three Cornered War* (New York: Scribner, 2020).
108 Michele Cunningham, *Mexico and the Foreign Policy of Napoleon III* (New York: Palgrave Macmillan, 2001).
109 Mallie Stafford, *The March of Empire through Three Decades Embracing Sketches of California History* (San Francisco: Spaulding & Co, 1884), 184–186.
110 Esther Mobley, "A Forgotten Whiskey from the S.F. Gold Rush is Staging a Comeback," *San Francisco Chronicle*, July 24, 2023.
111 Richard White, *Railroaded: The Transcontinentals and the Making of Modern America* (New York: Norton, 2011).
112 Jules Verne, *Around the World in Eighty Days* (New York: Oxford University Press, 1995), 159.
113 Report of Rear Adm. Bell, May 23, 1863, *ORN*, Series 1, Vol. 2, 215; Thomas Savage to Alex McKee, October 3, 1864, *ORN*, Series 1, Vol. 3, 302.
114 Report of Rear Adm. Bell June 23, 1864, *ORN*, Series 1, Vol. 3, 84.
115 James Waddell Diary, August 29, 1863, United States Naval Academy/Nimitz Library [hereafter USNA/NL], MS 144.

116 Bulloch Instructions to Waddell, October 5, 1864, *ORN*, Series 1, Vol. 3, 749; S. Baron to Mallory, Memo, August 19, 1864, *ORN*, Series 2, Vol. 2, 708.
117 "The Shenandoah," *Sacramento Daily Union*, March 31, 1865.
118 "The Pirate Shenandoah," *New York Times*, July 24, 1865; "The Pirate Reported to be Cruising off New-Zealand," *New York Times*, July 24, 1865.
119 "Pirate Steamship on Pacific Waters," *Merced County Sun*, July 29, 1865.
120 Charles James to Hugh McCulloch, July 20, 1865, *ORN*, Series 1, Vol. 3, 588.
121 "The Destruction of Whaleships by the Pirate Shenandoah," *New York Times*, August 4, 1865.
122 Captain D. McDougal to Gideon Welles, July 23, 1865, *ORN*, Series 1, Vol. 3, 571.
123 "The Shenandoah," *Sacramento Daily Union*, March 31, 1865.
124 G. F. Pearson to Gideon Welles, May 10, 1865, *ORN*, Series 1, Vol. 3, 513.
125 Gideon Welles to Captain D. McDougal, August 19, 1865, *ORN*, Series 1, Vol. 3, 587.
126 "Wholesale Destruction of American Whalers," *The Pacific Commercial Advertiser*, August 12, 1865.
127 "Statement of Capt. Hawes," *The Pacific Commercial Advertiser*, August 12, 1865.
128 Log of the CSS *Shenandoah*, *ORN*, Series 1, Vol. 3, 791.
129 Gene A. Smith, *Thomas Catesby Jones: Commodore of Manifest Destiny* (Annapolis: Naval Institute Press, 2000), 107–113; Edwin McClellan, "The Conquest of California," California, Z Files, Naval History and Heritage Command [hereafter NHHC].
130 Bruce Castleman, *Knickerbocker Commodore: The Life and Times of John Drake Sloat, 1781–1867* (New York: Suny Press, 2016).
131 Charles Chapman, *A History of California: The Spanish Period* (New York: The Macmillan Company, 1921), 443–444.
132 "The Confederate Cruiser Shenandoah in the Mersey," *Liverpool Mercury*, November 7, 1865.
133 "The Shenandoah," *New York Herald*, November 21, 1865.
134 Waddell, Notes, *ORN*, Series 1, Vol. 3, 836. John Baldwin and Ron Powers, *Last Flag Down* (New York: Three Rivers Press, 2007); Tom Chaffin, *Sea of Gray: The Around-the-World Odyssey of the Confederate Raider Shenandoah* (New York: Farrar, Straus & Giroux, 2006); Lynn Schooler, *The Last Shot* (New York: Harper Collins 2005).

2 The Pacific's Civil War Inheritance

1 James Henry Rochelle, *Life of Rear Admiral John Randolph Tucker* (Washington, DC: The Neale Publishing Company, 1903); David Werlich, *Admiral of the Amazon: John Randolph Tucker, His Confederate Colleagues and Peru* (Charlottesville: University of Virginia Press, 1990); David Shaw, *Sea Wolf of the Confederacy: The Daring Civil War Raids of Naval Lt. Charles W. Read* (New York: Free Press, 2004); James Hamilton Tomb, *Engineer in Gray: Memoirs of Chief Engineer James H. Tomb*, ed. Thomas Campbell (Jefferson, NC: McFarland & Co, 2005).

2 Sondhaus, *Naval War*, 139.
3 The standard secondary accounts deal with the war's aftereffects in short epilogs. Roberts, *Now for the Contest*; Luraghi, *A History of the Confederate Navy*; McPherson, *War on the Waters*. Silverstone, *Civil War Navies* provides the best reference on what became of vessels (though not personnel) after 1865.
4 Jay Luvaas, *The Military Legacy of the Civil War: The European Inheritance* (Lawrence: University of Kansas Press, 1959); Roberts, *Now for the Contest*, 170; *The United States and World Sea Power*, 389; Fuller, *Turret versus Broadside*, xxxi.
5 *Times* (London, UK) February 7, 1865, CCC/1 1862–1866, NMM/UK, Greenwich, United Kingdom.
6 Werlich, *Admiral of the Amazon*.
7 James Hamilton Tomb – Tucker's chief engineering officer – traveled to Brazil where he worked as a torpedo warfare. James Tomb, *Engineer in Gray*, 134. See also: James Hamilton Tomb Papers, University of North Carolina, Wilson Library, Special Collections [hereafter UNC/WL], Folder 1, Correspondence 1855–1899.
8 "Acciones Para Recibir a la Comisión Científica Española en el Perú," June 26, 1863, MREP, AC/10022.
9 William Columbus Davis, *The Last Conquistadores: The Spanish Intervention in Peru and Chile, 1863–1866* (Athens, GA: University of Georgia Press, 1950); Alberto Wagner de Reyna, *Las Relaciones Diplomáticas entre el Perú y Chile durante el Conflicto con España* (Lima: Ediciones del Sol, 1963).
10 Davis, *The Last Conquistadores*, 109.
11 Mallory to Davis, February 27, 1862, *ORN*, Series 2, Vol. 2, 151; José Manuel Pinto, September 10, 1866, *Memória de Marina de Chile, 1866* (Santiago: Imprenta Nacional, 1866), 5.
12 Vicuña Mackenna, August 25, 1866, *Memória de Marina, 1866*, 60.
13 Garcia y Garcia to Ministerio de la Marina, "Commission de Construcción Naval en Inglaterra Para la Fragata *Independencia*," AHMP, Sub-Series Comisiones de Adquirse Buques-b, Folio 2.
14 Mallory to Davis, February 27, 1862, *ORN*, Series 2, Vol. 2, 151.
15 December 13, 1864, Comisión de Construcción Naval En Francia, 1864–1865, AHMP, Folio 11; *Conway's All the World's Fighting Ships 1860–1905*, ed. Robert Gardiner, et al. (New York: Mayflower, 1979), 418. *Diario a bordo de la Corbeta* Unión, ed. Hernán Garrido-Lecca (Lima: La Casa Del Libro Viejo, 2008), 21. France also offered the ships to Chile, see: Legation de Chile en Britain to M. Carvallo, August 31, 1864, *Memória de Marina 1865*, 53–54.
16 Lawrence Clayton, *Grace: W.R. Grace & Co.: The Formative Years 1850–1930* (Ottawa, IL: Jameson Books, 1985), 112. Gideon Welles, *ARSN 1866*, 9.
17 Sullivan, "Phantom Fleet," 19–23; Silverstone, *Civil War Navies*, 162.
18 Captain Goldsborough to Gideon Welles, April 2, 1866, NARA-1, RG-45, M-125, "Letters to Secretary of the Navy from Captains," Roll 371.
19 Pareja to Thomson, October 12, 1865, No. 36, ENCL 3, TNA/FO 498/22.
20 Davis, *Last Conquistadors*, 245. Denman to Secretary of the Admiralty, February 2, 1866, No. 229, ENCL 1, TNA/FO 498/22.
21 "Spain," *Times* (London, UK) February 28, 1866.

22 Arnulf Becker Lorca, *Mestizo International Law* (Cambridge: Cambridge University Press, 2014), 66, 354.
23 Alvaro Covarrubias, Santiago, October 18, 1865, *Memória de Ministerio de Relaciones Exteriores de Chile* (Santiago: Imprenta Nacional, 1865), 66; Covarrubias to Thomson, February 27, 1866, No. 291, Encl. 1, TNA/FO 498/22.
24 F. X. Rosales to Ministro de Estado en el Departamento de Marina, April 14, 1865, *Memória de Marina de Chile 1865* (Santiago: Imprenta Nacional, 1865), 73.
25 "The Bombardment of Valparaiso," *New York Times*, March 29, 1866; Covarrubias to Thomson, April 7, 1866, No. 29, ENCL 3, TNA/FO 498/22.
26 Thomson to Covarrubias, February 14, 1866, No. 246, ENCL 2, TNA/FO 498/22.
27 Thomson to Clarendon, February 3, 1866, No. 243, TNA/FO 498/22; "The Meteor Case," *New York Herald*, April 7, 1866; "The Chilian War," *New York Times*, March 4, 1866.
28 Thomson to Clarendon, February 3, 1866, No. 243, TNA/FO 498/22.
29 Harvey to Thomson, February 14, 1866, No. 246, Encl. 1, TNA/FO 498/22.
30 "Valparaíso," *New York Herald*, May 10, 1866; Thomson to Clarendon, April 3, 1866, No. 357, TNA/FO 498/22; Eduardo Iriondo, *Impresiones del Viaje de Circunnavegación en la Fragata Blindada* Numancia (Valparaíso: Imprenta del Mercurio, 1868), 46.
31 Molins to Clarendon, May 12, 1866, No. 361, TNA/FO 498/22.
32 Covarrubias to Thomson, February 27, 1866, No. 291, Encl. 1, TNA/FO 498/22.
33 Circular Addressed to Chilean Representatives Overseas, April 1, 1866, No. 29, Encl. 1, TNA/FO 498/22.
34 *Mercurio del Vapor* (Valparaíso) April 16, 1867, NARA-1, RG-45, M-89, Roll 47.
35 Prado, No. 195, August 23, 1866, MREP, Serie Correspondencia, Caja 161, Carpeta 3, Código 5-4-, 1866, Folio 109.
36 Davis, *Last Conquistadors*, 304; Stephen Brown, "The Power of Influence in United States-Chilean Relations" (Ph.D. Diss., University of Wisconsin-Madison, 1983), 154. For "emporium" see: Circular Addressed to Chilean Representatives Overseas, April 1, 1866, No. 29, Encl. 1, TNA/FO 498/22.
37 Fuller, *Turret versus Broadside*, 304.
38 Covarrubias to Thomson, April 7, 1866, No. 29, Encl. 3, TNA/FO 498/22.
39 Ibid.
40 Powell to Admiralty, September 17, 1866, No. 190, Encl. 1, TNA/FO 498/22; "Chili," *New York Times*, September 20, 1866.
41 "Estado que Manifiesta la Artillería," October 22, 1864, AHMP, Marina del Callao 1864, Caja 5, Sobre 17, Folio 135; Romero, *Historia Marítima del Perú*, Tomo VIII, Vol. 2, 614.
42 Edwyn Gray, *Nineteenth-Century Torpedoes and Their Inventors* (Annapolis: Naval Institute Press, 2004).
43 S. P. Lee to Gideon Welles, August 25, 1863, ORN, Series 1, Vol. 9, 181; "John Lay Dies Destitute," *New York Times*, April 21, 1899.

44 McQuiston, *William B. Cushing in the Far East*, 44; Statistical Data of U.S. Ships, *ORN*, Series 2, Vol. 1, 213.
45 Gideon Welles, December 3, 1866, *ARSN 1866*, 12; Hagan *This People's Navy*, 176.
46 Vicuña Mackenna, *Diez Meses de Misión a los Estados Unidos* (Santiago, Chile: Imprenta de la Libertad, 1867), Vol. 1, 119.
47 Thomson to Clarendon, April 12, 1866, No. 287, TNA/FO 498/22.
48 "Spain," *Times* (London, UK), February 28, 1866.
49 Vicuña Mackenna, *Diez Meses de Misión a los Estados Unidos*, Vol. 1, 119.
50 John L. Lay to Perú Ministerio de la Marina, February 27, 1866 MREP, AC/11056, Folio 7.
51 Salcedo to Laird Brothers, December 27, 1864, V0321, WA/UK; Peruvian Legation (London) to Ministerio de Relaciones Exteriores, January 14, 1862, MREP, Servicio Diplomático del Perú Gran Bretaña 1862, Caja 134, C-1, Código 5-17-B, Folio 8.
52 Domingo Ortiz to the Comandancia de Marina, February 28, 1866, MREP, AC/11056, Folio 8–9.
53 Jose Galvez to Arsenal at Callao, March 5, 1866, MREP, AC/11056, Folio 10.
54 Bulloch to Mallory, December 18, 1862, *ORN*, Series 2, Vol. 2, 309.
55 Romero, *Historia Marítima del Perú*, Tomo VIII, Vol. 2, 522.
56 "Diagram of the Peruvian Iron-Clad," *New York Herald*, May 22, 1866.
57 Herbert Wilson, *Ironclads in Action*, Vol. 1 (Boston: Little Brown and Co., 1896), 255.
58 Rodgers to Gideon Welles, May 13, 1866, in *El 2 de Mayo de 1866* (Lima, Perú: Gil, S.A., 1941), 108; Pearson to Welles, May 3, 1866, NARA-1, RG-45, M-89, Roll 43, No. 46; Romero, *Historia Marítima del Perú*, Tomo VIII, Vol. 2, 523.
59 *The Journal and Letters of John M. Brooke*, ed. George M. Brooke (Columbia: University of South Carolina Press, 2002), 41; Request of Adolfo Rosenswig, May 26, 1870, MREP, "Solicitudes," Caja 190, File 6, Codigo 0-9, 1870, Folio 43–44.
60 Davis, *Last Conquistadors*, 311.
61 "Central and South America," *New York Times*, June 1, 1866.
62 Ibid.
63 Vicuña Mackenna, *Historia de la Guerra de Chile con España* (Santiago: Imprenta Victoria, 1883), 406; "Spain," *The Times* (London) August 20, 1869.
64 Pearson to Welles, May 10, 1866, NARA-1, RG-45, Roll 43, Target Two January 2–June 19, 1866.
65 Neale to Clarendon, June 2, 1866, No. 130, TNA/FO 498/22.
66 *Mercurio del Vapor* (Valparaiso) April 16, 1867, NARA-1, RG-45, M-89, Roll 47.
67 Iriondo, *Impresiones del Viaje*, 133; Commission of a Monument, June 26, 1866, MREP, AC/11064.
68 Gilbert Macdonald and Maria Reyes, January 13, 1870, MREP, "Solicitudes," Caja 190, File 6, Codigo 0-9, 1870, Folio 7.
69 Iriondo, *Impresiones del Viaje*, 89.
70 Vicuña Mackenna, *Diez Meses de Misión a los Estados Unidos*, Vol. 1, 119.
71 "John Lay Dies Destitute," *New York Times*, April 21, 1899.

72 De Novo i Colson, *Historia de la Guerra de Chile con España*, 393; Iriondo, *Impresiones del Viaje*, 69–70.
73 Comisión de Construcción Naval EU, September 21, 1867, AHMP, Caja 1, Sobre 3, N 1-A, Folio 14; Comisión de Construcción Naval EU, February 27, 1868, AHMP, Caja 1, Sobre 4, Folio 1.
74 Covarrubias to Peruvian Minister in Chile, September 15, 1866, MREP, Caja 161, Carpeta 8, Codigo 5-4-M, July–December, 1866, Folio 25; *El Diario Espanol* in "Chili," *New York Times*, September 20, 1866.
75 Vicuña Mackenna, *Diez Meses de Misión a los Estados Unidos*, 318, 344.
76 Glassell to Vicuna Mackenna, January 6, 1866, *Diez Meses de Misión a los Estados Unidos*, 344.
77 Rochelle, *Life of Rear Admiral John Randolph Tucker*, 27, 41–49; Werlich, *Admiral of the Amazon*, 88.
78 Andrew Harwood to Tucker, August 11, 1865, Folder 40, Tucker Papers, Old Dominion University, Special Collections [hereafter ODU/TP], Norfolk, VA.
79 "Salida de Contra Almirante Tucker Rumbo a Chile," July 12, 1866, MREP, AC/1109.
80 Secretaría de Guerra y Marina, "Instructions," July 12, 1866, MREP, AC/11096. See also: Rochelle, *Life of Rear Admiral John Randolph Tucker*, 57.
81 Foxhall Parker, translated by Domingo Salamanca, *Tácticas de Escuadras de Buques a Vapor* (Valparaíso: Imprenta de la Patria, 1872). In Peru, it was printed as *Táctica Naval* (likely by Aurelio Garcia y Garcia). See Werlich, *Admiral of the Amazon*, chapter 5, Note 89. Foxhall Parker, *Squadron Tactics under Steam* (New York: V. Nostrand, 1864).
82 Werlich, "Almirante Tucker," *Admiral of the Amazon*.
83 Note the articles in his personal papers: "Launch of a Turkish Ironclad," *Times* (London) December 15, 1864, Folder 39, ODU/TP; "Sir J. Elphinstone," *Times* (London), December 14, 1865, Folder 39, ODU/TP.
84 Toribio Pacheco y Rivero to José Pardo, June 26, 1866, MREP, AC/11407.
85 William Glassell, "Reminiscences of the Torpedo Service in Charleston Harbor," *SHSP*, Vol. 4 (1877): 228.
86 W. R. Butts, "American Officers in the Peruvian Navy," *Californian*, Vol. 6, No. 32 (August, 1882).
87 Commodore Powell to Admiralty, November 27, 1866, No. 248, ENCL 1, TNA/FO 498/22.
88 "Embarcado a la Independencia para su servicio venido del parque de Artillería," October, 1866, MREP, AC/11175, Folio 4; Werlich, *Admiral of the Amazon*, 104.
89 Barton to the Earl of Clarendon, No. 141, June 27, 1866, TNA/FO 498/22.
90 Barton to the Earl of Clarendon, No. 177, August 13, 1866, TNA/FO 498/22.
91 Thomson to Clarendon, June 13, 1866, TNA/FO 498/22, No. 137.
92 Prado to Tucker, August 17, 1866, MREP, Serie Correspondencia, Caja 161, Carpeta 3, Código 5-4-, 1866, Folio 85–86. During the War of 1898, Admiral George Dewey led the US against Manila, following the same logic. George Dewey, *Autobiography of George Dewey* (New York: Charles Scribner's and Sons, 1913), 168.

93 Powell to Secretary of the Admiralty, November 27, 1866, No. 248, ENCL 1, TNA/FO 498/22.
94 *Navigating the Spanish Lake: The Pacific in the Iberian World, 1521–1898*, Rainer Buschmann, et al. (Honolulu: University of Hawai'i Press, 2014).
95 Prado to Minister of Peru in Chile, August 17, 1866, MREP, Serie Correspondencia, Caja 161, Carpeta 3, Código 5-4-, 1866, Folio 87–90.
96 Thornton to Clarendon, May 7, 1866, No.52, TNA/FO 498/22.
97 Goldsborough to Welles, April 2, 1866, NARA-1, RG-45, M-125, "Letters to Secretary of the Navy from Captains," Roll 371.
98 "Central and South America," *New York Times*, June 1, 1866.
99 Rochelle, *Life of Rear Admiral John Randolph Tucker*, 60; Neale to Stanley, October 3, 1866, No. 196, TNA/FO 498/22.
100 Werlich, *Admiral of the Amazon*, 88.
101 Butts, *American Officers in the Peruvian Navy*, in *Californian*, August 1882, Vol. 6., No. 32. For Prado see: Prado to Tucker, March 26, 1867, Folder 8, ODU/TP.
102 *El Comercio* (Lima, Perú), March 20, 1868, Folder 39, ODU/TP.
103 Davis, The Last Conquistadors, 323.
104 Powell to Admiralty, November 27, 1866, No. 248, ENCL 1, TNA/FO 498/22.
105 Dahlgren, Report on the *David*, October 7, 1863, ORN, Series 1, Vol. 15, 14; Madeleine Vinton Dahlgren, *Memoir of John A. Dahlgren* (Boston: James R. Osgood and Co., 1882); Sherman to Dahlgren, February 14, 1866, LOC/DP, Box 18, Vol. 1, No. 283.
106 Dahlgren to Welles, October 12, 1866, No. 5, LOC/DP, Box 18, Vol. 1; U.S. Legation of Perú to Dahlgren, January 10, 1867, No. 58, LOC/DP, Box 18, Vol. 1.
107 Dahlgren to Welles, February 20, 1867, Squadron Letters, NARA-1, RG-45 M-89, Roll 47.
108 Welles to Dahlgren, November 9, 1866, LOC/DP, Box 6, General Correspondence.
109 Marquis de Molins to the Earl Clarendon, November 15, 1865, No. 14 TNA/FO 498/22.
110 Thomson to Russell, Santiago, October 10, 1865, TNA/FO 498/22.
111 Ibid.
112 "The Chilean War – Important Spanish Naval Movements," *New York Herald*, February 16, 1866.
113 "A Proclamation," *The London Gazette*, March 13, 1866, TNA/FO 498/22 Enclosure.
114 Police Commission to Foreign Office, January 15, 1866, TNA/OS 7800/14.
115 "The Chilian War," *New York Times*, March 4, 1866.
116 Vicuna Mackenna, *Diez Meses de Misión a los Estados Unidos*, December 10, 1865, 215; "The Accused Before the United States District Attorney," *New York Herald*, February 8, 1866.
117 Vicuña Mackenna, "Torpedos," *Memória de Marina de Chile*, 1866, 61.
118 H. H. Dotty, *Memória de Marina de Chile*, 1866, 76–80.
119 Benjamin Vicuna Mackenna, August 25, 1866, *Memória de Marina, 1866*, 60.

120 Hunter Davidson, "Electrical Torpedoes as a System of Defence," *SHSP*, Vol. 2 (1876): 3 (emphasis in original).
121 Hunter Davidson, "Davis and Davidson," *SHSP*, Vol. 24 (1896): 286.
122 Werlich, *Admiral of the Amazon*, 105; Commodore Powell to Secretary of the Admiralty, November 27, 1866, No. 248, ENCL 1, TNA/FO 498/22.
123 Dotty to Ministry of the Navy, July 24, 1866, *Memoria de Marina de Chile*, 1866, 76; "The Pacific," *Times* (London) September 13, 1866.
124 Dotty to Ministry of the Navy, July 24, 1866, *Memoria de Marina de Chile*, 1866, 80.
125 Correspondencia, Ministerio de Marina, July 31, 1866, Ministry of the Marine, Vol. 236, 1865–1866, Folio 85, Archivo Histórico Nacional De Chile, Ministerio de Marina [hereafter AHNC/MMAR], Santiago de Chile.
126 Davidson to Ministry of the Marine, August 27, 1866, AHNC/MMAR, Vol. 236, 1866, Folio 191.
127 Jose Ramon Lira to Ministry of the Marine, August 31, 1866, AHNC/MMAR, Vol. 236, Folio 186; "Chili," *New York Times*, September 20, 1866; Werlich, *Admiral of the Amazon*, 105.
128 "Hunter Davidson, CSN in Paraguay," *Confederate Veteran*, Vol. 14 (1906): 396; Hunter Davidson, "Electrical Torpedoes as a System of Defence," *SHSP*, Vol. 2 (1876): 3; Hunter Davidson, "Davis and Davidson," *SHSP*, Vol. 24 (1896): 286. Davidson's colleague Tomb engaged in similar debates. Superintendent Naval War Records to James H. Tomb, June 21, 1899, Folder 1, Correspondence 1855–1899, UNC-CH/WL; Edgar Stanton Maclay to Tomb June 22, 1899, Folder 1, Correspondence 1855–1899, UNC-CH/WL. For adjudication: Timothy Wolters, "Electric Torpedoes in the Confederacy: Reconciling Conflicting Histories," *The Journal of Military History*, Vol. 72, No. 3 (July 2008): 755–783.
129 "Torpedo Steam Launch," *Times* (London) February 1, 1875.
130 Eleanor C. Barnes, *Alfred Yarrow His Life and Work* (London: Edward Arnold & Co., 1923), 73.
131 Silverstone, *Civil War Navies*, 152.
132 Thomas J. Page, "Career of the Confederate Cruiser Stonewall," *SHSP*, Vol. 7 (1879): 263; "The Dano-Rebel Ram Sphynx," *New York Herald*, February 15, 1865; John Rodgers to Gideon Welles, September 9, 1864, *ORN*, Series 1, Vol. 3, 206–209.
133 *Warships of the Imperial Japanese Navy, 1869–1945*, ed. Hansgeorg Jentschura, Dieter Jung, and Peter Mickel (London: Arms and Armour Press, 1977), 12.
134 "Important if True," *Dallas Herald*, March 16, 1865; see also "Rumored Putting to Sea of Confederate Iron-Clads," *The Daily Dispatch* (Richmond, VA), February 16, 1865.
135 Thomas J. Page, "Career of the Confederate Cruiser Stonewall," *SHSP*, Vol. 7 (1879): 279.
136 W. Hunter to G. Garcia Y Tassara, October 5, 1865, *Foreign Relations of the United States* [hereafter *FRUS*] (Washington, DC: Government Printing Office, 1866), II, 576.
137 Gideon Welles, December 2, 1867, *ARSN 1867*, 20.

138 Stephen Howarth, *The Fighting Ships of the Rising Sun: The Drama of the Imperial Japanese Navy* (New York: Atheneum, 1983), 11.
139 *Diary of Gideon Welles*, ed. Howard Beale (New York: W.W. Norton, 1960), Vol. 2, 560–561; Valkenburg to Seward, February 19, 1867, *FRUS* II, 24.
140 Evans and Peattie, *Kaigun*, 10; John Curtis Perry, "Great Britain and the Emergence of Japan as a Naval Power," *Monumenta Nipponica*, Vol. 21, No. 3/4 (1966): 305–321.
141 J. Charles Schencking, *Making Waves: Politics, Propaganda, and the Emergence of the Imperial Japanese Navy, 1868–1922* (Stanford: Stanford University Press, 2005), 16.
142 Seward to Valkenburg, July 6, 1867, *FRUS 1867*, II, 45; "Japan a Great Field for American Enterprise," *New York Herald*, June 12, 1867.
143 "The Iron-Clad Market," *New York Herald*, May 30, 1867.
144 "The Steamer Stonewall," *New York Times*, May 11, 1868.
145 "The Stonewall," *The Pacific Commercial Advertiser* (Honolulu), March 8, 1868; "The Ram Stonewall," *New York Herald*, June 12, 1869; Dr. Samuel Pellman Boyer, *Naval Surgeon: The Diary of Dr. Samuel Pellman Boyer*, Vol. 1, ed. Elinor Barnes and James A. Barnes (Bloomington: Indiana University Press, 1963), 40.
146 Rowan to Welles, February 18, 1869, NARA-1, RG-45, M-89, Roll 254.
147 Rowan to Welles, July 16, 1868, "State of Affairs in Japan," NARA-1, RG-45, M-89, Roll 253.
148 Valkenburgh to Seward, April 28, 1868, No. 47, *FRUS* 1868; Seward to Valkenburgh, May 20, 1868, No. 52, *FRUS* 1868. For "Japanese" see: "Japan," *New York Herald*, November 6, 1868.
149 "Japan," *New York Herald*, November 6, 1868.
150 Mahan, Diary, May 29, 1868, *LPATM*, Vol. 1.
151 Cushing to Carter December 26, 1868, NARA-1, RG-45, M-89, Roll 253; Cushing to Rowan January 18, 1869, NARA-1, RG-45, M-89, Roll 254.
152 Rowan to Secretary of the Navy, February 14, 1869, NARA-1, RG-45, M-89, Roll 254; "Public Auction at Yokohama Japan," *Japan Gazette* (Yokohama) July 1869.
153 Rowan to Adolph Borie, Secretary of the Navy, April 18, 1869, NARA-1, RG-45, M-89, Roll 254; Rowan to Broie, May 13, 1869, NARA-1, RG-45, M-89, Roll 254.
154 "Japan," *New York Herald*, June 20, 1869.
155 Rowan to Broie, July 23, 1869, NARA-1, RG-45, M-89, Roll 254.
156 Bradford, "Report to Rowan," June 11, 1869, NARA-1, RG-45, M-89, Roll 254; Arai Ikunosuke to Enomoto, Bradford, "Report," ENCL 2, June 11, 1869, NARA-1, RG-45, M-89, Roll 254.
157 "Japan," *New York Herald*, August 1, 1869.
158 Rowan to Broie, July 23, 1869, NARA-1, RG-45, M-89, Roll 254; Bradford, "Report," June 11, 1869, NARA-1, RG-45, M-89, Roll 254.
159 "Important if True," *Dallas Herald*, March 16, 1865.
160 Rowan to Borie, June 26, 1869, NARA-1, RG-45, M-89, Roll 254.
161 Mahan, *From Sail to Steam*, 252.
162 *Kaijun Zushiki* [海軍圖識] (Tokyo: Okadaya Kashichi, 1870).
163 *North China Herald* (Beijing, China), August 29, 1874.

164 Charles H. Cramp, "The Coming Sea-Power," *The North American Review*, Vol. 165, No. 491 (1897).
165 Mahan, *From Sail to Steam*, 252.
166 Rawlinson, *China's Struggle for Naval Development*, 2; Bruce Elleman, *Modern Chinese Warfare, 1795–1989* (New York: Routledge, 2001), 33. 夏东元 [Xia Dongyuan] 《洋务运动》 [*The Foreign Affairs Movement*] (上海: 华东师范大学出版社, 1992), 304; 李平子 [Li Pingzi] 《从鸦片战争到甲午战争》 [*From the Opium War to the Sino-Japanese War*] (上海: 华东师范大学出版社, 1998), 118, 369. For earlier ideas, see: Ronald C. Po, *The Blue Frontier: Maritime Vision and Power in the Qing Empire* (Cambridge: Cambridge University Press, 2018).
167 Orville Schell and John Delury, *Wealth and Power: China's Long March to the Twenty-First Century* (New York: Random House, 2013).
168 The historian Li Pingzi criticized Qing reliance on "reason" over "force" as a consistent impediment to naval power [相信'理'而不相信'力'的作用], and credits Lin Zexu with rejecting that worldview. See: 李平子 [Li Pingzi] 《从鸦片战争到甲午战争》 [*From the Opium War to the Sino-Japanese War*], 115. See also: 关伟 [Guan Wei] 《北洋海军从筹建到覆灭的几点思考》 [Some Points of Thought on the Beiyang Navy from its Founding to its Demise], 40–41; 戚其章 [Qi Qizhang] 《北洋舰队覆没的历史反思》 [Reflections on the Annihilation of the Beiyang Navy], 10.
169 李鸿章 [Li Hongzhang] 创建轮船水师条款 [Conditions for Founding a Steamship Navy] January 2, 1867, 《清末海军史料》 [*Late Qing Navy Historical Materials*], 1; 夏东元 [Xia Dongyuan] 《洋务运动》 [*Foreign Affairs Movement*], 327. For Li and the Chinese Navy see: 钱钢 [Qian Gang] 《大清海军与李鸿章》 [*The Qing Navy and Li Hongzhang*] (香港: 中华书局, 1989, 2004); 王家俭 [Wang Jiajian] 《李鸿章与北洋舰队: 近代中国创建海军的失败与教训》 [*Li Hongzhang and the Beiyang Navy*] (北京: 三联书店, 2008).
170 戚其章 [Qi Qizhang] 《北洋舰队覆没的历史反思》 [Reflections on the Annihilation of the Beiyang Navy], 12; Jane Kate Leonard, *Wei Yuan and China's Rediscovery of the Maritime World* (Cambridge, MA: Harvard University Press, 1984), 5.
171 王家俭 [Wang Jiajian] 《中國近代海軍史論集》 [Discussions of Modern Chinese Naval History] (台北: 文史哲出版社, 1984), 1. Bruce Elleman, *The Chinese People's Liberation Army Navy and the History of Coastal Defence, in The Maritime Defence of China*, ed. Y. H. T. Sim (Singapore: Springer Nature Singapore, 2017), 116.
172 陈可畏 [Chen Kewei] 《1874年日本侵台事件与近代中国的东海危机》 [Japan's 1874 Invasion of Taiwan and the Modern Chinese Crisis in the East China Sea] 《浙江师范大学学报》 2014, 39 (1), 28–32; 夏东元 [Xia Dongyuan] 《洋务运动》 [*Foreign Affairs Movement*], 307. 王家俭 [Wang Jiajian] 《中國近代海軍史論集》 [*Discussions on Modern Chinese Naval History*], 1.
173 Paul D. Barclay, *Outcasts of Empire: Japan's Rule on Taiwan's "Savage Border," 1874–1945* (Los Angeles: University of California Press, 2018), 43–113; Edwin Pak-Wah Leung, "The Quasi-War in East Asia: Japan's Expedition to Taiwan and the Ryūkyū Controversy," *Modern Asian Studies*, Vol. 17, No. 2 (1983): 257–281.

174 H. H. Bell, "Skirmish with the Savages of Formosa," *ARSN 1867*, 55.
175 Gideon Welles, *ARSN 1867*, 8; CDR Belknap "Report," June 15, 1867, *ARSN 1867*, 56.
176 李鶴年 [Li Henian] 台湾防务大概情形 [General Situation of Taiwan's Defensive Affairs], June 14, 1874, 《清末海軍史料》 [*Late Qing Navy Historical Materials*], 2; Westad, *Restless Empire*, 92–93.
177 李鴻章 [Li Hongzhang], 籌議海防 [Establishing Maritime Defenses] 同治十三年十一月二日 (1874) 《洋务运动》第1冊 [*Foreign Affairs Movement*, Vol. 1] 45.
178 李鶴年 [Li Henian] 台湾防务大概情形 [General Situation of Taiwan's Defensive Affairs], June 14, 1874, 《清末海軍史料》 [*Late Qing Navy Historical Materials*], 2.《論英國近造火礮》 [Discussion on Newly Produced English Cannon], *Shenbao*, September 30, 1875;《論購造鐵甲船》 [Discussion of Purchasing Ironclad Warships], *Shenbao*, December 15, 1874.
179 总理衙门奏拟筹海防应办事 [Zongli Yamen, Memorial Proposing the Establishment of Coastal Defense and the Management of Affairs], November 5, 1874《清末海軍史料》 [*Late Qing Naval Historical Materials*], 5.
180 *North China Herald* (Beijing, China), August 29, 1874.
181 志剛 [Zhi Gan], 1868, 初使泰西記 [Journal of the First Mission to the West] in《洋务运动, 第8冊》 [*Foreign Affairs Movement*, Vol. 8], 260.
182 Viktor Von Scheliha, *A Treatise on Coast-Defence* (London: E. & F.N. Spon, 1868);《防海新论》 [New Theory of Coastal Defense] was published by the 江南制造局 [Jiangnan Arsenal] in 1874; 陈先松, 焦海燕 [Chen Xiansong, Jiao Haiyan]《北洋海军购置雷艇考述》 [A Study on the Purchasing of Torpedoes by Beiyang Navy]《安徽史学》 [*Anhui Historical Studies*], No. 1 (2017): 121–129.
183 "Literature," *London Illustrated News*, September 12, 1868. 李鴻章 [Li Hongzhang], 奏籌议海防折 [Memorial on the Establishment of Maritime Defense], December 10, 1874,《清末海軍史料》 [*Late Qing Naval Historical Materials*], 106.
184 Dean Mahin, *The Blessed Place of Freedom: Europeans in Civil War America* (Washington, DC: Brassey's, 2002), 75.
185 李鴻章 [Li Hongzhang], 籌議海防 [Establishing Maritime Defenses] 同治十三年十一月二日《洋务运动, 第1冊》 [*Foreign Affairs Movement*, Vol. 1], 45.
186 《論購造鐵甲船》 [Discussion of Purchasing and Manufacturing Ironclad Warships], *Shenbao*, December 12, 1874;《新到水雷》 [Newly arrived Torpedo-Mines] *Shenbao*, September 27, 1877.
187 李宗義 [Li Zongxi], 奏總理衙門 [Memorial to the Zongli Yamen], 1874,《洋务运动, 第1冊》 [*Foreign Affairs Movement*, Vol. 1], 71; an opinion echoed later almost word for word by 强汝询 [Qiang Ruxun] 海防議 [Coastal Defense Opinions],《洋务运动, 第1冊》 [*Foreign Affairs Movement*, Vol. 1], 358; 刘名誉 [Liu Mingyu] 越事備考 [Sino-French War],《洋务运动, 第3冊》 [*Foreign Affairs Movement*, Vol. 3], 424.
188 李鴻章 [Li Hongzhang],《李文忠公全書》 [Complete Works of Li Hongzhang], 光緒元年七月二十五日《洋务运动, 第3冊》 [*Foreign Affairs Movement*, Vol. 3], 291.

189 李鸿章 [Li Hongzhang], 奏筹议海防折 [Memorial on the Establishment of Maritime Defense], December 10, 1874,《清末海軍史料》[*Late Qing Naval Historical Materials*], 107; 志剛 [Zhi Gan], 1868, 初使泰西記 [Journal of the First Mission to the West] in《洋务运动, 第8册》[*Foreign Affairs Movement*, Vol. 8], 260.
190 李鶴年 [Li Henian] 台湾防务大概情形 [General Situation of Taiwan's Defensive Affairs], June 14, 1874,《清末海軍史料》[*Late Qing Naval Historical Materials*], 2.
191 Elleman, *Modern Chinese Warfare*, 85.
192 王家俭 [Wang Jiajian]《中國近代海軍史论集》[Discussions on Modern Chinese Naval History], 16.
193 《記津南兵情形》[Record of the Jinnan Military Situation], *Shenbao*, April 27, 1877;《水雷停買》[Halt to the Purchase of Torpedoes], *Shenbao*, October 11, 1877.
194 Sondhaus, *Naval War*, 139.
195 Gideon Welles, *ARSN 1868*, viii.
196 Dahlgren to Welles, February 20, 1867, Squadron Letters, NARA-1, RG-45, M-89, Roll 47.

3   Pacific Naval Races and the Old Steam Navy

1 Órdenes Generales, 1872, AHMP, Caja 10, Sobre 17, Folio 9; Gardiner, *The Japanese and Peru, 1873–1973*.
2 Legation of Perú and Japan and China, "Memorandum," March 5, 1873, MREP, Caja 216, Carpeta 6, Código 5–11, 42–44; November 12, 1872, No. 253, *FRUS 1872*, Vol. 1, 1873, 570; Gardiner, *The Japanese and Peru 1873–1973*, 17.
3 Navy of Japan, March 7, 1873, MREP, Oficios de la Legación del Perú en China y Japón, Caja 216, Capeta 6, Código 5–11, Folio 6.
4 Report to Ministerio de Relaciones Exteriores, January 15, 1874, MREP Servicio Consular del Perú in Hong Kong, Caja 228, Carpeta 16, Código 8-23-A, Folio 1.
5 Pedro Bustamante, July 28, 1878, *Memória del Rama de Guerra*, Vol. 2 (Lima: Imprenta Nacional, 1878), 9; 李宗羲 [Li Zongxi] 奏總理衙門 [Memorial, Zongli Yamen]《洋务运动, 第1册》[*Foreign Affairs Movement*, Vol. I], 69.
6 *The United States and World Sea Power*, 393; Rose, *Power at Sea*, 13.
7 Lance Crowther Buhl, "The Smooth Water Navy: American Navy Policy and Politics 1865–1876" (Ph.D. Diss., Harvard University, 1969); Hagan, *American Gunboat Diplomacy and the Old Navy*, 7.
8 Dahlgren to Welles, October 12, 1866, No. 5, LOC/DP, Box 18, Vol. 1; Dahlgren to Welles, February 20, 1867, Squadron Letters, NARA-1, RG-45 M-89, Roll 47; Rowan to Borie, June 26, 1869, NARA-1, RG-45, M-89, Roll 254.
9 Pomeranz, *The Great Divergence*.
10 Robert W. Shufeldt, *The Influences of Western Civilization in China* (Stamford, CT: William Gillespie & Co., 1868), 31.

11 Osterhammel and Petersen, *Globalization: A Short History*, 66; Osterhammel, *The Transformation of the World*, 394; Kennedy, *Rise and Fall of Great Powers*, 150; 李平子[Li Pingzi]《从鸦片战争到甲午战争》[*From the Opium War to the Sino-Japanese War*], 19.
12 Ferguson, *Civilization: The West and the Rest*.
13 Hobsbawm, *The Age of Empire*, 59.
14 Tai Ming Cheung, "Racing from Behind: China and the Dynamics of Arms Chases and Races in the Twenty-First Century," in *Arms Races in International Politics*, 247.
15 López, *La Guerra Del Pacífico*, 229; Barros, *Historia Diplomática de Chile, 1541–1938*, 326; *Arms Races in International Politics*, 6–7.
16 Van de Ven, "A Hinge in Time," *The Cambridge History of War*, 43–44; Grant T. Hammond, *Plowshares into Swords: Arms Races in International Politics, 1840–1991* (Columbia, SC: University of South Carolina Press, 1993), 36; Matthew Seligmann, *The Naval Route to the Abyss: The Anglo-German Naval Race, 1895–1914* (London: Routledge, 2015); David Herrmann, *The Arming of Europe* (Princeton: Princeton University Press, 1996); David Stevenson, *Armaments and the Coming of War: Europe, 1904–1914* (Oxford: Oxford University Press, 1996); Colin Gray, "The Urge to Compete: Rationales for Arms Racing," *World Politics*, Vol. 26, No. 2 (January, 1974): 207–223.
17 Samuel P. Huntington, "Arms Races: Prerequisites and Results," *Public Policy* (1958) 41.
18 Huntington, "Arms Races," 49.
19 Mahan to Ashe, May 21, 1875, *LPATM*, Vol. 1, 434.
20 David Stevenson, "Before 1914," in *Arms Races in International Politics*, ed. Thomas Mahnken, Joseph Maiolo, and David Stevenson (Oxford: Oxford University Press, 2016), 11–13; Jon T. Sumida "Naval Armaments Races, 1889–1922," *The Sea in History*, 151–156.
21 Jonathan A. Grant, *Rulers, Guns, and Money: The Global Arms Trade in the Age of Imperialism* (Cambridge, MA: Harvard University Press, 2007).
22 戚其章 [Qi Qizhang]《北洋舰队覆没的历史反思》[Rethinking the Annihilation of the Beiyang Navy] in《北洋海軍新探》[*Beiyang Navy: New Explorations …*].
23 Reynolds to Secretary of the Navy Thompson, December 4, 1877, NARA-1, M-89, Roll 263; Crosby to Walker, August 3, 1883, NARA-1, M-89, Roll 269; Peter A. Shulman, *Coal and Empire: The Birth of Energy Security in Industrial America* (Baltimore: Johns Hopkins University Press, 2015); David Allan Snyder, "Petroleum and Power: Naval Fuel Technology and the Anglo-American Struggle for Core Hegemony, 1889–1922" (Ph.D. Diss., Texas A&M University, 2001).
24 Gideon Welles, December 3, 1866, *ARSN 1866*, 23.
25 Rose, *Power at Sea*, 100; "Sheridan of the Sea," *The Mail* (New York), May 23, 1898, Union Ironworks Scrapbooks, National Maritime Resource Center/San Francisco [hereafter NMRC/SF].
26 Robeson, *ARSN 1869*, 5.
27 Albert Browne, "The Growing Power of the Republic of Chile," *Journal of the American Geographical Society of New York*, Vol. 16 (1884): 27; Edward

Melillo, "The First Green Revolution: Debt Peonage and the Making of the Nitrogen Fertilizer Trade, 1840–1930," *The American Historical Review*, Vol. 117, No. 4 (2012): 1028–1060.
28 Mario Barros, *Historia Diplomática de Chile, 1541–1938* (Santiago: Andrés Bello, 1970), 326.
29 LT J. F. Meigs, USN, "The War in South America," *Proceedings of the USNI*, Vol. 5 (1879): 463.
30 Concerns about Argentina were another impetus for naval investment. López, *Historia de la Marina de Chile*, 229–230.
31 López, *Guerra del Pacífico*, 15.
32 Brown, *The Power of Influence*, 154.
33 Mason, *The War on the Pacific Coast of South America*, 13.
34 J. Ramón Lira, *Memoria del Ministerio de Marina, 1871–1872* (Santiago: Imprenta Nacional, 1871), 7–8.
35 *Conway's All the World's Fighting Ships 1860–1905*, 410; A. Blest-Gana,"La construcción de los buques Almirante Cochrane, Valparaíso, Magallanes," AHNC/MMAR 129, Folio 1–6.
36 "Launch of a Chilian Ironclad," *Hull Times Office*, in Legacio de Chile to Departamento de Marina, May 20, 1875, AHNC/MMAR 130.
37 Mason, *The War on the Pacific Coast of South America*, 14; Ministerio de Marina Contratos Sobre Construcción de Buques en Inglaterra (1818–1882), AHNC/MMAR, Vol. 19, Nos. 44–45.
38 G. H. Preble to Secretary of the Navy Thompson, October 2, 1877, NARA-1, RG-45, M-89, Roll 65.
39 Silverstone, *Civil War Navies*, 18.
40 Mason, *The War on the Pacific Coast of South America*, 13.
41 Pedro Bustamante, July 28, 1878, *Memória del Rama de Guerra*, Vol. 2, 9.
42 López, *Guerra del Pacífico*, 16.
43 The *Abtao*, *O'Higgins*, *Chacabuco*, and *Esmeralda*; also the gunboats *Covadonga* and *Magallanes*. López, *Historia de la Marina de Chile*, 234. For torpedo-boats: Yarrow and Co. to Brown Esq, July 29, 1879, AHNC/MMAR, Vol. 369, loose-leaf at front of volume. See also: William Sater, *Andean Tragedy: Fighting the War of the Pacific, 1879–1884* (Lincoln: University of Nebraska Press, 2007), 113; Carlos Lopez Martinez, *Historia Maritima del Peru*, Tomo X (Lima: Instituto de Estudios Historico-Maritimos del Peru, 1988), 784.
44 "El Rol de los Vapores Mercantes," *Revista de Marina*, No. 6 (December, 1885): 657; Mason, *The War on the Pacific Coast of South America*, 16; Carlos Antunez, *Memoria de Ministro de Marina, 1885* (Santiago: Imprenta Nacional, 1885), lxix.
45 Preble to Thompson, October 2, 1877, NARA-1, RG-45, M-89, Roll 65.
46 "Inventory of Books at the Naval School 1870," AHNC/MMAR, Vol. 278, 1870.
47 Sater, *Andean Tragedy*, 111. According to the *Union's* official history, forty-three members of the crew (19 percent) were foreign, primarily of British or North American extraction. Hernán Garrido-Lecca, *Diario a bordo de la Corbeta* Unión, 19, 51, 105.
48 McCann Journal, October 13, 1881, McCann Papers, No. 6, USNA/NL.

49 "Launch of a Chilian Ironclad," *Hull Times Office*, in Legacio de Chile, May 20, 1875, AHNC/MMAR 130.
50 "Contract," July 2, 1874, AHNC/MMAR 130; "Conducción y Entrega del Almirante Cochrane," AHNC/MMAR 130.
51 "Story of the Career of Don Carlos M'Arti," *San Francisco Morning Call*, April 12, 1896. One of the many recruited by Peru; "Contracts," June–August 1874, Servicio Diplomático del Perú – Gran Bretaña, MREP, Caja 226, Carpeta 8, Código 5-17-R, 7–24; "James Whitehead," June 10, 1873, Servicio Diplomático del Perú – Gran Bretaña, MREP, Caja 217, Carpeta 4, Código 5-17-A, 99.
52 Peru's four ironclads (*Huáscar, Independencia, Manco Capac, Atahualpa*) all referenced Peruvian/Inca resistance to Spanish rule. *Cochrane* likewise referred to the British-born hero of the Chilean War of Independence.
53 Mason, *The War on the Pacific Coast of South America*, 16, 21.
54 Preble to Thompson, June 21, 1877, NARA-1, RG-45, M-89, Roll 65, No. 34; Preble to Thompson, ENCL 1 June 21, 1877, NARA-1, RG-45, M-89, Roll 65, No. 35.
55 Portal al Mayor de la 2nd Division, October 14, 1879, *Diario a bordo de la Corbeta* Union, 102.
56 Stockton "The Inter-Oceanic Canal," July 23, 1894, Staff Presentations 1886–1900, Record Group 14, Box 1, Naval Historical Collection, US Naval War College [hereafter USNWC-NHC], Newport, RI (emphasis in original); Kenneth Wenzer, "The U.S. Navy and the Conquest of the Pacific by Lt. Cmdr. Charles H. Stockton," *International Journal of Naval History*, Vol. 14, No. 2 (2018).
57 Robert Scheina, "Indigenous Latin American Sea Power" (Ph.D. Diss., Catholic University of America, 1974).
58 López, *Guerra del Pacífico*, 16.
59 Preble to Thompson, October 25, 1877, NARA-1, RG-45, M-89, Roll 65.
60 E. Le Leon, *Revue Maritime*, quoted in Browne, "The Growing Power of the Republic of Chile," 81.
61 Lopez, Ortiz, *Huáscar*, 18–19; RADM de Horsey to Graham, June 6, 1877, TNA/FO 881/3329, No. 8, ENCL 4.
62 Bedford, Diary, Friday May 11, 1877, Bedford Papers [hereafter BED] 5, NMM/UK; "The Revolutionary Movement," *South Pacific Times*, May 21, 1877, NARA-1, RG-45, M-89, Roll 65.
63 Bedford Letters, May 12, 1877, BED/7, NMM/UK.
64 De Horsey to Graham, June 6, 1877, TNA/FO 881/3329, No. 8, ENCL 4.
65 Bedford, Diary, Friday May 29, 1877, BED/5, NMM/UK.
66 De Horsey to Secretary of Admiralty, June 3, 1877, TNA/FO 881/3329, No. 9, ENCL 1; Bedford, Diary, June 1, 1877, BED/5, NMM/UK.
67 Don Enrique Gennario, June 19, 1877, MREP, Gran Bretaña 1877, Caja 149, File 20, Codigo 5-17-Q, Folio 5; "The Huáscar" *South Pacific Times* c. May 30, 1877, NARA-1, RG-45, M-89, Roll 65.
68 Bedford to de Horsey, May 29, 1877, TNA/FO 881/3329, No. 9, ENCL 10; Gray, *The Devil's Device*, 108; "Action between the Pirate Huáscar and HMS Shah and Amethyst, May 29, 1877," TNA/FO 881/3329, No. 9, ENCL 10.

69 "Orders Addressed to Captain Bedford, *Shah*, May 31, 1877," TNA/FO 881/3329, No. 9, ENCL 11; Don Enrique Gennario, June 19, 1877, MREP, Gran Bretaña 1877, Caja 149, File 20, Codigo 5-17-Q, Folio 6.
70 Charles Lindsay to Bedford, June 3, 1877, TNA/FO 881/3329, No. 9, ENCL 13; RADM de Horsey to Secretary of the Admiralty, June 3, 1877, TNA/FO 881/3329, No. 9, ENCL 1.
71 "Chile y Perú," *La Patria* (Lima, Perú), June 21, 1877, in NARA-1, RG-45, M-89, Roll 65; see also "Review for [sic] Abroad" *South Pacific Times*, June 14, 1877, in NARA-1, RG-45, M-89, Roll 65; "Version Ingles," *El Comercio* (Lima, Perú), September 11, 1877; "Protesta," MREP, Gran Bretaña 1877, Caja 149, File 20, Código 5-17-Q, Folio 97. See also: MREP, Caja 247, Carpeta 15, Código 2-0-E, 1877, Folio 9–10; "Los Sucesos del Perú," *Mercurio de Valparaíso*, June 16, 1877.
72 Gibbs to Evarts, July 20, 1877, *FRUS* 1877, No. 251; "Engagement Between the English Warship and the Rebel Huáscar," *South Pacific Times*, June 2, 1877, NARA-1, RG-45, M-89, Roll 65; "Los Sucesos del Perú," *Mercurio de Valparaíso*, June 16, 1877.
73 Gibbs to Evarts, July 20, 1877, *FRUS* 1877, No. 251.
74 Bedford Letters, May 1877, BED/7, NMM/UK.
75 March to Earl of Derby, June 9, 1877, TNA/FO 881/3329, No. 7.
76 *South Pacific Times*, June 13, 1877, NARA-1, RG-45, M-89, Roll 65.
77 "Peruvian Complications," *New York Herald*, July 7, 1877. See also: *South Pacific Times*, May 28, 1877, NARA-1, RG-45, M-89, Roll 65. For US coverage see: "The Naval Fight off Perú," *New York Times*, July 7, 1877; "Perú and Bolivia," *New York Herald*, June 25, 1877.
78 "Los Sucesos del Perú," *Mercurio de Valparaíso* (Valparaíso, Chile), June 16, 1877.
79 "The Shah and The Huascar" *Times* (London) July 17, 1877; RADM de Horsey to Secretary of the Admiralty, June 3, 1877, TNA/FO 881/3329 No. 9, ENCL 1.
80 Bedford Letters, May (undated), 1877, BED/7, NMM/UK.
81 Bedford Letters, June 1, 1877, BED/7, NMM/UK.
82 Dahlgren to Welles, February 20, 1867, Squadron Letters, NARA-1, RG-45 M-89, Roll 47.
83 王韜 [Wang Tao]記制造局 [Record of the Arsenal]《洋务运动，第8冊》[*Foreign Affairs Movement*, Vol. 8], 347. See also: Bruce Elleman, *Modern Chinese Warfare, 1795–1989*, 85; 王家儉 [Wang Jiajian],《李鴻章對於中國海軍近代化的貢獻》[Li Hongzhang's Program toward Naval Modernization],《歷史學報》[*Historical Studies Report*], June 1, 1988, 16期 (No. 16), 91–105.
84 直隸總督李鴻章奏摺 [Memorial of the Zhili Viceroy Li Hongzhang], 光緒五年十一月二十六日《洋务运动，第1冊》[*Foreign Affairs Movement*, Vol. 1], 203; 王先謙 [Wang Xianqian] 翰林院奏摺 [Memorial of the Hanlin Academy],《洋务运动，第1冊》[*Foreign Affairs Movement*, Vol. 1], 184. 世鐸奏 [Memorial of Shiduo] 光緒元年二月二十七日《洋务运动，第1冊》[*Foreign Affairs Movement*, Vol. 1], 118–119.
85 總理各國事務衙門奏 [Memorial of the Zongli Yamen] 同治十三年九月二十七日,《洋务运动，第1冊》[*Foreign Affairs Movement*, Vol. 1], 26; 總理衙門奕

訢奏 [Memorial of Prince Gong and the Zongli Yamen] 光緒三年六月十五日,《洋务运动, 第2冊》[*Foreign Affairs Movement*, Vol. 2], 372–373.

86 Westad, *Restless Empire*, 91; 两江总督曾国荃总遵旨筹议海防 [Viceroy of the Jiangnan and Jiangxi, Zeng Guoquan on the Founding of Maritime Defense], July 3, 1885,《清末海軍史料》[*Late Qing Naval Historical Materials*], 42. Though military matters were central, Qing reformers were also interested more broadly in industrial technology, see:《洋务运动》第1–8冊 [*Foreign Affairs Movement*, Vols. 1–8]; *Strengthen the Country and Enrich the People: The Reform Writings of Ma Jianzhong* (1845–1900), trans. Paul J. Bailey (Richmond, UK: Curzon Press, 1998).

87 李宗羲 [Li Zongxi] 奏總理衙門 [Memorial to the Zongli Yamen]《洋务运动, 第1冊》[*Foreign Affairs Movement*, Vol. 1], 69.

88 總理各國事務衙門奏 [Memorial of the Zongli Yamen] 同治十三年九月二十七日,《洋务运动, 第1冊》[*Foreign Affairs Movement*, Vol. 1], 26.

89 Rawlinson, *China's Struggle for Naval Development*, 1; Bruce A. Elleman "The Neglect and Nadir of Chinese Maritime Policy under the Qing," in *China Goes to Sea: Maritime Transformation in Comparative Historical Perspective*, ed. Andrew S. Erickson, Lyle J. Goldstein, and Carnes Lord (Annapolis: Naval Institute Press, 2009), 289; Elleman, *Modern Chinese Warfare*, 83–86; Richard J. Smith in *Li Hung-Chang and China's Early Modernization*, ed. Samuel C. Chu and Kwang-Ching Liu (London: East Gare Book, 1994), 135. Thomas Kennedy, *The Arms of Kiangnan Modernization in the Chinese Ordnance Industry 1860–1895* (Boulder: University of Colorado Press, 1978); Paul Cohen, *Between Tradition and Modernity: Wang T'ao and Reform in Late Ch'ing China* (Cambridge, MA: Harvard University Press, 1974); Wright, *The Last Stand of Chinese Conservatism*; Ralph Powell, *The Rise of Chinese Military Power* (Princeton: Princeton University Press, 1955). See also: 王家儉 [Wang Jiajian]《中國近代海軍史論集》[*Discussions of Modern Chinese Naval History*], 309; 李 [Li]《从鸦片战争到甲午战争》[*From the Opium War to the Sino-Japanese War*], 19.

90 王栻 [Wang Shi]《严复传》[*Biography of Yan Fu*] (上海: 上海人民出版社, 1975), 3.

91 宋德玲 Song Deling《日本海军的近代化》[Japanese Naval Modernization]《世界历史》[*World History*] (1993), 第2期, 102–109.

92 Benjamin Elman, "Naval Warfare and the Refraction of China's Self-strengthening Reforms into Scientific and Technological Failure, 1865–1895," *Modern Asian Studies*, Vol. 38, No. 2 (2004): 283–326; Meng Yue, "Hybrid Science versus Modernity: The Practice of the Jiangnan Arsenal," *East Asian Science, Technology, and Medicine*, No. 16 (1999): 13–52; Adam Chang, *Reappraising Zhang Zhidong: Forgotten Continuities During China's Self-Strengthening 1884–1901 Journal of Chinese Military History*, Vol. 6 (2017): 157–192.

93 Allen Fung, "Testing the Self-Strengthening: The Chinese Army in the Sino-Japanese War of 1894–95," *Modern Asian Studies*, Vol. 30, No. 4 (1996): 1007–1031. See also: 苏同炳 [Su Tongbing]《中国近代史上的关键人物》[*Key Figures in Modern Chinese History*] (台北: 百花文艺出版社, 2000), 294; 王 [Wang]《严复传》[Biography of Yan Fu], 3; S. C. M. Paine "Imperial Failure in the Industrial Age: China, 1842–1911," *The Sea in History*, 308–318.

94 David Pong, *Shen Pao Chen and China's Modernization in the Nineteenth Century* (Cambridge: Cambridge University Press, 1994), 2. For similar debates in the PRC, see: 戚其章 [Qi Qizhang]《北洋舰队覆没的历史反思》[Rethinking the Annihilation of the Beiyang Navy] in《北洋海軍新探》*[Beiyang Navy: New Explorations ...]*; 陈悦 [Chen Yue]《北洋海軍》*[The North Sea Fleet]* (济南: 山东画报出版社, 2015).
95 Adam Chang, "Reappraising Zhang Zhidong," *Journal of Chinese Military History*, Vol. 6 (2017): 157–192; Hodong Kim, *Holy War in China: The Muslim Rebellion and State in Chinese Central Asia, 1864–1877* (Stanford: Stanford University Press, 2004).
96 Kimberly to Rodgers, October 4, 1871, NARA-1, RG-45, M-89, Roll 257.
97 Encl to Reynolds, December 19, 1875, NARA-1, RG-45, M-89, Roll 261.
98 McNair to Reynolds, February 7, 1877, NARA-1, RG-45, Area Files M-625, Roll 348, 1861–1887; *North China Daily News*, December 10, 1875; *North China Herald*, September 5, 1874.
99 "Chinese Navy," *Daily Alta California* (San Francisco, CA), April 28, 1881.
100 Mullan to Asiatic Station, April 6, 1882, NARA-1, RG-45, M-89, Roll 268.
101 "Presentation to a Chinese Admiral," *Edinburgh Daily News*, August 9, 1881.
102 "Tyne-Built Vessels for the Chinese Navy," *York Herald* (York, UK), August 8, 1881.
103 "Chinese Gunboats," *Shields Daily Gazette* (South Shields, UK), August 8, 1881.
104 薛福成 [Xue Fucheng] 北洋海防水師章程 [Program of the Beiyang Navy and Coastal Defense]《洋务运动, 第3册》[*Foreign Affairs Movement*, Vol. 3], 361; 李鴻章 [Li Hongzhang] 北洋通商大臣 [North Sea Commercial Minister] 光緒九年二月八日,《洋务运动, 第2册》[*Foreign Affairs Movement*, Vol. 2], 532. 論英國近造火礟 [Discussion on Newly Produced English Cannon], *Shenbao*, September 30, 1875;《論購造鐵甲船》[Discussion of Purchasing Ironclad Warships], *Shenbao*, December 15, 1874.
105 《购办铁甲船消息》[News on the Purchase of an Ironclad] *Shenbao*, 1874年第677号;《购铁甲战舰》[Purchasing an Ironclad Warship] *Shenbao*, 1874年第695号.
106 陈[Chen]《北洋海军》[The North Sea Fleet], 57; Howarth, *The Fighting Ships of the Rising Sun*, 14.
107 李鸿章议复梅启照条陈折 [Li Hongzhang responding to Mei Qizhao's Proposal], January 1, 1881《清末海軍史料》[*Late Qing Navy Historical Materials*], 21.
108 舟欲行 [Zhou Yuxing] 黃传会 [Huang Chuanhui]《清末北洋海军纪实》*Record of the Late Qing Beiyang Navy* (北京: 学苑出版社, 2007), 166.
109 《中國在德國》[China in Germany], *Shenbao*, August 25, 1881;《輪船錫名》[Steamship Bestowed a Name], *Shenbao*, February 15, 1884;《吉秘續聞》[Chile and Peru, Additional News ...] *Shenbao*, June 18, 1879;《再述秘魯被兵事》[Additional Description of the Attack of Peru] *Shenbao*, June 20, 1879. "The Naval and Military Power of China," French Operations in China and Tonking, August 22 to October 15, The National Archives/War Office [hereafter TNA/WO] 106/66.

110 Elleman, "The Chinese People's Liberation Army Navy and the History of Coastal Defence," in *The Maritime Defence of China*, 121.
111 隸總督李鴻章奏 [Memorial of the Viceroy Li Hongzhang], 光緒十一年三月三日《洋务运动, 第2册》[*Foreign Affairs Movement*, Vol. 2], 167.
112 马军 [Ma Jun]《事迹与文献: 甲午黄海海战北洋水师中的洋员》 [Achievements and Documents: The Foreigners Employed by the North Sea Fleet in the Naval Battle of the Yellow Sea]《军事历史研究》[*Military History Research*] No. 4 (July, 2015): 108–116.
113 Reynolds to Robeson, November 7, 1875, NARA-1, RG-45, M-89, Roll 261.
114 Reynolds to Robeson, December 19, 1875, NARA-1, RG-45, M-89, Roll 261.
115 "Chinese Navigators," *The Celestial Empire* (Shanghai, China) December 4, 1875, in Encl to Reynolds to Robeson, December 19, 1875, NARA-1, RG-45, M-89, Roll 261.
116 Reynolds to Robeson, December 20, 1877, NARA-1, RG-45, M-89, Roll 263 (emphasis in original).
117 苏小东 Su Xiaodong 《北洋海军提督丁汝昌的身世及早年经历》[The Early Life Experiences of the Beiyang Fleet Commander Ding Ruchang] 安徽史学 [*Anhui History*] 2010年, 第1期, 106–111.
118 李鸿章 [Li Hongzhang] 奏接续遴材派赴各国留学谕 [Memorial on the Cultivation of Talent and the Dispatch of Students to Study Overseas], November 19, 1879《清末海軍史料》[*Late Qing Navy Historical Materials*], 388.
119 冯保善 [Feng Baoshan]《严复传》[*Biography of Yan Fu*] (北京: 团结出版社, 1998), 1–15.
120 "Naval Notes and News," *Portsmouth Telegraph*, September 22, 1880.
121 "Chinese Officers in the English Navy," *Edinburgh Evening News*, June 26, 1880.
122 王 [Wang]《严复传》[*Biography of Yan Fu*], 5–14.
123 Drake, *The Empire of the Sea*, xi.
124 Shufeldt Report, c. 1882, Shufeldt Papers, LOC, Box 24, Korean Treaty Items.
125 "Foh-kien Flotilla," August 12, 1881, Shufeldt Papers, LOC, Box 24, China Correspondence, 1880–1881. See also:《西報論中國水師事》[Western Reports Discuss Chinese Naval Affairs], *Shenbao*, June 4, 1881.
126 Drake, *The Empire of the Sea*, 257.
127 "Com. Shufeldt and the Chinese Navy," *Daily Alta California* (San Francisco, CA), March 26, 1881.
128 陈先松, 焦海燕 [Chen Xiansong, Jiao Haiyan]《北洋海军购置雷艇考述》[A Study on the Purchasing of Torpedoes by Beiyang Navy]《安徽史学》[*Anhui Historical Studies*], No. 1 (2017): 121–129; 李凤苞 [Li Fengbao] 使德日记 [Diary of the Emissary to Germany]《洋务运动, 第1册》[*Foreign Affairs Movement*, Vol. 1] 271.
129 Fish torpedo see: 鱼雷《副魚雷匠衣花》See: 北洋水师号衣图说 [Beiyang Navy Uniforms, Illustrations]《清末海軍史料》[*Late Qing Naval Historical Materials*], 469.
130 總理衙門奕訢爱新觉罗·奕訢奏 [Memorial of Shiduo] 光緒元年六月二十三日,《洋务运动, 第2册》[*Foreign Affairs Movement*, Vol. 2], 337.

131 Kimberly to Rodgers, October 4, 1871, ENCL 1, McClean Diagram, NARA-1, RG-45, M-89, Roll 257, No. 28. See also: "The Chinese Navy," *North China Herald*, December 16, 1875.
132 《在天津》[In Tianjin] *Shenbao*, March 3, 1877.
133 "China," *Torpedo Instruction School: Annual Report*, TNA/ADM 189/1, 72; "Captain of *Vernon*'s Remarks on LT Gamble's Report on Chinese Foreign Depot and Defence of Canton," *Torpedo Instruction School: Annual Report*, TNA/ADM 189/4.
134 秦缃业 [Qin Xiangye] 海防議 [Opinions on Maritime Defense], c. 1882, 《洋务运动，第1冊》[*Foreign Affairs Movement*, Vol. 1], 368; "Report on Chinese Mines, Progress" (1883) *Torpedo Instruction School*, TNA/ADM, 189/3, 190.
135 《數年以前南北花旗交戰時》[Several Years Ago during the US Civil War ...] *Shenbao*, September 7, 1877.
136 《美國人賴君》[The American John Lay], *Shenbao*, October 15, 1877; 《記津南過兵情形》[Record of Southern Tianjin Military Situation], *Shenbao*, April 27, 1877; 《述論魚水雷功用》[Discussing the Capabilities of Locomotive Torpedoes], *Shenbao*, March 3, 1877; 《在天津》 [In Tianjin ...] *Shenbao*, March 3, 1877.
137 《水雷停買》[Halt to the Purchase of Torpedoes], *Shenbao*, October 11, 1877.
138 U. S. Grant, *The Papers of Ulysses S. Grant: October 1, 1878–September 30, 1880* (Carbondale, IL: SIU Press, 1967), 163. For the meeting itself see: 《譯西報記李中堂禮賓事》[Translation of Western Papers Recording the Ceremonies of Li Hongzhang], *Shenbao*, July 4, 1879.
139 Gray, *19th Century Torpedoes and Their Inventors*, 43–44.
140 Mannix, Z Files, NHHC.
141 李鴻章 [Li Hongzhang] September 21, 1880, Shufeldt Papers, LOC, Box 24, China, Misc.
142 《西報論中國水師事》[Western Reports Discuss Chinese Naval Affairs], *Shenbao*, June 4, 1881.
143 Daniel Mannix III, *The Old Navy* (New York: Macmillan, 1983), 16.
144 Mannix III, *The Old Navy*, 23; 《津信彙錄》[Tianjin Record] *Shenbao*, April 14, 1884; *Congressional Record*, Vol. 17, June 8, 1886.
145 Schmidt and Co to Shufeldt, February 16, 1882, Shufeldt Papers, LOC, Box 24, Folder 1882.
146 "Specifications," Ericsson to Peruvian Construction Commission in New York, August 25, 1862, AHMP, Comisión de Construcción Naval en Estados Unidos (1862) 0382 Caja 1, Sobre 2, Folio 7.
147 李鴻章[Li Hongzhang] 奏续先学生出洋折 [Memorial on the Selection of Students to Send Overseas] December 2, 1881,《清末海軍史料》[*Late Qing Historical Materials*], 392; 直隸總督李鴻章奏 [Memorial of the Zhili Viceroy Li Hongzhang], 光緒五年十月十六日《洋务运动，第2冊》[*Foreign Affairs Movement*, Vol. 2] 420.
148 L. C. Arlington, *Through the Dragon's Eyes* (London: Constable & Co LTD, 1931), 15; H. E. Mullan to John M. B. Clitz, April 6, 1882, NARA-1, RG-45, M-89, Roll 268. See: Jonathan Spence, *To Change China: Western Advisers in China 1620–1960* (Boston: Little, Brown and Co., 1969).

Memoirs abound. James Allan, *Under the Dragon Flag* (New York: Frederick A. Stokes Company, 1898); *Robert Hart and China's Early Modernization*, ed. Richard Smith, John King Fairbank, and Katherine Frost Bruner (Cambridge, MA: Harvard University Press, 1991).

149 Shellen Xiao Wu, *Empires of Coal: Fueling China's Entry into the Modern World Order, 1860–1920* (Stanford, CA: Stanford University Press, 2015).

150 王先謙 [Wang Xianqian] 翰林院奏 [Memorial of Hanlin Academy] 光緒五年九月二十八日,《洋务运动,第1册》 [*Foreign Affairs Movement*, Vol. 1], 184.

151 Mullan to John M. B. Clitz, April 6, 1882, NARA-1, RG-45, M-89, Roll 268.

152 Mullan to John M. B. Clitz, April 6, 1882, NARA-1, RG-45, M-89, Roll 268. British Naval Intelligence in 1884 mirrored USN findings. "The Naval and Military Power of China," TNA/WO 106/66.

153 Mullan to John M. B. Clitz, April 6, 1882, NARA-1, RG-45, M-89, Roll 268.

154 Intelligence Branch, September 22, 1883, TNA/WO 106/66.

155 "China," *Torpedo Instruction School*, TNA/ADM, 189/4.

156 Robert Albion, *Makers of Naval Policy* (Annapolis: Naval Institute Press, 1980), 9.

157 Mahan, *From Sail to Steam: Recollections of a Naval Life*, 197.

158 Oscar Wilde, "The Canterville Ghost," *The Complete Works of Oscar Wilde* (London: Harper Collins, 2003), 197.

159 Robert Darnton, *The Great Cat Massacre and Other Episodes in French Cultural History* (New York: Basic Books, 1984).

160 D. D. Porter, October 2, 1871, *ARSN 1871*, 47.

161 "China for the Chinese," *New York Times*, March 30, 1882. For Wei Yuan see: 魏源 [Wei Yuan, 师夷长技以制夷 ["Study the Foreigners' Advanced Technologies and by Means of Them Control Them."] 《海国图志》 [Illustrated Treatise on the Maritime Kingdoms].

162 Steven Ericson, *The Sound of the Whistle: Railroads and the State in Meiji Japan* (Cambridge, MA: Harvard University Press, 1996).

163 "The War Cloud," *New York Herald*, December 7, 1873.

164 Silverstone, *Civil War Navies*, 162.

165 T. O. Selfridge, "Reconstruction of Our Navy," February 3, 1882, *Congressional Record*.

166 Rowan to Secretary of Navy, February 14, 1869, NARA, RG-45, M 89, Roll 254.

167 Cushing to Carter, December 26, 1868, NARA, RG-45, M 89, Roll 254.

168 Mahan to Ashe, December 27, 1875, *LPATM*, Vol. 1, 436.

169 Chisholm, *Waiting for Dead Men's Shoes*.

170 Mahan to Taylor, June 30, 1873, *LPATM*, Vol. 1, 385.

171 Karsten, *Naval Aristocracy*.

172 Hagan, *American Gunboat Diplomacy and the Old Navy*, 7.

173 Donald Canney, *The Old Steam Navy* (Annapolis: Naval Institute Press, 1990), 154.

174 Mobley, *Progressives in Navy Blue*, 26.

175 Mahan to Taylor, March 11, 1873, *LPATM*, Vol. 1, 377.
176 Karsten, *Naval Aristocracy*, 193; Mobley, *Progressives in Navy Blue*, 13; David Andersen, *Imperialism and Idealism: American Diplomats in China 1861–1898* (Bloomington: Indiana University Press, 1985).
177 Wolters, "Recapitalizing the Fleet," 103.
178 Gray, "The Urge to Compete," 224.
179 Hagan, *American Gunboat Diplomacy and the Old Navy*, 10.
180 Kennedy, *The Rise and Fall of British Naval Mastery*.
181 Gregory Cushman, *Guano and the Opening of the Pacific World: A Global Ecological History* (New York: Cambridge University Press, 2013); Arthur Power Dudden, *The American Pacific: From the Old China Trade to the Present* (New York: Oxford University, 1992).
182 "Reception and Entertainment of the Chinese Embassy by the City of Boston" (Boston: Alfred Mudge and Son, 1868), 20; *The First Chinese Embassy to the West: The Journals of Kuo Sung-T'ao, Liu Hsi-Hung and Chang Te-Yi*, translated by J. D. Frodsham (Oxford: Clarendon Press, 1974), 93. 余坚 [Yu Jian]《中美外交关系之研究》[*Research in Sino-US Diplomatic Relations*] (台北: 正中书局印行, 1973), 8. For primary accounts see: 初使泰西記 [First Journey to the West] 1868,《洋务运动, 第2册》[*Foreign Affairs Movement*, Vol. 2] 358. Also: Zheng Huangfu, "Internalizing the West: Qing Envoys and Ministers in Europe, 1866–1893" (Ph.D. Diss., UCSD, 2012).
183 Shufeldt, *The Influences of Western Civilization in China*, 10, 32.
184 William H. Seward, *New York Times*, February 25, 1871.
185 Paolino, *The Foundations of the American Empire*, 28.
186 Robeson, *ARSN 1871*, 4.
187 Gordon H. Chang, "Whose 'Barbarism'? Whose 'Treachery'? Race and Civilization in the Unknown United States–Korea War of 1871," *The Journal of American History*, Vol. 89, No. 4 (March, 2003): 1331–1365; Christoph Nitschke, "The U.S. Korean Conflict of 1871 and Imperial Commonality in the East Asian Arena," *Diplomatic History*, Vol. 46, No. 5 (2022): 929–959.
188 Robeson, *ARSN 1871*, 4.
189 Ibid., 13.
190 Ibid., 4.
191 McCann Journal, January, 1880, McCann Papers, Journal No. 5, USNA/NL.
192 McCann Journal, March 1, 1880, McCann Papers, No. 5, USNA/NL.
193 McCann Journal, February 18, 1880, McCann Papers, No. 5, USNA/NL.
194 McCann Journal, Date Unclear, McCann Papers, No. 5, USNA/NL.
195 McCann Journal, November 9, 1880, McCann Papers, No. 5, USNA/NL.
196 Bustamante, July 28, 1878, *Memória del Rama de Guerra*, Vol. 2 (Lima: Imprenta Nacional, 1878), 9.
197 李宗羲 [Li Zongxi] 奏總理衙門 [Memorial, Zongli Yamen]《洋务运动, 第1册》[*Foreign Affairs Movement*, Vol. 1], 69.
198 Mahan, *Influence*, 9.
199 李鸿章议复梅启照条陈折 [Li Hongzhang Responding to Mei Qizhao]《清末海軍史料》[*Late Qing Naval Historical Materials*], 24.

4 Pacific Wars and Their Lessons

1. Mahan, "Introduction," in Wilson, *Ironclads in Action*, Vol. 1, xiv–xv. Or, alternatively, the "test of practice," as opposed to theory. See: A. T. Mahan, "Naval Warfare," Lowell Institute Lectures, 1897, Mahan Papers, LOC, Box 5, Reel 4, Lecture 3, 96.
2. Chandler, *ARSN 1883*, 8.
3. Sater, *Andean Tragedy*; Lopez, *Guerra del Pacifico*; Bruce Farcau, *The Ten Cents War: Chile, Peru and Bolivia in the War of the Pacific 1879–1884* (Westport, CT: Praeger Publishers, 2000).
4. Department of State, *The Question of the Pacific: America's Alsace and Lorraine* (Washington, DC: Government Printing Office, 1919).
5. French Legation to Minister of Foreign Relations, October 29, 1897, *Informes Inéditos de Diplomáticos Extranjeros Durante la Guerra del Pacífico*, 270.
6. V. G. Kiernan, "Foreign Interests in the War of the Pacific," *The Hispanic American Historical Review*, Vol. 35, No. 1 (February, 1955): 14–36; Detail: "Heroes del Huáscar" Pacific Station in HMS Triumph, Album 0025, National Maritime Museum/Woolwich Arsenal [hereafter NMM/WA]. For history see: Diego Barros Arana, *Historia de la Guerra del Pacífico* (Santiago: Librería Central de Mariano Servat, 1880), Vols. 1–2; López, *Historia de la Marina de Chile*, 227–279; *Guerra del Pacífico*, ed. Pascual Ahumada (Santiago: Andrés Bello, 1982); López and Ortiz, *Monitor Huáscar: Una Historia Compartida*; Black, *Naval Warfare*, 18–19; Sondhaus, *Naval Warfare*, 128–132.
7. "Chile and Her Enemies," *New York Times*, December 12, 1879.
8. Legation of Chile in Panama, May 1879, Ministerio de Relaciones Exteriores [hereafter AMREC] Santiago, Chile, Vol. 62-D, Folios 182, 196, 276–283, 360–365; Legation of Chile in Panama, September 3, 1879, AMREC, Vol. 62-D, Folio 196.
9. Charles Flint, *Memories of an Active Life* (New York & London, G. P. Putnam 1923), 86; *Guerra del Pacífico*, Vol. 2, 279.
10. John Lay to Minister of War, January 26, 1882, AHNC/MMAR, Vol. 369, 27.
11. "Inventory of the Lay," Conflictos Internacionales Conflicto con Chile, AHMP, J, 5 Box 1, File 2, 0781; Cable, August 19, 1879 Callao, Manuel Palacios, *Guerra del Pacífico*, Vol. 1, 452.
12. "Inventory of the Lay," Conflictos Internacionales Conflicto con Chile, AHMP, J, 5 Box 1, File 2, 0781.
13. Grau to the Peruvian Commandant General, August 31, 1879, as used in *Diario a Bordo del Huáscar* ed. Robert Hunter (Buenos Aires: Francisco De Aguirre, S.A, 1977), 138.
14. Grau to Director de Marina, August 31, 1879, *Diario a Bordo del* Huáscar, 139.
15. 《水雷停買》 [Halt to the Purchase of Torpedoes], *Shenbao*, October 11, 1877.
16. Clements Markham, *War between Perú and Chile 1879–1882* (London: Sampson Low, Marston and Co. 1882), 222–223. Listing at the time: "gun torpedoes," Harvey towing torpedoes, "Ley [sic]" torpedoes, Hardley's torpedo, McEvoy's "outrigger torpedo."
17. "Chile and Her Enemies," *New York Times*, December 12, 1879.

18 Portal to Mayor del Departamento, November 29, 1879, *Diario a bordo de la Corbeta* Unión, 130. In addition to Lay Torpedoes, the *Union* also cruised with Harvey and McEvoy prototypes.
19 Ministerial Residence of Imperial Germany to Minister of State, September 9, 1879, *Informes Inéditos de Diplomáticos Extranjeros Durante la Guerra del Pacífico*, 30.
20 Melitón Carvajal Pareja, *Historia Marítima del Perú*, Tomo XI, Vol. 1 (Lima: Instituto de Estudios Histórico-Marítimos del Perú, 2004), 751.
21 Flint, *Memories of an Active Life*, 87; "Torpedo," *New York Times*, December 12, 1879.
22 John Evans to Peruvian Legation in London, January 11, 1881, Servicio Diplomático del Perú – Gran Bretaña, MREP, Caja 280, Carpeta 1, Código 5-17-L, 11 (emphasis in original).
23 "Ericsson's New Torpedo," *New York Times*, September 1, 1880.
24 Portal to Mayor del Departamento, November 29, 1879, *Diario a bordo de la Corbeta* Unión, 130.
25 "Peru," *Torpedo Instruction School* (1881), TNA/ADM 189/1, 72.
26 Winsor Statement, "Reconstruction of the Navy," Appendix to *Congressional Record*, January 24, 1882, 149.
27 "Ericsson's New Torpedo," *New York Times*, September 1, 1880.
28 Barnes, *Alfred Yarrow His Life and Work*, 73; "Torpedo Steam Launch," *Times* (London) February 1, 1875; Yarrow and Co. to Brown Esq., July 29, 1879; Articles in reference to Yarrow, c. 1879, AHNC/MMAR, Vol. 369, loose leaf at front of volume.
29 J. C. Julius Moller July 31, 1879, AHNC/MMAR, Vol. 369; Consulate of Chile San Francisco, November 3, 1879, AMREC, Vol. 62-D, Folio 73.
30 John Lay to Minister of War, January 26, 1882, AHNC/MMAR, Vol. 369, 27.
31 "Los Torpedoes," *Mercurio de Valparaiso* (Valparaíso, Chile), April 26, 1880; "Las Torpederas Como Medio de Defensa del Litoral," *Revista de la Marina*, August 1885, No. 2, 138–140; Jose Maria Santa Cruz "Resena de Defensa," *Revista de la Marina* October, 1885, No. 4.
32 Markham, *The War between Perú and Chile*, 189; "Cartas de la Escuadra," *Mercurio de Valparaiso* (Valparaíso, Chile), May 13, 1880.
33 "Cartas de la Escuadra," *Mercurio de Valparaiso* (Valparaíso, Chile), May 13, 1880; "Cartas de la Escuadra," *Mercurio de Valparaiso* (Valparaíso, Chile), May 14, 1880; Markham, *The War between Perú and Chile*, 222–223; "Chili," *Torpedo Instruction School*, TNA/ADM 189/1, 72.
34 Duncan Kennedy, "The Tactics of the Torpedo" 1888, USNWC-NHC, RG 14, Box 1.
35 刘名誉 [Liu Mingyu], 水雷艇策 [Torpedo-Boat Plans],《洋务运动, 第3册》[*Foreign Affairs Movement*, Vol. 3], 431; "Peru War," *Torpedo Instruction School* TNA/ADM, 189/1, 82–83.
36 Blume to Ministry of the Navy, December 3, 1879, Conflictos Internacionales, Conflicto con Chile, AHMP, J, 5, Box 1, 3; Robert Scheina, *Latin America: A Naval History 1810–1987* (Annapolis: Naval Institute Press, 1987), 36.

37 Watt Stewart, "Federico Blume's Peruvian Submarine," *The Hispanic American Historical Review*, Vol. 28, No. 3 (August, 1948): 468–478; Jorge Ortiz Sotelo, *Apuntes para la Historia de los Submarinos Peruanos* (Lima: Biblioteca Nacional del Peru, 2001).
38 Scheina, *Latin America: A Naval History*, 36.
39 Barros, *Historia de la Guerra del Pacífico*, Vol. 2, 197.
40 F. Stansbury Haydon, *Aeronautics in the Union and Confederate Armies* (Baltimore: Johns Hopkins University Press, 1941).
41 Barros Arana, *Historia de la Guerra del Pacífico*, Vol. 2, 61–65.
42 "VENGANZA! VENGANZA!" *Mercurio de Valparaiso* (Valparaiso, Chile), July 10, 1880.
43 "Covadonga," *Mercurio de Valparaiso* (Valparaiso, Chile), October 5, 1880.
44 "Notes on the Navies of Lesser-European, Asiatic and South and Central American States," Office of Naval Intelligence, Security Classified Publications, 1882–1954, NARA-1, Record Group 38, Box 26, Entry 141, 470.
45 "Notes on the Navies of Lesser-European, Asiatic and South and Central American States," Office of Naval Intelligence, Security Classified Publications, 1882–1954, NARA-1, Record Group 38, Box 26, Entry 141, 470.
46 E. Chouteau, *Revista de Marina*, No. 1, July 1885, 6–7 (emphasis in original).
47 "Chilian Circular to the Foreign Representatives," November 10, 1880, *FRUS* 1881, Encl 1. No. 181, 115; Frederick Pike, *The United States and the Andean Republics* (Cambridge, MA: Harvard University Press, 1977); Herbert Millington, *American Diplomacy and the War of the Pacific* (New York: Columbia University Press, 1948); "Annual Message of the President," *FRUS* 1881, vii; Brown, "The Power of Influence," 154.
48 McCann Journal, December 20, 1881, McCann Papers, No. 6, USNA/NL.
49 "Special Notice," *Los Angeles Herald*, December 15, 1881.
50 James Blaine to Arthur, February 3, 1882, Series 1, Library of Congress/Arthur Papers.
51 Chester Arthur, State of the Union, 1881, The American Presidency Project, U.C. Santa Barbara.
52 "The Navy without Ships," *New York Times*, December 4, 1882.
53 Frank Ninkovich, *Global Dawn: The Cultural Foundations of American Internationalism, 1865–1890* (Cambridge, MA: Harvard University Press, 2009), 313.
54 "Our Navy," *Harper's Magazine*, December 17, 1881, emphasis in original.
55 Preble to Thompson, June 21, 1877, NARA-1, RG-45, M-89, Roll 65, No. 34. Patricia Arancibia Clavel, Isabel Jara Hinojosa, and Andrea Novoa Mackenna, *La Marina en la Historia de Chile*, Tomo I (Santiago: Random House, 2005), 475; Alberto Silva Palma, *Crónicas de la Marina Chilena*, 2nd ed. (Santiago: Talleres de Estado Mayor Jeneral, 1913), 234; Vicuña Mackenna, "El Reparto del Pacífico," 68.
56 Hurlbut to Blaine, October 5, 1881, *FRUS 1881*, Nos. 572, 938; Blaine to Hurlbut, December 3, 1881, *FRUS 1881*, Nos. 584, 956–957; Balch to Hunt, October 19, 1881, NARA-1, RG-45, M-89, Roll 69.
57 Balch to Hunt, December 15, 1881, NARA-1, RG-45, M-89, Roll 69.

58 McCann Journal, December 3, 1881, McCann Papers, No. 6, USNA/NL.
59 McCann Journal, December 9, 1881, McCann Papers, No. 6, USNA/NL.
60 Vicuna-Mackenna, "El Reparto del Pacifico," *Revista de Marina*, No. 1, 1885, 65.
61 McCann Journal, January 2, 1882, McCann Papers, No. 6, USNA/NL, emphasis in original.
62 McCann Journal, April 13, 1882, McCann Papers, No. 6, USNA/NL.
63 McCann Journal, October 5, 1881, McCann Papers, No. 6, USNA/NL.
64 A. T. Mahan to S. Ashe, December 21, 1882, *LPATM*, Vol. 1, 543–544.
65 《秘魯續聞》 [Additional News from Peru], *Shenbao*, May 17, 1881;《秘魯虐待華佣事后》 [Aftermath of Perú's Abuse of Chinese Laborers], *Shenbao*, May 15, 1882; Spenser St. John to Earl Granville, June 27, 1881, No. 75, TNA/FO 881/4602.
66 吉秘續聞 [Chile and Perú News] *Shenbao*, June 18, 1879;《再述秘魯被兵事》 [Additional Description of the Attack of Peru] *Shenbao*, June 20, 1879. Historical accounts from the 1890s reference the war as well, see: 薛福成 [Xue Fucheng] 攻戰守具不用之用說《洋務运动，第1冊》 [*Foreign Affairs Movement*, Vol. 1], 387.
67 For general histories see: 龍章 [Long Zhang]《越南与中法战争》 [*Vietnam and the Sino-French War*] (臺北市：臺灣商務印書館, 1996); 李云泉 [Li Yunquan] 中法战争前的中法越南问题交涉与中越关系的变化 [Pre Sino-French War China-French-Vietnam Question Exchanges and Changes to Sino-Vietnamese Relations]《社会科学辑刊》No. 5 (2010): 150–55.
68 李文忠公全集光绪七年十二月二十二日 [Li Hongzhang Complete Works] in《中法戰爭, 第4冊》 [*Sino-French War*, Vol. 4] 邵循正 [Shao Xunzheng] (上海：新知出版社, 1955), 1.
69 War Office Correspondence, September 22, 1883, TNA/WO 106/66.
70 邵循正 [Shao Xunzheng],《中法战争资料叙列》 [Introduction, *Sino-French War Historical Materials*]《中法戰爭, 第1冊》 [*Sino-French War*, Vol. 1], 1; 钟启顺 周秋光 [Zhong Qishun and Zhou Qiuguang]《二十年来中法战争研究综述》 [Twenty Years digest of Research on the Sino-French War] 河池师专学报 [*Hechi Normal University Report*] Vol. 23, No. 1, March 2003
71 邵循正 [Shao Xunzheng],《中法战争资料叙列》 [Introduction, *Sino-French War Historical Materials*] in 《中法戰爭, 第1冊》 [*Sino-French War*, Vol. 1], 1–2.
72 Elleman, *Modern Chinese Warfare, 1795–1989*, 92.
73 Intelligence Branch, French Operations in Tong-King, TNA/WO 106/66, Part VII, 7.
74 "Admiral Courbet Official Report of the Sheipoo Affair," TNA/WO 106/66, Part VII, 27;《又有法國水雷船入》 [Additionally, There Were French Torpedo Boats That Entered ...], *Shenbao*, September 28, 1884.
75 刘名誉 [Liu Mingyu] 水雷艇策 [Torpedo Boat Plans]《洋务运动, 第3冊》 [*Foreign Affairs Movement*, Vol. 3], 431; "Memorial of Ho Superintendent of the Arsenal," *North China Herald* (Beijing, China), October 15, 1884.
76 Wilson, *Ironclads in Action*, Vol. 2, 11.
77 Duncan Kennedy, "The Tactics of the Torpedo" (1888) USNWC-NHC, RG-14, Box 1.

78 Rawlinson, *China's Struggle for Naval Development*, 1; *China's Quest for Modernization: A Historical Perspective*, ed. Fred Wakeman and Wang Xi (Berkeley: University of California Press, 1997); Lei Xianglin, *Neither Donkey nor Horse: Medicine in the Struggle over China's Modernity*, 260; See: Fan Fa-Ti, "Redrawing the Map Science in Twentieth-Century China," *Isis*, Vol. 98, No. 3 (2007): 524–538.
79 Intelligence Branch, French Operations in Tong-King, TNA/WO 106/66, Part V.
80 《法人狡計》 [The Cunning Plan of the French], *Shenbao*, October 8, 1884.
81 Intelligence Branch, French Operations in Tong-King, TNA/WO 106/66, Part V.
82 "The Naval Operations in Formosa," TNA/WO 106/66, Part VI, 17.
83 寄译署 [Translation Office] 光绪十年 6月十九日,《中法戰爭第4冊》 [*Sino-French War*, Vol. 4], 179.
84 《淡水軍信》 [Danshui/Tamsui Military Information], *Shenbao*, October 12, 1884.
85 "The Naval Operations in Formosa," TNA/WO 106/66, Part VI, 17; 寄译署 [Translation Office] 光绪十年九月二十三日,《中法戰爭, 第4冊,》 [*Sino-French War*, Vol. 4], 213.
86 W. H. Beehler, "The Capture of the Pescadores Islands," *Information from Abroad V* (Washington: Government Printing Office, 1886), 185.
87 Wu, *Empires of Coal*, 31.
88 "Affairs at Kelung," *North China Herald* (Beijing, China), November 5, 1884; 《厦門確電》 [Authentic Telegraphs from Xiamen], *Shenbao*, August 13, 1884.
89 "The Naval Operations in Formosa," TNA/WO 106/66, Part VI, 18.
90 Intelligence Branch, French Operations in Tong-King, TNA/WO 106/66, Part VI, 27.
91 《淡水勝仗指證》 [Evidence of the Glorious Victory at Danshui/Tamsui], *Shenbao*, October 15, 1884.
92 "The French Repulse at Tamsui," *New York Times*, October 20, 1884; "The French Repulsed," *North China Herald* (Beijing, China), October 15, 1884; "Bombardment of Tamsui," *North China Herald* (Beijing, China), October 22, 1884; James Wheeler Davidson, *Island of Formosa Past and Present* (New York: Macmillan & Co. 1903), 220.
93 Intelligence Branch, French Operations in Tong-King, TNA/WO 106/66, Part VII, 6.
94 Mallory to Bulloch May 7, 1863, *ORN*, Series 2, Vol. 2, 418.
95 《镇海保卫战》 directed by 张鑫 [Zhang Xin], 2013.
96 For Ningbo see:《海防加嚴》 [Maritime Defenses Tightened], *Shenbao*, August 20, 1884;《鎮海近聞》 [Recent News from Zhenhai], *Shenbao*, August 6, 1884;《鎮海近信》 [Recent Letter from Zhenhai], *Shenbao*, August 6, 1884;《鎮海防務》 [Zhenhai Defensive Matters], *Shenbao*, April 30, 1884.
97 《海防加嚴》 [Maritime Defenses Tightened], *Shenbao*, August 20, 1884.
98 《鎮海近聞》 [Recent News From Zhenhai], *Shenbao*, March 30, 1885;《甬事述聞》 [Description of the News of the Ningbo Affair], *Shenbao*, March 28, 1885.
99 《镇海保卫战》 directed by 张鑫 [Zhang Xin], 2013.

100 《中法战争镇海之役胜利纪念碑》
101 McGiffin, "China – The Celestial Empire," June 10, 1885, McGiffin Letters, USNA/NL.
102 李鸿章 [Li Hongzhang] 寄译署 [Translation Office] 光绪十年七月十日《中法戰爭, 第4冊》[Sino-French War, Vol. 4], 194; Arlington, *Through the Dragon's Eyes*, 42.
103 刘名誉 [Liu Mingyu] 水雷艇策 [Torpedo Boat Plans],《洋务运动, 第3冊》[Foreign Affairs Movement, Vol. 3], 431.
104 《以水雷敵阻勝以岸戰待敵説》[With Torpedo-Mines Restrict the Enemy …] *Shenbao*, October 25, 1884.
105 李鸿章 [Li Hongzhang] 寄译署 [Translation Office] 光绪十年七月十日,《中法戰爭, 第4冊》[Sino-French War, Vol. 4], 194.
106 Ibid.
107 刘名誉 [Liu Mingyu] 水雷艇策 [Torpedo Boat Plans],《洋务运动, 第3冊》[Foreign Affairs Movement, Vol. 3], 431.
108 John Lee Davis to Chandler, October 15, 1884, NARA-1, M-89, Roll 270.
109 津防信息 [News about the Defense of Tianjin] *Shenbao*, March 7, 1884.
110 "Narrative of the Naval Operations in Formosa," TNA/WO 106/66, Part VII, 36; "The Defense of Port Arthur," *The North China Herald* (Beijing, China), December 3, 1884.
111 薛福成 [Xue Fucheng] 出使英法義比四國日記 [Journal of Emissary to England, France …]《洋务运动, 第3冊》[Foreign Affairs Movement, Vol. 3], 299.
112 "Present and Prospective Ship-Building Policy of Foreign Nations," November, 1886, No. 119, TNA/ADM 231/10.
113 McGiffin, "China – The Celestial Empire," June 10, 1885, McGiffin Letters, USNA/NL.
114 For the Naval Attachés: Brian Crumley, "The Naval Attaché System of the United States, 1882–1914" (Ph.D. Diss., Texas A&M University, 2002), 22; Dorwart, *Office of Naval Intelligence*, 10; "Instructions in Regard to Intelligence Duty," 1892, NARA-1, RG-38, Naval Attaché Reports, 1886–1939, Box 1286.
115 Rosen, *Winning the Next War*, 75. See also: Charles Rogers, "Naval Intelligence," *Proceedings of the USNI*, Vol. 9 (1883): 659; *Knowing One's Enemy: Intelligence Assessment before the World Wars*, ed. Ernest May (Princeton, NJ: Princeton University Press, 1984); John Keegan, *Intelligence in War: Knowledge of the Enemy from Napoleon to Al-Qaeda* (New York: Knopf, 2003); Richard Betts, *Enemies of Intelligence: Knowledge and Power in American National Security* (New York: Columbia University Press, 2007).
116 Allan R. Millett, Williamson Murray, and Kenneth H. Watman, "The Effectiveness of Military Organizations," in *Military Effectiveness*, Vol. 1, 4. Similar pressures prompted the Admiralty to found the Naval Intelligence Department in 1887. See: Shawn Grimes, *Strategy and War Planning in the British Navy, 1887–1918* (Rochester: Boydell Press, 2012), 1.
117 James C. Scott, *Seeing like a State: How Certain Schemes to Improve the Human Condition Have Failed* (New Haven: Yale University Press, 1998).
118 Charles Rogers, "Naval Intelligence," *Proceedings of the USNI*, Vol. 9 (1883): 659.

119 A. T. Mahan to John Walker, March 18, 1884, *LPATM*, Vol. 1, 563–564.
120 "Seeking a Good Place for Capt. Mahan," *New York Times*, March 6, 1895; "Rumored Naval Changes," *Evening Star* (Washington, DC), February 24, 1896.
121 Paolo E. Coletta, *French Ensor Chadwick: Scholarly Warrior* (Lanham, MD: University Press of America, 1980), 11; Malcolm Muir, "French Ensor Chadwick: Reformer, Historian, Outcast," in *Admirals of the New Steel Navy: Makers of the American naval tradition, 1880–1930*.
122 Dorwart, *Office of Naval Intelligence*, 9.
123 Dorwart, *Office of Naval Intelligence*, 9; Wyman H. Packard, *A Century of U.S. Naval Intelligence* (Washington: Department of the Navy, 1996); Johnson, *Thence Round Cape Horn*, 137.
124 Rodgers, "Orders," October 14, 1879, NARA-1, RG 45, M-89, Roll 67.
125 Rodgers to Secretary of the Navy, October 24, 1879, NARA-1, RG 45, M-89, Roll 67.
126 Mason, "The War on the Pacific Coast of South America," *Information from Abroad*, War Series, No. 2, 13; "Report of a Board of U.S. Naval Officers on the Injuries Received by the Ironclad *Huáscar* in the Battle of Angamos," October 20, 1879, NARA-1, RG-38, Naval Attaché Reports, Box 832; A. T. Mahan to Robert U. Johnson, June 2, 1895, *LPATM*, Vol. 2.
127 "Paper on the Employment of Torpedoes in Steam Launches against Men-of-War," trans. Theodorus Mason, 1880, NARA-1, RG-38, Naval Attaché Reports, Box 832; Packard, *A Century of U.S. Naval Intelligence*, 2.
128 T. B. Mason, "The Capture of the Peruvian Monitor Ram Huáscar by the Chilian Squadron off Mejillones de Bolivia" (1880), Naval Attaché Reports, Chile-Peru War, NARA-1, RG 38, Box 832; "Official Reports of Battle of Angamos," in "Plans and Drawings in Reference to the Battle of Angamos," Naval Attaché Reports, Chile-Perú War, NARA-1, RG 38, Box 832.
129 Admiral Frederick Rodgers to Secretary of the Navy, October 24, 1879, NARA-1, RG 45, M-89, Roll 67, 102. "Professional Notes, Details Concerning the Capture of the Huascar," *Proceedings of the USNI*, No. 6 (1880): 295–99; "Answers and Questions Relating to the Battle of Angamos," Naval Attaché Reports, Chile–Peru War, NARA-1, RG 38, Box 832.
130 J. W. King, *Warships and Navies of the World* (Boston: Williams and Company, 1881), 439–441.
131 Theodorus Mason, "The War on the Pacific Coast of South America," *Information from Abroad*, War Series, No. 2 (1883): 13; William Bainbridge-Hoff, "Examples, Conclusions, and Maxims of Modern Naval Tactics," General Information Series, No. 3 (Washington: Government Printing Office, 1884); Luis Uribe Y Orrego, "The Naval Combats in the War of the Pacific, 1879–1881," *Proceedings of the USNI*, Vol. 13 (1887): 688–693.
132 Albert Parker Niblack, *The History and Aims of the Office of Naval Intelligence* (Washington, DC: GPO, 1920), 2; Packard, *A Century of U.S. Naval Intelligence*, 2.
133 See: Freeman, *The Pacific*; Steel, *Oceania under Steam*; *Pacific Histories: Ocean, Land, People*, ed. David Armitage and Alison Bashford; Matsuda, *Pacific Worlds*.

134 Kennedy, *The Rise and Fall of Great Powers*, 147.
135 Hammond, *Plowshares to Swords*, 85.

5 The Californian Case for a New Navy

1. "Our Little Navy," *United Service*, Vol. 11 (1884): 305. See also: "Chili, China, Japan, Spain or any of the inferior nations when compared with ours could wipe out every seacoast city that we have got," Henry Teller, *Congressional Record*, Vol. 18, February 2, 1887, 1274; the US "[c]annot resist a first-class ship of China, Japan, Chili or any one of the nations of Europe," Joseph Hawley, *Congressional Record*, Vol. 19, 5677; Franklin Bartlett, *Congressional Record*, Vol. 27, February 16, 1895, 2307; S. B. Luce, "Report of Board on a Post-Graduate Course," June 13, 1884, *ARSN 1885*, 100; D. D. Porter, "Report of the Admiral of the Navy," *ARSN 1888*, 16; "Torpedo Vessels," *New York Times*, September 2, 1889; Charles A. Sumner, *Congressional Record*, Vol. 15, March 5, 1884, 1636–1637; T. O. Selfridge, "Reconstruction of the Navy," Appendix to *Congressional Record*, January 24, 1882, 95.
2. Chamber of Commerce of San Francisco, Resolution to Congress, *Congressional Record*, Vol. 15, April 24, 1884, 3330.
3. Lotchin, *Fortress California*, 3.
4. Karp, *This Vast Southern Empire*, 31–33.
5. "The Defenses of San Francisco," *Sacramento Daily Record Union*, December 31, 1881; Petitions, *Congressional Record*, Vol. 15, February 21, 1884, 1285; Petitions, *Congressional Record*, Vol. 15, April 24, 1884, 3330.
6. Chandler, *ARSN 1882*, 6.
7. ONI, "Security Classified Publications, 1882–1954," NARA-1, RG 38, Box 26, Entry 141, 470.
8. For a similar argument about British politics see: David G. Morgan-Owen, *The Fear of Invasion: Strategy, Politics, and British War Planning, 1880–1914* (New York: Oxford University Press, 2017). For "civilization" in elite US politics: Ninkovich, *Global Dawn*, 18.
9. Chandler, *ARSN 1883*, 33; Shulman, *Navalism*, 32; Bonker, *Militarism in a Global Age*; For "pejorative," see: E. L. Godkin, "Navalism," *Nation*, Vol. 54 (January, 1892): 44; and "Militarism in a Republic," *Nation*, Vol. 62 (March, 1896): 190.
10. Paullin, *History of Naval Administration 1775–1911*, 392. Ashore, ONI (1882) and the Naval War College (1884) came in. Jeffery Dorwart, *Office of Naval Intelligence* (Annapolis: Naval Institute Press, 1979), 9; Spector, *Professors of War*.
11. Herrick, *The American Naval Revolution*.
12. "Present and Prospective Shipbuilding Policy of the Principal Maritime Nations" (1889) TNA/ADM 231/15.
13. Benjamin Harris, *Congressional Record*, January 24, 1883, 1562.
14. J. D. Kelley, *Our Navy* (Hartford: The American Publishing Company, 1897), 180; "Our New Navy," *Evening World* (New York), May 21, 1891.
15. "In Special Session," *New York World*, November 26, 1891.

16 See: Introduction, n. 52–n. 54. See also: Shulman, *Navalism*, 6–9.
17 Mullins, *The Transformation of American and British Naval Policy in the Pre-Dreadnought Era*, 217; Mobley, *Progressives in Navy Blue*, 238.
18 Love, *History of the U.S. Navy*, Vol. 1, 345; Hagan, *This People's Navy*, 180–185. Surveys also commonly mention Chile's effect as a matter of rhetoric. Green, *By More than Providence*, 74.
19 Davis, *A Navy Second to None*, 32 (emphasis in original).
20 Herrick, *The American Naval Revolution*, 23; Hagan, *American Gunboat Diplomacy and the Old Navy*, 140; Wicks, "New Navy and New Empire," 126; Brian Loveman, *No Higher Law: American Foreign Policy and the Western Hemisphere since 1776* (Chapel Hill, NC: University of North Carolina Press, 2010), 145. See also: Davis, *A Navy Second to None*, 35; Robert Seager, "Ten Years before Mahan: The Unofficial Case for the New Navy, 1880–1890," *The Mississippi Valley Historical Review*, Vol. 40, No. 3 (1953): 491–512. Mark Russell Shulman's work on the 1880s highlighted changes in US attitudes toward the Pacific as an influence on naval expansion, but nonetheless framed threats from a "minor power" like Chile as incidental. Shulman, *Navalism*, 177.
21 Brown, "The Power of Influence," 272; Emilio Meneses Ciuffardi, *El Factor Naval en las Relaciones Entre Chile y Los Estados Unidos 1881–1951* (Santiago: Hachette, 1989); William Sater, *Chile and the United States: Empires in Conflict* (Athens: University of Georgia Press, 1990).
22 Braisted, *The United States Navy in the Pacific*; Jeffery Dorwart, *The Pigtail War* (Amherst: University of Massachusetts Press, 1975); Stephen R. Platt, *Autumn in the Heavenly Kingdom* (New York: Alfred A. Knopf, 2012); David Silbey, *The Boxer Rebellion and the Great Game in China* (New York: Hill and Wang, 2012); Schoonover, *Uncle Sam's War of 1898 and the Origins of Globalization*. An exception is the institutional history: Johnson, *Far China Station: The U.S. Navy in Asian Waters 1800–1898*.
23 Erika Lee, *At America's Gates: Chinese Immigration During the Exclusion Era* (Chapel Hill: UNC Press, 2003); Xu Guoqi, *Chinese and Americans* (Cambridge, MA: Harvard University Press, 2014); Elliott Young, *Alien Nation: Chinese Migration in the Americas from the Coolie Era through World War II* (Chapel Hill: UNC Press, 2014); Yen Ching-Hwang, *Coolies and Mandarins* (Singapore: Singapore National University Press, 1985); Watt Stewart, *Chinese Bondage in Peru* (Durham, NC: Duke University Press, 1951); Steffen Rimner, "Chinese Abolitionism: The Chinese Educational Mission in Connecticut, Cuba, and Peru," *Journal of Global History*, Vol. 11, No. 3 (2016): 344–64; Yong Chen, *Chinese San Francisco, 1850–1943: A Trans-Pacific Community* (Stanford: Stanford University Press, 2000); *Remapping Asian American History*, ed. Sucheng Chan (New York: Alta Mira Press, 2003).
24 Caspar T. Hopkins, "Report on Shipping and Shipbuilding" (San Francisco: Crocker and Co., 1885), 29, NMRC/SF.
25 As used by Lambert, *Seapower States* (New Haven: Yale University Press, 2018), 7.
26 Mallie Stafford, *The March of Empire through Three Decades Embracing Sketches of California History* (San Francisco: Spaulding & Co, 1884), 188–189.

27 Robert Louis Stevenson, *Across the Plains* (New York Charles Scribner's Sons, 1897), 98.
28 Josiah Strong, *Our Country* (New York: Baker and Taylor Co. 1891), 43. For vulnerability, see: H. M. Stephens, "President's Address," *The Pacific Ocean in History*, ed. H. Morse Stephens and Herbert E. Bolton (New York: Macmillan Company, 1917), 23. See also: Earl Pomeroy, *The Pacific Slope* (New York: Alfred Knopf, 1965), 255–258. For contemporaneous naval officers objecting, see: LT Edward W. Very, "The Type of Vessel Best Suited to the Present Needs of the United States," in *Proceedings of the USNI*, 7 (1880), 43; W. I. Chambers, "The Reconstruction and Increase of the Navy," *Proceedings of the USNI*, Vol. 11 (1885): 34.
29 J. R. Thomas, *Congressional Record*, March 1, 1884, 1532.
30 D. D. Porter, "Report of the Admiral of the Navy," *ARSN 1887*, 39–41.
31 W. T. Sampson, "Outline of a Scheme for the Naval Defense of the Coast," *Proceedings*, Vol. 15, No. 2 (1889): 208.
32 "Chilian Circular to the Foreign Representatives," November 10, 1880, *FRUS* 1881, Encl 1. No. 181, 115.
33 For Tahiti, see: "Descripción de la Isla de Pascua," *Revista de Marina*, No. 4 (1885): 369; "Islas de Sociedad," *Revista de Marina*, No. 22 (March, 1887): 269. For Argentina and Patagonia, see: Barros, *Historia Diplomática de Chile, 1541–1938*; López, *Historia de la Marina de Chile*; Kristine L. Jones, "Warfare, Reorganization, and Readaptation at the Margins of Spanish Rule: The Southern Margin (1573–1882)," in *The Cambridge History of the Native Peoples of the Americas*, ed. Frank Salomon and Stuart B. Schwartz (Cambridge: Cambridge University Press, 1999), 178–187. For US, see: "The American and Chilian Navies," *Times* (London), October 30, 1891.
34 E. Chouteau, *Revista de Marina*, No. 1 (1885): 3.
35 Vicuna-Mackenna, "El Reparto del Pacífico," *Revista de Marina*, No. 1 (1885): 67; Carlos Condell, "Defensa de Nuestro Litoral," *Revista de la Marina*, No. 2 (August, 1885): 135.
36 "The Chile of To-Day," *Omaha Daily-Bee*, June 3, 1884; Edward Dallam Melillo, *Strangers on Familiar Soil: Rediscovering the Chile–California Connection* (New Haven: Yale University Press, 2015), 137.
37 Nicolás Palacios, *Raza Chilena* (Santiago: Imprenta Universitaria, 1918); Jeffrey L. Klaiber, "Los 'Cholos' y los 'Rotos': Actitudes Raciales Durante la Guerra del Pacífico," *Histórica Peru*, No. 1 (1978): 27–38.
38 "Por Qué Chile Es Más Fuerte Que el Perú," *El Mercurio* (Valparaiso, Chile), December 14, 1881; Cumings, *Dominion from Sea to Sea*, 104.
39 Horace Fisher to Long, May 3, 1898, *Papers of John Davis Long*, 111.
40 Palacios, *Raza Chilena*, 34, 65. See also: Hugo Alberto Maureira, "'Valiant Race, Tenacious Race, Heroic, Indomitable and Implacable': The War of the Pacific (1879–1884) and the Role of Racial Ideas in the Construction of Chilean Identity" (M.A. Thesis, Queen's University, 2002), 4.
41 Gerald C. Langley, "Chili: Navy, Coast Defences, &c" (1890) TNA/ADM 231/19.
42 "Discursos," *El Mercurio* (Valparaiso, Chile) March 16, 1881.
43 Carlos Condell, "Defensa de Nuestro Litoral," *Revista de Marina*, No. 2 (August, 1885): 135 (emphasis in original).

44 "Importante Juicio Sobre Chile," *El Mercurio* (Valparaiso, Chile) May 30, 1883.
45 "Por Qué Chile Es Más Fuerte Que el Perú," *El Mercurio* (Valparaíso, Chile), December 14, 1881.
46 Benjamin Vicuña Mackenna, *Historia de la Campana de Tarapacá* (Santiago: Litografía de Pedro Cadot, 1880), 241.
47 Ricardo Ferrando Keun, *Y Así Nació la Frontera* (Santiago: Editorial Antártica, 1986); Juan Carlos Walther, *La Conquista del Desierto* (Buenos Aires: Universitaria de Buenos Aires, 1970).
48 "Una Carta que Honra al País y a su Autor," *El Mercurio* (Valparaiso, Chile) October 17, 1883.
49 "Economías de Nuestra Escuadra," *El Mercurio* (Valparaiso, Chile) October 8, 1885.
50 Melillo, *Strangers on Familiar Soil*, 132.
51 Sondhaus, *Naval Warfare*, 132–133; *Conway's All the World's Fighting Ships 1860–1905*, 233. For construction, see: *Memoria del Ministerio de Marina* (Santiago, Imprenta Nacional, 1884), viii; Juan Lopez to Ministerio de Marina, June 9, 1885, AHNC/MMAR, Vol. 453, Folio 2.
52 *Memoria de Ministerio de Marina* (Santiago: Imprenta Nacional, 1884), vi.
53 Officials in Qing China commented on the *Esmeralda*'s [爱斯马而达] speed as "the fastest of all" the world's warships. See: 吴大澂 [Wu Daji] 奏海防条议 [Memorial on Coastal Defense Conditions] 《清末海軍史料》 [*Late Qing Navy Historical Materials*], 46–47; *25 de Mayo*, as noted by the Legacion de Chile, Paris to Ministerio de Marina, November 11, 1890, AHNC/MMAR, Vol. 520; "A Fast Warship," *Times* (London, UK), November 10, 1890; W. Noble, Elswick Shipyard to Chilean Minister, London, December 2, 1891, AHNC/MMAR, Vol. 520; N. H. White to William Armstrong, November 29, 1884, DF.A/1/37, Tyne and Wear Archive [hereafter TWA/UK], Newcastle, UK; N. H. White to William Armstrong, November 23, 1884 DF.A/1/37, TWA/UK; Rendel to Armstrong, December 5, 1884, DF.A/1/275-7, TWA/UK; "The Esmeralda" in General Information Series, ONI, Series No. 4, 1885, 121, USNWC/NHC.
54 John Wilson to William Armstrong, October 1, 1884, DF.A/3/21, TWA/UK; J. O. Hopkins to William Armstrong, October 7, 1884, DF.A/3/11, TWA/UK; Rendel to Armstrong, December 5, 1884, DF.A/1/275-7, TWA/UK. Chilean observers likewise referred to ships of the "Esmeralda type": "Movimiento del Material," *Revista de Marina*, No. 12 (June 1886).
55 White to Armstrong, November 28, 1884, DF.A/1/37, TWA/UK; White to Armstrong, November 23, 1884, DF.A/1/37, TWA/UK. See also: E. J. Reed, "The Navy Question" *Times*, London, December 1, 1884.
56 William Chandler, *ARSN 1882*, 6.
57 *ARSN 1884*, 62.
58 Mahan, *The Interest of America in Sea Power*, 13; A. T. Mahan, "Naval War College," October 4, 1887, *ARSN 1887*, 164; "Programme of Naval War College," *ARSN 1888*, 101; Federico Chaigneau, "Parte del Viaje de la Corbeta *Chacabuco* a la Comandancia General de Marina," *Revista de Marina*, No. 34 (March, 1888): 244; "Tráfico Probable por el Canal de Panamá," *Revista de Marina*, No. 15 (September, 1886).

59 "Table of Distances: Panama to Puerto Montt," in *Revista de Marina*, No. 30 (November, 1887): 586.
60 Legation of Colombia in Washington, April 4, 1885, *FRUS* 1885–1886, 245.
61 Daniel Wicks, "Dress Rehearsal: United States Intervention on the Isthmus of Panama, 1885," *Pacific Historical Review*, January 1, 1980: 49.
62 Robert Seager II, "Alfred Thayer Mahan: Christian Expansionist, Navalist, and Historian," *Admirals of the New Steel Navy*, 27.
63 Sims, April 12, 1885, Library of Congress, Sims Papers [hereafter LOC/SP], Box 12. See also: Wicks, "Dress Rehearsal," 581–582.
64 Lopez to Ministerio de Marina, June 9, 1885, AHNC/MMAR, Vol. 453, Folio 9–10.
65 Vicuna Mackenna, "El Reparto del Pacífico," *Revista de Marina*, No. 1 (July 1885): 68. For Minister of Marine, see: Carlos Condell, "Defensa de Nuestro Litoral," *Revista de Marina*, No. 2 (August 1885): 135.
66 "Movimiento del Material de la Armada," *Revista de Marina*, No. 1 (July, 1885): 63; Lopez to Ministerio de Marina, June 9, 1885, AHNC/MMAR, Vol. 453, Folio 4; C. S. Norton to Department of Navy, May 6, 1885, NARA-1, RG-45, M-125, Roll 413. See also: Carlos Tromben, "Naval Presence," *International Journal of Naval History*, Vol. 1, No. 1 (2002).
67 Vicuna Mackenna, "El Reparto del Pacífico," *Revista de Marina*, No. 1 (July, 1885): 68.
68 Lopez to Ministerio de Marina, AHNC/MMAR, Vol. 453, Folio 3.
69 "La Ocupación de Panamá Por Fuerzas Norteamericanas," *El Telégrafo de Guayaquil* (Guayaquil, Ecuador) as printed in *El Mercurio de Valparaíso* (Valparaíso, Chile) May 27, 1885.
70 Upshur to Chandler Valpo December 6, 1884, NARA-1, RG-45, M-89, Roll 72; "Descripción de la Isla de Pascua," *Revista de Marina*, No.4 (1885): 369; "Notas sobre Isla de Pascua," *Revista de Marina*, No. 16 (1886): 392; "Islas de Sociedad," *Revista de Marina*, No. 22 (March, 1887): 269.
71 Ridgley Hunt, "Notes on the Commerce of Chile," NARA-1, RG-38, Box 19, NM-63, Entry 141; "Informe Sobre el Actual Estado de la Isla de Juan Fernández," *Revista de Marina*, No. 108 (June, 1895): 1194–1206.
72 "La Isla de Pascua," *El Mercurio* (Valparaíso, Chile), February 19, 1889; "Idolos de la Isla de Pascua," *El Mercurio* (Valparaíso, Chile), October 22, 1888.
73 Matsuda, *Pacific Worlds*, 227. For Chilean naval perceptions of Easter Islanders, see: Ignacio Gana, "Descripción de la Isla de Pascua," *Revista de Marina*, No. 4 (October 1885).
74 "Naval Station Pago Pago, Samoa," *ARSN 1889*, 266; Paul Kennedy, *The Samoan Tangle: A Study in Anglo-German-American Relations, 1878–1900* (New York: Barnes & Noble, 1974).
75 "Battleships a Necessity for the Defence of Cities," *San Francisco Morning Call*, February 16, 1890; "A Real Need," *Los Angeles Herald*, February 16, 1882; "Need of an Adequate Navy," *St. Louis Globe-Democrat*, February 23, 1890.
76 *London Standard*, as used by "The United States and Chili," *New York Times*, November 23, 1881.
77 B. Mackenna, "El Reparto del Pacífico," *Revista de Marina*, No. 1 (1885): 68.

78 D. D. Porter, "Report of the Admiral of the Navy," *ARSN 1887*, 39.
79 Brown, "The Power of Influence," 309–310; "Naval Estimate of the Republic of Chile," NARA-1, RG-38, Box 740.
80 D. D. Porter, "Report of the Admiral of the Navy," *ARSN 1883*, 393.
81 Eugene Hale, *Congressional Record*, July 5, 1884, 6082.
82 W. I. Chambers, "The Reconstruction and Increase of the Navy," *Proceedings of the USNI*, Vol. 11 (1885): 34.
83 "Pacific Station," 1883 TNA/ADM 231/4.
84 Hagan, *American Gunboat Diplomacy*, 139.
85 Westad, *Restless Empire*, 43. John Fairbank, *Trade and Diplomacy on the China Coast: The Opening of the Treaty Ports, 1842–1854* (Cambridge, MA: Harvard University Press, 1953).
86 "Graduation Address," 1885, RG-16, Box 3, USNWC-NHC.
87 Theodorus Mason, *The War on the Pacific Coast of South America*, ONI Information from Abroad, War Series, No. 2; Caspar Goodrich, *Report of the British Naval and Military Operations in Egypt, 1882*, ONI Information from Abroad, War Series, No. 3; Mahan, "Plans of Operations in Case of War with Great Britain" (1891), NARA-1, RG-45, Box 453.
88 Robert Erwin Johnson, *Thence Round Cape Horn* (Annapolis: Naval Institute Press, 1963), 122.
89 J. M. Ellicott, *The Composition of the Fleet*, in *Proceedings of the USNI*, Vol. 22 (1896), 542; *Los Angeles Daily Herald*, February 18, 1882; "The Coast Defense Ship," *The Morning Press* (Santa Barbra, CA), May 7, 1889.
90 "Naval Estimate of the Republic of Chile," NARA-1, RG-38, Box 740.
91 "La Flota Nueva," *Revista de Marina*, No. 108 (June, 1895): 1174.
92 Porter, "Report of the Admiral of the Navy," *ARSN 1884*, 62; Chandler, *ARSN 1884*, 7.
93 *Congressional Record – House*, February 23, 1885, 2037; *Congressional Record – House*, February 20, 1885, 1971.
94 Lopez to Ministerio de Marina, June 9, 1885, AHNC/MMAR, 453, Folio 3; Whitney, *ARSN 1886*, 5–6; Porter, "Report of the Admiral of the Navy," *ARSN 1884*, 272.
95 "The New Warships," *New York Times*, October 6, 1885.
96 "The New Cruisers," *New York Times*, December 10, 1884.
97 "Present and Prospective Ship-Building Policy of Foreign Nations 1886," November 1886, TNA/ADM 231/10.
98 Kennedy, *The Rise and Fall of British Naval Mastery*, 177; Rear Admiral John Wilson to Armstrong, October 1, 1884, TWA/UK, DF.A/3/20.
99 John Wilson to Armstrong, October 1, 1884, TWA/UK, DF.A/3/20; *Revista Militar y Naval* used in "La Esmeralda," *El Mercurio* (Valparaiso, Chile) March 14, 1885.
100 J. D. Kelley, 42; W. Whitney, *ARSN 1887*, xxxvi.
101 Carlos Herrera, "Las Torpederas Como Medio de Defensa del Litoral," *Revista de la Marina*, No. 2 (August, 1885): 138–140; Carlos Condell "Defensa de Nuestro Litoral," *Revista de la Marina*, No. 2 (August, 1885): 137; "Guerra Franco-China: Notables Ataques con Torpedos," *Revista de la Marina*, No. 2 (August, 1885); A. Blest-Gana to Ministro de Marina January 28, 1887, AHNC/MMAR, Vol. 466.

102 "Blanco Encalada," *Revista de Marina*, No. 8 (February, 1886): 243; Alberto Fuentes, "Oficiales Artilleros y Torpedistas," *Revista de Marina*, No. 57 (February, 1890); Edwyn Gray, *The Devil's Device: Robert Whitehead and the History of the Torpedo* (Annapolis: Naval Institute Press, 1991).
103 E. Sanchez, *Memoria de Marina 1889*, xx. In 1891, ONI reckoned the number had grown to twenty-one. "Torpedo Boats," ONI, NARA-1, RG 38, Entry 141, Box 23, NM-63 Entry 141, 359–362.
104 "Torpedo Vessels," *New York Times*, September 2, 1889; B. F. Tracy, *ARSN 1891*, 6; "Building a Torpedo Boat," *Omaha Daily Bee*, October 2, 1892.
105 Porter, "Report of the Admiral of the Navy," *ARSN 1888*, 16.
106 For definition of torpedo cruisers vs torpedo boats, see: B. F. Tracy, *ARSN 1891*, 36.
107 Rendel to Armstrong, December 5, 1884, DF.A/1/275-7, TWA/UK; J. M. Valdes Carrera, *Memória* (Santiago: Imprenta Nacional, 1889), xxxvi.
108 "Sunk by Torpedoes," *New York Times*, April 28, 1891.
109 "Chile's Sea-Going David," *New York Times*, April 28, 1891; "The Torpedoes at Caldera," *New York Times*, May 10, 1891; "Chile's Great Naval Battle," *New York Times*, July 8, 1894.
110 "Report of Bureau of Construction and Repair," *ARSN 1891*, 295; B. F. Tracy, *ARSN 1892*, 35–36.
111 B. F. Tracy, *ARSN 1891*, 36; Hillary Herbert, *ARSN 1893*, 35; Long, *The New American Navy*, 43.
112 D. D. Porter, "Report of the Admiral of the Navy," *ARSN 1884*, 59–62; "The Year's Naval Progress," *Information from Abroad X*, ONI (1891), 411; "United States of America," Torpedo School Reports, ADM 189/11, 132.
113 J. M. Valdes Carrera, *Memória* (Santiago: Imprenta Nacional, 1889), xxxviii.
114 J. D. Kelley, *Our Navy*, 176.
115 Isidoro Errazuriz, *Memória del Ministro de Marina 1893* (Santiago: Imprenta Nacional, 1893), xxiv; E. Sanchez, *Memória del Ministro de Marina 1888* (Santiago: Imprenta Nacional, 1888), xxiii.
116 "Electrical Fittings of the *Capitan Prat*," Torpedo School Reports, TNA/ADM 189/14, 226; *Revista de Marina*, No. 73 (June, 1892): 609; *Revista de Marina*, No. 83 (April, 1893): 373; *Revista de Marina*, No. 92 (January, 1894): 25.
117 "El Acorazado Chileno," *Mercurio de Valparaíso*, March 21, 1892; "The Captain Pratt [sic]," *Los Angeles Herald*, January 21, 1892; *Seattle Post-Intelligencer*, January 21, 1892. For Reed: Legación de Chile, Paris to Ministerio de Marina, March 6, 1891, AHNC/MMAR, Vol. 520; Legación de Chile, London to Ministerio de Marina, December 9, 1891, AHNC/MMAR, Vol. 520.
118 "Pride of the Chilian Navy," *New York Times*, April 15, 1894.
119 T. Roosevelt, "Naval War College Closing Address," June 2, 1897, RG-16, Box 3, Graduation or Closing Addresses, USNWC-NHC; A. T. Mahan to T. Roosevelt, May 6, 1897, *LPATM*, Vol. 2, 507.
120 D. D. Porter "Report of the Admiral of the Navy," *ARSN 1886*, 61; D. D. Porter to Senate, NARA-1, RG-46, Box No. 40, Folder 272.

121 McCauley to Whitney, December 12, 1885, NARA-1, RG-45, M-89, R-73.
122 McCauley to Whitney, December 12, 1885, NARA-1, RG-45, M-89, R-73. By 1890, even the Chilean naval school had its own US-designed machine gun for training purposes. Arsenal de Marina, April 19, 1890, AHNC/MMAR, Vol. 520.
123 Whitney, *ARSN 1885*, xxxvii. A tradition by then. "Specifications," Ericsson to Peruvian Construction Commission, August 25, 1862, AHMP, Comisión de Construcción Naval en Estados Unidos (1862) 0382, Caja 1, Sobre 2, Folio 7; Schmidt and Co. to Shufeldt, February 16, 1882, Shufeldt Papers, LOC, Box 24, Folder 1882; D. D. Porter "Report of the Admiral of the Navy," *ARSN 1886*, 61.
124 *Army and Navy Gazette* (London, UK), February 10, 1866, CCC/1 1862-1866, NMM/UK; Cowper P. Coles, *Journal of the Royal United Service Institution*, Vol. 11 (1868): 436.
125 Hunt, *Ideology and U.S. Foreign Relations*; Kramer, "Empires, Exceptions, and Anglo-Saxons," 1315–1353. See also: Stuart Anderson, *Race and Rapprochement: Anglo-Saxonism and Anglo-American Relations, 1895–1904* (Rutherford: Fairleigh Dickinson University, 1981); Anders Stephanson, *Manifest Destiny: American Expansionism and the Empire of Right* (New York: Hill and Wang, 1995).
126 E. Chouteau, *Revista de Marina*, No. 1 (1885): 3.
127 Stephen B. Luce, "Christian Ethics an Element of Military Education," *United Service*, January, 1883, 1; Benjamin Tracy in "In Special Session," *New York World*, November 26, 1891; J. D. Kelley, *Our Navy*, 176.
128 Shulman, *Navalism*, 3.
129 Mason, *The War on the Pacific Coast of South America*, 6; Palacios, *Raza Chilena*, 329; See also: Pike, *Chile and the United States*, 61.
130 Karsten, *The Naval Aristocracy*, 116.
131 Mahan to J. B. Sterling, February 13, 1896, *LPATM*, Vol. 2, 445. A term used by Mahan well in advance of the figures cited in Kramer, "Empires, Exceptions, and Anglo-Saxons."
132 "Extract from the Chilean Times," January 24, 1891, No. 91, Encl. 5, TNA/FO 881/6186.
133 "The Destiny of America," September 24, 1853, *The Works of William H. Seward*, Vol. 4, 124.
134 Belknap to Balch December 11, 1881, NARA-1, RG-45, M-89, Roll 69.
135 Albert Browne, "The Growing Power of the Republic of Chile," *Journal of the American Geographical Society of New York*, Vol. 16 (1884): 27.
136 "Defenseless Against Chile," *The Seattle Post-Intelligencer*, November 2, 1891.
137 Mahan to S. Ashe, March 11, 1885, *LPATM*, Vol. 1, 592.
138 Mahan to Bouverie Clark, May 22, 1891, *LPATM*, Vol. 2, 47.
139 "That Wonderful Navy," *Dallas Herald*, December 3, 1881.
140 Benjamin, *The End of New York*, 140.
141 Mahan to Samuel Ashe, March 11, 1885, *LPATM*, Vol. 1, 592.
142 Mahan, *The Interest of America in Sea Power*, 39.

143 "And Now Chile Kicks Us," *Sacramento Daily Record Union*, November 25, 1880; "The Chilean Imbroglio," *Sacramento Daily Record Union*, December 7, 1881; "Coast Defenses," *Sacramento Daily Record Union*, December 7, 1881; *Los Angeles Daily Herald*, February 18, 1882; "Cassandra," *Sacramento Daily Record Union*, March 25, 1882; "Doctrine Full of Difficulties," *Sacramento Daily Record Union*, December 17, 1881.
144 "Belligerent Chile and Our Navy," *Sacramento Daily Record Union*, November 6, 1880.
145 李鶴年 [Li Henian] 台湾防务大概情形 [General Situation of Taiwan's Defensive Affairs], June 14, 1874, 《清末海軍史料》[*Late Qing Navy Historical Materials*], 2.
146 Melillo, *Strangers of Familiar Soil*, 68–69; Belich, *Replenishing the Earth*, 320.
147 T. Roosevelt to Henry Cabot Lodge, January 22, 1880, in *Selections from the Correspondence of Theodore Roosevelt and Henry Cabot Lodge, 1884–1918*, Vol. 1, 63.
148 Rodgers to Thompson, November 11, 1879, NARA-1, RG-45, M-89, Roll 67.
149 Mahan to Samuel Ashe, March 11, 1885, *LPATM*, Vol. 1, 592. Emphasis on "8" included in the original copy of the letter. Mahan to Ashe, March 11, 1885, Correspondence 1876–1886, RL/DU.
150 "*Wachusett*," Z Files, NHHC.
151 Mahan, *From Sail to Steam*, 277; A. T. Mahan to Roy Marston, February 19, 1897, *LPATM*, Vol. 2, 441. See also: Larrie D. Ferreiro, "Mahan and the 'English Club' of Lima, Peru," *The Journal of Military History*, Vol. 72, No. 3 (July, 2008): 901–906.
152 John Bassett Moore, "Recollections of Admiral Mahan," Mahan Z-File, NHHC.
153 Herrick, *The American Naval Revolution*, 23; Hagan, *American Gunboat Diplomacy*, 140; Davis, *A Navy Second to None*, 35; Brown, "The Power of Influence," 272; Meneses, *El Factor Naval*, 51–52; Sater, *Chile and the United States*, 42–53; Lopez, *Historia de la Marina de Chile*, 335.
154 "Senator Stanford's Views," *Sacramento Daily Record Union*, February 13, 1886.
155 "The American Navy," *The Daily Astorian* (Astoria, Oregon), August 5, 1884.
156 "The Senate Commission," *Los Angeles Daily Herald*, September 27, 1884; *Congressional Record – Senate*, March 2, 1885, 2345.
157 Walter LaFeber, *The Cambridge History of American Foreign Relations* (New York: Cambridge University Press, 2013); J. D. Kelley, *Our Navy*, 9.
158 Chandler, *ARSN 1883*, 8–9. See also: Whitney, *ARSN 1885*, xxvii. Citing: J. Fenimore Cooper, *The History of the Navy of the United States of America* (Philadelphia: Lea & Blanchard, 1839).
159 *Los Angeles Daily Herald*, February 18, 1882.
160 Porter, "Report of the Admiral of the Navy," *ARSN 1884*, 62.
161 William Oates, *Congressional Record*, February 26, 1887, 2344. For Critics, see Shulman, *Navalism*, chapter 8; E. Berkeley Tompkins, *Anti-Imperialism in the United States: The Great Debate 1890–1920* (Philadelphia: University of Pennsylvania Press, 1970), 13.

162 Elman, "Naval Warfare and the Refraction of China's Self-Strengthening Reforms into Scientific and Technological Failure, 1865–1895," 283–326.
163 La Fayette Grover, *Congressional Record*, Vol. 13, March 2, 1882, 1545.
164 Lee, *At America's Gates*, 22.
165 Lee, *At America's Gates*, 11–13; 余坚 [Yu Jian] 《中美外交关系之研究》 [*Research in Sino-U.S. Diplomatic Relations*], 8–10; Dong Wang, *The United States and China* (New York: Rowman and Littlefield Publishers, 2013), 77.
166 Stephen B. Luce, "Christian Ethics an Element of Military Education," *United Service*, January 1, 1883.
167 Shufeldt Papers, LOC, Box 24, China Miscellany, Box 30 Newspaper Clippings China/Japan; *Daily Evening Bulletin* (San Francisco, CA), March 21, 1882.
168 Drake, *Empire of the Sea*, 257.
169 "China for the Chinese," *New York Times*, March 30, 1882.
170 Shufeldt to Chandler, July 30, 1882, Chandler Papers, LOC, Box 54. For "letter" see: May 17, 1882, NARA-1, M-89, Roll 268; "China for the Chinese," *New York Times*, March 30, 1882; *Daily Evening Bulletin* (San Francisco, CA), March 21, 1882; "Commodore Shufeldt on the Chinese," *Seattle Daily Post-Intelligencer*, May 5, 1882;《美國禁止華人新例》[America Prohibits Chinese Immigrants, New Regulations], *Shenbao*, May 30, 1882;《書西報載美將致美員信後》[Western Reports after the American Official Letter Reached America], *Shenbao*, May 18, 1882;《論美将式君書中》[Discussing the Contents of Shufeldt's Letter], *Shenbao*, October 31, 1882; *North China Herald*, May 26, 1882.
171 "China for the Chinese," *New York Times*, March 30, 1882. Unsurprisingly, Shufeldt's son became a noted white supremacist. R. W. Shufeldt, *The Negro: A Menace to American Civilization* (Boston: Gorham Press, 1907).
172 "A Valuable Witness," *Daily Evening Bulletin* (San Francisco, CA) March 21, 1882.
173 See: 两江总督曾国荃总遵旨筹议海防 [Viceroy of Jiangnan and Jiangxi Zeng Guoquan Memorial on the Establishment of Maritime Defense], July, 13, 1885《清末海軍史料》[*Late Qing Naval Historical Materials*], 42.
174 "A Valuable Witness," *Daily Evening Bulletin* (San Francisco, CA) March 21, 1882. For "failure" see: Elleman, *Modern Chinese Warfare, 1795–1989*, 92.
175 Arlington, *Through the Dragon's Eyes*, 30, 42.
176 "China for the Chinese," *New York Times*, March 30, 1882. Many Chinese reformers echoed that critique (a formula later Marxists historians would reverse). 李鸿章 [Li Hongzhang] 寄译署 [Translation Office] 光绪十年七月十日,《中法戰爭, 第4冊》[*Sino-French War*, Vol. 4] 194; 邵循正 [Shao Xunzheng]《中法战争资料叙列》[Introduction, Sino-French War Historical Materials] in《中法戰爭第1冊》[*Sino-French War*, Vol. 1] 2.
177 "France and China," *New York Times*, April 22, 1883.
178 "A Valuable Witness," *Daily Evening Bulletin* (San Francisco, CA) March 21, 1882.
179 Stevens, May 5, 1881, NARA-1, RG-45, M-89, Roll 69; D. D. Porter, "Report of the Admiral of the Navy," *ARSN 1887*, 60.
180 "China for the Chinese," *New York Times*, March 30, 1882.

181 Chester Holcombe to Shufeldt, November 26, 1881, Shufeldt Papers, LOC, Box 24.
182 Mahan to Ashe, July 11, 1870, *LPATM*, Vol. 1, 354.
183 Dooner, *Last Days of the Republic*, 103; Bruce Franklin, *War Stars: The Superweapon and the American Imagination* (New York: Oxford University Press, 1988), 21.
184 John Russell Young, "New Life in China," *The North American Review*, Vol. 153 (July 1, 1891): 430.
185 Mahan to *New York Times* January 30, 1893, *LPATM*, Vol. 2, 92.
186 T. Roosevelt to Cecil Arthur, August 5, 1896, *The Letters of Theodore Roosevelt* [hereafter *TR Letters*], ed. Elting Morison (Cambridge, MA: Harvard University Press, 1951), Vol. 1, 553; H. J. Mackinder, "The Geographical Pivot of History," *The Geographical Journal*, Vol. 23, No. 4 (1904): 421–437.
187 Mahan to Ellen Mahan, November 13, 1894, *LPATM*, Vol. 2, 360; Singer, "Hawaiian Islands," February, 1, 1893, Tracy Papers, LOC, Box 31. See also: William Michael Morgan, *Pacific Gibraltar* (Annapolis: Naval Institute Press, 2011).
188 "China for the Chinese," *New York Times*, March 30, 1882.
189 Mahan to *New York Times* January 30, 1893, *LPATM* Vol. 2, 92.
190 "Hawaiian Islands," February 1, 1893, Tracy Papers, LOC, Box 31.
191 Sims, January 10, 1894, LOC/SP, Box, 3.
192 George F. Seward, "Mongolian Immigration," *North American Review*, Vol. 134, No. 307 (June, 1882): 576.
193 Washington Whitthorne, *Congressional Record*, January 24, 1883.
194 直隸總督李鴻章奏 [Memorial of Zhili Viceroy Li Hongzhang] 光緒十三年二月五日《洋务运动第3册》[*Foreign Affairs Movement*, Vol. 3], 39–41; 李鴻章 [Li Hongzhang] 北洋通商大臣李鴻章 [Beiyang Trade Minister Li Hongzhang 光緒九年二月八日《洋务运动第2册》[*Foreign Affairs Movement*, Vol. 2], 532; 电谕李鸿章购钢面铁甲快船 [Telegraph from Li Hong Zhang Ordering Steel Plated Cruisers]《清末海軍史料》[*Late Qing Naval Historical Materials*], 117; Arthur Grant to Armstrong, July 21, 1882, DF/A/3/8, TWA/UK.
195 "Notes on the Chinese Navy," NARA-1, RG-38, Entry 141, Box 26.
196 薛福成 [Xue Fucheng] 議北洋海防水師章程 (1881) [Discussing the Plans of the Beiyang Navy and Coast Defense]《洋务运动, 第3册》[*Foreign Affairs Movement*, Vol. 3], 361. 左宗棠 [Zuo Zongtang] 总理各国事务衙门遵旨会议海防折 [Zongli Yamen Meeting on Maritime Defenses], 1885《清末海軍史料》[*Late Qing Naval Historical Materials*], 62.
197 "Notes on the Chinese Navy," RG-38, Entry 141, Box 26; "Introduction to Notes on the Imperial Japanese Navy," RG-38, Entry 141, Box 26.
198 Richard N. J. Wright, *The Chinese Steam Navy 1862–1945* (London: Chatham, 2000), 51–55; 醇親王 [Prince Chun] 光緒十二年五月一日《洋务运动, 第3册》[*Foreign Affairs Movement*, Vol. 3], 553–555; "Ting-Yuen," *Diagrams of Typical War-Ships* (1888), NARA-1, RG 38, Entry 141, Box 29.
199 《钢船试验》[Ironclad Testing] *Shenbao*, August 25, 1881.

200 "Recent Naval Progress," *Information from Abroad VI*, Navy Department, ONI (1887), 277.
201 直隸總督李鴻章 [Zhili Viceroy Li Hongzhang] 光緒十三年二月五日《洋務运动, 第3冊》 [*Foreign Affairs Movement*, Vol. 3], 46; ICN *Zhiyuan* (致遠) and ICN *Jingyuan* (靖遠). 直隸總督李鴻章奏 [Memorial of the Zhili Viceroy Li Hongzhang] 光緒年十五四月二十二日,《洋务运动, 第3冊》 [*Foreign Affairs Movement*, Vol. 3], 104. See also: Wright, *The Chinese Steam Navy*, 67–84; ICN *Jingyuan* (經遠) and ICN *Laiyuan* (來遠).
202 "Present and Prospective Ship-Building Policy of Foreign Nations 1886," November 1886, TNA/ADM 231/10; 直隸總督李鴻章片 [Note from the Zhili Viceroy Li Hongzhang], 光緒年十五四月二十二日,《洋务运动, 第3冊》 [*Foreign Affairs Movement*, Vol. 3], 111; John Hay, Certification to Charles Cheshire, NAI/3/27, NMM/UK; Sah Ching Ping to Charles Cheshire, NAI/3/27, NMM/UK; 直隸總督李鴻章 [Zhili Viceroy Li Hongzhang], 光緒十二年九月四日,《洋务运动, 第3冊》 [*Foreign Affairs Movement*, Vol. 3], 37.
203 詹事志 [Zhan Shizhi] 光緒十五年其餘二十七日《洋务运动, 第3冊》 [*Foreign Affairs Movement*, Vol. 3], 120. Though some Chinese resented them. 薛福成 [Xue Fucheng] 出使英法義比四國日記 [A Diary of an Emissary to Four Countries] 《洋务运动, 第8冊》 [*Foreign Affairs Movement*, Vol. 8], 296–297.
204 Shufeldt, *The Influences of Western Civilization in China*, 15. See also: Shulman, *Navalism*, 63–64.
205 "Keeping Account," *Puck*, September 16, 1885.
206 A. T. Mahan, *Naval Strategy* (Boston: Little Brown and Co, 1911), 447.
207 Charles A. Sumner, *Congressional Record*, Vol. 15, March 5, 1884, 1636–1637.
208 Orville Platt, *Congressional Record*, Vol. 17, March 24, 1886, 2692.
209 J. D. Kelley, *Modern Ships of War* (New York: Harper's Brothers 1888), 241.
210 Theodore S. Wilkinson, *Congressional Record*, Vol. 21, April 9, 1890, 3218.
211 Dooner, *Last Days of the Republic*, 22; Woltor, *A Short and Truthful History of the Taking of Californian and Oregon by the Chinese in the Year AD 1889*.
212 《一八九四-甲午大海战》Directed by [Feng Xiaoning] 冯小宁, 中国电影集团公司 [China Film Group, LTD], 2011.
213 Hughes to Chandler, September 2, 1883, NARA-1, RG-45, M-89, Roll 71.
214 Upshur to Chandler, July 21, 1884, NARA-1, RG-45, M-89, Roll 72; Upshur to Chandler November 15, 1884, NARA-1, RG-45, M-89, Roll 72.
215 Report of USS *Pinta* to Whitney, October 19, 1888, NARA-1, Area Files, M-625, Roll 294.
216 Sims, January 29, 1895, LOC/SP, Box 3; Sims, February 7, 1895, LOC/SP, Box 3.
217 Hagan, *This People's Navy*, 185; Drake, *The Empire of the Sea*, 312.
218 Drake, *The Empire of the Sea*, xi.
219 伊原泽周《北洋舰队1891年访日问题的再检讨》[Reexamination of Questions Surrounding the 1891 Visit of the Beiyang Fleet to Japan] 《北洋海軍新探》[*Beiyang Navy: New Explorations* …], 432. See also: 《海東耀武》[Our Glorious Military on the Eastern Sea] *Shenbao*, July 5, 1891.

220 *The North China Herald*, July 31, 1891; *North China Herald*, July 24, 1891.
221 李伯相 [Li Boxiang] 奏設水師書 [Memorial on the Establishment of a Naval Handbook] 1881,《洋务运动, 第1册》 [*Foreign Affairs Movement*, Vol. 1], 431.
222 Loveman, *No Higher Law*, 151–152.
223 Hoganson, *Fighting for American Manhood*, 1; Richard Hofstadter, *The Paranoid Style in American Politics* (New York: Vintage Books, 1967), 150–57.
224 Maier, *Among Empires*.

6   The US New Navy Wins a Race – Finally

1 Benjamin F. Tracy to Harrison, August 6, 1891, Library of Congress, Harrison Papers [hereafter LOC/HP], Series 1; Tracy to Harrison, August 15, 1891, LOC/HP, Series 1; James J. Beach to Benjamin Harrison, September 26, 1891, ENCL Newspapers, LOC/HP, Series 1; Benjamin Cooling, *Benjamin Franklin Tracy: Father of the Modern American Fighting Navy* (Hamden, CT: Archon Books, 1973); "Cabinet Officers Present," *Portland Daily Press* (Portland, ME), August 14, 1891.
2 Tracy to Harrison, August 19, 1891, LOC/HP, Series 1.
3 "Yankee Tars Racing," *Portland Daily Press* (Portland, ME), August 18, 1891; "At Bar Harbor," *Daily Kennebec Journal* (Augusta, ME), August 18, 1891.
4 "Fleet Gathering," *Portland Daily Press* (Portland, ME), August 21, 1891.
5 "Present and Prospective Shipbuilding Policy of the Principal Maritime Nations," 1889, TNA/ADM 231/15. See also: J. D. Kelley, *Our Navy*, 180; "Our New Navy," *Evening World* (New York), May 21, 1891.
6 T. Roosevelt, "Naval War College, Closing Address," June 2, 1897, USNWC-NHC, RG-16, 21.
7 *New York Herald* as used in *Life and Letters of Rear Admiral Stephen B. Luce*, ed. Albert Gleaves (New York: G. P. Putnam's Sons, 1925), 221; Seth Milliken, *Congressional Record*, April 24, 1884, 3364–3365.
8 Shulman, *Navalism*, chapter 8.
9 "Cronica," *Revista de Marina*, No. 30 (November, 1887): 580. See also: "La Flota Nueva," *Revista de Marina*, No. 108 (June, 1895): 1174.
10 Tracy, *ARSN 1889*, 49.
11 "The American and Chilian Navies," *Times* (London) October 30, 1891.
12 Tracy to Harrison, September 4, 1891, LOC/HP, Series 1.
13 Harrison to Tracy, September 5, 1891, LOC/HP, Series 1.
14 A. T. Mahan to Bouverie Clark, May 22, 1891, *LPATM*, Vol. 2, 47. For similar language see: A. T. Mahan to Horace Scudder, October 11, 1890, *LPATM*, Vol. 2, 28.
15 Cooling, *Benjamin Franklin Tracy*, 157.
16 Shulman, *Navalism*, 2.
17 Rose, *Power at Sea*, 1–4; US State Department, Office of the Historian, "Milestones: Mahan."
18 A. T. Mahan, *Influence*, 71.
19 Field, "American Imperialism," 667.

20 Mobley, *Progressives in Navy Blue*, 12.
21 Tracy, *ARSN 1889*, 3–11; "The Vessels of the New Navy" Hearing, *Congressional Record*, January 15–February 25, 1890.
22 John Reilly and Robert Scheina, *American Battleships 1886–1923: Predreadnought Design and Construction* (Annapolis: Naval Institute Press, 1980), 21.
23 Tracy, *ARSN 1889*, 11.
24 Baer, *One Hundred Years of Sea Power*, 18.
25 "Union Iron Works," *The Wave*, April 1, 1899, NMRC/SF.
26 *Notables of the West* (New York: International News Service, 1915), 255.
27 "Where the Oregon and Ohio were Built," *The Evening Post*, May 18, 1901, NMRC/SF.
28 *A Century of Progress: San Francisco Yard Bethlehem Steel Company 1849–1949*.
29 Scott Testimony, "The Vessels of the New Navy," *Congressional Record*, January 15–February 25, 1890.
30 "Cruiser No. 2," *Los Angeles Herald*, February 6, 1887.
31 "The Cruiser Charleston a Perfect Success," *Morning Tribune* (San Luis Obispo, CA) July 20, 1888; "The Charleston Launched," *San Jose Mercury News*, July 20, 1888.
32 "Building War Ships," *Daily Alta California*, October 21, 1887.
33 Johnson, *Thence Round Cape Horn*, 224.
34 Alejandro San Francisco, *La Guerra Civil de 1891* (Santiago: Ediciones Centro de Estudios Bicentenario, 2007); Maurice Hervey, *Dark Days in Chile: An Account of the Revolution of 1891* (London: Edward Arnold, 1892).
35 "The *Itata*," *New York Times*, May 8, 1891; US Legation Paris to Blaine, May 22, 1891, LOC/HP, Series 1; US Legation Paris to Blain, July 23, 1891, LOC/HP, Series 1.
36 Clayton, *Grace: W. R. Grace and Company, 1850–1930*, 210. See also: "Chili and the United States," *Times* (London, UK), May 12, 1891. Part of a series of neutrality complaints relevant to the war, see: Elswick Shipyard to Chilean Minister, London, December 2, 1891, AHNC/MMAR, Vol. 520; Elswick Works to Chilean Minister, London, December 19, 1891, AHNC/MMAR, Vol. 520; John North to Salisbury, May 15, 1891, No. 301, TNA/FO 881/6186.
37 "The United States and Chile," *New York Times*, May 7, 1891. See also: "Foster's Many Masters," *New York Times*, July 4, 1892; Clayton, *Grace and Co.*, 212; The Chiefs of the Revolutionary Party to RADM Hothman, March 20, 1891, No. 321, ENCL 2, TNA/FO 881/6186.
38 Alvah Pendleton to Harrison, May 4, 1891, LOC/HP, Series 1.
39 Miller to Harrison, May 7, 1891, LOC/HP, Series 1.
40 Miller to Harrison, May 8, 1891, LOC/HP, Series 1.
41 B. F. Tracy, *ARSN 1891*, 25; López, *Historia de la Marina de Chile*, 329; Miller to Harrison, May 8, 1891, Harrison Papers, Series 1.
42 "Our Cruisers in Pursuit," *New York Times*, May 12, 1891; "Itata Returns to U.S.," *Times* (London) May 23, 1891; *Voz de Mexico* (Mexico City), July 7, 1891; "El Charleston y el Esmeralda," *El Siglo Diez y Nueve* (Mexico City) May 28, 1891.

43 "The Charleston's Mission," *The Record Union* (Sacramento, CA) May 12, 1891; "The Charleston and the Esmeralda," *Times* (London, UK), Friday, May 15, 1891; "Let Them Fight," *Los Angeles Herald*, May 12, 1891.
44 Remey to Secretary of the Navy, May 16, 1891, NARA-1, Area Files, M-625, Roll 299. For earlier comparisons, see: D. D. Porter, "Report of the Admiral of the Navy," November 12, 1884, in *ARSN 1884*, 62; "The New Cruisers," *New York Times*, December 10, 1884; "The New Warships," *New York Times*, October 6, 1885; *Congressional Record – House*, February 23, 1885, 2037; *Congressional Record – House*, February 20, 1885, 1971; "Lanzamiento al agua del Crucero Americano Charleston," *Revista de Marina*, November 1888, No. 42, 393.
45 "The War in Chili," *Times* (London), Monday, May 18, 189; "Corsario Chileno," *La Voz de México* (Mexico City), May 16, 1891; Remey to Secretary of the Navy, May 16, 1891, NARA-1, Area Files, M-625, Roll 299.
46 "Let Them Fight," *The Los Angeles Herald*, May 12, 1891.
47 McCaskey to Dept. of States, May 18, 1891, Copy of Telegram A, Harrison Papers, Series 1.
48 Isidoro Errazuriz to Admiral Brown, May 13, 1891, *ARSN 1891*, 26.
49 Jenner to Salisbury, June 26, 1891, No. 458, TNA/FO 881/6186.
50 Cooling, *Benjamin Franklin Tracy*, 157.
51 RADM McCann to Secretary of the Navy, June 12, 1891, NARA-1, Area Files, M-625, Roll 300.
52 *Warspite* Report to Admiralty, June 8, 1891, No. 439, ENCL 1, TNA/FO 881/6186.
53 McCann Journal, December 20, 1881, McCann Papers, No. 6, USNA/NL; "Special Notice," *Los Angeles Herald*, December 15, 1881.
54 *Baltimore*, Z Files, NHHC; Johnson, *Thence Round Cape Horn*, 145.
55 Lopez to Ministerio de Marina, AHNC/MMAR 453, Folio 3.
56 Harrison to Tracy, August 12, LOC/HP, Series 1; Soley to Harrison, August 13, 1891, LOC/HP, Series 1.
57 Soley to Harrison, August 13, 1891, LOC/HP, Series 1.
58 Tracy, *ARSN 1891*, 31.
59 Board of Investigation, October 19, 1891, NARA-1, Area Files, M-625, Roll 301; B. F. Tracy, *ARSN 1891*, 21–22.
60 Cooling, *Benjamin Franklin Tracy*; Goldberg, *The Baltimore Affair*; Hervey, *Dark Days*.
61 May, *Imperial Democracy*, 10; Herring, *From Colony to Superpower*, 294; Loveman, *No Higher Law*, 145–147.
62 Schley to Tracy, October 22, 1891, LOC/HP, Series 1.
63 A. Ross to Ministerio de Relaciones Exteriores, January 22, 1892, AMREC/95, No. 106.
64 Hervey, *Dark Days*, 307.
65 Robley D. Evans, *A Sailor's Log* (New York: Appleton and Company, 1901), 285.
66 "Looks like a Chilean War," *New York Times*, December 24, 1891.
67 Evans, *A Sailor's Log*, 262.
68 A. T. Mahan to Bouverie Clark, May 22, 1891, *LPATM*, Vol. 2, 47.
69 Hoganson, *Fighting for American Manhood*, 1.

70 "Cause of Chile's Delay," *New York Times*, January 18, 1892.
71 James Harrison to Benjamin Harrison, January 18, 1892, LOC/HP, Series 1 (emphasis in original).
72 George Edward Graham, *Schley and Santiago* (Chicago: Conkey Publishers, 1902), 36–37.
73 A. T. Mahan to Luce, January 10, 1892 *LPATM*, Vol. 2, 63; A. T. Mahan to T. Roosevelt, May 6, 1897, *LPATM*, Vol. 2, 507.
74 Timothy Wolters, "Recapitalizing the Fleet: A Material Analysis of Late-Nineteenth-Century U.S. Naval Power," *Technology and Culture*, Vol. 52, No. 1 (2011): 103–126; Goldberg, *The Baltimore Affair*, ix.
75 "The American and Chilian Navies," *Times* (London, UK), October 30, 1891; Hervey, *Dark Days*, 308.
76 Lopez, *Historia de la Marina de Chile*, 335. US planners were more skeptical, citing the duration and "hard service" of the Civil War. See: "The United States and Chilian Navies," *The Buenos Aires Herald*, Tracy Papers, LOC, Box 31, Folder 2; Report of RADM McCann to Secretary of the Navy, May 25, 1891, NARA-1, Area Files, M-625, Roll 299. A report he echoed in August 1891. RADM McCann to Secretary of the Navy August 15, 1891, NARA-1, Area Files, M-625, Roll 300; LT C. C. Rogers, "Notes on the Defenses and Military Resources of the Republic of Chile," NARA-1, RG-38, Box 19, NM-63, Entry 141; R. D. Evans to Tracy, December 4, 1891, NARA-1, Area Files, M-625, Roll 301; Evans, *A Sailor's Log*, 263; Dorwart, *Office of Naval Intelligence*, 43.
77 RADM George Brown to B. F. Tracy, December 14, 1891, NARA-1, Area Files, M-625, Roll 301.
78 Harrison to Tracy, June 15, 1891, LOC/HP, Series 1; James Soley to Bering Strait Force, August 8, 1891, LOC/HP, Series 1.
79 Tracy to Harrison, August 20, 1891, LOC/HP, Series 1.
80 Schley to Tracy, October 31, 1891, LOC/HP, Series 1.
81 Johnson, *Thence Round Cape Horn*, 146.
82 Grant to Blaine, January 7, 1892, LOC/HP, Series 1; O. L. Hein to Secretary of War, February 1, 1892, LOC/HP, Series 1.
83 A. T. Mahan to S. B. Luce, January 10, 1892, *LPATM*, Vol. 2, 63; Ernest Spencer to Salisbury, May 15, 1891, No. 289, TNA/FO 881/6186. An opinion he held in common with T. Roosevelt for years thereafter. A. T. Mahan to T. Roosevelt, May 6, 1897, *LPATM*, Vol. 2, 507. T. Roosevelt, "Naval War College, Closing Address," June 2, 1897 (Washington, DC: Government Printing Office, 1897). See also: RG-16, Box 3, USNWC-NHC.
84 E. Reed to Captain Valenzuela Day, December 24, 1891, AHNC/MMAR, Vol. 520; W. Noble, Elswick Shipyard to Chilean Minister, London, December 2, 1891, AHNC/MMAR, Vol. 520; Nobel, Elswick Works to Chilean Minister, London, December 19, 1891, AHNC/MMAR, Vol. 520.
85 Pitkin to Blaine, January 25, 1892, LOC/HP, Series 1; Naval Attaché Reports, 1892, NARA-1, RG-38, Box 925, 13825 H-5-c 93/196; "Las Fortificaciones de Valparaíso," *Revista de Marina*, No. 4 (October 1885): 459.
86 Bradley Fiske, *From Midshipman to Rear Admiral* (New York: The Century Co., 1919), 168.

87 "Sunk by Torpedoes," *New York Times*, April 28, 1891; J. D. Kelley, *Our Navy*, 47; "Guerra Franco-China: Notables Ataques Con Torpedos," *Revista de la Marina*, No. 2, August 1885; Guerra del Pacífico, *Revista de la Marina*, No. 3 (September, 1885): 256; C. H. Davis, "Notes on the Defenses and Military Resources of the Republic of Chile," NARA-1, RG-38, Box 19, NM-63, Entry 141; "Extracts from Letter of Captain of 'Admiral Lynch' to Captain R King R.N.," TNA/ADM 189/11, 159; RADM Hotham to Admiralty, May 9, 1891, TNA/FO 881/6186.
88 Boulding, *Conflict and Defense*, 262.
89 A. T. Mahan to Luce, January 10, 1892, *LPATM*, Vol. 2, 63.
90 A. T. Mahan, "Necessity and Objects of a Naval War College," August 6, 1888, Box 1, Folder 2, US Naval USNWC-NHC; B. F. Tracy, *ARSN 1891*, 33.
91 Harrison to Blaine, December 31, 1891, LOC/HP, Series 1.
92 Yrigoyen, as used by Valdivieso, *El Incidente del "USS* Baltimore," 84. See also: A. Ross to Ministerio de Relaciones Exteriores, January 22, 1892, AMREC/95, No. 106; A. T. Mahan, "Iquique for the Purposes of Invasion" (1891) Tracy Papers, LOC Box 31.
93 Blaine to Harrison, January 2, 1892, LOC/HP, Series 1.
94 "Preparations to Meet Chile," *New York Times*, December 27, 1891.
95 "Defenseless against Chile," *Seattle Post-Intelligencer*, November 2, 1891.
96 Mahan to Luce, January 10, 1892, *LPATM*, Vol. 2, 63; Mahan to Luce, November 26, 1891, *LPATM*, Vol. 2, 60.
97 "The American and Chilian Navies," *Times* (London, UK), October 30, 1891.
98 "The President's Message," *New York Times*, December 10, 1891; Goldberg, *The Baltimore Affair*, 124.
99 Egan to Blaine, Letter, November 11, 1891, LOC/HP; Egan to Blaine, Telegraph, November 11, 1891, LOC/HP, Series 1.
100 Goldberg, *The Baltimore Affair*, 125; Dorwart, *Office of Naval Intelligence*, 43.
101 Egan to Blaine, January 25, 1892, LOC/HP, Series 1.
102 Blaine Draft to Egan, January 29, 1892, LOC/HP, Series 1, strikethrough in original. Though Harrison's draft was more generous. See: Harrison to Blaine, January 29, 1892, LOC/HP, Series 1.
103 Harrison to W. H. Seward, January 29, 1892, LOC/HP, Series 1.
104 Johnson, *Thence Round Cape Horn*, 224.
105 Wicks, "New Navy and New Empire," 296.
106 B. F. Tracy, *ARSN 1889*, 49.
107 A. T. Mahan to S. B. Luce, January 28, 1892, *LPATM*, Vol. 2, 65. For "nucleus" see: T. Roosevelt, "Naval War College, Closing Address," June 2, 1897, USNWC-NHC, RG-16, 21.
108 Pitkin to Blaine, January 25, 1892, LOC/HP, Series 1.
109 Brown, "The Power of Influence," 1; Sater, *Empires in Conflict*, 69.
110 Mahan to Soley, October 29, 1892, *LPATM*, Vol. 2, 82; Cooling, *Benjamin Franklin Tracy*, 122.
111 Alberto Linacre, "El Progreso de la Marina Norte-Americana," *Revista de Marina*, No. 82 (March, 1893): 269; "La Flota Nueva," *Revista de Marina*, No. 108 (June, 1895): 1174.

112 Dept. of Navy, "Veteran Minelayer Baltimore Offered for Sale," Z Files, Baltimore, NHHC.
113 Harrison to Grant, May 18, 1891, LOC/HP, Series 2; International Railway Commission to Blaine, May 5, 1891, LOC/HP, Series 1.
114 Blaine to Harrison, August 10, 1891, LOC/HP, Series 1.
115 Stevens to Blaine, September 5, 1891, LOC/HP, Series 1.
116 Shulman, *Navalism*, 2. Ignoring, for unclear reasons, the *Baltimore* Incident (1891). See: Morgan, *Pacific Gibraltar*, 136. Tom Coffman, *Nation Within: The History of the American Occupation of Hawai'i* (Kihei, HI: Koa Books, 1998), 135–141; William Russ, *The Hawaiian Revolution* (Selinsgrove, PA: Susquehanna University Press, 1959); Noenoe K. Silva, *Aloha Betrayed: Native Hawaiian Resistance to American Colonialism* (Durham, NC: Duke University Press, 2004), 164–203.
117 Wilste to Tracy, January 18, 1893, LOC/HP, Series 1.
118 A. T. Mahan, "Hawaii and Our Future Sea Power," in *The Interest of America in Sea Power*, 31, 39; "Hawaii and Our Future Sea Power," *New York Times*, March 1, 1893; "Needed as a Barrier to Protect the World from an Invasion of Chinese Barbarism," *New York Times*, February 1, 1893.
119 "Opinion of Leading Newspapers on the Hawaiian Question," Tracy Papers, LOC, Box 31. Staff included carefully reworded critical assessments as well. As in *Boston Advertiser*, January 31, 1894; *Baltimore Morning Herald*, February 1, 1894.
120 *Philadelphia Inquirer*, February 1, 1893, in "Opinion of Leading Newspapers on the Hawaiian Question," Tracy Papers, LOC, Box 31.
121 *Chicago Inter-Ocean*, January 30, 1894, in "Opinion of Leading Newspapers on the Hawaiian Question," Tracy Papers, LOC, Box 31.
122 "Hawaii in our System," *New York Daily Tribune*, February 6, 1893, in LOC/HP, Series 1.
123 May, *Imperial Democracy*, 13.
124 Telegram to Cleveland, April 28, 1893, Library of Congress/Grover Cleveland [hereafter LOC/GC], Series 2.
125 Irish to Cleveland April 15, 1893, LOC/GC, Series 2. Boosterism in the California press was, indeed, considerable. "Kaiulani," *San Francisco Morning Call*, January 30, 1893; May, *Imperial Democracy*, 13.
126 Irish to Cleveland April 15, 1893, LOC/GC, Series 2.
127 Coffman, *Nation Within*, 141–148; Herring, *From Colony to Superpower*, 305–306. The Chinese vernacular press transmitted critical pieces about the US "coveting" Hawaii and plotting to drive out its rulers; 《檀君失國》 [The Monarch of Hawaii Loses Her Kingdom], *Shenbao*, March 6, 1893;《檀事近述》 [Further Description of Events in Hawaii] *Shenbao*, December 20, 1893.
128 Coffman, *Nation Within*, 135; Liliuokalani to US House of Representatives December 19, 1898; NARA-1, RG-233, HR-55A-H28.3.
129 "The Crowning Shame of the Hawaiian Business," *New York Tribune*, January 7, 1894.
130 A. T. Mahan to Ellen E. Mahan, November 13, 1894, *LPATM*, Vol. 2, 360.
131 T. Roosevelt to Anna Roosevelt, January 27, 1895, *TR Letters*, Vol. 1, 423; T. Roosevelt to C. Lodge October 27, 1894, *Selections from the Correspondence*

of Theodore Roosevelt and Henry Cabot Lodge, Vol. 1, 139; T. Roosevelt to A. T. Mahan, May 3, 1897, *TR Letters*, 607.
132 *Revista de Marina*, December 1885, No. 6, 732. "Sketches of Warships Constructed by G. W. Armstrong for the Imperial Japanese Navy," D/VA/21/2, TWA/UK.
133 David Trask, "William Sowden Sims: The Victory Ashore," *Admirals of the New Steel Navy: Makers of the American Naval Tradition, 1880–1930*, ed. James Bradford (Annapolis, MD: Naval Institute Press, 1990); "Papers on Squadrons of Evolutions and the Recent Development of Naval Materiel," *Information from Abroad V*, Navy Department, Office of Naval Intelligence (1886), 77; Sims to Parents, April 5, 1894, Sims Papers, Box 3, Personal Correspondence, LOC.
134 Sims to Parents, October 11, 1894, LOC/SP, Box 3.
135 Evans and Peattie, *Kaigun*, 19.
136 R. W. Mitchill to B. F. Tracy, August 18, 1891, NARA-1, Area Files, M-625, Roll 300; E. W. Halford to Tracy April 21, 1892, Box 23, "Special Correspondence," Tracy Papers, LOC.
137 The *Charleston* had in fact completed a series of port calls in California in the summer of 1891, drumming up support for the New Navy following the Chase of the *Itata*. Remey to Secretary of the Navy, August 5, 1891, NARA-1, M-625, Roll 300. "Columbia River Celebration," *Dalles Weekly Chronicle*, April 15, 1892; "Astoria's Jubilee" *Evening Capital Journal* (Salem, OR) May 12, 1892.
138 "Long Cruises Ended," February 28, 1893, *New York Times*.
139 "Will Want to See the Cruisers," *Dalles Daily Chronicle*, April 16, 1892. See also: "Columbia River Celebration," *Dalles Weekly Chronicle*, April 15, 1892; "Astoria's Jubilee," *Evening Capital Journal* (Salem, OR) May 12, 1892.
140 "Will Want to See the Cruisers," *Dalles Daily Chronicle*, April 16, 1892.
141 "The International Columbian Navy Rendezvous and Review of 1893," *Information from Abroad XII*, Office of Naval Intelligence (1893); "Report of Leiut. Richard Rush, November 23, 1888," *Report of the Secretary of the Navy, 1888*, 543.
142 "The Naval Parade and Review," NARA-1, RG-45, Box 460.
143 "Boatswain Riggin Buried," *New York Times*, August 15, 1892.
144 "Long Cruises Ended," *New York Times*, February 28, 1893.
145 Schley to Harrison, March 18, 1892, LOC/HP, Series 1; Baltimore, Z Files, NHHC.
146 Harrison, State of the Union Address, 1892.
147 "Naval Review in New York Harbor," *Providence News*, April 20, 1893.
148 "The Great Naval Review," *Morning Call* (San Francisco), April 28, 1893.
149 "Naval Review Fleet," May 22, 1893, NARA-1, RG-45, Box 460; Hillary Herbert, *ARSN 1893*, 58.
150 Hillary Herbert, *ARSN 1893*, 58.
151 "The Naval Review at Spithead," *The Sunday Times* (London, UK), July 24, 1887; "Plan of the Naval Review at Spithead," *Times* (London, UK), July 24, 1887. Though in part designed to demonstrate the need for *British* naval expansion. See: Jeffery Lant, "The Spithead Naval Review of 1887," *The Mariner's Mirror*, February, 1976.

152 "The Great Naval Review at New York," *Times* (London, UK), April 28, 1893.
153 Brian Lane Herder, *US Navy Armored Cruisers 1890–1933* (Oxford: Osprey, 2022), 5.
154 "The Navies of the Great Powers," *Times* (London, UK), June 1, 1893.
155 Fenton R. McCreery to Isidoro Errazuriz, September 22, 1892, NARA-1, RG-45, Box 460; Isidoro Errazuriz to F. McCreery, January 3, 1893, NARA-1, RG-45, Box 460; "Vessels of Many Nations," *New York Times*, April 9, 1893.
156 Joseph Smith, *Brazil and the United States: Convergence and Divergence* (Athens, GA: University of Georgia Press, 2010), 40; Joseph Smith, *Unequal Giants: Diplomatic Relations Between the United States and Brazil 1889–1930* (Pittsburgh: University of Pittsburgh Press, 1991), 3–34; Steven Topik, *Trade and Gunboats: The United States and Brazil in the Age of Empire* (Stanford: Stanford University Press, 1996), 121–154.
157 Loveman, *No Higher Law*, 150.
158 Topik, *Trade and Gunboats*, 138.
159 Smith, *Unequal Giants*, 23.
160 "Benham's Gallant Fight," *New York Tribune*, January 31, 1894.
161 "The Old Flag," *Morning Call* (San Francisco), January 31, 1894.
162 Flint, *Memories of an Active Life*, 100. For comparable efforts see: Confederacy in Europe (1861–1865) or the Lay-Osborne Flotilla in China (1862–1863).
163 "Memories of a Propper-Up of Tottering Thrones," *New York Times*, December 9, 1923.
164 Topik, *Trade and Gunboats*, 167.
165 "Shows His Hand," *The Morning Call* (San Francisco), November 18, 1893.
166 "Last Edition," *The World* (New York), November 2, 1893.
167 "May Stop El Cid," *The World* (New York), November 6, 1893.
168 Flint, *Memories of an Active Life*, 91–96.
169 Topik, *Trade and Gunboats*, 155.
170 Flint, *Memories of an Active Life*, 101; Topik, *Trade and Gunboats*, 175.
171 George Boynton, *The War Maker* (Chicago: A. C. McClurg, 1911), 335.
172 Boynton, *The War Maker*, 350.
173 Topik, *Trade and Gunboats*, 175; "Notes on the Year's Naval Progress," ONI (Washington, DC: Government Printing Office, 1894).
174 "John Wilde's Awful Scheme," *New York Times*, December 13, 1894.
175 Smith, *Brazil and the United States*, 44; Topik, *Trade and Gunboats*, 121; "Discussing Benham's Action," *New York Daily Tribune*, January 31, 1894.
176 "The Old Flag," *The Morning Call* (San Francisco), January 31, 1894.
177 Smith, *Unequal Giants*, 3–34.
178 Sater, *Empires in Conflict*.
179 Smith, *Brazil and the United States*, 30.
180 Ibid., 45.
181 Topik, *Trade and Gunboats*, 177.
182 Clowes, *Four Modern Naval Campaigns*, 187.
183 Wilson, *Ironclads in Action*, Vol. 2, 51.

184 Boynton, *The War Maker*, 339.
185 A. T. Mahan to Luce, January 10, 1892, *LPATM*, Vol. 2, 63; A. T. Mahan to Luce, November 26, 1891, *LPATM*, Vol. 2, 60; RADM George Brown to B. F. Tracy, December 14, 1891, NARA-1, Area Files, M-625, Roll 301.
186 Harrison to Blaine, December 31, 1891, LOC/HP, Series 1; A. T. Mahan, "Iquique for the Purposes of Invasion" (1891) Tracy Papers, LOC Box 31.
187 Sater, *Empires in Conflict*, 69.
188 May, *Imperial Democracy*, 10.
189 Timothy Wolters, "Recapitalizing the Fleet: A Material Analysis of Late-Nineteenth-Century U.S. Naval Power," *Technology and Culture*, Vol. 52, No. 1 (2011): 103–126.
190 W. T. Sampson, "Outline of a Scheme for the Naval Defense of the Coast," *Proceedings of the United States Naval Institute*, Vol. 15, No. 2 (1889): 170.
191 USS *Kearsarge* (1862–1894), NH61669, NHHC.

7 The Sino-Japanese War and New "Yankees" in the Pacific

1 马军 [Ma Jun]《事迹与文献： 甲午黄海海战北洋水师中的洋员》 [Achievements and Documents: The Foreigners Employed by the North Sea Fleet in the Naval Battle of the Yellow Sea]《军事历史研究》[*Military History Research*] July 2015, No. 4, 108–116.
2 Lee McGiffin, *Yankee of the Yalu: Philo Norton McGiffin* (New York: E. P. Dutton & Co., 1968), 115.
3 S. C. M. Paine, *The Sino-Japanese War of 1894–1895* (Cambridge: Cambridge University Press, 2003); Dorwart, *The Pigtail War*;《中日戰爭：中国近代史资料丛刊》[*The Sino-Japanese War: Chinese Modern Historical Materials Series*] 第1册, ed. 邵循正 [Shao Xunzheng] (上海：人民出版社, 1956), 1; 钱钢 [Qian Gang]《大清海军于李鸿章》[*The Qing Navy and Li Hongzhang*, 240; 戚其章 [Qi Qizhang]《甲午战争史》[*History of the Sino-Japanese War*] (北京：人民出版社, 1990), 587.
4 Mahan to Luce, January 28, 1892, *LPATM*, Vol. 2, 65. For "Yankees" see: Mason, *The War on the Pacific Coast of South America*, 6; William Curtis, *Yankees of the East: Sketches of Modern Japan* (New York: Stone and Kimball, 1896), 1.
5 Sims, May 26, 1894, LOC/SP, Box 3. Chinese observers shared that chauvinism, see: 李鸿章奏校阅海军事 [Li Hongzhang Inspection and Review of Naval Affairs] May 29, 1894《清末海軍史料》[*Late Qing Navy Historical Materials*], 279.
6 陈悦 [Chen Yue]《北洋海军》[*The Beiyang Navy*], 57.
7 梅启照奏筹议海防拟 [Mei Qizhao Memorial on the Establishment of Maritime Defenses] 1880,《清末海軍史料》[*Late Qing Naval Historical Materials*], 15; 李鸿章议复梅启照条陈折 [Li Hongzhang, Responding to Mei Qizhao's Proposal] 1881,《清末海軍史料》[*Late Qing Naval Historical Materials*], 21;《论战事将成》[Discussion of the Impending Military Affairs] *Shenbao*, July 10, 1894.
8 Lambert, *Seapower States*, 7; Evans and Peattie, *Kaigun*, 19.

9 Shufeldt Report, c. 1882, Shufeldt Papers, LOC, Box 24, Korean Treaty Items.
10 《论战事将成》 [Discussion of the Impending Military Affairs] *Shenbao*, July 10, 1894.
11 李鸿章奏校阅海军事 [Li Hongzhang, Inspection and Review of Naval Affairs] May 29, 1894,《清末海軍史料》 [*Late Qing Navy Historical Materials*], 279.
12 陈悦 [Chen Yue]《北洋海军》 [*The Beiyang Navy*], 68–69. 醇親王 [Memorial of Prince Chun] 光緒十二年五月一日《洋务运动，第3册》 [*Foreign Affairs Movement*, Vol. 3], 555:《钢船试验》 [Ironclad Testing] *Shenbao*, August 25, 1881; "Germany," *London and China Telegraph*, July 30, 1883; "The Chinese Pei-Yang Squadron," *North China Herald*, May 7, 1886; "Rumors," *North China Herald*, July 20, 1894.
13 李鸿章议复梅启照条陈折 [Li Hongzhang, Responding to Mei Qizhao's Proposal] 1881,《清末海軍史料》 [*Late Qing Naval Historical Materials*], 26; "Present and Prospective Ship-Building Policy of Foreign Nations," November, 1886, No. 119, TNA/ADM 231/10.
14 *Notes on the Navies of the Lesser-European, Asiatic and South and Central American States* (1887), ONI, NARA-1, RG 38, Box 26, Entry 141; "Japan: Coast Defence, Dockyards, etc.," August, 1894, No. 386, TNA/ADM 231/24; *Revista de Marina*, No. 47 (April, 1889): 366.
15 "Japan: Naval and Commercial Ports," July 1885, No. 70, TNA/ADM 231/6.
16 *Notes on the Navies of the Lesser-European, Asiatic and South and Central American States* (1887), ONI, NARA-1, RG 38, Entry 141, Box 26, NM-63 Entry 141.
17 "The Chinese Navy," *North China Herald*, September 21, 1894. Though many Chinese officers were more dubious. 薛福成 [Xue Fucheng] 出使英法義比四國日記 [Diary of the Mission to Four Nations] January 3, 1891,《洋务运动，第8册》 [*Foreign Affairs Movement*, Vol. 8], 296–297.
18 关飞 [Guan Fei] 为中国海军而死的美国青年 [The Young American Who Died for the Chinese Navy]《文史博览》19.
19 《海東耀武》 [Military Radiance on the Eastern Sea] *Shenbao*, July 5, 1891.
20 "Rumors," *North China Herald*, July 20, 1894;《西人論華兵可用》 [Westerners Discuss Chinese Military Capabilities] *Shenbao*, August 12, 1894.
21 "Kaikoku Nippon," Evans and Peattie, *Kaigun*, 19; Inagaki Manjirō, *Japan and the Pacific* (London: Fisher Unwin, 1890), 34.
22 舟欲行，黄传会 [Zhou Yuxing and Huang Chuanhui]《龙旗:清末北洋海军纪实》 [*Dragon Flag: History of the Late Qing Beiyang Navy*] (北京: 学苑出版社, 2007), 101.
23 *Notes on the Navies of the Lesser-European, Asiatic and South and Central American States* (1887), ONI, NARA-1, RG 38, Entry 141, Box 26, NM-63, Entry 141. See also: "Ships Built for Japan, 1880–1905," D.VA/21/1, TWA/UK; "Sketches of Warships Constructed by G. W. Armstrong for the Imperial Japanese Navy," D/VA/21/2, TWA/UK.
24 伊原泽周《北洋舰队1891年访日问题的再检讨》 [Reexamination of Questions Surrounding the 1891 Visit of the Beiyang Fleet to Japan] in《北洋海军新探》 [*Beiyang Navy: New Explorations …*] 432; 汤正东

[Tang Zhengdong]《浅析李鸿章的海防思想》[Preliminary Analysis of Li Hongzhang's Thinking on Maritime Defense] 郧阳师范高等专科学校学报 [*Journal of Yunyang Normal University*] 36, No. 4 (2016): 111.
25. ONI, *Information from Abroad X* (1891), 60; ONI, *Information from Abroad XI* (1892), 51; "Naval Budget, 1892" in "Japan: Coast Defences, Dockyards, etc.," August 1894, No. 386, TNA/ADM 231/24.
26. 钱钢 [Qian Gang]《大清海军于李鸿章》[*The Qing Navy and Li Hongzhang*], 88, 127.
27. 李鸿章奏校阅海军事 [Li Hongzhang, Inspection and Review of Naval Affairs] May 29, 1894,《清末海军史料》[*Late Qing Navy Historical Materials*], 279. For similar complaints see also: 薛福成 [Xue Fucheng] 出使英法義比四國日記 [Diary of the Mission to Four Nations]《洋务运动, 第8册》[*Foreign Affairs Movement*, Vol. 8], 290; 李鸿章订购新式小快船旨 [Li Hongzhang, Supplemental Directive to Purchase New Style, Small Cruisers]《清末海军史料》[*Late Qing Navy Historical Materials*], 125.
28. 李鸿章奏为海军铁甲快练各船拟分年添购快炮陆续付款折 [Li Hongzhang, Memorial on Purchasing Quick Firing Guns] March 31, 1894《清末海军史料》[*Late Qing Navy Historical Materials*], 124.
29. 李鸿章通筹扩充海军以出洋攻战 [Li Hongzhang, Proposes Expanding Maritime Forces to Wage War on the Open Sea] August 7, 1894,《清末海军史料》[*Late Qing Navy Historical Materials*], 84.
30. Bridge to Foreign Office, July 16, 1894, TNA/FO-881/6594. See also: O'Conor to Foreign Office, July 26, 1894, No. 414, TNA/FO-881/6594; "The Sea of War in the Far East," *Sunday Times* (London, UK), August 5, 1894.
31. Paine, *Sino-Japanese War*, 15; Westad, *Restless Empire*, 101.
32. O'Conor to Foreign Office, July 26, 1894, No. 414, TNA/FO-881/6594; O'Conor to Foreign Office July 3, 1894, No. 322, TNA/FO-881/6594.
33. Bridge to Foreign Office, July 16, 1894, TNA/FO-881/6594.
34. No. 407, ENCL 2, June 26, 1894, TNA/FO-881/6594. See also: "The Sea of War in the Far East," *Sunday Times* (London, UK), August 5, 1894.
35. Hilary Conroy, *The Japanese Frontier in Hawaii, 1868–1898* (Los Angeles: University of California Press, 1953); Akira Iriye, *Japan and the Wider World: From the Mid-nineteenth Century to the Present* (New York: Longman, 1997), 27.
36. Juan Lopez to Ministerio de Marina, June 9, 1885, AHNC/MMAR, Vol. 453, Folio 10; B. Vicuna Mackenna, "El Reparto del Pacífico," *Revista de Marina*, No. 1 (July 1885): 68.
37. Coffman, *Nation Within*, 255.
38. "Memorandum for the Secretary of the Navy: Hawaiian Islands," Tracy Papers, LOC, Box 31.
39. Juan Lopez to Ministerio de Marina, June 9, 1885, AHNC/MMAR, Vol. 453, Folio 10.
40. "Rumors of War," *The Pacific Commercial Advertiser* (Honolulu, HI) March 21, 1893; "Another Japanese Cruiser," *Hawaiian Gazette* (Honolulu, HI) March 23, 1894; "The Japanese Cruiser," *Hawaii Holomua* (Honolulu, HI) April 26, 1894.

41 "The American Flag!" *Daily Pacific Commercial Advertiser* (Honolulu, HI) April 3, 1893; "Hawaiian Annexation," *Hawaiian Gazette* (Honolulu, HI), May 23, 1893.
42 "The Flag Down," *Hawaiian Star* (Honolulu, HI), April 1, 1893.
43 John L. Stevens, *Congressional Record*, December 13, 1893.
44 "The Japanese Cruiser Naniwa," *Pacific Commercial Advertiser* (Honolulu, HI) March 27, 1893.
45 Thompson, "Exaggeration of American Vulnerability."
46 D. D. Porter, "Report of the Admiral of the Navy," November 12, 1884, *ARSN 1884*, 62; "The Charleston and the Esmeralda," *Times* (London, UK), Friday, May 15, 1891.
47 *Revista de Marina*, No. 6 (December 1885): 732; "Sketches of Warships Constructed by G. W. Armstrong for the Imperial Japanese Navy," D/VA/21/2, TWA/UK; Fred S. Cozzens, 1892, "USS *Charleston* and USS *San Francisco*" (Detail), J. D. Kelley, *Our Navy*, 46. See also: "Naniwa-Kan" Album 655, NMM/WA.
48 "Papers on Squadrons of Evolutions and the Recent Development of Naval Materiel," *Information from Abroad V*, Navy Department, Office of Naval Intelligence (1886), 77.
49 "Another Japanese Cruiser," *Hawaiian Gazette* (Honolulu, HI), March 23, 1894; "Another Japanese Cruiser," *Pacific Commercial Advertiser* (Honolulu, HI), March 22, 1894; William Sims, April 5, 1894, LOC/SP, Box 3.
50 David Trask, "William Sowden Sims: The Victory Ashore," *Admirals of the New Steel Navy*; *21st Century Sims: Innovation, Education, and Leadership for the Modern Era*, ed. Benjamin Armstrong (Annapolis: Naval Institute Press, 2015).
51 Sims, December 21, 1893, LOC/SP, Box 2.
52 Sims, April 5, 1894, LOC/SP, Box 3; William Sims, October 11, 1894, LOC/SP, Box 3.
53 Paine, *The Sino-Japanese War*, 302.
54 LaFeber, *The Clash*, 45: "Interred with Honors," *Hawaiian Gazette* (Honolulu, HI), April 10, 1894; "Took a Fatal Plunge," *Pacific Commercial Advertiser* (Honolulu, HI), April 6, 1894.
55 Sims, May 26, 1894, LOC/SP, Box 3; William Sims, December (no date indicated) 1894, LOC/SP, Box 3.
56 Sims, May 26, 1894, LOC/SP, Box 3.
57 "The Japanese Cruiser," *Hawaiian Gazette* (Honolulu, HI), May 25, 1894.
58 Sims, May 26, 1894, LOC/SP, Box 3.
59 The visiting Japanese students at the US Naval Academy impressed Sims. William Sims, December 25, 1894, LOC/SP, Box 3.
60 "Wharf and Wave," *Pacific Commercial Advertiser* (Honolulu, HI), June 20, 1894.
61 Sims Biography, Z File, NHHC.
62 "The Korean Question," as Sims called it. William Sims, September 11, 1894, LOC/SP, Box 3; "Correspondence Korea and the War between China and Japan," TNA/FO 881/6594; "The Corean Affair," *Japan Daily Mail* (Tokyo), June 9, 1894.

63 Sometimes "Kowshing."
64 《德員述高陞被擊事》[German Official Describing the Attack on the Gaosheng], *Shenbao*, August 7, 1894;《烟臺訪事人信述中日交兵事》[Visitors to Yantai Describe Sino-Japanese Military Affairs], *Shenbao*, August 3, 1894; Fremantle to Admiralty, August 13, 1894, No. 298, ENCL 1, TNA/FO-881/6594; W. H. Wilkinson to O'Conor, July 28, 1894, No. 478, ENCL 1, TNA/FO 881/6594.
65 O'Conor to Foreign Office, July 3, 1894, No. 322, TNA/FO-881/6594; "The War," *North China Herald*, August 17, 1894. Douglas Howland, "The Sinking of the S. S. Kowshing," *Modern Asian Studies*, Vol. 42, No. 4 (July, 2008): 673–703.
66 Paine, *Sino-Japanese War*; 戚其章 [Qi Qizhang]《甲午战争史》[*History of the Sino-Japanese War*]; 李平子 [Li Pingzi]《从鸦片战争到甲午战争》[*From the Opium War to the Sino-Japanese War*], 609–627; 张明金 [Zhang Mingjin]《落日下的龙旗: 1894–1895 年中日战争纪实》[*The Sunset of the Dragon Banner*]; Benjamin Lai, *Chinese Battleship vs Japanese Cruiser: Yalu River 1894* (London: Osprey, 2019).
67 "Battle of the Yalu," Naval Attaché, Tokio, Received May 21, 1895, NARA-1, RG-45, Box 460.
68 Roosevelt to Hilary Herbert, December 12, 1894, "Deductions Drawn from the Yaloo Fight," NARA-1, RG-45, Box 460; H. B. Bristow to O'Conor, September 21, 1894, TNA/ADM-125/112; "The Chinese Ironclad Battle-Ship 'Chen-Yuen' Undergoing Repairs at Port Arthur," *Illustrated London News*, November 24, 1894.
69 Roosevelt to Hilary Herbert, December 12, 1894, "Deductions Drawn from the Yaloo Fight," NARA-1, RG-45, Box 460. See also: 陈兆锵所记中日战役情形 [Chen Zhaoqiang's Remembrance of the Details of the Sino-Japanese War]《清末海軍史料》[*Late Qing Navy Historical Materials*], 349.
70 "China-Japan War," March 1895, No. 416, TNA/ADM 231/25.
71 Bristow to O'Conor, September 21, 1894, TNA/ADM-125/112; "Ships Built for Japan, 1880–1905," D.VA/21/1, TWA/UK. See also: "Sketches of Warships Constructed by G. W. Armstrong for the Imperial Japanese Navy," D/VA/21/2, TWA/UK; "Chih Yuan," NMM/WA, Album 655.
72 李鸿章奏为海军铁甲快练各船拟分年添购快炮陆续付款折 [Li Hongzhang Memorial on Purchasing Quick Firing Guns], March 31, 1894,《清末海軍史料》[*Late Qing Navy Historical Materials*], 124.
73 Fremantle to Admiralty, October 30, 1894, No. 437, TNA/FO-881/6605.
74 李鸿章奏请添威海大连湾水雷栅 [Li Hongzhang's Memorial to Increase the Torpedo Defenses at Dalian and Weihaiwei], August 6, 189《清末海軍史料》[*Late Qing Navy Historical Materials*], 277. 夏东元 [Xia Dongyuan]《洋务运动》[*Foreign Affairs Movement*], 372; "Foochow District: Local Notice to Mariners," TNA/ADM 125/112; "Torpedoes in Min River," August 13, 1894, ADM 125/112.
75 "The English Mail Papers," *North China Herald* (Shanghai), October 5, 1894.
76 Sims, February 1, 1895, LOC/SP, Box 3; "China Coast and River Defences," June 1887, TNA/ADM 231/11; Nowell Simon, "China Coast and River Defences," January 1889, TNA/ADM 231/15.

77 Sims, February 28, 1895, LOC/SP, Box 3; "The Chinese Navy," *North China Herald* (Shanghai), September 21, 1894. For the Royal Navy scheme: "The War Between China and Japan," Appendix G, TNA/ADM 189/15; E. Simpson, October 25, 1895 (USS *Concord*), "Report on the Kiangnan Arsenal," NARA-1, RG-38, Box 392, noting indigenously produced torpedoes for the "late war." "The Chinese Navy," *North China Herald* (Shanghai), September 21, 1894; 《遠購魚雷》[Purchases of Locomotive Torpedoes] *Shenbao*, June 4, 1893.

78 Roosevelt to Herbert, December 12, 1894, "Deductions Drawn from the Yaloo Fight," NARA-1, RG-45, Box 460; Luce, "Naval Warfare under Modern Conditions," *North American Review*, Vol. 162 (1896): 70.

79 《甲午战争有关奏折史料》[Memorials and Historical Materials Relating to the Sino-Japanese War] in《清末海軍史料》[*Late Qing Navy Historical Materials*], 336; Rawlinson, *China's Struggle for Naval Development*, 189.

80 Trench to Foreign Office, October 24, 1894, No. 386, TNA/FO-881/6605. A long-held Japanese ambition: "China-Japan War," March 1895, No. 416, TNA/ADM 231/25; "Notes on Yaloo from Japanese Officers," US Legation Tokyo, May 21, 1895, NARA-1, RG-45, Box 460.

81 "War between China and Japan," *Annual Report of the Torpedo School*, TNA/ADM 189/15. 陈兆锵所记中日战役情形 [Chen Zhaoqiang Remembrances of the Details of the Sino-Japanese War]《清末海軍史料》[*Late Qing Navy Historical Materials*], 127.

82 Sims, February 25, 1895, "Condition of the Chinese Vessels after Their Capture by the Japanese at Wei Hai Wei," NARA-1, RG-45, Box 460.

83 《殲倭記》[Record of the Annihilation of the Japanese], *Shenbao*, February 17, 1895;《倭人詭計》[The Cunning Plan of the Japanese], *Shenbao*, January 18, 1895; Fremantle to Admiralty, February 9, 1895, TNA/ADM 125/112; "War Between China and Japan," *Annual Report of the Torpedo School*, TNA/ADM 189/15.

84 张之洞筹款购铁快船只谕 [Zhang Zhidong Memorial on the Creation of Funds for the Purchase of Armored Cruisers], February, 13, 1895《清末海軍史料》[*Late Qing Navy Historical Materials*], 127.

85 薛福成 [Xue Fucheng] 出使英法義比四國日記 [Diary of the Mission to Four Nations], January 3, 1891《洋务运动, 第8冊》[*Foreign Affairs Movement*, Vol. 8], 316; Carpenter, August 6, 1895, NARA-1, RG-45, Box 469, Operations of the Pacific Station 1887–1902.

86 Allan, *Under the Dragon Flag*, 35–51.

87 Annual Report of the Torpedo School, Japan, TNA/ADM 189/5, xx.

88 《電傳戰耗》[Telegraphic Reports of News from the War] *Shenbao*, February 14, 1895, noting the persistence of the Japanese torpedo boats. 刘名誉 [Liu Mingyu] 水雷艇策 [Torpedo Boat Plan]《洋务运动, 第3冊》[*Foreign Affairs Movement*, Vol. 3], 431–432; 醇親王 [Memorial of Prince Chun] 光緒十二年五月一日《洋务运动, 第3冊》[*Foreign Affairs Movement*, Vol. 3], 555.

89 刘名誉 [Liu Mingyu] 水雷議 [Opinions on Torpedoes]《洋务运动, 第3冊》[*Foreign Affairs Movement*, Vol. 3], 432.

Notes to pages 161–163 253

90 李鴻章 [Li Hongzhang], 籌議海防 [Establishing Maritime Defenses] 同治十三年十一月二日《 洋务运动, 第1册》[*Foreign Affairs Movement*, Vol. 1], 45; Lee Hsi-ming (李喜明), *Taiwan's Plan for Victory: An Asymmetric Strategy to Use the Small to Control the Large: All of Taiwan Should Understand the Overall Defense Concept* (《臺灣的勝算：以小制大不對稱戰略, 全臺灣人都應了解的整體防衛構想》) (2022), 300.
91 "John Wilde's Awful Scheme," *New York Times*, December 12, 1894; *New York Times*, February 24, 1895; Jeffery Dorwart, "Providence Conspiracy of 1894," *Rhode Island History*, Vol. 32, No. 3 (1973): 91.
92 "The Esmeralda Reaches Japan," *New York Times*, February 6, 1895; "Esmeralda Gone to Japan," *Pacific Commercial Advertiser* (Honolulu, HI), January 22, 1895.
93 "The *Esmeralda*," Album 655, NMM/WA; *Izumi* (ex-*Esmeralda*), in "Sketches of Warships Constructed by G. W. Armstrong for the Imperial Japanese Navy," D/VA/21/2, TWA/UK.
94 In 1884–1885, the steel cruiser *Arturo Prat* was recommissioned as the *Tsukushi*. See: Sondhaus, *Naval Warfare*, 132–133; "Japan" *General Information Series*, No. 4, 1885, 121.
95 "Statement of Facts," August 1894, No. 397, TNA/FO-881/6594; India Office to Foreign Office, September 12, 1894, No. 404, TNA/FO-881/6594.
96 December 22, 1893, Flint Papers, Business Correspondence, Box 1, New York Public Library [hereafter NYPL]; "List of Vessels Sold to the Brazilian Government," May 1, 1895, Flint Papers, Business Correspondence, Box 4, NYPL.
97 Flint, *Memories of an Active Life*, 64, 180.
98 "Anexo a La Unión," *Diario de la Unión*, December 13, 1894, Vol. 20, Archivo Histórico de la Armada [hereafter AMC], Valparaíso, Chile; J. M. P. Caamano to Luis Cordero, October 19, 1894, "A Mis Conciudadanos: Explicación Circunstanciada de lo Ocurrido en el Odioso Asunto del Crucero *Esmeralda*" (Cuenca: Imprenta de José Ma. Montesinos e Hijos, 1896), 9.
99 Flint, *Memories of an Active Life*, 181; Minister of Chile in France to Ministry of the Marina, November 29, 1894, AMREC, Vol. 227, 1895, Folio 44; Legation of Chile in Washington to Legation of Chile in Paris, November 26, 1895, AMREC, Vol. 95, 1883–1899, Folio 269; Japanese Legation to Chilean Ministry in Washington, DC, AMREC, November 30, 1894 in Vol. 45, 1872–1899, Folio 97.
100 Flint, *Memories of an Active Life*, 181. "The Sale of the Esmeralda," *Times* (London, UK), February 2, 1895.
101 "Is There an Alliance?" *New York Times*, March 26, 1895; Servicio Consular Del Peru, Guayaquil, Ecuador (January–April), 1895, MREP, Caja 418, C-1, Codigo 8-12-A, Folio 8.
102 Servicio Consular Del Peru, Guayaquil, Ecuador (January–April), 1895, MREP, Caja 418, C-1, Codigo 8-12-A, Folio 8.
103 "Ecuador's National Honor Riot," *New York Times*, May 4, 1895; Cordero, *Asunto del Crucero*, 28; Editorial, *Grito del Pueblo*, Guayaquil, Ecuador, January 26, 1895, republished in *Diario de la Unión*, February 14, 1895, Vol. 21, January–June 1895, AMC.

104 Representatives attempted to buy the ship from Chile while it was being fitted out. It became the forerunner of the *Jingyuan* and *Zhiyuan*. See: 陈悦 [Chen Yue]《北洋海军》[*The Beiyang Navy*], 94.
105 李鸿章电总理衙门智利出售兵船 [Li Hongzhang Telegram to the Zongli Yamen on Chile's Offer to Sell Warships]《清末海軍史料》[*Late Qing Navy Historical Materials*], 125; 上谕 [Imperial Edict] September 14, 1894, attached to 李鸿章电总理衙门智利出售兵船 [Li Hongzhang Telegram to the Zongli Yamen on Chile's Offer to Sell Warships], October 12, 1894,《清末海軍史料》[*Late Qing Navy Historical Materials*], 126; 陈悦 [Chen Yue]《北洋海军》[*The Beiyang Navy*], 96.
106 吴大澂奏海防条议 [Wu Daji Memorial on Measures for Maritime Defense], August 21, 1885,《清末海軍史料》[*Late Qing Navy Historical Materials*], 47.
107 《西報談兵》[Western Reports Discussing Weapons] *Shenbao*, February 21, 1895;《西報談兵》[Western Reports Discussing Weapons], *Shenbao*, December 21, 1895.
108 陈悦 [Chen Yue]《北洋海军》[*The Beiyang Navy*], 96;《困倭人》[Hampering the Japanese] *Shenbao*, December 27, 1894.
109 Teh Moo Sim, Legation of Korea to Flint & Co., February 24, 1904, Flint Papers, Box 1, NYPL.
110 Henry Cabot Lodge, January 21, 1895, *Congressional Record*. See also: "Warship Esmeralda in Port," *Pacific Commercial Advertiser* (Honolulu, HI), January 11, 1895; "Man-of-War in Port," *The Hawaiian Star* (Honolulu, HI), January 10, 1895.
111 Henry Cabot Lodge, January 22, 1895, *Congressional Record*; Henry Cabot Lodge, March 2, 1895, *Congressional Record*, 3107; "The American Flag!" *Daily Pacific Commercial Advertiser* (Honolulu, HI), April 3, 1893.
112 Tracy, *ARSN 1891*, 31; *Memoria de Ministerio de Marina* (Santiago, 1884), vi.
113 "Is There an Alliance?" *New York Times*, March 26, 1895.
114 Legation of Chile in Washington to Ministry of Foreign Affairs, January 15, 1883, AMREC, Vol. 93, 1883, Folio 13; M. Terashima to Joaquin Godoy, January 11, 1883, Legation of Chile (US), AMREC, Vol. 45, 1872–1899, Folio 9; Japanese Legation in Washington to Chilean Legation, November 11, 1883, AMREC, Legation of Chile (US), Vol. 45, 1872–1899, Folio 20.
115 "Is There an Alliance?" *New York Times*, March 26, 1895.
116 Ienaga Saburō, *The Pacific War: World War II and the Japanese, 1931–1945* (New York: Pantheon Books, 1978).《中日戰爭: 中国近代史资料丛刊》[*The Sino-Japanese War: Chinese Modern Historical Materials Series*] 第1冊, 1; 李平子 [Li Pingzi]《从鸦片战争到甲午战争》[*From the Opium War to the Sino-Japanese War*], 609–627; 张明金 [Zhang Mingjin]《落日下的龙旗: 1894–1895 年中日战争纪实》[*The Sunset of the Dragon Banner*] (北京: 燕山出版社, 1998), 483.
117 Paine, *The Sino-Japanese War of 1894–1895*, 3–4; S. C. M. Paine, *The Japanese Empire: Grand Strategy from the Meiji Restoration to the Pacific War* (Cambridge: Cambridge University Press, 2017), 39–46; Westad, *Restless Empire*, 100–101; Rawlinson, *China's Struggle for Naval Development*, 198; Thomas G. Otte, *The China Question: Great Power Rivalry and British Isolation, 1894–1905* (Oxford: Oxford University Press, 2007), 30.

118 Paine, *The Sino-Japanese War*, 3–4; Paine, *The Japanese Empire*, 39–46.
119 Dorwart, *The Pigtail War*, 136.
120 Herring, *From Colony to Superpower*, 299–336; LaFeber, *The New Cambridge History of American Foreign Relations*, 111–114; May, *Imperial Democracy*, 25.
121 LaFeber, *The Clash*, 45–57; Edward Miller, *War Plan Orange: The U.S. Strategy to Defeat Japan, 1897–1945* (Annapolis: Naval Institute Press, 1991), 21; Charles Neu, *The Troubled Encounter: The United States and Japan* (New York: John Wiley, 1975), 33–34; William Nester, *Power Across the Pacific* (New York: New York University Press, 1996), 62–67; Sadao Asada, *From Mahan to Pearl Harbor: The Imperial Japanese Navy and the United States* (Annapolis: Naval Institute Press, 2013), 3–21.
122 Morgan, *Pacific Gibraltar*, 4, 173. See also: William Morgan, "The Anti-Japanese Origins of the Hawaiian Annexation Treaty of 1897," *Diplomatic History*, Vol. 6, No. 1 (January 1, 1982): 23; Iriye, *Pacific Estrangement*, 54; Kees van Dijk, *Pacific Strife: The Great Powers and Their Political and Economic Rivalries in Asia and the Western Pacific, 1870–1914* (Amsterdam: Amsterdam University Press, 2015), 382; Coffman, *Nation Within*, 196.
123 Iriye, *Pacific Estrangement*, 39–40; Gardiner, *The Japanese and Peru, 1873–1973*.
124 Iriye, *Pacific Estrangement*, 49–50.
125 Morgan, *Pacific Gibraltar*, 4, 173; See also: Morgan, "The Anti-Japanese Origins of the Hawaiian Annexation Treaty of 1897," *Diplomatic History*, Vol. 6, No. 1 (January 1, 1982): 23; Iriye, *Pacific Estrangement*, 54.
126 A. T. Mahan, *Retrospect and Prospect* (Boston: Little, Brown and Co., 1902), 144.
127 Yoshida to George Balch, June 18, 1881, George Balch Papers, Box 1, Folder 7, UNC-CH/WL; George Balch to Yoshida, July 25, 1881, George Balch Papers, Box 1, Folder 7, UNC-CH/WL.
128 Blaine to Balch, May 10, 1882, George Balch Papers, Box 1, Folder 7, UNC-CH/WL; Consulate of Japan San Francisco to George Balch, May 18, 1882, George Balch Papers, Box 1, Folder 7, UNC-CH/WL.
129 Terashima to Godoy, January 11, 1883, Legation of Chile in the United States, AMREC, Vol. 45, 1872–1899, Folio 9.
130 Anthony O'Higgins, February 7, 1895, *Congressional Record*, Vol. 27, 1894.
131 H. C. Lodge, March 2, 1895, *Congressional Record*, Vol. 27, 3107.
132 John M. Palmer, February 7, 1895, *Congressional Record*, Vol. 27, 1891.
133 H. C. Lodge, March 2, 1895, *Congressional Record*, Vol. 27, 3107.
134 《美國防倭》 [The United States Guards Against Japan] *Shenbao*, April 10, 1895; Shelby Collum, *Congressional Record*, December 10, 1895, 112.
135 Mannix, *The Old Navy*, 36; Sims, May 10, 1895, LOC/SP, Box 3; "Expects Another War," *Commercial Gazette*, Pittsburgh, PA, October 30, 1895, United States Naval Academy/McGiffin Papers [hereafter USNA/MP].
136 "The Warning of Wei-Hai-Wei," *Spectator* (London, UK), February 16, 1895; ENCL to Anthony O'Higgins, *Congressional Record*, March 2, 1895, 3109.
137 "The English Mail Papers," *North China Herald*, September 7, 1894.
138 Evans and Peattie, *Kaigun*, 24.

139 *Conway's All the World's Fighting Ships 1860–1905*, 217.
140 "Naval Estimates of Foreign Countries," May 1896, No. 447, TNA/ADM 231/26; LT J. M. Ellicott, *The Composition of the Fleet*, in *Proceedings of the USNI*, Vol. 22 (1896): 546; "List of Ships Projected in Foreign Countries," Intelligence Department (No. 441) December 1895, TNA/ADM 231/26.
141 Kelley, *Our Navy*, 185.
142 "Commander McGiffin," *The Democrat* (Washington, PA), November 6, 1895, in USNA/MP.
143 Shelby Collum, *Congressional Record*, December 10, 1895, 112.
144 Sims, January 29, 1895, LOC/SP, Box 3; Goschen to Foreign Office, October 10, 1894, No. 93, TNA/FO-881/6605.
145 Sims, January 29, 1895, LOC/SP, Box 3; Sims, February 5, 1895, LOC/SP, Box 3. For Mahan see: Mahan to Samuel Ashe, March 11, 1885, *LPATM*, Vol. 1, 592.
146 Mahan to James R. Thursfield, November 21, 1895, *LPATM*, Vol. 2.
147 Charles H. Cramp, "The Coming Sea-Power," *The North American Review*, Vol. 165, No. 491 (1897).
148 Ibid.
149 Consulate General of Japan to Balch, George Balch Papers, Folder 9, Box 1, UNC-CH/WL; H. P. Goddard, "Reminiscences of Commodore M. G. Perry's Japan Expedition by our Oldest Admiral," George Balch Papers, Folder 9, UNC-CH/WL.
150 Mahan to J. B. Sterling, February 13, 1896, *LPATM*, Vol. 2, 445. See also: Kramer, "Empires, Exceptions, and Anglo-Saxons."
151 H. C. Lodge, March 2, 1895, *Congressional Record*, Vol. 27, 3107.
152 Paine, *Sino-Japanese War*, 39.
153 LaFeber, *The Clash*, 45.
154 Pike, *Chile and the United States*, 61; Mason, *The War on the Pacific Coast of South America*, 6.
155 Carpenter to Secretary of the Navy, August 6, 1895, Operations of the Pacific Squadron 1887–1902, NARA-1, RG-45, Box 469; Thomas Fremantle, "Naval Aspects of the China Japan War," *Journal of the Royal United Service Institute*, in NARA-1, RG-45, Box 460.
156 Edwin Dun to Gresham December 30, 1894, *FRUS 1894*, Appendix I, 85; *New York Times*, December 12, 1894; "Port Arthur Massacre," *The Evening World*, December 20, 1894.
157 William Sims, December 25, 1894, LOC/SP, Box 3.
158 Allan, *Under the Dragon Flag*, 89.
159 O'Higgins, February 7, 1895, *Congressional Record*, 1894.
160 Mahan to J. B. Sterling, February 13, 1896, *LPATM*, Vol. 2, 445.
161 "The Triumph of Civilisation!" *Punch*, August 11, 1894.
162 H. C. Taylor, "Report of the President of the Naval War College and Torpedo School," *ARSN 1895*, 167; Li Hongzhang to Robert Wilson Shufeldt, September 20, 1881, Shufeldt Papers, Box 24, LOC.
163 Kelley, *Our Navy*, 179.
164 H. Herbert, *ARSN 1894*, 17.

165 McAdoo, "Opening Address," June 4, 1895, RG-16, Box 1, USNWC-NHC.
166 McAdoo, "Opening Address," June 2, 1896, RG-16, Box 1, USNWC-NHC.
167 Roosevelt to William Clowes, August 3, 1897, *TR Letters*, Vol. 1, 637.
168 Sims, February 5, 1895, LOC/SP, Box 3.
169 Herbert, *ARSN 1895*, lvii.
170 Sims, March 24, 1895, LOC/SP, Box 3.
171 Roosevelt to Herbert, December 12, 1894, "Deductions Drawn from the Yaloo Fight Sketch of the Ting-Yuen Showing Punishment Received," NARA-1, RG-45, Box 460.
172 Herbert, *ARSN 1896*, 4; J. D. Kelley, *Our Navy*, 179.
173 Roosevelt to Lodge, April 24, 1896, *Selections from the Correspondence of Theodore Roosevelt and Henry Cabot Lodge*, Vol. 1, 217.
174 John Frederick Pike, "1894 Battle of the Yalu, Logbook," NMM/UK, Log/N/D/15/2.
175 "Pride of the Chilean Navy," *New York Times*, April 15, 1894.
176 Herbert, *ARSN 1896*, 9; "Cruisers vs. Battleships," *Los Angeles Times*, September 24, 1894.
177 Herbert, *ARSN 1895*, lvii.
178 May, *Imperial Democracy*, 33; Karsten, *Naval Aristocracy*, 116.
179 Bradford Perkins, *The Great Rapprochement: England and the United States, 1895–1914* (New York: Athenaeum, 1968); Kori Schake, *Safe Passage* (Cambridge, MA: Harvard University Press, 2017); G. S. Clarke, "A Naval Union with Great Britain: A Reply to Mr. Andrew Carnegie," *The North American Review*, Vol. 158 (1894): 362; Mahan to G. S. Clarke, July 29, 1894, *LPATM*, Vol. 2; A. T. Mahan, "Naval Warfare," Lowell Institute Lectures, March 24–April 24, 1897, Mahan Papers, LOC, Box 5, Reel 4.
180 Mahan to George Sydenham Clarke, November 5, 1892, *LPATM*, Vol. 2, 83; Mahan to James Ford Rhodes, April 26, 1897, *LPATM*, Vol. 2.
181 "Memorandum for the Secretary of the Navy: Hawaiian Islands," Tracy Papers, LOC, Box 31.
182 Mahan to James Thursfield, February 1, 1897, *LPATM*, Vol. 2, 529. For related opinion see: Mahan to Walter Hines Page, July 23, 1897, *LPATM*, Vol. 2, 520; T. Roosevelt to Charles Arthur Moore, February 14, 1898, *TR Letters*, Vol. 2, 772; Fiske, *From Midshipman to Rear Admiral*, 227.
183 "Three Cheers All," *The Pacific Commercial Advertiser* (Honolulu, HI), August 6, 1897.
184 Mahan to Roosevelt, May 1, 1897, *LPATM*, Vol. 2, 505–506.
185 Mahan to Roosevelt, May 6, 1897, *LPATM*, Vol. 2, 507.
186 Roosevelt, "Naval War College Closing Address," June 2, 1897, RG-16, Box 3, USNWC-NHC.
187 "China for the Chinese," *New York Times*, March 30, 1882; A. T. Mahan to *New York Times*, January 30, 1893, *LPATM*, Vol. 2, 92; Henry Blair, *Congressional Record*, February 3, 1894.
188 Lodge, March 2, 1895, *Congressional Record*, 3107; O'Higgins, February 7, 1895, *Congressional Record*, 1894.
189 Mahan to Roosevelt, May 6, 1897, *LPATM*, Vol. 2, 507. See also: Iriye, *Pacific Estrangement*, 49–50.

190 "Japanese Scare in Hawaii," *New York Times*, June 28, 1897; "American News," *Daily Mail* (London), April 13, 1897.
191 LaFeber, *The Clash*, 56; "Japan's Protest against Annexation," *Los Angeles Herald*, July 25, 1897.
192 "No Arbitration," *The Pacific Commercial Advertiser*, May 6, 1897; "The Naniwa," *The Independent* (Honolulu, HI), May 4, 1897; "Japan and Hawaii," *The Independent* (Honolulu, HI), May 4, 1897; "Serious Possibilities," *Evening Bulletin* (Honolulu, HI), May 3, 1897.
193 Roosevelt to James Bryce, September 10, 1897, *TR Letters*, Vol. 1, 676; "More Americans Needed," *Hawaiian Gazette*, March 23, 1897.
194 Henry Teller, *Congressional Record*, February 16, 1898.
195 Roosevelt to W. McKinley, April 22, 1897, *TR Letters*, Vol. 1, 601.
196 "No Arbitration," *Pacific Commercial Advertiser* (Honolulu, HI), May 6, 1897.
197 "Preparing for Trouble," *Hawaiian Star* (Honolulu, HI), April 10, 1897; "Is It Annexation?" *Hawaiian Gazette* (Honolulu, HI), April 13, 1897.
198 Michael Vlahos, "The Naval War College and the Origins of War-Planning Against Japan," *Naval War College Review*, Vol. 33, No. 4 (1980): 24–25. See also: Roosevelt to C.F. Goodrich, June 26, 1897, *TR Letters*, Vol. 1, 626.
199 Roosevelt to McKinley, April 22, 1897, *TR Letters*, Vol. 1, 601.
200 RADM McCann to Secretary of the Navy, June 12, 1891, NARA-1, Area Files, M-625, Roll 300; Roosevelt to Cabot Lodge, December 1, 1894, *Selections from the Correspondence of Theodore Roosevelt and Henry Cabot Lodge*, Vol. 1, 140.
201 Roosevelt, "Naval War College Closing Address," June 2, 1897, RG-16, Box 3, USNWC-NHC.
202 LaFeber, *The Clash*, 57; Iriye, *Pacific Estrangement*, 52–53.
203 "On the Cruiser," *Hawaiian Gazette* (Honolulu, HI), May 21, 1897.
204 "On the Cruiser," *Pacific Commercial Advertiser* (Honolulu, HI), May 20, 1897.
205 "On the Philadelphia," *Pacific Commercial Advertiser* (Honolulu, HI), June 17, 1897.
206 S. B. Luce to Hilary Herbert, October 14, 1897, *Life and Letters of Rear Admiral Stephen B. Luce, U.S. Navy*, 321.
207 Mahan to Roosevelt, May 1, 1897, *LPATM*, Vol. 2, 505–506.
208 Roosevelt to Mahan, May 3, 1897, *TR Letters*, Vol. 1, 608; Roosevelt to Mahan, June 9, 1897, *TR Letters*, Vol. 1, 622; Roosevelt, "Naval War College Closing Address," June 2, 1897, RG-16, Box 3, USNWC-NHC.
209 J. D. Kelley, *Our Navy*, Vol. 2, 14.
210 Roosevelt to Bowman Hendry McCalla, August 3, 1897, *TR Letters*, Vol. 1, 636. See also: Roosevelt to John Long, September 30, 1897, *TR Letters*, Vol. 1, 695.
211 John Long, *ARSN 1897*, 11; T. Roosevelt to John Long, September 30, 1897, *TR Letters*, Vol. 1, 695; "Japan's Army and Navy," *Daily Mail* (London), July 20, 1897.
212 T. Roosevelt to Hermann Speck von Sternberg, January 17, 1898, *TR Letters*, Vol. 1, 763.

213 Cumings, *Dominion from Sea to Sea*, 137; Morison, *Two Ocean War*, 17; Theodore Roosevelt, *Thomas Hart Benton* (Boston, MA: Houghton, Mifflin, and Co., 1886), 52.
214 May, *Imperial Democracy*, 10.
215 Dorwart, *The Pigtail War*; Farcau, *The Ten Cents War*.
216 Dewey, *Autobiography of George Dewey*, 168. Ronald Spector, *Admiral of the New Empire: The Life and Career of George Dewey*, (Baton Rouge: Louisiana State University Press, 1974).

Conclusion

1 Daniel Immerwahr, *How to Hide an Empire: A History of the Greater United States* (New York: Farrar, Straus, and Giroux, 2019).
2 Hendrix, *Theodore Roosevelt's Naval Diplomacy*; Adam Tooze, *The Deluge: The Great War, America, and the Remaking of the Global Order, 1916–1931* (New York: Penguin, 2014), 35–36; Jeffery. J Safford, *Wilsonian Maritime Diplomacy 1913–1921* (New Brunswick, NJ: Rutgers University Press, 1978); Chase Untermeyer, *Inside Reagan's Navy: The Pentagon Journals* (College Station: Texas A&M Press, 2015).
3 Epstein, *Torpedo*, 12.
4 "Our Little Navy," *United Service*, Vol. 11 (1884): 305.
5 Jordan, "Seacoast Defenses of Southern Carolina and Georgia," *SHSP*, Vol. 1 (June, 1876): 404.
6 Clowes, *Captain of the* Mary Rose, xiii.
7 Mahan, "Introduction," in Wilson, *Ironclads in Action*, Vol. 1, xiv–xv.
8 Brent Sterling. *Other People's Wars: The US Military and the Challenge of Learning from Foreign Conflicts* (Washington, DC: Georgetown University Press, 2021).
9 Fuller, *Turret versus Broadside*, 281.
10 Hoganson, *Fighting for American Manhood*.
11 Schencking, *Making Waves*, 1–4.
12 Ryan D. Wadle, *Selling Sea Power: Public Relations and the U.S. Navy, 1917–1941*. (Norman: University of Oklahoma Press, 2019).
13 "La Flota Nueva," *Revista de Marina*, No. 108 (1895): 1174.
14 H. C. Lodge, March 2, 1895, *Congressional Record*, 3107.
15 Holger Herwig, "The Battlefleet Revolution, 1885–1914," in *The Dynamics of Military Revolution*, 115. See: Daniel Headrick, *The Tools of Empire* (New York: Oxford University Press, 1981); Daniel Headrick, *The Tentacles of Empire* (New York: Oxford University Press, 1988).
16 Black, *Naval War a Global History*, 25.
17 Erez Manela, "International Society as a Historical Subject," *Diplomatic History*, Vol. 44, No. 2 (April, 2020): 184–209.
18 Akira Iriye, *Global Community: The Role of International Organizations in the Making of the Contemporary World* (Berkeley: University of California Press, 2002); Amy Sayward, *The Birth of Development: How the World Bank, Food and Agriculture Organization, and World Health Organization Changed the World, 1945–1965* (Kent, OH: Kent State University Press, 2006); Matthew Connelly, *Fatal Misconception: The Struggle to Control World Population*

(Cambridge, MA: Harvard University Press, 2008); Nick Cullather, *The Hungry World: America's Cold War Battle against Poverty in Asia* (Cambridge, MA: Harvard University Press, 2010); David C. Engerman, *The Price of Aid: The Economic Cold War in India* (Cambridge, MA: Harvard University Press, 2018).

19 Pomeranz, *The Great Divergence*; Hobsbawm, *The Age of Empire*, 59.
20 Clifford Rogers, "The Military Revolutions of the Hundred Years' War," *The Journal of Military History*, Vol. 57 (April, 1993): 241–278.
21 *The Dynamics of Military Revolution, 1300–2050*, ed. Macgregor Knox and Williamson Murray (Cambridge: Cambridge University Press, 2001), 13.
22 Nicholas Lambert, *Sir John Fisher's Naval Revolution* (Columbia, SC: University of South Carolina Press 1999); Baxter, *The Introduction of the Ironclad Warship*.
23 For interest in disruptive technologies, see: Andrew Krepinevich, *The Origins of Victory: How Disruptive Military Innovation Determines the Fates of Great Powers* (New Haven: Yale University Press, 2023). For competition, see: United States National Security Strategy (October, 2022) www.whitehouse.gov/wp-content/uploads/2022/10/Biden-Harris-Administrations-National-Security-Strategy-10.2022.pdf.
24 Ernest May, *"Lessons" of the Past: The Use and Misuse of History in American Foreign Policy* (New York: Oxford University Press, 1975).
25 Wilson, *Ironclads in Action*, Vol. 2, 136.
26 Peter Singer and August Cole, *Ghost Fleet: A Novel of the Next World War* (Boston: Houghton Mifflin Harcourt, 2015); *Future Wars: The Anticipations and Fears*, ed. David Seed (Liverpool: Liverpool University Press, 2012).
27 David Armitage and Jo Guldi, *The History Manifesto* (Cambridge: Cambridge University Press, 2014), i.
28 Melville, *Moby Dick*, 397; Seward, "The Physical, Moral and Intellectual Development of the American People" (1854), 165.
29 高技术条件下的局部战争. See: *China's Military in Transition*, ed. David Shambaugh (Oxford: Oxford University Press, 1997); *Forging China's Military Might: A New Framework for Assessing Innovation*, ed. Tai Ming Cheung (Baltimore, MD: Johns Hopkins University Press, 2014); Taylor M. Fravel, *Active Defense: China's Military Strategy since 1949* (Princeton, NJ: Princeton University Press, 2019).
30 《舰载武器》 [*Shipborne Weapons*] (2005), No. 4, 67–72; "Company News: Grumman in China," *New York Times*, August 24, 1987.

Bibliography

Archival Repositories, United States

National Archives, Washington, DC (NARA-1)
- RG-38 (Records of the Chief of Naval Operation; Naval Attaché Reports)
- RG-45 (Collections of the Office of Naval Records)
- RG-46 (Records of the United States Senate)

Library of Congress, Washington, DC (LOC)
- George Belknap Papers
- James Blaine Papers
- William Chandler Papers
- Grover Cleveland Papers
- John Dahlgren Papers
- George Dewey Papers
- Benjamin Harrison Papers
- Alfred Thayer Mahan Papers
- Robert W. Shufeldt Papers
- William Sims Papers
- Benjamin Franklin Tracy Papers

New York Public Library, Special Collections (NYPL)
- Charles Flint Papers

U.S. Naval War College, Newport, RI (USNWC-NHC)
- RG-12 (Student Problems and Solutions)
- RG-14 (Faculty and Staff Presentations)
- RG-15 (Naval War College Lectures)
- RG-16 (Opening and Closing Addresses)

U.S. Naval Academy, Nimitz Special Collection Library (USNA/NL)
- William McCann Papers
- James Waddell Papers
- Philo McGiffin Papers

Wilson Library, Special Collections, University of North Carolina (UNC-CH/WL)
- George Balch Papers
- James H. Tomb Papers

Rubenstein Library, Duke University (RL/DU)
- Samuel Ashe Papers

Old Dominion University, Norfolk, VA (ODU)
- John Randolph Tucker Papers

Southern Illinois University, Special Collections Research Center, Carbondale, IL (SIU/SCRC)
- F. L. Barreda Correspondence

National Marine Resource Center, San Francisco, CA (NMRC/SF)
- Union Iron Works Collection

Naval History and Heritage Command, Washington, DC (NHHC)
- Z Files

Archival Repositories, South America

Ministerio de Relaciones Exteriores, Lima, Perú (MREP)
- Serie Correspondencia (1866–1895)
- Comunicación Ministerio de Guerra y Marina
- Servicio Diplomático del Perú en Gran Bretaña
- Oficios de la Legación del Perú en China y Japón
- Servicio Diplomático del Perú en España
- Servicio Diplomático del Perú en Ecuador
- Servicio Consular del Perú en New York

Archivo de la Marina del Perú, Callao (AHMP)
- Comisión de Construcción Naval en Inglaterra
- Comisión de Construcción Naval en Francia
- Comisión de Construcción Naval en EE.UU
- Conflictos Internacionales, Conflicto con Chile
- Departamento de Marina del Callao (1864–1880)
- Comandancia General de la Escuadra (1879–1880)
- Escuadra Alida (1866)

Archivo Histórico de la Armada, Valparaíso, Chile (AMC)
- *Revista de Marina* (1885–1900)

Ministerio de Relaciones Exteriores, Santiago, Chile (AMREC)
- Legación de Chile en EE.UU.
- Legación de Chile en Paris
- Fondo Historico Vol 227 (*Esmeralda*)

Biblioteca Nacional, Santiago, Chile (AHNC)
- Ministerio de Marina Files (AHNC/MMAR)
- Ministerio de Relaciones Exteriores (AHNC/MREL)

Archival Repositories, United Kingdom

National Archives, Kew, U.K., (TNA)
- Admiralty Files (TNA/ADM)
- War Office Files (TNA/WO)
- Foreign Office Files (TNA/FO)

National Maritime Museum, Caird Library, Greenwich (NMM/UK)
- Cowper Coles Papers (CCC)
- Frederick G.D. Bedford Papers
- William Laird Clowes Letters
- John Frederick Pike Logbook

Wirral Archive, Birkenhead, U.K., (WA/UK)
- Dimensions of Particular Vessels (ZCL)
- Papers Relating to the *Huascar*
- Papers Relating to Vessel 572
- Papers Relating to the Laird Rams

Tyne and Wear Archive, Newcastle (TWA/UK)
- Letters to Lord Armstrong (DF.A)
- Sketches of Warships for Imperial Japanese Navy
- Postcard Album, Battleships (AS.IES)

Archival Repositories Regarding East Asia

National Library (国家图书馆) Beijing, PRC.
- *Shenbao* (申報)

Harvard-Yenching Library (East Asia Collection), Cambridge, MA.

Official Publications

Annual Reports of the Secretary of the Navy [*ARSN*]. Washington, DC: Government Printing Office, 1862–1900.
Congressional Record. Washington, DC: Government Printing Office, 1882–1900.
Foreign Relations of the United States [*FRUS*]. Washington, DC: Government Printing Office, 1861–1900.
Information from Abroad. Washington, DC: Government Printing Office, 1886–1892.
Memoria de Guerra i Marina Presentada al Congreso Nacional por el Ministro del Ramo. Ministerio de Guerra y Marina Santiago de Chile: Imprenta Nacional, 1875–1892.
Memória de Marina de Chile. Santiago: Imprenta Nacional, 1865–1893.
Memória del Ramo de Guerra. Lima: Imprenta Nacional, 1878–1884.
Memoria del Ramo de Marina. Lima: Imprenta Nacional, 1865–1880.

Memória de Ministerio de Relaciones Exteriores de Chile. Santiago: Imprenta Nacional, 1865–1892.
Navy Yearbook. Washington, DC: Government Printing Office, 1904–1910.
Notes on the War between China and Japan. Washington, DC: Government Printing Office, 1896.
Official Records of the Union and Confederate Navies in the War of the Rebellion [*ORN*]. Washington, DC: Government Printing Office 1894–1922.

Published Collections of Primary Documents

Diario a bordo de la Corbeta Unión: *Guerra del Pacifico: Testimonios Inéditos*, ed. Hernán Garrido-Lecca. Lima: La Casa Del Libro Viejo, 2008.
El 2 de Mayo de 1866: Documentos Esenciales para el estudio de la Consolidación de la independencia Americana. Lima, Perú: Gil, S.A., 1941.
Guerra del Pacífico: Recopilación completa de todos los documentos oficiales, correspondencias i demás publicaciones referentes a la guerra que ha dado a luz la prensa de Chile, Perú i Bolivia, conteniendo documentos inéditos de importancia, ed. Moreno, Pascual Ahumada. Valparaiso: Imprenta del Progreso, 1894.
Huáscar Las Cartas Perdidas 1879–1884. Santiago, Chile: Ril Editores, 2003.
History of the War between Japan and China, trans. Major Jikemura and Arthur Lloyd. Tokyo: Kinkodo Publishing Co., 1904.
Informes Inéditos de Diplomáticos Extranjeros Durante la Guerra del Pacífico. Santiago, Chile: Andrés Bello, 1980.
Letters and Papers of Professor Sir John Knox Laughton 1830–1915, ed. Andrew Lambert. Burlington, VT: Ashgate Publishing, 2002.
Letters and Papers of Alfred Thayer Mahan [*LPATM*], ed. Robert Seager II and Doris Maguire. Annapolis, MD: Naval Institute Press, 1975.
The Letters of Theodore Roosevelt [*TR Letters*], ed. Elting Morison, Cambridge, MA: Harvard University Press, 1951.
Life and letters of Rear Admiral Stephen B. Luce, U.S. Navy, ed. Albert Gleaves. New York: G. P. Putnam's & Sons, 1925.
Papers of John Davis Long, 1897–1904, ed. Gardner Weld Allen. Boston, MA: Massachusetts Historical Society, 1939.
Selections from the Correspondence of Theodore Roosevelt and Henry Cabot Lodge, 1884–1918. New York: Charles Scribner's Sons, 1925.
Voices of the Confederate Navy: Articles, Letters, Reports and Reminiscences, ed. Thomas Campbell. Jefferson, NC: McFarland & Co. 2007.
The Works of William H. Seward, ed. George Baker. Boston, MA: Houghton Mifflin Harcourt, 1884.
《洋务运动》第1-8册 [*Foreign Affairs Movement*, Vol 1–8] 上海：上海人民出版社, 1961.
《清末海軍史料》 [*Late Qing Naval Historical Materials*] 张侠, ed. Zhang Xia, et al. 北京：海洋出版社, 1982.
《中法戰爭第》1-8册 [*Sino-French War*, Volume I–VIII] 邵循正, ed. Shao Xunzheng. 上海：新知出版社, 1961.
《中日戰爭》第1-7册 [*Sino-Japanese War*, Volume I–VII] 邵循正, ed. Shao Xunzheng. 上海：上海人民出版社, 1956.

《外国冒险家与南台湾的土著》 [*Foreign Adventurers and the Aborigines of Southern Taiwan*] 《台湾史料丛刊》 [*Compilation of Historical Taiwanese Materials*] Taipei: Academia Sinica, 2005.

Primary-Source Histories and Memoirs

Allan, James. *Under the Dragon Flag: My Experiences in the Chino-Japanese War.* New York: Frederick A. Stokes Company, 1898.
Arlington, L. C. *Through the Dragon's Eyes.* London: Constable & Co LTD, 1931.
Barros, Diego Arana. *Historia de la Guerra del Pacífico.* Santiago: Librería Central de Mariano Servat, 1880.
Belloc, Hilarire. "The Modern Traveler," 1898.
Benjamin, Park. "The End of New York," in *Stories by American Authors*, Vol 5. New York: Scribner's Sons, 1900.
Boyer, Samuel Pellman. *Naval Surgeon: The Diary of Dr. Samuel Pellman Boyer*, Vol I, ed. Elinor Barnes and James A. Barnes. Bloomington, IN, 1963.
Brooke, John. *The Journal and Letters of John M. Brooke*, ed. George M. Brooke. Columbia: University of South Carolina Press, 2002.
Butts, Walter Raleigh. *American Officers in the Peruvian Navy*, in *Californian*, August 1882, Vol VI., No. 32.
Clowes, W. Laird. *Four Modern Naval Campaigns: Historical, Strategical and Tactical.* New York: Unit Library, 1902.
Curtis, William. *Yankees of the East: Sketches of Modern Japan.* New York: Stone & Kimball, 1896.
Dahlgren, John, *Memoir of John A. Dahlgren*, ed. Madeleine Vinton Dahlgren. Boston, MA: James R. Osgood and Co., 1882.
Davidson, James Wheeler. *Island of Formosa Past and Present.* New York: Macmillan & Co., 1903.
De Novo, Pedro y Colson. *Historia de la Guerra de Chile con España.* Santiago: Victoria, 1883.
Dewey, George. *Autobiography of George Dewey.* New York: Charles Scribner's Sons, 1913.
Dooner, Pierton. *Last Days of the Republic.* San Francisco: Alta California Publishing House, 1879.
Eastlake, Warrington. *A History of the War between China and Japan.* Washington, DC: University Publications of America, 1979.
Evans, Robley D. *A Sailor's Log: Recollections of Forty Years of Naval Life.* New York: D. Appleton & Company, 1901.
The First Chinese Embassy to the West: The Journals of Kuo Sung-T'ao, Liu Hsi-Hung and Chang Te-Yi, translated by J. D. Frodsham. Oxford: Clarendon Press, 1974.
Fiske, Bradley. *From Midshipman to Rear Admiral.* New York: The Century Co., 1919.
Flint, Chares. *Memories of an Active Life: Men Ships and Sealing Wax.* New York & London: G. P. Putnam's & Sons, 1923.
Goodrich, Caspar F. *Rope Yarns from the Old Navy.* New York: Naval History Society, 1931.

Grant, Ulysses S. *The Papers of Ulysses S. Grant*, ed. John Y. Simon, and John F. Marszalek. Carbondale, IL: Southern Illinois University Press, 1967.
Grau, Miguel. *Diario a Bordo del Huáscar*, ed. Robert Hunter. Buenos Aires: Francisco De Aguirre, S.A, 1977.
Hervey, Maurice. *Dark Days in Chile: An Account of the Revolution of 1891.* London: Edward Arnold, 1892.
Inagaki, Manjirō. *Japan and the Pacific, and a Japanese View of the Eastern Question.* London, 1890.
Iriondo, Eduardo. *Impresiones del Viaje de Circunnavegación en la Fragata Blindada Numancia.* Valparaíso: Imprenta del Mercurio, 1868.
Jane, Fred, T. *All the World's Fighting Ships.* London: Sampson Low, Marston & Co., 1898–1904.
Jomini, Antoine Henri. *A Critical and Military History of the Wars of Frederick the Great, as Contrasted with the Modern System.* New York: D. Van Nostrand, 1865.
Kelley, J. D. *A Desperate Chance.* New York: Charles Scribner's Sons, 1886.
Kelley, J. D. *Modern Ships of War.* New York: Harper's Brothers, 1888.
Kelley, J. D. *Our Navy.* Hartford: The American Publishing Company, 1897.
King, James Wilson. *The War-Ships and Navies of the World.* Boston, MA: A. Williams, 1880.
Long, John. *The New American Navy.* New York: Outlook Co., 1903.
Luce, Stephen. *The Writings of Stephen B. Luce*, ed. John D. Hayes, and John B. Hattendorf. Newport, RI: Naval War College Press, 1977.
Ma, Jianzhong. *Strengthen the Country and Enrich the People: The Reform Writings of Ma Jianzhong (1845–1900)*, trans. Paul J. Bailey. Richmond, UK: Curzon Press, 1998.
Mackinder, H. J. "The Geographical Pivot of History," *The Geographical Journal*, Vol. 23, No. 4, (1904): 421–437.
Mahan, Alfred Thayer. *The Influence of Sea Power Upon History.* Boston, MA: Little, Brown and Company, 1890.
Mahan, Alfred Thayer. *The Interest of America in Sea Power.* Boston, MA: Little, Brown and Company, 1897.
Mahan, Alfred Thayer. *The Life of Nelson: The Embodiment of the Sea Power of Great Britain.* Boston, MA: Little, Brown and Company, 1900.
Mahan, Alfred Thayer. *Retrospect and Prospect: Studies in International Relations, Naval and Political.* Boston, MA: Little, Brown and Company, 1902.
Mahan, Alfred Thayer. *The Influence of Sea Power Upon the French Revolution and Empire, 1793–1812.* Boston, MA: Little, Brown and Company, 1902.
Mahan, Alfred Thayer. *From Sail to Steam: Recollections of a Naval Life.* New York: Harper Brothers, 1907.
Mahan, Alfred Thayer. *Naval Strategy.* Boston, MA: Little, Brown and Company, 1911.
Mahan on Naval Warfare: Selections from the Writings of Rear Admiral Alfred Thayer Mahan, ed. Allan Westcott. Boston, MA: Little, Brown and Company, 1918.
Mannix, Daniel, *The Old Navy.* New York: Macmillan, 1983.
Markham, Clements. *War between Perú and Chile 1879–1882.* London: Sampson Low, Marston & Co., 1882.

Marx, Karl. *The Portable Karl Marx,* ed. Eugene Kamenka. New York: Penguin Books, 1983.
Mason, Theodorus B. M. *The War on the Pacific Coast of South America between Chile and the Allied Republics of Peru and Bolivia.* Washington, DC: Government Print Office, 1883.
Melville, Herman. "A Utilitarian View of the Monitor's Fight," in *Battle Pieces and Aspects of the Civil War.* New York: Harper and Brothers, 1866.
Melville, Herman. *White Jacket: Or the World in a Man-of-War.* New York: A. L. Burt, 1892.
Melville, Herman. *Moby Dick.* London: Wordsworth Classics, 1993.
The Naval Annual 1895, ed. T. A. Brassey. Portsmouth: Griffin & Co., 1895.
Palmer, John Henry. *The Invasion of New York: Or How Hawaii Was Annexed.* New York: F. Tennyson Neely, 1897.
Parker, Foxhall. *Squadron Tactics Under Steam.* New York: V. Nostrand, 1864.
Roosevelt, Theodore. *The Naval War of 1812.* New York and London: G. P. Putnam's & Sons, 1882.
Roosevelt, Theodore. *Thomas Hart Benton.* Boston, MA: Houghton Mifflin Harcourt, 1886.
Roosevelt, Theodore. *The Strenuous Life: Essays and Addresses.* Philadelphia: Gebbie, 1903.
Scharf, Thomas. *History of the Confederate Navy.* New York: Rogers and Sherwood, 1887.
Semmes, Ralph. *The Confederate Raider Alabama,* ed. Philip van Doren Stern. Bloomington: University of Indiana Press, 1962.
Shufeldt, Robert W. *The Influences of Western Civilization in China.* Stamford, CT: William Gillespie & Co., 1868.
Soley, James Russell. *The Boys of 1812 and Other Naval Heroes.* Boston, MA: Estes and Lauriat, 1887.
Strong, Josiah. *Our Country.* New York: Baker and Taylor Co. 1891.
Tomb, James Hamilton. *Engineer in Gray: Memoirs of Chief Engineer James H. Tomb,* ed. Thomas Campbell. Jefferson, NC: McFarland & Co., 2005.
Vicuña Mackenna, Benjamin. *Diez Meses de Misión a los Estados Unidos de Norte América Como Ajente Confidencial de Chile.* Santiago: Imprenta de la Libertad, 1867.
Vicuña Mackenna, Benjamin. *Historia de la Guerra de Chile con España.* Santiago: Imprenta Victoria, 1883.
Von Scheliha, Viktor. *A Treatise on Coast-Defence.* London: E. & F.N. Spon, 1868.
Welles, Gideon. *Diary of Gideon Welles,* ed. Howard Beale. New York: W. W. Norton & Company, 1960.
Wilde, Oscar. "The Canterville Ghost," in *The Complete Works of Oscar Wilde.* London: Harper Collins, 2003.
Williams, Rebolledo Juan. *Guerra del Pacifico.* Valparaiso: Imprenta Nacional, 1882.
Wilson, Herbert, *Ironclads in Action: A Sketch of Naval Warfare from 1855 to 1895.* London: Low, Martson and Company, 1896.
Woltor, Robert. *A Short and Truthful History of the Taking of Californian and Oregon by the Chinese in the Year AD 1889.* San Francisco, CA: Bancroft, 1882.

Secondary Materials

Allison, Graham. *Destined for War: Can America and China Escape the Thucydides' Trap?* Boston, MA: Houghton Mifflin Harcourt, 2017.
Amrith, Sunil. *Crossing the Bay of Bengal*. Cambridge, MA: Harvard University Press, 2013.
Anderson, Benedict. *Imagined Communities*. London: Verso, 1983.
Anderson, Stuart. *Race and Rapprochement: Anglo-Saxonism and Anglo-American Relations, 1895–1904*. Rutherford: Fairleigh Dickinson University, 1981.
Anderson, Warwick. *Colonial Pathologies: American Tropical Medicine, Race, and Hygiene in the Philippines*. Durham, NC: Duke University Press, 2016.
Arancibia Clavel, Patricia, Jara Hinojosa, Isabel, and Novoa Mackenna, Andrea. *La Marina en la Historia de Chile*. Santiago: Random House, 2005.
Armitage, David and Guldi, Jo. *The History Manifesto*. Cambridge: Cambridge University Press, 2014.
Armstrong, Benjamin. *21st Century Sims: Innovation, Education, and Leadership for the Modern Era*. Annapolis, MD: Naval Institute Press, 2015.
Asada, Sadao. *From Mahan to Pearl Harbor: The Imperial Japanese Navy and the United States*. Annapolis, MD: Naval Institute Press, 2013.
Baer, George W. *One Hundred Years of Sea Power: The U.S. Navy, 1890–1990*. Stanford, CA: Stanford University Press, 1994.
Barclay, Paul. *Outcasts of Empire: Japan's Rule on Taiwan's "Savage Border," 1874–1945*. Los Angeles: University of California Press, 2018.
Barnes, Eleanor C. *Alfred Yarrow His Life and Work*. London: Edward Arnold & Co., 1923.
Barros, Mario. *Historia Diplomática de Chile, 1541–1938*. Santiago: Andrés Bello, 1970.
Baxter, James. *The Introduction of the Ironclad Warship*. Cambridge, MA: Harvard University Press, 1933.
Beard, Charles. *The Navy: Defense or Portent?* New York: Harper & Brothers, 1932.
Beckert, Sven. *Empire of Cotton: A Global History*. New York: Alfred A. Knopf, 2014.
Beeler, John. *Birth of the Battleship: British Capital Ship Design 1870–1881*. Annapolis, MD: Naval Institute Press, 2001.
Bernstein, Richard and Munro, Ross. *The Coming Conflict with China*. New York: Alfred A. Knopf, 1997.
Berube, Claude. *On Wide Seas: The U.S. Navy in the Jacksonian Era*. Tuscaloosa: University of Alabama Press, 2021.
Betts, Richard. *Enemies of Intelligence: Knowledge and Power in American National Security*. New York: Columbia University Press, 2007.
Biddle, Stephen. *Military Power: Explaining Victory and Defeat in Modern Battle*. Princeton, NJ: Princeton University Press, 2004.
Black, Jeremy. *War and the World: Military Power and the Fate of Continents 1450–2000*. New Haven, CT: Yale University Press, 1998.
Black, Jeremy. *Naval Warfare: A Global History since 1860*. Lanham, MD: Rowman & Littlefield, 2017.

Bönker, Dirk. *Militarism in a Global Age: Naval Ambitions in Germany and the United States Before World War I.* Ithaca, NY: Cornell University Press, 2012.

Boulding, Kenneth. *Conflict and Defense.* New York and London: Harper & Row, 1963.

Bradford, James, ed. *Admirals of the New Steel Navy: Makers of the American Naval Tradition, 1880–1930.* Annapolis, MD: Naval Institute Press, 1990.

Braisted, William. *The United States Navy in the Pacific.* Austin: University of Texas Press, 1958.

Braudel, Fernand. *The Mediterranean and the Mediterranean World in the Age of Philip II.* New York: Harper & Row, 1972.

Bravo, German Valdivieso. *El Incidente del "USS Baltimore."* Santiago: Ediciones Altazor, 2002.

Brodie, Bernard. *Sea Power in the Machine Age.* Princeton, NJ: Princeton University Press, 1941.

Campbell, Thomas. *Hunters in the Night.* Shippensburg, PA: Burd Street Press, 2000.

Captains of the Old Steam Navy: Makers of the American Naval Tradition, 1840–1880, ed. James C. Bradford. Annapolis, MD: Naval Institute Press, 1986.

Carvajal, Melitón Pareja. *Historia Marítima del Perú,* Tomo XI, Vol I. Lima: Instituto de Estudios Histórico-Marítimos del Perú, 2004.

Chaffin, Tom. *Sea of Gray: The Around-the-World Odyssey of the Confederate Raider Shenandoah.* New York: Hill & Wang, 2006.

Chen, Yong. *Chinese San Francisco, 1850–1943: A Trans-Pacific Community.* Stanford, CA: Stanford University Press, 2000.

China Goes to Sea: Maritime Transformation in Comparative Historical Perspective, ed. Andrew S. Erickson, Lyle J. Goldstein, and Carnes Lord. Annapolis, MD: Naval Institute Press, 2009.

China's Military in Transition, ed. David Shambaugh. Oxford: Oxford University Press, 1997.

China's Quest for Modernization: A Historical Perspective, ed. Fred Wakeman and Wang Xi. Berkeley: University of California Press, 1997.

Ching-Hwang, Yen. *Coolies and Mandarins.* Singapore: Singapore National University Press, 1985.

Chisholm, Donald. *Waiting for Dead Men's Shoes: Origins and Development of the U.S. Navy's Officer Personnel System, 1793–1941.* Stanford, CA: Stanford University Press, 2001.

Clayton, Lawrence. *Grace: W.R. Grace & Co.: The Formative Years, 1850–1930.* Ottawa, IL: Jameson Books, 1985.

Coffman, Tom. *Nation Within: The History of the American Occupation of Hawai'i.* Kihei, HI: Koa Books, 1998.

Cohen, Paul. *Between Tradition and Modernity: Wang T'ao and Reform in Late Ch'ing China.* Cambridge, MA: Harvard University Press, 1974.

Coletta, Paolo E. *French Ensor Chadwick: Scholarly Warrior.* Lanham, MD: University Press of America, 1980.

Coletta, Paolo E. *A Survey of U.S. Naval Affairs.* London: University Press of America, 1987.

Colonial Crucible: Empire in the Making of the Modern American State, ed. A. W. McCoy and Francisco A. Scarano. Madison, WI: University of Wisconsin Press, 2009.

Connelly, Matthew. *Fatal Misconception: The Struggle to Control World Population.* Cambridge, MA: Harvard University Press, 2008.

Conroy, Hilary. *The Japanese Frontier in Hawaii, 1868–1898.* Los Angeles: University of California Press, 1953.

Conway's all the World's Fighting Ships 1860–1905, ed. Robert Gardiner, et al. New York: Mayflower, 1979.

Cooling, Benjamin. *Benjamin Franklin Tracy: Father of the Modern American Fighting Navy.* Hamden, CT: Archon Books, 1973.

Cooling, Benjamin. *Gray Steel and Blue Water Navy.* Hamden, CT: Archon Books, 1979.

Cullather, Nick. *The Hungry World: America's Cold War Battle against Poverty in Asia.* Cambridge, MA: Harvard University Press, 2010.

Cumings, Bruce. *Dominion from Sea to Sea: Pacific Ascendency and American Power.* New Haven, CT: Yale University Press, 2009.

Cushman, Gregory. *Guano and the Opening of the Pacific World: A Global Ecological History.* New York: Cambridge University Press, 2013.

Dalzell, George. *The Flight from the Flag: The Continuing Effect of the Civil War Upon the American Carrying Trade.* Chapel Hill: University of North Carolina Press, 1940.

Darnton, Robert. *The Great Cat Massacre and Other Episodes in French Cultural History.* New York: Basic Books, 1984.

Davis, George. *A Navy Second to None: The Development of Modern American Naval Policy.* New York: Harcourt, Brace and Company, 1940.

Davis, William Columbus. *The Last Conquistadores: The Spanish Intervention in Peru and Chile, 1863–1866.* Athens: University of Georgia Press, 1950.

Delay, Brian. *War of a Thousand Deserts: Indian Raids and the U.S.-Mexican War.* New Haven, CT: Yale University Press, 2008.

Delury, John and Schell, Orville, *Wealth and Power: China's Long March to the Twenty-First Century.* New York: Random House, 2013.

Dorwart, Jeffery. *The Pigtail War: American Involvement in the Sino-Japanese War, 1894–1895.* Amherst: University of Massachusetts Press, 1975.

Dorwart, Jeffery. *Office of Naval Intelligence: The Birth of America's First Intelligence Agency, 1865–1918.* Annapolis, MD: Naval Institute Press, 1979.

Doyle, Don H. *The Cause of all Nations: An International History of the American Civil War.* New York: Basic Books, 2015.

Drake, Frederick. *The Empire of the Sea: A Biography of Rear Admiral Robert Wilson Shufeldt, USN.* Honolulu: University of Hawaii Press, 1984.

DuBois, W. E. B. *The Suppression of the African Slave Trade to the United States of America, 1638–1870.* New York: Oxford University Press, 1895/2007.

The Dynamics of Military Revolution, 1300–2050, ed. Macgregor Knox and Williamson Murray. Cambridge: Cambridge University Press, 2001.

Eastman, Lloyd. *Throne and Mandarins: China's Search for a Policy during the Sino-French Controversy, 1880–1885.* Cambridge, MA: Harvard University Press, 1967.

Elleman, Bruce. *Modern Chinese Warfare, 1795–1989*. New York: Routledge, 2001.
Engerman, David. *The Price of Aid: The Economic Cold War in India*. Cambridge, MA: Harvard University Press, 2018.
Epstein, Katherine, *Torpedo: Inventing the Industrial-Military Complex in the United States and Britain*. Cambridge, MA: Harvard University Press, 2014.
Ericson, Steven. *The Sound of the Whistle: Railroads and the State in Meiji Japan*. Cambridge, MA: Harvard University Press, 1996.
Evans, David and Peattie, Mark. *Kaigun: Strategy, Tactics and Technology in the Imperial Japanese Navy 1887–1941*. Annapolis, MD: Naval Institute Press, 1997.
Fairbank, John. *Trade and Diplomacy on the China Coast: The Opening of the Treaty Ports, 1842–1854*. Cambridge, MA: Harvard University Press, 1953.
Farcau, Bruce. *The Ten Cents War: Chile, Peru, and Bolivia in the War of the Pacific 1879–1884*. Westport, CT: Praeger Publishers, 2000.
Ferguson, Niall. *Civilization: The West and the Rest*. New York: Penguin Press, 2011.
Ferrando, Ricardo Keun. *Y Así Nació la Frontera: Conquista, Guerra, Ocupación, Pacificación, 1550–1900*. Santiago: Editorial Antártica, 1986.
Fighting in the Dark: Naval Combat at Night, 1904–1944, ed. Vincent P. O'Hara and Trent Hone. Annapolis, MD: Naval Institute Press, 2023.
Forging China's Military Might: A New Framework for Assessing Innovation, ed. Tai Ming Cheung. Baltimore, MD: Johns Hopkins University Press, 2014.
Franklin, Bruce. *War Stars: The Superweapon and the American Imagination*. New York: Oxford University Press, 1988.
Fravel, Taylor. *Active Defense: China's Military Strategy since 1949*. Princeton, NJ: Princeton University Press, 2019.
Freeman, Donald B., *The Pacific*. New York: Routledge, 2010.
Fry, Joseph. *Dixie Looks Abroad: The South in U.S. Foreign Relations*. Baton Rouge: Louisiana State University Press, 2002.
Fuller, Howard. *Turret versus Broadside: An Anatomy of British Naval Prestige, Revolution and Disaster 1860–1870*. Warwick, UK: Helion & Company, 2020.
Future Wars: The Anticipations and Fears, ed. David Seed. Liverpool: Liverpool University Press, 2012.
Gamio, Jose Valdizan. *Historia Naval Del Perú*, Vols 1–4. Lima, Perú: Dirección General De Intereses Marítimos, 1987.
Gardiner, Harvey. *The Japanese and Peru 1873–1973*. Albuquerque: University of New Mexico Press, 1975.
Geissler, Suzanne. *God and Sea Power: The Influence of Religion on Alfred Thayer Mahan*. Annapolis, MD: Naval Institute Press, 2015.
Goldberg, Joyce. *The Baltimore Affair*. Lincoln: University of Nebraska Press, 1986.
Graebner, Norman. *Empire on the Pacific: A Study in American Continental Expansion*. New York: Ronald Press, 1955.
Grant, Jonathan A. *Rulers, Guns, and Money: The Global Arms Trade in the Age of Imperialism*. Cambridge, MA: Harvard University Press, 2007.

Gray, Edwyn. *The Devil's Device: Robert Whitehead and the History of the Torpedo.* Annapolis, MD: Naval Institute Press, 1991.
Gray, Edwyn. *Nineteenth-Century Torpedoes and Their Inventors.* Annapolis, MD: Naval Institute Press, 2004.
Green, Michael. *By More Than Providence: Grand Strategy and American Power in the Asia Pacific Since 1783.* New York: Columbia University Press, 2017.
Grimes, Shawn. *Strategy and War Planning in the British Navy, 1887–1918.* Rochester: Boydell Press, 2012.
Guerra del Pacífico, ed. Pascual Ahumada. Santiago: Andrés Bello, 1982.
Hackemer, Kurt. *The U.S. Navy and the Origins of the Military-industrial Complex, 1847–1883.* Annapolis, MD: Naval Institute Press, 2001.
Hagan, Kenneth. *American Gunboat Diplomacy and the Old Navy.* Westport, CT: Greenwood Press, 1973.
Hagan, Kenneth. *This People's Navy: The Making of American Sea Power.* New York: Free Press, 1991.
Hämäläinen, Pekka. *The Comanche Empire.* New Haven, CT: Yale University Press, 2008.
Hammond, Grant T. *Plowshares into Swords: Arms Races in International Politics, 1840–1991.* Columbia: University of South Carolina Press, 1993.
Harding, Richard. *Modern Naval History: Debates and Prospects.* New York: Bloomsbury Academic, 2016.
Haydon, F. Stansbury. *Aeronautics in the Union and Confederate Armies.* Baltimore, MD: Johns Hopkins Press, 1941.
Headrick, Daniel. *The Tools of Empire.* New York: Oxford University Press, 1981.
Headrick, Daniel. *The Tentacles of Empire.* New York: Oxford University Press, 1988.
Healy, George. *U.S. Expansionism: The Imperialist Urge in the 1890s.* Madison: University of Wisconsin Press, 1970.
Hendrix, Henry. *Theodore Roosevelt's Naval Diplomacy: The U.S. Navy and the Birth of the American Century.* Annapolis, MD: Naval Institute Press, 2009.
Henson, Curtis. *Commissioners and Commodores: The East India Squadron and American Diplomacy in China.* Tuscaloosa: University of Alabama Press, 1982.
Herder, Brian Lane. *U.S. Navy Armored Cruisers 1890–1933.* Oxford: Osprey, 2022.
Herrick, Walter. *The American Naval Revolution.* Baton Rouge: Louisiana State University Press, 1967.
Herring, George. *From Colony to Superpower: U.S. Foreign Relations since 1776.* New York: Oxford University Press, 2008.
Herrmann, David. *The Arming of Europe.* Princeton, NJ: Princeton University Press, 1996.
Hietala, Thomas. *Manifest Design: American Exceptionalism and Empire.* Ithaca, NY: Cornell University Press, 2003.
Hobsbawm, Eric. *The Age of Empire.* New York: Random House, 1987.
Hofstadter, Richard. *The Paranoid Style in American Politics.* New York: Vintage Books, 1967.
Hoganson, Kristin. *Fighting for American Manhood: How Gender Politics Provoked the Spanish-American and Philippine-American Wars.* New Haven, CT: Yale University Press, 1998.

Hollett, David. *Men of Iron: The Story of Cammell Laird Shipbuilders 1828–1991*. Rock Ferry, UK: Countyvise Limited, 1992.
Howarth, Stephen. *The Fighting Ships of the Rising Sun: The Drama of the Imperial Japanese Navy*. New York: Atheneum, 1983.
Howarth, Stephen. *To Shining Sea: A History of the United States Navy, 1775–1991*. New York: Random House, 1991.
Hunt, Michael. *Ideology and U.S. Foreign Relations*, 2nd ed. New Haven, CT: Yale University Press, 2009.
Ienaga, Saburō. *The Pacific War: World War II and the Japanese, 1931–1945*. New York: Pantheon Books, 1978.
Igler, David. *The Great Ocean: Pacific Worlds from Captain Cook to the Gold Rush*. Oxford: Oxford University Press, 2013.
Immerwahr, Daniel. *How to Hide an Empire: A History of the Greater United States*. New York: Farrar, Straus and Giroux, 2019.
In Peace and War: Interpretations of American Naval History 1775–1978, ed. Kenneth Hagan. Greenwood, CT: Westport Press, 1978.
Iriye, Akira. *Pacific Estrangement: Japanese and American Expansion*. Cambridge, MA: Harvard University Press, 1972.
Iriye, Akira. *Japan and the Wider World: From the Mid-Nineteenth Century to Present*. London: Longman, 1997.
Iriye, Akira. *Global Community: The Role of International Organizations in the Making of the Contemporary World*. Berkeley: University of California Press, 2002.
James, Alan, Zaforteza, Carlos Alfaro, and Murfett, Malcolm. *European Navies and the Conduct of War*. London: Routledge, 2018.
Japan and the Pacific, 1540–1920, ed. Mark Caprio and Matsuda Koichirō. Burlington, VT: Ashgate, 2006.
Johnson, Robert Erwin. *Thence Round Cape Horn: The Story of United States Naval Forces on Pacific Station 1818–1923*. Annapolis, MD: Naval Institute Press, 1963.
Johnson, Robert Erwin. *Rear Admiral John Rodgers*. Annapolis, MD: Naval Institute Press, 1967.
Johnson, Robert Erwin. *Far China Station: The U.S. Navy in Asian Waters 1800–1898*. Annapolis, MD: Naval Institute Press, 1979.
Johnson, Walter. *River of Dark Dreams: Slavery and Empire in the Cotton Kingdom*. Cambridge, MA: Belknap Press, 2013.
Karsten, Peter. *The Naval Aristocracy: The Golden Age of Annapolis and the Emergence of Modern American Navalism*. New York: Free Press, 1972.
Keegan, John. *The Price of Admiralty: The Evolution of Naval Warfare*. New York: Viking, 1988.
Keegan, John. *Intelligence in War: Knowledge of the Enemy from Napoleon to Al-Qaeda*. New York: Knopf, 2003.
Kennedy, Paul. *The Samoan Tangle: A Study in Anglo-German-American Relations, 1878–1900*. New York: Barnes & Noble, 1974.
Kennedy, Paul. *The Rise and Fall of British Naval Mastery*. New York: Scribner, 1976.
Kennedy, Paul. *The Rise of the Anglo-German Antagonism, 1860–1914*. Boston, MA: Allen & Unwin, 1980.

Kennedy, Paul. *The Rise and Fall of Great Powers*. New York: Random House, 1987.

Kennedy, Thomas. *The Arms of Kiangnan Modernization in the Chinese Ordnance Industry 1860–1895*. Boulder: University of Colorado Press, 1978.

Knowing One's Enemy: Intelligence Assessment before the World Wars, ed. Ernest May. Princeton, NJ: Princeton University Press, 1984.

Knox, Dudley. *A History of the United States Navy*. New York: G. P. Putnam's & Sons, 1936.

Krepinevich, Andrew F. *The Origins of Victory: How Disruptive Military Innovation Determines the Fates of Great Powers*. New Haven, CT: Yale University Press, 2023.

LaFeber, Walter. *The New Empire: An Interpretation of American Expansion 1860–1898*, 35th Year Edition. Ithaca, NY: Cornell University Press, 1963/1998.

LaFeber, Walter. *The Clash: U.S.-Japanese Relations throughout History*. New York: W. W. Norton & Company, 1997.

LaFeber, Walter. *The Cambridge History of American Foreign Relations: The American Search for Opportunity*. New York: Cambridge University Press, 2013.

Lai, Benjamin. *Chinese Battleship vs Japanese Cruiser: Yalu River 1894*. London: Osprey, 2019.

Lambert, Andrew. *Sea Power States: Maritime Culture, Continental Empires, and the Conflict that Made the Modern World*. New Haven, CT: Yale University Press, 2018.

Lambert, Nicholas. *Sir John Fisher's Naval Revolution*. Columbia: University of South Carolina Press, 1999.

Lee, Erika. *At America's Gates: Chinese Immigration during the Exclusion Era*. Chapel Hill: University of North Carolina Press, 2003.

Leeman, William. *The Long Road to Annapolis: The Founding of the Naval Academy and the Emerging American Republic*. Chapel Hill: University of North Carolina Press, 2010.

Lei, Xianglin. *Neither Donkey nor Horse: Medicine in the Struggle over China's Modernity*. Chicago: University of Chicago Press, 2014.

Li Hung-Chang and China's Early Modernization, ed. Samuel C. Chu and Kwang-Ching Liu. London: East Gare Book, 1994.

Lotchin, Roger. *Fortress California, 1910–1961: From Warfare to Welfare*. New York: Oxford University Press, 1992.

Lopez, Carlos Martinez. *Historia Marítima del Peru*. Lima: Instituto de Estudios Historico-Maritimos del Peru, 1988.

López, Carlos Urrutia. *Historia de la Marina de Chile*. Santiago: Editorial Andrés Bello, 1969.

López, Carlos Urrutia. *La Guerra Del Pacífico*. Madrid: Ristre Media, 2003.

López, Carlos and Ortiz, Jorge. *Monitor Huáscar: Una Historia Compartida*. Lima: Association de Historia Marítima Y Naval Iberoamericana, 2005.

Lorca, Arnulf Becker. *Mestizo International Law: A Global Intellectual History 1842–1933*. Cambridge: Cambridge University Press, 2014.

Love, Eric. *Race over Empire: Racism and U.S. Imperialism, 1865–1900*. Chapel Hill: University of North Carolina Press, 2004.

Love, Robert Jr. *History of the U.S. Navy*, Vol I, 1775–1941. Harrisburg, PA: Stackpole Books, 1992.

Loveman, Brian. *No Higher Law: American Foreign Policy and the Western Hemisphere since 1776*. Chapel Hill: University of North Carolina Press, 2010.

Luraghi, Raimondo. *A History of the Confederate Navy*. Annapolis, MD: Naval Institute Press, 1996.

Luvaas, Jay. *The Military Legacy of the Civil War: The European Inheritance*. Lawrence: University of Kansas Press, 1959/1988.

Mahin, Dean. *The Blessed Place of Freedom: Europeans in Civil War America*. Washington, DC: Brassey's, 2002.

Maier, Charles. *Among Empires: American Ascendancy and Its Predecessors*. Cambridge, MA: Harvard University Press, 2006.

The Maritime Defence of China, ed. Y. H. T. Sim. Singapore: Springer Nature Singapore, 2017.

Matsuda, Matt. *Pacific Worlds: A History of Seas, Peoples and Cultures*. New York: Cambridge University Press, 2012.

May, Ernest. *Imperial Democracy: The Emergence of America as a Great Power*. New York: Harcourt, Brace and World, 1961.

May, Ernest. *Lessons of the Past: The Use and Misuse of History in American Foreign Policy*. New York: Oxford University Press, 1975.

May, Robert. *Manifest Destiny's Underworld*. Chapel Hill: University of North Carolina Press, 2002.

McBride, William. *Technological Change and the United States Navy, 1865–1945*. Baltimore, MD: Johns Hopkins University Press, 2000.

McCormick, Thomas. *China Market: America's Quest for Informal Empire 1893–1901*. Chicago: Quadrangle Books, 1967.

McDougall, Walter. *Let the Sea Make a Noise: A History of the North Pacific from Magellan to MacArthur*. New York: Basic Books, 1993.

McGiffin, Lee. *Yankee of the Yalu: Philo Norton McGiffin, American Captain in the Chinese Navy*. New York: E. P. Dutton & Co., 1968.

McPherson, James. *Battle Cry of Freedom: The Civil War Era*. New York: Oxford University Press, 1988.

McQuiston, Julian. *William B. Cushing in the Far East: A Civil War Naval Hero Abroad, 1865–1869* Jefferson, NC: McFarland & Co., 2013.

Melillo, Edward Dallam. *Strangers on Familiar Soil: Rediscovering the Chile-California Connection*. New Haven, CT: Yale University Press, 2015.

Meneses, Emilio Ciuffardi. *El Factor Naval en las Relaciones Entre Chile y Los Estados Unidos 1881–1951*. Santiago: Hachette, 1989.

Merk, Frederick. *Manifest Destiny and Mission in American History: A Reinterpretation*. New York: Alfred Knopf, 1963.

Merli, Frank. *Great Britain and the Confederate Navy, 1861–1865*. Bloomington: Indiana University Press, 1970.

Merli, Frank. *The Alabama, British Neutrality, and the American Civil War*. Bloomington: University of Indiana Press, 2004.

Military Effectiveness, ed. Allan R. Millett and Williamson Murray. Vol I. Boston, MA: Allen & Uwin, 1988.

Miller, Edward. *War Plan Orange: The U.S. Strategy to Defeat Japan 1897–1945*. Annapolis, MD: Naval Institute Press, 1991.

Millington, Herbert. *American Diplomacy and the War of the Pacific*. New York: Columbia University Press, 1948.

Mobley, Scott. *Progressives in Navy Blue: Maritime Strategy, American Empire and the Transformation of U.S. Naval Identity, 1873–1897*. Annapolis, MD: Naval Institute Press, 2018.

Morgan, William Michael. *Pacific Gibraltar: U.S.-Japanese Rivalry over the Annexation of Hawai'i, 1885–1898*. Annapolis, MD: Naval Institute Press, 2011.

Morison, Elting. *Admiral Sims and the Modern American Navy*. Boston, MA: Houghton Mifflin Harcourt, 1942.

Navigating the Spanish Lake: The Pacific in the Iberian World, 1521–1898, Rainer Buschmann, et al. Honolulu: University of Hawai'i Press, 2014.

Nester, William. *Power Across the Pacific*. New York: New York University Press, 1996.

Neu, Charles. *The Troubled Encounter: The United States and Japan*. New York: John Wiley, 1975.

Niblack, Albert Parker. *The History and Aims of the Office of Naval Intelligence*. Washington, DC: Government Printing Office, 1920.

Oceanic History, ed. David Armitage, Alison Bashford, Sujit Sivasundaram. Cambridge: Cambridge University Press, 2018.

O'Connell, Robert L. *Sacred Vessels: The Cult of the Battleship and the Rise of the U.S. Navy*. Boulder, CO: Westview Press, 1991.

Ortiz, Jorge. *Miguel Grau, El Hombre Y El Mar*. Lima: Fondo Editorial Del Congreso Del Perú, 2003.

Ortiz, Jorge. *La Armada En La Guerra Del Pacífico: Aproximación Estratégica-operacional*. Lima, Perú: Asociación De Historia Marítima Y Naval Iberoamericana, 2017.

Osterhammel, Jurgen. *Transformation of the World: A Global History of the Nineteenth Century*. Princeton, NJ: Princeton University Press, 2015.

Osterhammel, Jurgen and Petersen, Niels. *Globalization: A Short History*. Princeton, NJ: Princeton University Press, 2005.

Otte, Thomas G. *The China Question: Great Power Rivalry and British Isolation, 1894–1905*. Oxford: Oxford University Press, 2007.

Packard, Wyman H. *A Century of U.S. Naval Intelligence*. Washington: Department of the Navy, 1996.

Pacific Histories: Ocean, Land, People, ed. David Armitage and Alison Bashford. New York: Palgrave Macmillan, 2014.

The Pacific Ocean in History, ed. H. Morse Stephens and Hebert E. Bolton. New York: Macmillan & Co., 1917.

Paine, S. C. M. *The Sino-Japanese War of 1894–1895: Perceptions, Power, and Primacy*. Cambridge: Cambridge University Press, 2003.

Paine, S. C. M. *The Japanese Empire: Grand Strategy from the Meiji Restoration to the Pacific War*. Cambridge: Cambridge University Press, 2017.

Palacios, Nicolás. *Raza Chilena*. Santiago: Imprenta Universitaria, 1918.

Paolino, Ernest N. *The Foundations of the American Empire: William Henry Seward and U.S. Foreign Policy*. Ithaca, NY: Cornell University Press, 1973.

Paullin, Charles. *History of Naval Administration 1775–1911*. Annapolis, MD: Naval Institute Press, 1968.
Peattie, Mark. "The Japanese Colonial Empire, 1895–1945," *The Cambridge History of Japan* Cambridge: Cambridge University Press, 1989.
Pedisich, Paul Everett. *Congress Buys a Navy: Politics, Economics, and the Rise of American Naval Power, 1881–1921*. Annapolis, MD: Naval Institute Press, 2016.
Perkins, Bradford. *The Great Rapprochement: England and the United States, 1895–1914*. New York: Athenaeum, 1968.
Perry, Milton. *Infernal Machines: The Story of Confederate Submarine and Mine Warfare*. Baton Rouge: Louisiana State University Press, 1965.
Pike, Frederick. *The United States and the Andean Republics*. Cambridge, MA: Harvard University Press, 1977.
Platt, Stephen R. *Autumn in the Heavenly Kingdom: China, the West, and the Epic Story of the Taiping Civil War*. New York: Alfred A. Knopf, 2012.
Po, Ronald C. *The Blue Frontier: Maritime Vision and Power in the Qing Empire*. Cambridge: Cambridge University Press, 2018.
Pomeranz, Kenneth. *The Great Divergence: China, Europe, and the Making of the Modern World Economy*. Princeton, NJ: Princeton University Press, 2000.
Pomeroy, Earl. *The Pacific Slope: A history of California, Oregon, Washington, Idaho, Utah, and Nevada*. New York: Alfred Knopf, 1965.
Pong, David. *Shen Pao Chen and China's Modernization in the Nineteenth Century*. Cambridge, UK: Cambridge University Press, 1994.
Powell, Ralph. *The Rise of Chinese Military Power*. Princeton, NJ: Princeton University Press, 1955.
Power, Arthur Dudden. *The American Pacific: From the Old China Trade to the Present*. New York: Oxford University Press, 1992.
Rappaport, Armin. *The Navy League of the United States*. Detroit, MI: Washington State University Press, 1962.
Rawlinson, John. *China's Struggle for Naval Development, 1839–1895*. Cambridge, MA: Harvard University Press, 1967.
Register of the Officers of the Confederate States Navy. Washington, DC: Government Printing Office, 1931.
Reilly, John and Scheina, Robert. *American Battleships 1886–1923: Predreadnought Design and Construction*. Annapolis, MD: Naval Institute Press, 1980.
Remapping Asian American History, ed. Sucheng Chan. New York: Alta Mira Press, 2003.
Resende-Santos, Joao. *Neorealism, States and the Modern Mass Army*. New York: Cambridge University Press, 2007.
Robert Hart and China's Early Modernization, ed. Richard Smith, John King Fairbank, and Katherine Frost Bruner. Cambridge, MA: Harvard University Press, 1991.
Roberts, William. *Now for the Contest: Coastal and Oceanic Naval Operations in the Civil War*. Lincoln: University of Nebraska Press, 2004.
Rochelle, James. *Life of Rear Admiral John Randolph Tucker*. Washington: The Neale Publishing Company, 1903.

Rogaski, Ruth. *Hygienic Modernity: Meanings of Health and Disease in Treaty-port China*. Berkeley: University of California Press, 2004.

Romero, Fernando Pintado. *Historia Marítima del Perú*. Lima: Estudios Histórico-Marítimos del Perú, 1984.

Rosen, Stephen Peter. *Winning the Next War: Innovation and the Modern Military*. Ithaca, NY: Cornell University Press, 1991.

Rouleau, Brian. *With Sails Whitening Every Sea*. Ithaca: Cornell University Press, 2014.

Russ, William. *The Hawaiian Revolution*. Selinsgrove, PA: Susquehanna University Press, 1959.

Safford, Jeffery. *Wilsonian Maritime Diplomacy 1913–1921*. New Brunswick, NJ: Rutgers University Press, 1978.

Salomon, Frank and Schwartz, Stuart B., eds. *The Cambridge History of the Native Peoples of the Americas*. Cambridge: Cambridge University Press, 1999.

San Francisco, Alejandro. *La Guerra Civil de 1891*. Santiago: Ediciones Centro de Estudios Bicentenario, 2007.

Santiago Sanz, Luis. *El Caso Baltimore*. Buenos Aires: Instituto de Publicaciones Navales, 1998.

Sater, William. *Chile and the United States: Empires in Conflict*. Athens: University of Georgia Press, 1990.

Sater, William. *Andean Tragedy: Fighting the War of the Pacific, 1879–1884*. Lincoln: University of Nebraska Press, 2007.

Sayward, Amy. *The Birth of Development: How the World Bank, Food and Agriculture Organization, and World Health Organization Changed the World, 1945–1965*. Kent, OH: Kent State University Press, 2006.

Schafer, Louis. *Confederate Underwater Warfare*. Jefferson, NC: McFarland & Co., 1996.

Schake, Kori. *Safe Passage: The Transition from British to American Hegemony*. Cambridge, MA: Harvard University Press, 2017.

Scheina, Robert. *Latin America: A Naval History 1810–1987*. Annapolis, MD: Naval Institute Press, 1987.

Schencking, Charles. *Making Waves: Politics, Propaganda, and the Emergence of the Imperial Japanese Navy, 1868–1922*. Stanford, CA: Stanford University Press, 2005.

Schoonover, Thomas. *Uncle Sam's War of 1898 and the Origins of Globalization*. Lexington: University Press of Kentucky, 2003.

Scott, James, C. *Seeing like a State: How Certain Schemes to Improve the Human Condition Have Failed*. New Haven, CT: Yale University Press, 1998.

The Sea in History: The Modern World, ed. Nicholas A. M. Rodger. Woodbridge, UK: The Boydell Press, 2017.

Seager, Robert. *Alfred Thayer Mahan: The Man and His Letters*. Annapolis, MD: Naval Institute Press, 1977.

Seligmann, Matthew. *The Naval Route to the Abyss: The Anglo-German Naval Race, 1895–1914*. London: Routledge, 2015.

Shaw, David. *Sea Wolf of the Confederacy: The Daring Civil War Raids of Naval Lt. Charles W. Read*. New York: Free Press, 2004.

Sherry, Michael. *In the Shadow of War: The United States Since the 1930s*. New Haven, CT: Yale University Press, 1995.

Shulman, Mark R. *Navalism and the Emergence of American Sea Power*. Annapolis, MD: Naval Institute Press 1995.
Shulman, Peter. *Coal & Empire: The Birth of Energy Security in Industrial America*. Baltimore, MD: Johns Hopkins University Press, 2015.
Silbey, David. *The Boxer Rebellion and the Great Game in China*. New York: Hill & Wang, 2012.
Silva, Alberto Palma. *Crónicas de la Marina Chilena*. Santiago: Talleres de Estado Mayor Jeneral, 1913.
Silva, Noenoe K. *Aloha Betrayed: Native Hawaiian Resistance to American Colonialism*. Durham, NC: Duke University Press, 2004.
Singer, Peter and Cole, August. *Ghost Fleet: A Novel of the Next World War*. Boston, MA: Houghton Mifflin Harcourt, 2015.
Smith, Jason. *To Master the Boundless Sea: The U.S. Navy, the Marine Environment, and the Cartography of Empire*. Chapel Hill: University of North Carolina Press, 2018.
Smith, Joseph. *Unequal Giants: Diplomatic Relations Between the United States and Brazil 1889–1930*. Pittsburgh: University of Pittsburgh Press, 1991.
Smith, Joseph. *Brazil and the United States: Convergence and Divergence*. Athens: University of Georgia Press, 2010.
Sondhaus, Lawrence. *Naval War 1815–1914*. New York: Routledge, 2001.
Spector, Ronald. *Admiral of the New Empire: The Life and Career of George Dewey*. Baton Rouge: Louisiana State University Press, 1974.
Spector, Ronald. *Professors of War: The Naval War College and the Development of the Naval Profession*. Newport, RI: Naval War College Press, 1977.
Spence, Johnathan. *To Change China: Western Advisers in China 1620–1960*. Boston, MA: Little, Brown and Company, 1969.
Spencer, Warren. *The Confederate Navy in Europe*. Tuscaloosa: University of Alabama Press, 1983.
Sprout, Harold and Sprout, Margaret. *The Rise of American Naval Power*. Princeton, NJ: Princeton University Press, 1939/1967.
Steel, Frances. *Oceania under Steam: Sea Transport and the Cultures of Colonialism, C. 1870–1914*. New York: Manchester University Press, 2011.
Stein, Stephen K. *From Torpedoes to Aviation: Washington Irving Chambers & Technological Innovation in the New Navy 1876 to 1913*. Tuscaloosa: University of Alabama Press, 2007.
Stephanson, Anders. *Manifest Destiny: American Expansionism and the Empire of Right*. New York: Hill & Wang, 1995.
Sterling, Brent L. *Other People's Wars: The US Military and the Challenge of Learning from Foreign Conflicts*. Washington, DC: Georgetown University Press, 2021.
Stevenson, David. *Armaments and the Coming of War: Europe, 1904–1914*. Oxford: Oxford University Press, 1996.
Stewart, Watt. *Chinese Bondage in Peru*. Durham, NC: Duke University Press, 1951.
Still, William. *Iron Afloat: The Story of the Confederate Armorclads*. Nashville: Vanderbilt Press, 1971.
Sumida, Jon. *In Defence of Naval Supremacy: Finance, Technology, and British Naval Policy 1889–1914*. Boston, MA: Unwin Hyman, 1989.

Surdam, David. *Northern Naval Superiority and the Economics of the American Civil War.* Columbia: University of South Carolina Press, 2001.

Symonds, Craig. *The Civil War at Sea.* Oxford: Oxford University Press, 2012.

Tooze, Adam. *The Deluge: The Great War, America, and the Remaking of the Global Order, 1916–1931.* New York: Penguin, 2014.

Topik, Steven. *Trade and Gunboats: The United States and Brazil in the Age of Empire.* Stanford, CA: Stanford University Press, 1996.

United States, Department of State. *The Question of the Pacific: America's Alsace and Lorraine.* Washington, DC: Government Printing Office, 1919.

Untermeyer, Chase. *Inside Reagan's Navy: The Pentagon Journals.* College Station: Texas A&M Press, 2015.

Van de Ven, Hans. "A Hinge in Time," in *The Cambridge History of War*, Vol 4. Cambridge: Cambridge University Press, 2012.

Van Dijk, Kees. *Pacific Strife: The Great Powers and Their Political and Economic Rivalries in Asia and the Western Pacific, 1870–1914.* Amsterdam: Amsterdam University Press, 2015.

Vegas, Manuel. *Historia de la Marina de Guerra del Perú.* Lima, Perú: Instituto De Estudios Histórico-Marítimos Del Perú, 2014.

Verney, Michael. *A Great and Rising Nation: Naval Exploration and Global Empire in the Early US Republic.* Chicago: University of Chicago Press, July 2022.

Wadle, Ryan. *Selling Sea Power: Public Relations and the U.S. Navy, 1917–1941.* Norman: University of Oklahoma Press, 2019.

Wagner de Reyna, Alberto. *Las Relaciones Diplomáticas entre el Perú y Chile durante el Conflicto con España.* Lima: Ediciones del Sol, 1963.

Waldron, Arthur. *From War to Nationalism: China's Turning Point.* London: Cambridge University Press, 1995/2003.

Wallerstein, Immanuel. *World-Systems Analysis: An Introduction.* Durham, NC: Duke University Press, 2004.

Walther, Juan Carlos. *La Conquista del Desierto.* Buenos Aires: Universitaria de Buenos Aires, 1970.

Wang, Dong. *The United States and China.* New York: Rowman & Littlefield Publishers, 2013.

Warships of the Imperial Japanese Navy, 1869–1945, ed. Hansgeorg Jentschura, Dieter Jung, and Peter Mickel. London: Arms and Armour Press, 1977.

Werlich, David. *Admiral of the Amazon: John Randolph Tucker, His Confederate Colleagues and Peru.* Charlottesville: University of Virginia Press, 1990.

West, Richard Sedgwick. *Admirals of the American Empire: The Combined Story of George Dewey, Alfred Thayer Mahan, Winfield Scott Schley and William Thomas Sampson.* Indianapolis: Bobbs-Merrill Co., 1948.

Westad, Odd Arne. *Restless Empire: China and the World Since 1750.* New York: Basic Books, 2012.

White, Richard. *The Middle Ground: Indians, Empires, and Republics in the Great Lakes Region, 1650–1815.* New York: Cambridge University Press, 1991.

Wilson, Walter and McKay, Gary. *James D. Bulloch: Secret Agent and Mastermind of the Confederate Navy.* Jefferson, NC: McFarland & Co., 2012.

Woodman, Harold. *King Cotton & His Retainers: Financing & Marketing the Cotton Crop of the South, 1800–1925.* Lexington: University of Kentucky Press, 1968.

Wright, Mary. *The Last Stand of Chinese Conservatism*. Stanford, CA: Stanford University Press, 1962.
Wright, Richard. *The Chinese Steam Navy 1862–1945*. London: Chatham, 2000.
Wu, Shellen Xiao. *Empires of Coal: Fueling China's Entry into the Modern World Order, 1860–1920*. Stanford, CA: Stanford University Press, 2015.
Xu, Guoqi. *Chinese and Americans*. Cambridge, MA: Harvard University Press, 2014.
Young, Elliott. *Alien Nation: Chinese Migration in the Americas from the Coolie Era through World War II*. Chapel Hill, NC: University of North Carolina Press, 2014.
《北洋海軍新探北洋海军成军120周年国际学术研讨会论文集》[*The Beiyang Navy: New Explorations …*], ed. 张荣国 [Zhang Rongguo]. 北京: 中华书局, 2012.
陈悦 [Chen Yue]《北洋海军》[*The North Sea Fleet/The Beiyang Navy*] 济南: 山东画报出版社, 2015.
樊百川 [Fan Baichuan]《清季的洋务新政》[*New Foreign Affairs Polices of the Late Qing*] 上海: 上海书店出版社, 2009.
李喜明 [Lee Hsi-ming] *Taiwan's Plan for Victory: An Asymmetric Strategy to Use the Small to Control the Large: All of Taiwan Should Understand the Overall Defense Concept* (臺灣的勝算: 以小制大不對稱戰略, 全臺灣人都應了解的整體防衛構想) (2022) ISBN: 978-957-08-6508-0 (EPUB).
李平子 [Li Pingzi]《从鸦片战争到甲午战争》[*From the Opium War to the Sino-Japanese War*] 上海: 华东师范大学出版社, 1998.
龍章 [Long Zhang]《越南與中法戰爭》[*Vietnam and the Sino-French War*] 臺北市: 臺灣商務印書館, 1996.
戚其章 [Qi Qizhang]《甲午战争史》[*History of the Sino-Japanese War*] 北京: 人民出版社, 1990.
钱钢 [Qian Gang]《大清海军与李鸿章》[*The Qing Navy and Li Hongzhang*] 香港: 中华书局, 1989/2004.
苏同炳 [Su Tongbing]《中国近代史上的关键人物》[*Key Figures in Modern Chinese History*] 台北: 百花文艺出版社, 2000.
王家俭 [Wang Jiajian]《李鸿章与北洋舰队: 近代中国创建海军的失败与教训》[*Li Hongzhang and the Beiyang Navy: The Failure of China to Found a Modern Fleet and Its Lessons*] 北京: 三联书店, 2008.
夏东元 [Xia Dongyuan]《洋务运动》[*The Foreign Affairs Movement*] 上海: 华东师范大学出版社, 1992.
余坚 [Yu Jian]《中美外交关系之研究》[*Research in Sino-U.S. Diplomatic Relations*] 台北: 正中书局印行, 1973.
张明金 [Zhang Mingjin]《落日下的龙旗: 1894–1895 年中日战争纪实》[*The Sunset of the Dragon Banner*] 北京: 燕山出版社, 1998.
《中国海关与中法战争》[*Chinese Customs and the Sino-French War*] 北京: 科学出版社, 1957.
周建波 [Zhou Jianbo]《洋務運動與中國早期現代化思想》[*The Foreign Affairs Movement and the Early Chinese Modernization Ideology*] 濟南市: 山東人民出版社, 2001.
舟欲行, 黄传会 [Zhou Yuxing and Huang Chuanhui《龙旗:清末北洋海军纪实》[*Dragon Flag: History of the Late Qing Beiyang Navy*] 北京: 学苑出版社, 2007.

Articles

Allard, Dean. "Admiral William S. Sims and the United States Naval Policy in World War I," *The American Neptune*, Vol. 35, No. 2 (1975): 97.

Bessner, Daniel and Logevall, Fredrik. "Recentering the United sates in the Historiography of American Foreign Relations," *Texas National Security Review*, Vol. 3, No. 2 (Spring, 2020): 39–55.

Bonner, Robert. "The Salt Water Civil War: Thalassological Approaches, Ocean-Centered Opportunities," *Journal of the Civil War Era*, Vol. 6, No. 2 (June 2016): 243.

Botsman, Daniel. "Freedom Without Slavery? 'Coolies,' Prostitutes, and Outcastes in Meiji Japan's 'Emancipation Moment,'" *The American Historical Review*, Vol. 116, No. 5 (2011): 1323–1347.

Chang, Gordon. "Whose 'Barbarism'? Whose 'Treachery'? Race and Civilization in the Unknown United States – Korea War of 1871," *Journal of American History*, Vol. 89, No. 4 (March 2003): 1331–1365.

Dorwart, Jeffery. "Providence Conspiracy of 1894," *Rhode Island History*, Vol. 32, No. 3 (1973): 91.

Elman, Benjamin. "Naval Warfare and the Refraction of China's Self-Strengthening Reforms into Scientific and Technological Failure, 1865–1895," *Modern Asian Studies*, Vol. 38, No. 2 (2004): 283–326.

Ferreiro, Larrie D. "Mahan and the 'English Club' of Lima, Peru: The Genesis of the Influence of Sea Power upon History," *The Journal of Military History*, Vol. 72, No. 3 (July 2008): 901–906.

Fung, Allen. "Testing the Self-Strengthening: The Chinese Army in the Sino-Japanese War of 1894–95," *Modern Asian Studies*, Vol. 30, No. 4 (1996): 1007–1031.

Gluck, Carol. "The End of Elsewhere: Writing Modernity Now," *The American Historical Review*, Vol. 116, No. 3 (2011): 676–687.

Gordon, Andrew. "Consumption, Leisure and the Middle Class in Transwar Japan," *Social Science Japan Journal*, Vol. 10, No. 1 (April 2007): 1–21.

Gray, Colin. "The Urge to Compete: Rationales for Arms Racing," *World Politics*, Vol. 26, No. 2 (January, 1974): 207–223.

Howland, Douglas. "The Sinking of the S. S. Kowshing: International Law, Diplomacy, and the Sino-Japanese War," *Modern Asian Studies*, Vol. 42, No. 4 (July 2008): 673–703.

Kiernan, V. G. "Foreign Interests in the War of the Pacific," *The Hispanic American Historical Review*, Vol. 35, No. 1 (February 1955): 14–36.

Klaiber, Jeffrey L. "Los 'Cholos' y los 'Rotos': Actitudes Raciales Durante la Guerra del Pacífico," *Histórica Peru*, Vol. 2, No. I (1978): 27–38.

Kramer, Paul. "Empires, Exceptions, and Anglo-Saxons: Race and Rule between the British and United States Empires, 1880–1910," *Journal of American History*, Vol. 88, No. 4 (2002): 1315–1353.

Lant, Jeffery. "The Spithead Naval Review of 1887," *The Mariner's Mirror*, February, 1976.

Leung, Edwin Pak-Wah. "The Quasi-War in East Asia: Japan's Expedition to Taiwan and the Ryūkyū Controversy," *Modern Asian Studies*, Vol. 17, No. 2 (1983): 257–281.

Manela, Erez. "International Society as a Historical Subject," *Diplomatic History*, Vol. 44, No. 2 (April 2020): 184–209.

Melillo, Edward. "The First Green Revolution: Debt Peonage and the Making of the Nitrogen Fertilizer Trade, 1840–1930," *The American Historical Review*, Vol. 117, No. 4 (2012): 1028–1060.

Meng, Yue. "Hybrid Science versus Modernity: The Practice of the Jiangnan Arsenal," *East Asian Science, Technology, and Medicine*, No. 16 (1999): 13–52.

Morgan, William. "The Anti-Japanese Origins of the Hawaiian Annexation Treaty of 1897," *Diplomatic History*, Vol. 6, No. 1 (January 1, 1982): 23.

Perry, John Curtis. "Great Britain and the Emergence of Japan as a Naval Power," *Monumenta Nipponica*, Vol. XXI, No. 3/4 (1966): 305–321.

Rogers, Clifford. "The Military Revolutions of the Hundred Years' War," *The Journal of Military History*, Vol. 57, No. 2 (1993): 241–278.

Rüegg, Jonas. "Mapping the Forgotten Colony: The Ogasawara Islands and the Tokugawa Pivot to the Pacific," *Cross-Currents: East Asian History and Culture Review*, Vol. 23 (2017): 108–157.

Sater, William F. "Chile during the First Months of the War of the Pacific," *Journal of Latin American Studies*, Vol. 5, No. 1 (1973): 133–158.

Seager, Robert. "Ten Years Before Mahan: The Unofficial Case for the New Navy, 1880–1890," *The Mississippi Valley Historical Review*, Vol. 40, No. 3 (1953): 491–512.

Shulman, Mark Russell. "The Influence of History Upon Sea Power: The Navalist Reinterpretation of the War of 1812," *The Journal of Military History*, Vol. 56, No. 2 (1992): 183–206.

Shulman, Mark Russell. "The Rise and Fall of American Naval Intelligence, 1882–1917," *Intelligence and National Security*, Vol. 8, No. 2 (1993): 214–226.

Sumida, Jon. "Sir John Fischer and the Dreadnought: The Sources of Naval Mythology," *The Journal of Military History*, Vol. 59 (1995): 619–638.

Sumida, Jon. "Fisher's Naval Revolution," *Naval History*, July, 1996.

Sumida, Jon. "Gunnery, Procurement, and Strategy in the Dreadnought Era," *The Journal of Military History*, Vol. 69, No. 4 (2005): 1179–1187.

Steffen, Rimner. "Chinese Abolitionism: The Chinese Educational Mission in Connecticut, Cuba, and Perú," *Journal of Global History*, Vol. 11, No. 3 (2016): 344–364.

Stewart, Watt. "Federico Blume's Peruvian Submarine," *The Hispanic American Historical Review*, Vol. 28, No. 3 (August 1948): 468–478.

Thompson, John. "Exaggeration of American Vulnerability," *Diplomatic History*, Vol. 16, No. 1 (January 1992): 23–43.

Tromben, Carlos. "Naval Presence: The Cruiser Esmeralda in Panama," *International Journal of Naval History*, Vol. I, No. 1 (2002). www.ijnhonline.org/wp-content/uploads/2012/01/pdf_tromben_english.pdf

Van De Ven, Hans J. "War in the Making of Modern China," *Modern Asian Studies*, Vol. 30, No. 4 (1996): 737–756.

Van Evera, Stephen. "The Cult of the Offensive and the Origins of the First World War," *International Security*, Vol. 9, No. 1 (Summer 1984): 58–107.

Vlahos, Michael. "The Naval War College and the Origins of War-Planning against Japan," *Naval War College Review*, Vol. 33, No. 4 (1980): 24–25.

Wenzer, Kenneth. "The U.S. Navy and the Conquest of the Pacific by Lt. Cmdr. Charles H. Stockton," *International Journal of Naval History*, Vol. 14, No. 2 (2018). www.ijnhonline.org/the-u-s-navy-and-the-conquest-of-the-pacific-by-lt-cmdr-charles-h-stockton/

Wicks, Daniel. "Dress Rehearsal: United States Intervention on the Isthmus of Panama, 1885," *Pacific Historical Review*, Vol. 49, No. 4 (January 1, 1980): 581–605.

Wolters, Timothy. "Electric Torpedoes in the Confederacy: Reconciling Conflicting Histories," *The Journal of Military History*, Vol. 72, No. 3 (July 2008): 755–783.

Wolters, Timothy. "Recapitalizing the Fleet: A Material Analysis of Late-Nineteenth-Century U.S. Naval Power," *Technology and Culture*, Vol. 52, No. 1 (2011): 103–126.

《舰载武器》[*Naval Weapons*] No. 4 (2005): 67–72.

陈可畏 [Chen Kewei]《1874年日本侵台事件与近代中国的东海危机》[Japan's 1874 Invasion of Taiwan and the Modern Chinese Crisis in the East China Sea]《浙江师范大学学报》(社会科学版), Vol. 39, No. 1 (2014): 28–32.

陈先松，焦海燕，[Chen Xiansong, Jiao Haiyan]《北洋海军购置雷艇考述》[A Study on the Purchasing of Torpedoes by Beiyang Navy]《安徽史学》[*Anhui Historical Studies*], No. 1 (2017): 121–129.

李云泉 [Li Yunquan]. 中法战争前的中法越南问题交涉与中越关系的变化 [Pre Sino-French War China-French-Vietnam Exchanges and Changes to Sino-Vietnamese Relations]《社会科学辑刊》No. 5 (2010): 150–155.

汤正东 [Tang Zhengdong]《浅析李鸿章的海防思想》[Preliminary Analysis of Li Hongzhang's Thinking on Maritime Defense]《郧阳师范高等专科学校学报》[*Journal of Yunyang Normal University*], Vol. 36, No. 4 (2016): 111.

王家儉 [Wang Jiajian]《李鴻章對於中國海軍近代化的貢獻》[Li Hongzhang's Program toward Chinese Naval Modernization]《歷史學報》[*Historical Studies Report*], 1988-06-01, 16 期 No. 16: 91–105.

王琰 [Wang Yan] 甲午战争战败原因之悖论 [The Paradoxical Reasons Why China Lost the Sino-Japanese War]《深圳大学学报》Vol. 31, No. 6. (November 2014).

钟启顺 周秋光 [Zhong Qishun and Zhou Qiuguang]《二十年来中法战争研究综述》[Twenty Years digest of Research on the Sino-French War] 河池师专学报 [*Hechi Normal University Report*] Vol. 23, No. 1 (March 2003).

Ph.D. Dissertations and M.A. Theses

Bartlett, Laurence Wood. "Not Merely for Defense: The Creation of the New American Navy." Ph.D. Dissertation, Texas Christian University, 2011.

Brown, Stephen. "The Power of Influence in United States-Chilean Relations." Ph.D. Dissertation, University of Wisconsin-Madison, 1983.

Buhl, Lance Crowther. "The Smooth Water Navy: American Navy Policy and Politics 1865–1876." Ph.D. Dissertation, Harvard University, 1969.

Costello, Christopher. "A Vast Consolidation: Everyday Agents of Empire, the United States Navy, and the Processes of Pacific Expansion, 1784–1861." Ph.D. Dissertation, UC San Diego, 2022.

Crumley, Brian. "The Naval Attaché System of the United States, 1882–1914." Ph.D. Dissertation, Texas A&M University, 2002.

Maureira, Hugo Alberto. "'Valiant Race, Tenacious Race, Heroic, Indomitable and Implacable': The War of the Pacific (1879–1884) and the Role of Racial Ideas in the Construction of Chilean Identity." M.A. Thesis, Queen's University, 2002.

Scheina, Robert. "Indigenous Latin American Sea Power." Ph.D. Dissertation, Catholic University of America, 1974.

Sexton, Donald. "Forging the Sword: Congress and the American Naval Renaissance, 1880–1900." Ph.D. Dissertation, University of Tennessee, 1976.

Snyder, David Allan. "Petroleum and Power: Naval Fuel Technology and the Anglo-American Struggle for Core Hegemony, 1889–1922." Ph.D. Dissertation, Texas A&M University, 2001.

Stevens, Carter. "When the Confederates Terrorized Maine: The Battle of Portland Harbor." Honors Thesis. Colby College, 2013.

Stewart, Daniel Wayne. "The Greatest Gift to Modern Civilization: Naval Power and Moral Order in the United States and Great Britain, 1880–1918." Ph.D. Dissertation, Temple University, 1999.

Wicks, Daniel H. "New Navy and New Empire: The Life and Times of John Grimes Walker." Ph.D. Dissertation, University of California, Berkeley, 1979.

Zheng, Huangfu. "Internalizing the West: Qing Envoys and Ministers in Europe, 1866–1893." Ph.D. Dissertation, UCSD, 2012.

Index

Age of Empire, 9, 61
airship, 90
Alaska, 81, 125, 128
Alexandria, bombardment of, 113
America, 37
Angamos, Battle of, 11, 87–88, 100–101, 108, 160–161, 177, 180
   US observations, 101
Anglo-Saxonism, 105, 107–108, 112, 117, 159
Aquidaban, 149
Argentina, 50, 108, 138–139
   competition with Chile, 211
Armstrong, 10, 40, 65, 72, 115, 159, 167
Arthur, Chester, 92
Asiatic Squadron, 81
Atacama Desert, 20, 63, 86
Atahualpa, 37

Balch, George, 93, 166, 168
Balmaceda, Jose Manuel, 133
Baltimore Crisis, 14, 128, 135, 138–140, 142, 144–145, 149–150, 153, 168, 170–171, 179
   contingency, 137
   underlying motivations, 136
Bedford, Frederick, 68–69
Belknap, George, 117
Bello, Andres, 39
Benham, Andrew, 147
Birkenhead. *See* Liverpool
Blaine, James, 92, 127, 134, 138, 140
Blanco Encalada, 64, 87, 91, 116
Blume, Federico, 90
Bolivia, 63, 108, 117
Boshin War, 3, 5, 13, 36, 51
Bouchard, Hippolyte, 32
Boynton, George, 148
Brazilian Naval Revolt, 129, 147, 149–150. *See also* Brazilian Civil War
Britain, 27, 32, 40. *See also* Royal Navy
   military intelligence, 96, 98, 106, 113, 154, 167
   naval expansion, 40
   Rapprochement, 170
   threat perception, 3, 10, 130
Brown, George, 137
Bulloch, James, 16–17, 19, 22–27, 31, 33, 42, 46, 148
Burlingame Mission, 55, 81
Butts, Walter Raleigh, 45

Caldera, Battle of, 11, 116, 160, 177, 182
California, 5, 7–8, 82, 107, 178
   isolation, 30–31, 107
   vulnerability, 113
Callao, 90, 113
   port defense, 41
Callao, Battle of, 6, 39, 43, 53, 65, 85, 95, 139, 182
Canada, 128
Cape Horn, 52, 62
Capitan Prat, 116, 137, 164, 170
Charleston, 35, 39, 42, 45, 47
chemical warfare, 149, 161
Chile
   comparison to Japan, 171, 174
   comparison with Japan, 172
   geography, 20, 64
   identity, 39. *See also Raza Chilena*
   Navy, 19
   Sino-Japanese War, 163
Chilean Civil War, 3, 105, 115, 117, 133, 135, 147
Chilean Navy, 47, 49, 52
   Academy, 65
   armored warships, 64
   coastal defenses, 65
   deployment to Panama, 111
   as newly made navy, 66, 94
   Oceania, 111
   regional power, 13, 66
   technological progress, 110

286

torpedo boat, 65, 90
victory in War of Pacific, 87
Chimbote, 93–94, 111
China, 128
  Black Flag, 95
  China Dream, 54
  Foreign Affairs Movement, 70, 95
  geography, 20, 75
  immigration, 81, 94, 105, 107, 120, 171
  Taiping Civil War, 54, 73
  Tongzhi Restoration, 70
Chinese Exclusion Act, 14, 105, 120
Chinese Navy
  arsenal, 54, 70–71, 74
  assessments, 76
  battleships, 72, 159
  Beiyang Fleet, 74, 123–124, 152, 155, 159
  CSN influence, 55
  foreign acquisitions, 71, 98, 123
  foreign experts, 76, 152
  Naval Academy, 73, 152
  as navy to construct, 54
  as newly made navy, 74, 124
  overseas students, 73
  South Sea Fleet, 95
  torpedo mines, 56
  training, 72
Civil War. *See* US Civil War
Clark, Bouverie, 117
Cleveland, Grover, 143, 146
Clowes, William Laird, 6, 150
coal, 66, 76, 138
coastal defense artillery, 42–43, 97, 138
Cochrane, 64, 66, 87, 91
Coles, Cowper, 22, 25, 65, 117
Columbia River Centennial, 144–145
Condell, 115
Confederacy, 12
  coastal defense, 28
  geography, 21
  ports, 19, 21
  technology demands, 27
  template of resistance, 33, 43
Confederate States Navy (CSN), 17
  Cottonclads, 22
  Naval Academy, 19
  as newly made navy, 16
  self-strengthening, 36
  strategy, 20
  technological asymmetry, 51
  torpedo boat attacks, 41
  veterans, 38, 44–45, 47, 49
Confederate Veteran, 49
Congress, 3, 10, 119, 130, 139
cotton, 8, 18, 22, 36, 48
Courbet, Amédée, 95

Covadonga, 38, 91
Covarrubias, Alvaro, 39
Cramp, Charles, 167
CSS *Alabama*, 12, 16, 22, 24, 48, 114, 133, 150–151
CSS *Albemarle*, 41
CSS *David*, 28–29
CSS *Hunley*, 28, 90
CSS *Shenandoah*, 31–33, 51, 62, 107, 113, 138
CSS *Stonewall*. *See* Stonewall
CSS *Virginia*, 21–23, 25, 45
Cuba, 46, 48, 78, 141, 151, 165, 173
Cushing, William, 41, 52

Dahlgren, John A., 29, 47, 57
  controversey with Tucker, 47
Davidson, Hunter, 28, 35, 47–50, 89
Davis, Jefferson, 20
Destroyer, 76, 148
Dewey, George, 1, 46, 174
Ding, Ruchang, 73, 161
Dingyuan, 72, 123, 154–155, 159–160
Dotty, H. H., 48–49
dynamite gun, 148

Easter Island, 108, 111
Ecuador, 43, 163
Elswick, 138
Enomoto, Takeaki, 52
Ericsson, John, 24, 76, 89, 116, 145, 148
Esmeralda, 110–111, 114, 116, 119–120, 134–135, 144, 153, 157, 162
  in Hawaii, 164
Europe. *See also* North Atlantic
  supplying CSN, 22
Evans, Robley, 136
exaggeration of vulnerability, 7, 104, 107

filibuster, 143
Fiske, Bradley, 138
Fiume, Austria, 115
Flint, Charles, 148, 162, 164
  "new navy," 148
Floriano, Peixoto, 147–148
  asymmetric weapons, 149
Foreign Affairs Movement, 70.
  See also China
Foreign Enlistment Act, 16, 24
Formosa expedition, US, 54
Fox, Gustavus, 24
France, 128, 137
  intervention in Mexico, 37
  Mexico intervention, 30
  shipyard, 51
  Southeast Asia, 95

Fucheng, Xue, 72
Fuzhou. *See* Sino-French War
Fuzhou, Battle of, 95, 98
Fuzhou Naval College, 73

Gaosheng, 159
Garcia y Garcia, Aurelio, 10, 25–26, 37, 41, 59, 61, 63, 68, 87
Garfield, James, 121
Gatling-guns, 116
Germany, 3, 128, 154
Glassell, William, 28–29, 33, 44
Gold Rush, 30, 81, 132
Grace and Co., 133
Grant, Ulysses, 75
Grau, Miguel, 87–88
great divergence, 9, 83, 181
Great White Fleet, 127, 136
guano, 81, 94, 134
guerre de course, 48

Hampton Roads, 21, 23, 42, 67, 69
Harper's, 92, 140
Harrison, Benjamin, 127, 133, 135, 137–139, 145
Hawaii, 7, 15, 121, 129, 140, 153, 156, 170–171
  annexation debate, 143, 146, 153
  coup, 1893, 128, 142
  Crisis, 1897, 171–172
  flag, 88, 163
  Republic of, 163
Hayashi, Shihei, 195
Henrietta, 49
Herbert, Hilary, 169–170
history
  area studies, 9, 102, 166, 176
  imperial turn, 9
  international, 8
  International Society, 180
  New Military History, 8
  oceanic, 9, 11, 102
  transnational, 9
HMS *Shah*, 68
Hokkaido, 50–51
Honolulu, 142
Huáscar, 12, 24–26, 37–38, 42, 44–47, 64, 66–70, 87–88, 90, 100–101, 115, 161, 177, 181

Independencia, 37–38, 44–45, 47, 59, 70
indigenous peoples
  Chile, 109
  North American Indians, 31, 55
  Patagonia, 108
  Taiwan, 55

Influence of Sea Power upon History, 5, 10, 91, 99, 106, 129, 167
international law, 38–40, 159
Islas de Lobos, 134
Itata, 14, 128, 133–137, 139–140, 144, 150

James River, 19, 28, 48
Japan, 15
  comparison to Chile, 171, 174
  comparison with Chile, 172
  immigration to Hawaii, 156
  as newly made navy, 168
  racism toward, 168
Japanese Navy. *See also* Yalu, Battle of; Weihaiwei, Battle of
  cruiser diplomacy, 157
  as navy to construct, 51
  as newly made navy, 53
  port call in Chile, 164
  US threat perception, 167
Jefferson, Thomas, 142
jingoism, 143, 165

Keelung, 96
Kelley, J. D., 124, 167
Kit Carson, 30
Korea, 81, 121, 164
Kotetsu. *See Stonewall*
Krupp, 73, 148

Laird Brothers, 16, 18, 22, 24, 38, 115, 177
Laird Rams, 23–24, 27, 31–32, 46, 90
Lang, William, 154
Latin America. *See* South America
Lay, John, 10, 35, 41, 43, 49, 75, 88–89, 162
  in China, 57
Lay Torpedo, 75, 88–89
Lay-Osborne Flotilla, 24, 246
Li, Fengbao, 123
Li, Hongzhang, 10–11, 19–20, 54–56, 70–76, 88–89, 95, 98, 154–156, 159–160, 163, 166–167, 184
Lili'uokalani, 142–143, 156–157
Lin, Zexu, 54
Liverpool, 16, 24, 38, 48
Lodge, Henry Cabot, 7, 118, 164, 166, 170–171
Long, John, 7, 173
Lopez, Juan, 111
Luce, Stephen, 7, 138–139, 172
Lynch, 115

Mahan, Alfred Thayer, 5, 7–8, 11, 20, 22, 52, 54, 79, 85, 94, 100, 105, 116–119, 122, 125, 128–130, 136–137, 142–143, 167, 171, 173

Index

Mallory, Stephen, 19–20, 27, 29, 46
Manco Capac, 37
Manifest Destiny, 5
Manila Bay, 1, 46, 173–175
Mannix, Daniel, 75–76
Manuel Pinto, José, 20
Mare Island, 31, 119
Mason, Theodorus, 5–6, 64, 100–101
McAdoo, William, 169
McCann, William, 82, 93–94
McCorkel, Porter, 45
McGiffin, Philo, 152, 155, 166–167
McKinley, William, 171
Meiji, 20, 51–53, 56, 125, 155, 164, 171.
   See also Japan
  Restoration, 36, 52
Melville, Herman, 183
Méndez-Núñez, Casto, 38–39, 43–44
mercenary, 23, 57, 66, 97, 152
Meteor, 48
Mexican American War, 30, 32
missionaries, 121
Miyako Bay, Battle of, 53
Monroe Doctrine, 37, 40, 43, 64, 69, 80
Monterey, 32, 107

Nagasaki, 73, 79, 125
Naniwa, 115, 143, 157, 171
Nation, 92
nationalism, 46, 69, 181
nativism, 107, 120, 122
Naval Advisory Board, 125
Naval Attaché, 100, 109
naval modernity, 11, 47, 86, 102, 161, 182
naval race, 2, 3, 7, 13, 59, 62, 80, 83, 94,
   99, 179
  Chile/Peru, 60, 65
  China/Japan, 60, 70–71, 125, 147, 152,
   155, 158
  humiliation as motive, 118, 126
  United States and Chile, 107–108, 119,
   128, 133, 142, 150
  United States and Japan, 153
navalism, 4, 19, 60, 105–106, 130
  Chilean variant, 108, 119
  Chinese variant, 11
  Japan variant, 154
  regional variation, 104
New Navy, 1, 7, 10
  balance of Pacific and Atlantic, 173
  Bar Harbor review, 127
  battleship, 63, 72, 116, 132
  Chinese serving in, 125
  comparisons to China, 72
  cruiser diplomacy, 128, 133–134,
   139, 151

  cruiser gap with Chile, 114
  emphasis on North Atlantic, 10
  great power defense thesis, 2, 129,
   149, 176
  history of, 10
  imperial preparation thesis, 2, 129, 176
  as reaction to Pacific, 105, 179
  Squadron of Evolution, 127
  torpedo boats, 115
New York Naval Review, 128, 145
Newcastle, 110, 123, 159, 162, 167
newly made navy, 2, 5, 12, 24, 34
Numancia, 43, 46

Oceania, 111
Office of Naval Intelligence, 6, 86, 91, 99,
   113–114, 122, 137, 154, 178
  chief intelligence officer, 100–101
Old Navy, 2, 7, 13, 60, 71, 77, 86
  comparisons with China, 74
  comparisons with Pacific, 61, 78–79, 86,
   104, 178
  gunboat imperialism, 79, 92
  inferiority to Chile, 94, 110, 112
  as a joke, 77, 92, 118, 140
  as police force, 80–81, 83
Old Steam Navy. *See* Old Navy
Opium War, 11–12, 54, 70, 78, 113
  Second Opium War, 54
Oregon, 5, 120, 133, 178

Pacific Ocean
  history, 11, 102
  regional order, 53, 66, 85, 91, 108, 130
  trans-oceanic, 52, 183
  wars, 2, 86
Pacific Squadron, 32, 92, 100
Pacocha, Battle of, 3, 11, 47, 60, 69, 80,
   85, 96, 102, 137, 139, 177, 181–182
  Allegory, 69
Page, Thomas J., 51
Panama, 10, 88, 110, 114
  Canal, 10, 30, 149
  expedition, 1885, 110, 156
Pareja, José Manuel, 38
Parker, Foxhall, 45, 53
Pearson, George, 43
People's Republic of China, 95, 170, 184
Pérez, Jose Joaquin, 39
Perry, Matthew, 20, 51, 125, 153, 167
Peru
  arsenal, 42
  coastal defense, 41
  foreign weapons, 43
  ironclads, 42–43
  Japan visit, 59

Peru (cont.)
  naval innovation, 37
  as newly made navy, 38, 44, 63
  torpedo boat, 88
  US Civil War connections, 38
Philippine Insurrection, 140
Philippines, 48
Piérola, Nicolas, 68, 90
Port Arthur, 76, 98, 160
  capture of, 160, 168
Portal, Nicolas, 89
Porter, D. D., 77, 108, 110, 112, 115, 120
Portland, 144
Prado, Mariano Ignacio, 44
Preble, George, 65
privateer, 31, 40, 48
Progressives, 6, 82
Prussia, 25
Puck, 140
Puerto Rico, 141
Punch, 168
Punta Gruesa, 87

Qing, 24, 55, 70. *See also* China

Raza Chilena, 105, 109, 117
Read, Charles, 6, 23, 89
Reed, Edward, 25, 116
Rendel, George, 110
Revista de Marina, 4, 10, 91, 94, 108, 116–117, 128
Robeson, George, 63, 82
Rodgers, Christopher, 100
Rodgers, John, 81
Roosevelt, Theodore, 1, 7, 16, 105, 116, 118, 122, 169–170, 173
Rowan, Stephen, 53
Royal Navy, 27, 40, 68, 85, 94
  Greenwich, 73
  Spithead review, 146
Russia, 122, 139, 157, 165, 182
Russo-Japanese War, 157, 165, 182
Ryukyus, 54, 56, 70, 153

Salcedo, Jose Maria, 25
Samoa, 80, 129, 137
Sampson, William, 108, 151
Samuda Brothers, 25, 72
San Francisco, 1, 12, 14, 31
  defenses, 7, 104
  as entrepot, 107
  industry, 131
  vulnerability, 8
Sandwich Islands. *See* Hawaii
Sargent, Aaron, 121

Scharf, Thomas, 23–24
Scheliha, Viktor von, 161
Schley, Winfield Scott, 135, 137, 145
Scott, Irving, 132
security dilemma, 13, 61, 63
self-strengthening, 13–14, 17–18, 21, 27, 34, 36–37, 44, 53–54, 59–60, 62–63, 67, 70–71, 86, 95, 97, 106, 120, 174
  California, 132–133
  China, 6, 54
  Confederacy, 12, 20, 25
  and naval race, 13, 15
  reassesment, 99, 152
  US New Navy, 151
Semmes, Raphael, 48
Seward, William, 5, 48, 81, 117, 139
Shipu, Battle of, 95
Shufeldt, Robert, 10, 20, 60, 74, 76, 78, 82, 121, 124, 154, 184
Sims, William, 5, 6, 100, 111, 122, 144, 158, 166–167, 169
Sino-French War, 3, 14, 85, 120–121
  Chinese success, 97
Sino-Japanese War, 3, 14, 60, 152, 159, 170
  comparison to War of the Pacific, 152, 166
  Esmeralda, 162
  regional order, 165
  and the United States, 165
slavery, 5, 19, 104
Somerscales, Thomas, 67
South America, 8, 43, 48, 55, 66, 76, 87–88, 91, 101–102, 105, 114, 116–118, 138–139, 152–153, 164, 178
South Sea Fleet. *See* Sino-French War
Soviet Union, 170, 175, 183–184
Spain. *See also* War Against Spain
  empire, 36, 44–48
  navy, 36, 39, 167
  Virginius affair, 78
spar torpedo, 49, 75, 102
Sputnik Moment, 114
Squadron Tactics under Steam, 45, 57
Stanford, Leland, 119
Stevens, John, 142
Stevenson, Robert Louis, 107
Stonewall, 6, 35, 50–53, 55, 58–59, 79, 162, 174, 176, 181
strategy
  asymmetric, 6, 13, 27, 45, 54, 69, 74, 91, 98, 161, 177
  symmetrical, 6, 64, 72
submarine, 28, 44, 89–90

Index

Taiwan Expedition, Japan, 3, 54, 58, 70, 73, 78, 153
Takachiho, 144, 157
  reception, 158
Tamsui, Battle of, 85, 95–96
technology
  change as opportunity, 6, 75, 83, 106, 162
  demand from Pacific, 43, 72
  foreign dependency, 76, 132
  gap, 9, 12, 83
  innovation, 180
  observations, 99
  as progress, 117, 121, 126, 158
  proliferation, 5, 50, 54, 116, 165
Tianjin, 57, 73, 75, 88, 98
  Chinese torpedo school, 75, 184
  Naval Academy, 152
Tōgō, Heihachirō, 72, 157, 159
Tokugawa, 20, 51–53
Tomb, James Hamilton, 28–29
Toro Submarino, 90
torpedo, 42, 44, 68
torpedo automobile, 11, 74, 88
torpedo boats, 49, 115
torpedo cruiser, 115
torpedo mine, 27, 41, 48
Tracy, Benjamin Franklin, 73, 106, 116, 127, 133, 135, 144
  1889 Report, 130
transcontinental railroad, 30, 81
transwar, 8, 17, 35–36, 57, 86, 104, 129, 165, 174, 176
Tucker, John Randolph, 11, 35, 44–47, 53, 65, 174

Unión, 37, 59, 65, 88
Union Iron Works, 114, 131–133, 145
United States
  Brazil Relations, 150
  comparison to Chile, 119
  comparison to China, 169, 178
  comparison to Japan, 165
  empire, 5, 79, 81, 104, 153, 156
  marines, 14, 54, 75, 82, 142–143
  New Empire, 5, 12, 81
  post-Civil War demobilization, 4, 41, 51, 60, 77
US Civil War, 3, 8, 12, 33
  blockade, 22
  Chinese observations, 55
  Hampton Roads, 25
  Monitor, 21, 30, 37, 145
  surplus, 37, 51, 78
  veterans, 45, 48, 57, 75, 87, 148, 180

US Naval Academy, 79, 100, 159
US Naval Institute, 10, 113
US Naval War College, 7–8, 10, 66, 90, 99, 113, 140, 171–172
US-Korean War, 81
USS *Baltimore*, 134–137, 140, 144–145, 172
USS *Boston*, 142–143
USS *Charleston*, 115, 130, 132–135, 140, 144, 149–150, 157, 159, 162, 172
USS *Detroit*, 148
USS *Indiana*, 116
USS *Iroquois*, 137
USS *Kearsarge*, 151
USS *Lancaster*, 32
USS *Monterey*, 131–132
USS *New Ironsides*, 28–29
USS *Oregon*, 63, 132, 145, 172
USS *Pensacola*, 92–93, 135
USS *Philadelphia*, 158, 172
USS *Ranger*, 82
USS *San Francisco*, 131–132
USS *Ticonderoga*, 82
USS *Trenton*, 79
USS *Wachusett*, 118
USS *Yorktown*, 136, 145

Valparaiso, 38–39, 54
  bombardment of, 39, 63, 113
  coastal defense artillery, 138
Van Valkenburgh, Robert, 52
Venezuelan Crisis, 173
Vicuña Mackenna, Benjamin, 7, 43–44, 48, 94, 108, 112
Virginius, 78
von Scheliha, Viktor, 56

Waddell, James, 31–33
Wallerstein, Immanuel, 9
War against Spain, 3, 13, 26, 37–38
war fiction, 7, 118, 122, 124, 183
War of 1898, 1, 129, 135, 173
War of the Pacific, 3, 5, 44, 60, 67, 85–86, 100, 108, 115, 126, 148
  comparison to Sino-Japanese War, 152, 166
War Plan Orange, 165
Washington Naval Treaty, 140
Wei, Yuan, 11, 54, 78, 166, 184
Weihaiwei, Battle of, 6, 11, 159–161, 182
  torpedo boat, 160
Welles, Gideon, 47
whaling, 31, 81, 107
whiskey, 30
Whitehead, Robert, 88

Whitehead torpedo, 115
Wilde, John, 149, 161
Wilde, Oscar, 77
Wilson, Herbert, 150
World War I, 11, 29, 86, 161, 182
World-Systems Theory, 9, 18, 66

Xue, Fucheng, 97, 123

Yalu, Battle of, 11, 124, 155–156, 159–161, 163, 170, 175, 182
Yan, Fu, 73
Yangwu, 71, 73

Yarrow and Hedley, 50, 65
Yashima, 170
Yellow Peril, 14, 105, 120, 122
Yokohama, 125

Zeng, Guoquan, 121
Zhang, Zhidong, 95
Zhenhai, Battle of, 85, 95, 97–98, 102, 121, 137, 181
Zhenyuan, 72, 123, 154–155, 159, 161
Zongli Yamen, 55
Zuo, Zongtang, 19, 54, 70, 73, 183

For EU product safety concerns, contact us at Calle de José Abascal, 56–1°,
28003 Madrid, Spain or eugpsr@cambridge.org.

www.ingramcontent.com/pod-product-compliance
Lightning Source LLC
Chambersburg PA
CBHW020250090925
32316CB00002B/18